T0230416

Lecture Notes in Computer Science 940
Edited by G. Goos, J. Hartmanis and J. van Leeuwen

Springer
Berlin
Heidelberg
New York
Barcelona
Budapest
Hong Kong
London
Milan
Paris
Tokyo

Carole Goble John Keane (Eds.)

Advances in Databases

13th British National Conference on Databases
BNCOD 13
Manchester, United Kingdom, July 12-14, 1995
Proceedings

Series Editors

Gerhard Goos
Universität Karlsruhe
Vincenz-Priessnitz-Straße 3, D-76128 Karlsruhe, Germany

Juris Hartmanis
Department of Computer Science, Cornell University
4130 Upson Hall, Ithaca, NY 14853, USA

Jan van Leeuwen
Department of Computer Science, Utrecht University
Padualaan 14, 3584 CH Utrecht, The Netherlands

Volume Editors

Carole Goble
Department of Computer Science, University of Manchester
Oxford Road, Manchester M13 9PL, United Kingdom

John Keane
Department of Computation, UMIST
P.O.Box 88, Manchester M60 1QD, United Kingdom

CIP data applied for

Die Deutsche Bibliothek - CIP-Einheitsaufnahme

Directions in databases : proceedings / 13th British National Conference on Databases, BNCOD 13, Manchester, United Kingdom, July 12 - 14, 1995. Carole Goble ; John Keane (ed.). - Berlin ; Heidelberg ; New York : Springer, 1995
(Lecture notes in computer science ; Vol. 940)
ISBN 3-540-60100-7
NE: Goble, Carole [Hrsg.]; BNCOD <13, 1995, Manchester>; GT

CR Subject Classification (1991): H.2-5

ISBN 3-540-60100-7 Springer-Verlag Berlin Heidelberg New York

Typesetting: Camera-ready by author
Printed on acid-free paper SPIN 10486347 06/3142 – 5 4 3 2 1 0

FOREWORD

This volume continues the theme of directions in database research established by the British National Conference on Databases, containing the proceedings of the thirteenth conference (BNCOD 13) held in Manchester, UK in July 1995.

The conference enhanced its record of excellence and internationalism: in all 64 technical paper submissions were received from 18 countries including Australia, Brazil, Korea, New Zealand, Singapore and USA. Each paper received at least three reviews. Of the 64 papers, 14 were accepted for presentation at the conference, together with two internationally respected invited speakers.

The database field is now an established one with regard to conventional applications and structured data types, yet a progressive and exciting one for new applications, such as multimedia, document management, and CAD. These applications demand sophisticated and powerful models, and new operational approaches.

Although the relational model continues to dominate the commercial sector, object-oriented data databases (OODB) are maturing and are increasingly influential in both the commercial and research sectors. This is reflected by the first invited speaker, *Rick Cattell* of SunSoft, USA, and a leader in the field of OODB standardisation. He discusses *object databases and standards*, exploring object database technology and product market directions, comparing object and relational technology, and presenting the ODMG-93 standard for object DBMSs.

One of the chief new application areas that requires the expressivity and sophistication of the OODB is multimedia. The second invited speaker, *Arif Ghafoor* of Purdue University, USA, considers *multimedia database management.* He argues that multimedia database systems will need data models both more powerful and more versatile than the relational model. He suggests that two key requirements for multi-media databases are the process of spatio-temporal modelling and the computational needs for automatic-indexing of spatio-temporal data.

The first group of technical papers continues the exploration of new modelling formalisms through functional database languages. *Courtenage & Poulovassilis* consider extending a functional database language to support subtyping, inheritance and method overloading, whilst *Sutton & Small* discuss the update operations implemented in the functional database programming language PFL and the linear type system which regulates their use.

Not only have database applications become more demanding, but so have database users. The first point of contact for a user is the database interface, and surprisingly little attention has been paid to this essential area. *Nordbotten & Crosby* investigate user understanding of graphic models: their study in graphic data perception indicates that many details are seen by less than half of the readers and that graphic style is an influence. *Haw et al.* analyse the communicative process of enquiry and present GUIDANCE, a system based on ideas derived from the human communicative practices and conventions. Finally *Mitchell et al.* propose a conceptual approach to defining interfaces which uses the features of a fully object-oriented data language to specify interface objects combined with database objects.

Work remains to be done at the system-level of databases; an area addressed in the third group of papers. *Sieg et al.* describe and analyse query scheduling policies that use knowledge of the number of available system buffers and the various hot points of the queries to provide more efficient processing. *Veenhof et al.* consider the optimisation of n-way spatial joins using filters, showing that a filter sequence can reduce the number of calls to spatial operations. Finally, *Gukal et al.* present a dynamic transient-versioning method which both increases concurrency among transactions and reduces storage overhead.

Concurrency, distributed environments, and data types such as text provide challenges to, and support for, retrieval and transactions. *Hussak & Keane* discuss how transactions that access different types (*tiers*) of data offer greater scope for concurrent execution by allowing the standard serializability condition to be weakened, whilst *Kim et al.* consider the problem of finding an optimal global plan for a tree query in a distributed database, the aim being the minimisation of total processing time. At a different level, *Kaufmann & Schek* describe the realisation of a preprocessor for simple text retrieval on top of a relational database.

The ubiquity and evolutionary growth of databases have altered the database environment to one of federated systems rather than centralised stand-alone systems. *Alzahrani et al.* present a software tool to help resolve conflicts between local integrity specifications in a heterogeneous federated system. Databases that have accumulated, and continue to accumulate, terabytes of data are commonplace; new applications such as satellite information and scientific data collect information on an immense scale. Parallel machines offer some solutions to the scale and performance issues. *Watson & Catlow* discuss the requirements on such machines of commercial database processing, and consider how the ICL GOLDRUSH MegaSERVER meets these requirements. Finally, *Kerridge et al.* present an interface between the relational processing part and the storage system of a parallel machine, the aim being to perform low-level SQL processing as close to the data storage as possible.

Acknowledgements

Many people have assisted in the staging of BNCOD 13: the other members of the Organising Committee – Ferzana Butt, Mary Garvey, Babis Theodoulidis and Brian Warboys – have all made invaluable contributions to the organisation; the members of the Programme Committee who ensured that all papers had at least three referees; the members of the Steering Committee; the authors who responded on time to the deadline; the British Computer Society for their support; and Alfred Hofmann and Springer-Verlag for continued interest in publishing these proceedings in the *Lecture Notes in Computer Science* series. Finally, thanks to our respective departments – Computer Science at the University of Manchester and Computation at UMIST – for use of their facilities, and to all our colleagues.

Manchester, UK, May 1995 *Carole Goble & John Keane*

CONFERENCE COMITTEES

ORGANISING COMMITTEE

Carole Goble	(Chair)	University of Manchester
Ferzana Butt	(Administrator)	University of Manchester
Mary Garvey	(Publicity)	University of Wolverhampton
John Keane	(Proceedings)	UMIST
Babis Theodoulidis	(Exhibition)	UMIST
Brian Warboys		University of Manchester

PROGRAMME COMMITTEE

Brian Warboys	(Chair)	University of Manchester
Andy Bailey		Oracle
Tim Bourne		SIAM Ltd
David Bowers		University of Surrey
Richard Cooper		University of Glasgow
Barry Eaglestone		University of Bradford
Bill Edisbury		TSB Bank
Carole Goble		University of Manchester
Alex Gray		University of Wales, Cardiff
Peter Gray		University of Aberdeen
Frances Grundy		University of Keele
Mike Jackson		University of Wolverhampton
Keith Jeffrey		DRAL
Mike Kay		ICL
John Keane		UMIST
Jessie Kennedy		Napier University
Jon Kerridge		University of Sheffield
Mark Levene		University College London
Rob Lucas		Keylink Computers
Sue Malaika		IBM (UK)
Simon Monk		University of Central Lancashire
Ken Moody		University of Cambridge
Bill Olle		T.William Olle Associates
Norman Paton		Heriot-Watt University
Alex Poulovassilis		Kings College, London
Norman Revell		Middlesex University
Phill Robinson		Sybase
Mike Shave		University of Liverpool
Babis Theodoulidis		UMIST
Sarah Wilkinson		Integrated Computer Technologies Ltd
Geoff Young		NATWEST Bank

STEERING COMMITTEE

Alex Gray	(Chair)	University of Wales, Cardiff
Tim. Bourne		SIAM Ltd
David Bowers		University of Surrey
Carole Goble		University of Manchester
Peter Gray		University of Aberdeen
Mike Jackson		University of Wolverhampton
Mike Worboys		University of Keele

CONTENTS

Object Databases and Standards

R.G.G. Cattell, SunSoft, Inc
1500 Salado Drive, Mountain View, CA 94043 USA

Object DBMSs are an interesting new technology now reaching some degree of maturity. This paper explores object database technology, product market directions, comparisons to object-relational technology, and the ODMG standard for object DBMSs.

1. Introduction

For the purposes of this paper, an object-oriented DBMS, sometimes called an object DBMS, is a DBMS that adds database capability to an existing object-oriented programming language such as C++ or Smalltalk. An object DBMS differs in several ways from the other most popular way to incorporate "object" capabilities in databases, *object-relational DBMSs,* in which SQL-based DBMSs are extended with object programming language capabilities.

In the commercial arena, examples of object DBMSs include GemStone from Servio, O_2 from O_2 Technologies, Objectivity/DB for Objectivity, ObjectStore from Object Design, ONTOS from Ontos Corporation, POET from POET Software, and VERSANT from Versant Object Technology. In contrast, Oracle, Sybase and other major relational vendors are evolving towards object-relational DBMSs, and new start-ups such as Illustra and UniSQL have also introduced products in the object-relational market.[1]

Object DBMSs generally provide the following features:

- An object-oriented data model, including object identifiers, attributes, methods, and type inheritance.
- Integration with an object-oriented programming language, with transparent or semi-transparent fetch and store of objects.
- A declarative query language similar to the ones provided by other DBMSs, usually a SQL derivative.
- Advanced data sharing mechanisms, including long transactions, optimistic concurrency control, multiple versions of data, and private data check-out.

The object DBMS products differ in a variety of specific details. Also, simple object managers, database system generators, semantic/functional DBMSs, and other approaches have been taken in addition to object-relational and object DBMSs. A number of good sources are available comparing the approaches [3,4].

---

[1] Yes, these product names are all trademarks of their respective companies.

2. Contrast of Approaches

There is some debate about the future market directions for object DBMSs, particularly about the likely success of object DBMSs versus object-relational DBMSs, however a fair amount of this debate may simply result from financial investments of the parties involved.

There are certainly compelling arguments for the object-relational approach. Most notably, there is substantial investment in SQL-based relational DBMSs, so an evolutionary approach that preserves that investment is very attractive. Object-relational DBMSs based on existing products such as Oracle or Sybase boast many years investment in the robustness, application development tools, data security, transaction processing performance, and day-to-day business requirements such as online backup.

Nevertheless, there are reasons to believe that there is a substantial market for object DBMSs over the next decade, even as object modeling capabilities are added relational systems:

- Object DBMSs provide a simpler way for programmers familiar with an object-oriented programming language to use databases; it is not necessary to split applications into parts written in the programming language and parts written in the database language (SQL), and it is not necessary to explicitly translate data from the database to programming language data structures and vice versa.
- In addition to supporting conventional DBMS functionality, object DBMSs deal with complex data with substantially higher performance; these benefits stem primarily from client-side caching and seamless integration with the programming language environment [2].
- Projections from market firms such as IDC indicate that the object database market is experiencing revenue growth very closely parallel to that of the early relational industry. As with relational systems a decade earlier, object DBMSs now offer revolutionary advantages that are not likely to be achieved through evolutionary development of their predecessors.

Despite these advantages, it is unlikely that object DBMSs will completely overcome the evolutionary advantages that extensions to relational systems have for business applications in the near future. Thus, I believe object DBMSs and object-relational DBMSs will co-exist for the remainder of this decade. They will likely be used for different kinds of applications, just as different programming languages are popular for different kinds of applications. As an example, SunSoft has incorporated both object DBMS and relational DBMS access into its DOE distributed object environment.

3. ODMG Standard

The importance of a standard for new technology is often underestimated. The success of relational database systems did not result simply from a better level of data independence and a simpler data model than previous systems. Much of their success came from the standardization that they offered. The acceptance of the SQL standard allowed a high degree of portability and interoperability between systems, simplified learning new relational DBMSs, and probably most importantly, represented a wide endorsement of the relational approach.

All of these factors are as important for object DBMSs today as they were for relational systems a decade ago. In fact, these factors are even more important, because most of the products in this area are offered by young companies: portability and endorsement of the approach are essential to a customer investing in applications on these DBMSs. In the case of object DBMSs the scope of the customer's investment is even more far-reaching than with relational DBMSs, because one environment encompasses all of an application's operations and data. A standard is critical to making applications practical.

In addition to the benefits of standardization, the introduction of ODMG-93 has relieved another impediment to the use of object DBMSs, namely the existence of a powerful query language. The OQL language in ODMG-93 is more powerful than SQL, as we shall see, while the query languages in many of the object DBMS products had been substantially weaker than SQL, or non-existent. Object DBMS vendors committed to much more query capability in conjunction with ODMG-93.

In 1993 the Object Database Management Group (ODMG) defined a standards specification, ODMG-93, designed for object DBMSs [1, 5]. Consistent with our definition of object DBMSs, the ODMG architecture includes bindings to provide transparent persistence and database capability in object-oriented programming languages, specifically C++ and Smalltalk.

On the object-relational front, the ANSI X3H2 (SQL) group has been working on SQL3, which is not yet to "draft standard" stage this year. The thrust of the SQL3 work is aimed at extending the SQL type system and adding procedural capability to the SQL language. There is little overlap between the ODMG and SQL3 work, except in the query language portion (Chapter 4 of the ODMG-93 specification, and the SELECT statement of SQL3).

The ODMG and X3H2 groups have had several ad hoc meetings to decrease differences in the query language syntax and semantics in their respective standards. Two actions have resulted from these meetings:

1. The ODMG OQL language has been revised to make it as compatible as possible with SQL2 (with ODMG object extensions).
2. Change proposals are being made to X3H2 to reduce differences in the SQL3 and OQL object extensions. The most fundamental remaining difference is that

SQL3 still treats tables as the only "top level" type, while OQL treats all types as equivalent (the result of a query or a named top level entity can be of any type).

ODMG was founded because no progress had been made towards standards for object DBMSs several years after their successful deployment. OMG had formed a database special interest group and had begun work toward database-related standards in the Object Services Task Force, ANSI had formed an Object-Oriented Database Task Force which resulted in ANSI X3H7, and various ad hoc attempts were made between vendors, but nothing resulted in standards for object DBMS products.

ODMG was formed in late 1991, at my invitation to a meeting at SunSoft. The ODMG work was done by a small group of five vendor employees who committed one week per month to the ODMG work over two years. As a result, the work progressed very quickly compared to traditional standards groups. A first draft for all the major components was produced during 1992, and the accepted version was published in 1993. The intense ODMG effort gave the object database industry a "jump start" toward standards that would otherwise have taken many years.

Since the introduction of the standard, the ODMG group has expanded significantly; it now includes Object Design, Objectivity, Ontos, O_2 Technologies, POET Software, Servio, Versant, American Management Systems, Anderson Consulting, EDS, Fujitsu, Hewlett-Packard, Intellitic, MITRE, Persistence Software, Sybase, UniData, and Texas Instruments. The voting members of ODMG (the first seven in the list) are committed to support the ODMG-93 standard this year, and as of this writing several of the vendors have already released partial implementations. Thus, ODMG-93 is likely to become a de facto standard for the object DBMS industry.

There are some lessons to be learned about technology and the standards process from the ODMG history. It is very difficult to do substantial creative work within a large standards group, given the number of people and the politics involved. It is generally necessary to choose a de facto standard as a starting point, and then make incremental modifications. Unfortunately, unlike SQL in the relational DBMS world, no accepted starting point existed for object DBMSs. Instead, the ODMG work is derived by creatively combining the strongest components of a number of products currently available. These products provided demonstrated implementations of the standards components that had been tried in the field.

4. ODMG Architecture

ODMG defines a common architecture for object DBMS products. The programmer writes declarations for the application schema (both data and operations) plus a source program for the application implementation.

The source program is written in a programming language such as C++, which has been extended to provide a full database manipulation language including transactions and object query. The schema declarations may be written in an extension of the programming language syntax, called the programming language

ODL (object definition language), or may be written in a programming language-independent ODL that ODMG defines. The latter ODL might be used as a higher-level design language, or to allow schema definition independent of programming language.

The programmer's declarations and source program are compiled and linked with the DBMS runtime to produce the running application. The application accesses a new or existing database, whose types must conform to the declarations. Databases may be shared with other applications on a network; the DBMS provides a shared service for transaction and lock management, allowing data to be cached in the application.

The chapters of the ODMG-93 specification correspond to the main components of the standard:

- Architecture: The first chapter defines a common architecture for an object DBMS as just described. This agreement on the architecture and approach to object DBMSs was essential to making this work possible.
- Object Model: ODMG defines a common data model to be supported by object DBMSs. A subset of the object model provides interoperability across programming languages, e.g. allowing the same database to be shared by a C++ and Smalltalk program.
- Object Definition Language: ODMG defines an object definition language (ODL) as a syntax for the object model. ODL may be used to define an application schema; the schema can subsequently be translated into declarations in the desired programming language.
- Object Query Language: ODMG defines a declarative object query language (OQL) for querying database objects. OQL can be used by end-users or from within a programming language. OQL is based on SQL syntax wherever possible.
- C++ and Smalltalk Bindings: The remaining chapters of the ODMG specification define programming language bindings, also known as the object manipulation language (OML). Currently bindings have been defined for C++ and Smalltalk. OML binding chapters for SQL3, C, LISP, and IDL are being considered.

5. Object Model and Definition Language

Much of the ODMG work is based on Object Management Group (OMG) specifications [6]. In particular, the ODMG object model is designed as a superset of the OMG object model.

The ODMG model is based on objects, with object identifiers. Objects can be categorized into types. All objects of a given type exhibit common behavior and a common range of states. The behavior of objects is defined by a set of operations that can be executed on an object of the type. The state of objects is defined by the values they carry for a set of properties. These properties may be either attributes of the object itself or relationships between the object and one or more other objects.

As with variables in programming languages, human-meaningful names may be given to ODMG objects. A name must refer uniquely to a single object within the scope of the definition of the name; currently the only name scope defined is a database. Note that these names differ from primary keys in a relational DBMS; they are more like relation names, except that they can refer to objects of any type (not just tables).

Operation signatures define the operations that objects of a given type support. As in most programming languages, each signature defines the name of the operation, the name and type of any arguments, the name and type of any returned values, and the names of any exceptions (error conditions) the operation can raise.

Attributes of object types are similarly specified with attribute signatures. Each signature defines the name of the attribute and the type of its legal values. Attributes take literals as values, e.g., strings, numbers, etc.

Relationship signatures specify the relationships in which objects of a given type can participate. Each signature defines the type of the other object or set of objects involved in the relationship and the name of a traversal function (an *inverse attribute*) used to refer to the related object or set of objects. Relationships are binary and are defined between two types of objects (as opposed to attributes that are defined between an object and a literal). The cardinality of the relationship can be one-to-one, one-to-many, and many-to-many.

ODMG defines a number of collection types: sets, bags, lists, and arrays. Named instances of these types can be used to group objects; for example, hourly_employees might be the employees who are paid by the hour. Thus, there may be many pre-defined collections of each type, not just the extent of the type (e.g., the employee table).

ODMG supports inheritance between types in a subtype/supertype graph. All of the attributes, relationships, and operations defined on a supertype are inherited by a subtype. The subtype may add additional properties and operations to introduce behavior or state unique to instances of a subtype. Multiple inheritance is supported.

The extent of a type can automatically be maintained by the object DBMS, as in relational DBMSs. The type definer can request that the system automatically maintain an index to the members of this set. Keys can also be defined on type extents, in which case the DBMS guarantees the uniqueness of the key attributes within the type extent.

ODMG defines an object definition language (ODL) that is the syntax for the object model. ODL is intended to define object types that can be implemented in a variety of programming languages; it is not tied to the syntax or semantics of one programming language.

There are a number of benefits to having a programming language-independent ODL. ODL allows the same database to be shared across multiple programming languages, and allows an application to be ported to a new programming language without rewriting the data schema description. ODL can also be used by design and analysis tools that must describe an application's data and operations independently of programming language. The resulting design can then be used directly or translated into a data description language of the programmer's choice. Also, a schema specified in ODL will be supported by any ODMG-compliant DBMS.

In addition to the programming language-independent ODL, the ODMG programming language bindings (currently C++ and Smalltalk) describe optional ODL syntaxes designed to fit smoothly into the declarative syntax of their host programming language. Due to the differences inherent in the object models native to these programming languages, it is not always possible to achieve 100% consistent semantics across the programming-language specific versions of ODL. ODMG's goal has been to maximize database schema portability across programming languages. In the ODMG specification, each programming language binding documents any extensions or shortfalls with respect to the common ODMG model.

ODL's syntax is based on OMG's Interface Definition Language (IDL) developed as part of the Common Object Request Broker Architecture (CORBA). ODMG used IDL rather than invent yet another language syntax. ODL adds to IDL the constructs required to specify the complete semantics of the ODMG object model, in particular, referential integrity and collections. An example ODL definition looks something like this:

```
interface Professor: Employee {
    extent professors;
    attribute String office_number;
    attribute enum rank {full, associate, assistant};
    relationship Set<Course> teaches inverse is_taught_by;
    grant_tenure() raises (ineligible);
};
```

This declaration defines professors to be a subtype of employee with a named extent, two attributes, a relationship to courses named teaches (the inverse attribute of courses is named is_taught_by), and an operation to grant tenure.

6. Object Query Language

There are two ways to retrieve objects out of an ODMG database:

1. Objects may be retrieved implicitly by navigating relationships in OML (the programming language), or

2. Objects may be retrieved through the ODMG object query language (OQL), by identifying objects through predicates defined on their characteristics.

Simple OQL queries are based on a predicate applied to a collection, selecting the members of a collection that satisfy the predicate. However, more complex queries may be performed: OQL can perform the equivalent of relational joins, and more. OQL need not produce an object or a table — it may result in an integer, a list of object references, a structure, a set of sets of real numbers, or any data structure that can be defined in the ODMG object model.

OQL queries objects starting with their names, which act as entry points into a database. In this sense, OQL is like SQL; however, in OQL a name may denote any kind of object: atomic, structure, collection, or literal. As an embedded language, OQL allows you to query objects which are supported by the native language through expressions yielding atoms, structures, collections, and literals.

The ODMG object model is used as the basis for OQL. The semantics of OQL are formally defined in the ODMG specification.

OQL differs from SQL2 and the planned SQL3 in some important respects. In keeping with the object paradigm of encapsulation, OQL does not provide explicit update operators; it relies on methods defined on objects for this purpose. Also, OQL is a declarative query language; it contains no procedural operations as in SQL3. OQL can be easily optimized by virtue of its declarative nature.

OQL's syntax is based on SQL, because of the prevalence of this language in the DBMS world. However, ODMG did not feel constrained to SQL syntax or semantics in cases where it would compromise the simplicity or power of OQL. Other concrete OQL syntaxes will be defined in order to merge the query language into programming languages. For example, ODMG plans to define a syntax for preprocessed C++ that is a natural extension of the language as opposed to an embedded foreign syntax.

OQL provides high-level primitives to deal with collections of objects, but OQL is not exclusively centered on the set construct as is SQL. OQL provides primitives to deal with structures and lists, and treats all such constructs with the same efficiency and convenience. As an illustration of the scope and nature of OQL, the following are valid queries:

```
2+3

president.subordinates

list ( joe, harry ) union
    select x from x in employees where x.salary > 50000

exists x in professors : x.spouse in x.advisees
```

7. Programming Language Bindings

A "programming language binding" in ODMG is quite different than in SQL. The ODMG binding is based on extending a programming language's syntax and semantics in order to provide database capabilities rather than embedding statements in SQL or another language. It is the goal of an ODMG programming language binding that the programmer feel there is one language, not two separate languages with arbitrary boundaries between them.

ODMG's goal of programming language integration results in several general principles. There is a single unified type system across the programming language and the database; individual instances of these common types can be persistent or transient. The programming language-specific binding respects the syntax and semantics of the base programming language into which it is being inserted. The binding is structured as a small set of additions to the base programming language; it does not introduce sublanguage-specific constructions that duplicate functionality already present within the base language. Expressions in the OML and OQL can be composed freely with expressions from the base programming language and vice versa.

An ODMG programming language binding has three components: OML, ODL, and OQL. In the C++ binding, ODL is expressed as a class library and an extension to the standard C++ class definition grammar. The class library provides classes and functions to implement the concepts defined in the ODMG object model. The OML, or object manipulation language, is used for retrieving and operating upon objects from the database. The C++ OML syntax and semantics are those of standard C++ in the context of the standard class library. The C++ OQL provides a way to retrieve data based on predicates.

In the case of C++, a completely seamless interface between the programming language and the ODL, OML, and OQL technically requires a preprocessor, due to constraints of the current C++ language. Because some customers dislike a preprocessor, ODMG chose to limit the ODMG-93 standard in some minor ways. ODMG-93 requires only an ODL preprocessor. A nearly seamless OML solution is possible without C++ changes, and a short-term OQL solution is possible with procedure calls. This allows vendors to get a standard API out quickly to customers, and to get some experience with it.

In addition to the query facilities and data modelling extensions such as collections and inverse attributes, ODMG extends programming language operations with database and transaction operations. All access, creation, modification, and deletion of persistent objects must be done within a transaction on an open database. Operations are defined on pre-defined database and transaction types. A database application generally will begin by opening a database and accessing one or more named objects, proceeding from there. These objects are in some sense "root" objects, in that they lead to interconnected webs of other objects.

The following is an example C++ ODL declaration for a professor class. The declaration could be written by a programmer, or a vendor's processor could be used to generate this declaration from the programming language-independent ODL:

```
class Professor : public  Employee {
    int age;
    int id_number;
    char* office_number;
    char* name;
    Ref<Department> dept inverse professors;
    Set<Student> advisees inverse Student::advisor;
    void grant_tenure ();
    void assign_course (course);
    }
```

An instance of type professor is declared as:

```
profP: Ref<Professor>
```

Standard C++ access syntax works on persistent objects:

```
profP->grant_tenure();
profP->age = 35;
deptRef = profP->dept;
```

Objects can be created, deleted, and modified. Objects are created in C++ OML using the C++ new operator, which is overloaded to allow additional arguments specifying the lifetime of the object.

A dereference operation on an object reference always guarantees that the object referred to is returned or that an exception is raised. If an object (persistent or transient) refers to a second, persistent, object that is not in memory when the dereference is executed, the second object, if it exists, will be retrieved automatically from disk, mapped into memory, and returned as the result of the dereference. If the supposedly referenced object does not exist, an appropriate exception is raised. References to transient objects work exactly the same as references to persistent objects, as far as the programmer is concerned.

8. Summary

Object DBMSs represent a new way of using databases. Essentially, they are an evolution of object-oriented programming languages to become "database programming languages," as opposed to an evolution of database languages to add object-oriented programming language capabilities. Object DBMSs provide important capabilities not present in other DBMSs:

- the programmer sees one seamless programming language and type system rather than two, and

- the architecture puts the bulk of the DBMS on the client side, offloading the server and allowing orders of magnitude faster cached data access.

ODMG defined a standard for object DBMSs; without this standard it is likely that object DBMSs would not have been viable in the market. Some lessons about effective standards definition can be learned from this experience. I posit that nearly all successful standards are defined in cases where three preconditions hold true:

1. A relatively small group of people write the standards specification.
2. These people have products that are already close to the standard, and their products collectively dominate the market.
3. There is a level of personal trust and investment in the group, with aggressive leadership to divide and track the work.

ODMG-93 was defined remarkably quickly using these principles, and many successful standards began in a similar way. However, not all standards can be defined in this way, and most standards activities (including ODMG) will have to abandon some of these principles as the technology matures, moving to a slower, more incremental process.

Bibliography

[1] R. G. G. Cattell, Editor, with contributions from T. Atwood, J. Duhl, G. Ferran, M. Loomis, and D. Wade: *The Object Database Standard: ODMG-93*, Morgan-Kaufmann, 1993, Revised 1994.

[2] R. G. G. Cattell and J. Skeen, "An Engineering Database Benchmark", *ACM Transactions on Database Systems,* April 1992.

[3] R. G. G. Cattell, *Object Data Management,* Addison-Wesley, 1991, revised 1994 (covers two dozen systems in some detail, plus an annotated bibliography of other sources).

[4] M. Loomis, *Object Databases: The Essentials,* Addison-Wesley, 1994 (provides good introductory discussion of object-oriented DBMSs, with contrasts to the object-relational approach).

[5] ODMG: Automated response providing the most up-to-date status and contacts for ODMG can be obtained by sending an empty email message to info@odmg.org.

[6] OMG: Object Management Architecture, 1995; send a request to info@omg.org or call +1-508-820-4300 for more information about OMG and about OMG documents.

Multimedia Database Management: Perspectives and Challenges

Arif Ghafoor

Distributed Multimedia Systems Laboratory,
School of Electrical Engineering,
Purdue University, West Lafayette, IN 47907, USA

1 Introduction

The areas which hope to benefit enormously from the emerging multimedia technologies include advanced information management systems for a broad range of applications, remote collaboration via video teleconferencing, improved simulation methodologies for all disciplines of science and engineering, and better human-computer interfaces [1]. There is a potential for developing vast libraries of information including arbitrary amounts of text, video, pictures, and sound usable more efficiently than traditional book, record, and tape libraries of today. These applications are just a sample of the kinds of things that may be possible with the development and use of multimedia. As the need for multimedia information systems is growing rapidly in various fields, management of such information is becoming a focal point of research in the database community. This also explains partly why there is an explosion of research in the areas related to the understanding, development and utilization of multimedia-related technologies.

With all the euphoria surrounding the potential benefits of the coming multimedia revolution, computer scientists and engineers are faced with real technological challenges pushing the limits of both the available hardware and the ingenuity of human thought. Some of the hardware problems faced include the following. Storage devices, which are usable online with the computers, are not "big" enough. The speed of retrieval from the available storage devices, including disks, is not sufficiently fast to cope with the demands of many multimedia applications. Conversely, storing multimedia data on disk is also relatively slow. Cache memories are a precious resource, but they are too small when it comes to multimedia, hence even greater demands for efficient resource management. Communication bandwidth tends to be another problem area for multimedia applications. A single object may demand large portions of bandwidth for extended periods of time. The problems of communication are compounded because of the delay-sensitive nature of multimedia. Storage problems for multimedia and for similar high-performance applications have been identified as deserving high priority.

From the systems point of view, storage, transportation, display and in general, management of multimedia data must have considerably more functionalities and capabilities than the conventional information management systems, due to the heterogeneous nature of the data. The fundamental issues faced by the multimedia database management researchers/designers are as follows:

- Development of models for capturing the media synchronization requirements. Integration of these models with the underlying database schema will be required. Subsequently, in order to determine the synchronization requirements at retrieval time, transformation of these models into a meta-schema is needed. This entails designing of object retrieval algorithms for the operating systems. Similarly, integration of these models with higher level information abstractions such as Hypermedia or object-oriented models, may be required.
- Development of conceptual models for multimedia information, especially for video, audio and image data. These models should be rich in their semantic capabilities for abstraction of multimedia information, be able to provide canonical representations of complex images, scenes, events in terms of objects and their spatio-temporal behavior.
- Design of powerful indexing, searching, accessing and organization methods for multimedia data. Search in multimedia databases can be quite computationally intensive, especially if content-based retrieval is needed for image and video data stored in compressed or uncompressed form. Occasionally, search may be fuzzy or based on incomplete information. Some form of classification/grouping of information may be needed, to help the search process.
- Design of efficient multimedia query languages. These languages should be capable of expressing complex spatio-temporal concepts, should allow imprecise match retrieval and be able to handle various manipulation functions for multimedia objects.
- Development of efficient data clustering and storage layout schemes to manage real-time multimedia data, for both single and parallel disk systems.
- Design and development of a suitable architecture and operating system support for a general purpose database management system
- Management of distributed multimedia data and coordination for composition of multimedia data over a network

In this paper, we elaborate on these issues and discuss the prospects of meeting the technical challenges involved in this development. We start our discussion with data modeling in Section 2 and 3. In Sections 4 and 5 we look at the issues in data indexing and the computational challenges involved. Section 6 discusses the role of query languages and user interfaces to access multimedia data. A brief overview of physical storage management is given in Section 7.

2 Spatio-Temporal Dimensions of Multimedia Data: Composition vs Semantic Modeling

Space and time are important dimensions of multimedia data. A large number of multimedia queries can be expressed in some form of interplay among objects in the course of time and their relationship in space. These objects may include physical objects such as persons, buildings, vehicles, etc., or events identified in a multimedia database. Many multimedia applications may require to store and access information about the worldly knowledge of these objects that can be expressed by complex spatio-temporal events. A video database, is a typical replica of this worldly environment.

The spatio-temporal specification process is sort of reversed while composing multimedia information. In this case, a user synthetically creates interplay among various media objects (akin to physical objects), both in space and time. In multimedia database these objects may represent individual data entities that serve as components of a multimedia document [1, 2].

In either case, it is essential that the user should be able to identify and address different objects and be able to express their relationship in time and space and represent them in a suitable structure that is powerful enough to develop higher-level semantics and event abstractions. It is, therefore, desirable that a general framework for spatio-temporal modeling should be available that can ultimately be integrated within a database management system. For such modeling, substantial benefits can be reaped from the AI area, since the AI community has been struggling for decades for solving complex semantic problems.

A number of attempts have been made to develop synchronization models for representing temporal ordering of objects in a multimedia document. Most of these models focus on the compositional aspects of multimedia information rather than on the semantic modeling of multimedia data [1]. There is a pressing need to develop and even standardize a general framework for such modeling and address the implementation issues within the realm of database environment. A number of attempts have been made towards this goal. The most prominent success is the hypermedia based HyTime/SGML standard. However, this standard is also aimed at composition of multimedia document rather than data semantic representation. An approach based on spatio-temporal logic is possible. However, this approach has limitations in terms of its capability for expressing many real-world events.

3 Object-Orientation in Multimedia System and Pitfalls of the Relational Model

Implementation of multimedia integration models with a database management systems is a challenging problem. Using meta-schema for this purpose and developing a unified family of schema is non-trivial, since the application domain for the multimedia applications can be quite complex and ill-structured. Moreover, the meta-schema may also require the incorporation of some unconventional information, eg. the quality of service requirements for presentation, such as speed, volume, resolution, etc. It is, therefore, essential to scrutinize the possible implementation approaches of integration. These approaches can be classified into two categories:

- Using the conventional data model, such as relational, the way we have used it for the last fifteen years,

- or semantic-based object-oriented solution, which will prevail throughout this decade and onwards.

From integration point of view, the conventional data modeling techniques lack the ability of managing composition of multimedia objects in a heterogeneous multimedia database environment. Semantic-based integration of different types of data may be required for a large number of multimedia applications. The relational model has a drawback of losing semantics which can cause erroneous interpretation of multimedia data. It is still being debated in the database community whether or not integration problems of even textual databases can be solved through schema integration alone. A family of solutions using the notion of external and internal schema have been proposed. This approach has its own strengths and weaknesses. Although, some relational DBMS have started supporting access to multimedia objects in form of pointing to BLOBs (Binary Large Objects), there is no provision for interactively accessing various portion of objects, as a BLOB is treated as a single entity in its entirety.

The object-oriented technology, on the other hand, can provide a powerful paradigm to meet the requirements of multimedia composition and developing semantic models. Its data and computational encapsulation features offer elegant semantic modeling capabilities at various levels of information granularity in multimedia database systems [15].

Limitation of the the relational model is also obvious when we deal with the semantic model of time-dependent multimedia data, such video or audio. The key characteristic of this data is the spatial/temporal semantics associated with it, making this data quite different from static data such as text, pictures, and images. A user of audio/video database can generate queries containing both temporal and spatial concepts. Moreover, considerable semantic heterogeneity may exist among users of such data due to differences in their pre-conceived interpretations or intended use of the information given in a video/audio clip. Semantic heterogeneity has been a difficult problem for conventional database, and even today this problem is not clearly understood. Consequently, providing a comprehensive interpretation of time-dependent data is a complex problem. However, also in this case, the semantic-based object-oriented models can provide a richer set of abstractions that is particularly useful using with a top-down design approach. This approach can allow users to extract/define view of information at various levels and can help them develop their own custom-tailored access tools without mis-interpreting the underlying meta-level concepts. Through such an approach, real meaning of attributes can be captured using common concepts and thus can provide a highly interactive environment.

For video data, Figure 1 describes how abstraction hierarchies in space and time need to be generated. Such a hierarchy provides a set of design specifications for the development of an automated video database management system. The figure also highlights the complex integration of various diverse technologies including computer vision and image processing (CVIP), AI, and database man-

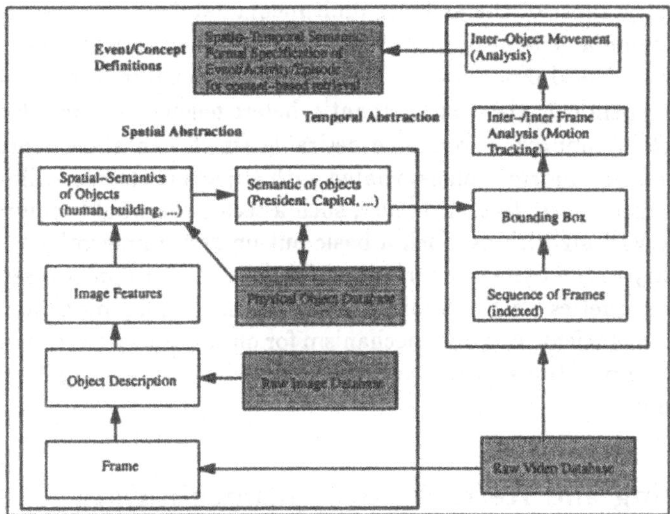

Fig. 1. An Architecture for an Automated Video/Image Database Management System for On-Line Query Processing

agement system. The generation of these hierarchies require a broad spectrum of computations that are intermingled with data and entities at various levels. Integration and management of heterogeneous computation with data entities at these levels would be clumsy if we attempt to use a relational model. As mentioned earlier, the data/computation encapsulation feature of object-oriented technology would be more suitable for such purpose.

Abandoning the relational model altogether for the implementation of a general purpose multimedia database system can cause a serious dilemma, as extensive management of a large number of indices, the meta-schema, and physical databases (eg. shown in Figure 1), as well as interfacing with the operating system for real-time retrieval can be technologically challenging. Since, most of the management data itself is textual in nature, it can be efficiently managed using the traditional relational database technology. However, if we insist on using the relational technology as the bases of the whole system, the capabilities of the relational model need to be expanded at least in the following three dimensions, in order to overcome the problem of mismatch between the relational and object-oriented technologies:

-multimedia schema architecture can be influenced by the use of an object-oriented common data model,

-the system architecture can be based on the fundamentals of the heterogeneous object-based architecture

-encapsulation concept of object-oriented technology can be used to integrate spatio-temporal composition with the components of multimedia information.

In summary, most of the existing multimedia database approaches lack the ability to provide a general-purpose, automatic mechanism which can render itself to semantic-based description of data. In order to address the issues related to a user-independent view and semantic heterogeneity, a ***semantically unbiased abstraction*** approach would be desirable which can allow representation of spatio-temporal information associated with objects (persons, buildings, vehicles, etc.) at some ***basic level***. However, such a technique would require effective and robust CVIP algorithms. Such a basic but unified framework can provide a good flexibility to the users to express and for the system to process semantically heterogeneous queries on the unbiased encoded data. This modeling approach can provide an efficient indexing mechanism for on-line query processing without performing computations on the raw video data since such computation can be quite extensive.

4 Indexing and Retrieval of Multimedia Data

Most of the existing multimedia database systems (especially video and image) either employ limited image processing techniques for semi-automated indexing of data or use manual approaches to generate keywords or annotated textual descriptors. In a semi-automated image processing based systems, special emphasis is given to content-based analysis of the data [5, 4, 3, 6, 7, 11]. For example, in [3], images are indexed using average histograms information as features and retrieval is performed based on similarity matching of these features. Similarly, in [6, 7], the content of an image is described by a language based on encoding the positional relationship (=, <) among the projections of the objects on the x-y axes of the image coordinate system. Thus each image is described by a 2D string and retrieval is based on the string matching. This approach is extended in [8], where objects in a frame having the same relationship in the 2D string are grouped in sets, and changes between subsequent frames are expressed through a set of operations such as addition/deletion or merging/splitting. Although, these systems are intended for managing still images only, their techniques have recently been extended for handling video data. For example, in [12], modeling of movements in a image sequence using spatio-temporal logic is proposed. In this approach moving objects in a scene are mapped to a set of processes through temporal logic, and models based on spatial logic are used to specify spatial relationships among the objects in the scene.

A manual approach can provide an alternate scheme for indexing multimedia data using keywords and textual descriptions. Such a scheme, based on a generalization hierarchy in an object-oriented realm, has been suggested in [14]. In this approach, video segments can be joined or concatenated based on the semantics of this hierarchy. However, this approach is very tedious since the perception of video contents is done manually by users, not through an automatic image processing mechanism. A video system that automatically parses video data into scenes using a color histogram comparison routine has been proposed in [13]. To locate frames containing desired objects, a method based on comparing the color histogram maps of objects is used. In [9], a hierarchical video stream model is proposed, that uses a template or histogram matching technique to identify scene change in a video segment. A video segment is thus divided into several subsegments. In each subsegment, a frame-based model is used to index the beginning frame of a subsegment from which objects are identified. In this system a video stream is parsed, and the information is stored in the database. However, this system has many limitations. First, the textual descriptions are manually associated with video segments. Second, the system provides parsing only for a specific type of video.

In general, for any automated system, we need to provide extensive computational facilities to index and access multimedia data. These computational challenges are discussed in the next section.

5 Multimedia Database Computational Challenges

The first step in the modeling of multimedia databases is extraction of information about the objects of interest that are present in the input data such as their identity, position, size, orientation, depth, and occlusions with respect to each other. The extraction of these features is a comprehensive process and requires extensive use of numerous computer vision/image processing, and speech processing techniques. Their consideration is critical however, for two main reasons: (i) accurate recognition of objects relies on the features employed and (ii) indexing and retrieval capability of the database system depends on these features.

In the detection of the *orientation* of the objects, models of objects are widely used. Fortunately, most of the recognition schemes available are capable of handling the orientation of the objects in the input images. The changes in orientation in subsequent scenes is used to represent the rotary motion. This information enables a database system to deal with rotations of the objects and answer the related queries.

The *depth* of an object is another feature, that makes it possible to answer queries involving the 3-D positions of the objects. For example, queries like "Find the video clips where Glenn Robinson scores a 3 pointer" are easy to process for the clips taken by a camera located near the basket. Depth information can be obtained either by using the motion of objects or by means of geometric projective properties of generic shapes when only a single image is available for recognition [18]. Texture analysis is a third technique used for the same purpose; if the floor for the indoor scenes or the ground for the outdoor scenes is visible then that can be used to arrange the objects according to depth.

A feature closely related to depth is the *occlusion* of objects which is especially important when multiple objects are present in a scene. An example query for partial occlusion of objects is "Find the clips where clouds partially cover the sun". Occlusion feature is also a useful means to detect the depth information for the objects [22].

5.1 Object Recognition

Recognition of objects consists of two phases: *detection* and *identification*. Scenes that contain a specified class of objects are searched for in the detection phase and information such as the size and location of the detected objects is extracted. The objects detected in each scene are later identified as known objects to complete the recognition process. Due to vast variety of objects that may be present in the data, classification of objects into groups is useful. That can enable us both to recognize them efficiently during the initial processing of data and to process database queries efficiently at the later phases. In other words, grouping objects into classes will make it possible to know what to look for during recognition and what to ask for at the database management level. As an example, recognition of a person in the video is done in two steps: Using the model of the class "men" that is available in the database, scenes that contain men are detected in the first step. Using more detailed data, all "familiar faces" in the database under class "men" are compared to the detected objects to identify them as one of the pre-recognized persons in the second step.

Although recognition of objects is highly case-dependent, several robust methods have been proposed in the literature. Generally, the techniques which are implemented sequentially are classified into two groups; non-correspondence matching and correspondence matching [17].

Non-correspondence matching deals with only global features and makes use of transformations from the object model to the image. Correspondence matching, or feature matching, on the other hand, involves finding a correspondence between local features of the object model and the image. Several techniques that differ in terms of matching primitives as well as matching criteria and searching methods have been developed in feature matching. Detailed references to various object recognition techniques can be found in [17].

The above mentioned methods and several connectionist approaches to object recognition have numerous advantages and disadvantages over each other depending on the different conditions of the problem. We believe, however, that most of the cases that may be faced in the multimedia applications are solvable by the currently available recognition technology.

5.2 Face Recognition

Since any multimedia database system should be capable of handling queries involving humans, automated detection and identification of humans is of vital importance, and that can only be accomplished by recognition of faces. This, however, constitutes an extremely difficult problem, because faces are highly complex multi-dimensional natural objects.

Several methods for face recognition have been developed incorporating feature matching. In the early stages of the recognition technology, semi-automatic techniques were used that requires human involvement at certain steps such as feature extraction or marking of the images [16]. Fully automated techniques followed in mid 70's that used local feature template and a global measure of fit to find and measure facial features. In [23] this method is further developed and a strategy is used based on "deformable templates" which are parameterized models of the face and its features in which the parameter values are determined by interactions with the image.

Number of connectionist techniques for fast and intelligent recognition of human faces have also been developed. In [19], an associative neural network is proposed that classifies and identifies face images in a noisy environment. WISARD system is able to recognize both identity and expression of faces and has been applied with some success [20]. In contrast to their advantage of being parallel schemes, connectionist systems have no ability to handle configurational properties of a face. Furthermore, they are not extensible to larger and more complex problems.

The EIGENFACE approach [21], is probably one of the most reliable schemes developed for face recognition. The approach is highly sensitive to variations of the geometry in the input images. In this method, the set of sample images is represented by a certain number of most "important" eigenvectors (eigenfaces) and face classes are formed by projecting the sample faces onto these vectors. Faces are recognized according to their representation in the feature space with respect to the ones of the face classes initially formed.

6 Multimedia Queries and User Interface

The query language of a database system is strongly related to the underlying data model. For multimedia applications, a highly interactive environment is needed which can allow content-based search or partial match retrieval. For content-based retrieval, a query in its simplest form can be based on keywords/descriptors or some formal spatio-temporal expression. The other extreme is to allow user to sketch images or to draw examples of spatio-temporal events. Such query-by-example (QBE) capability places stringent requirements on the design of user interface. For this purpose a graphical interface or visual language is more useful and friendly than the conventional textual query language, such as SQL, since the former can allow representation of objects by images or icons and it is easy to use [5].

As we expect, object-oriented schemes may be used as a toolkit for developing such interfaces. The integration of these components, data definition languages, and database programming languages pose major challenges in designing the query language of the system.

7 Storage Management in Multimedia Databases

There are certain characteristics of multimedia data objects which make their storage an unusual problem. Multimedia objects can be very large. Indeed, in most real-world systems, we may expect multimedia objects to be a few orders of magnitude larger on the average than other objects (typically text files and binary files). Further, multimedia objects tend to have hard real-time timing constraints during display. This is unlike most non-multimedia data objects, where temporal constraints are either missing (such as electronic mail) or very soft (such as user expectations on display terminals). Typical multimedia objects which need a high degree of temporal management are real-time visual displays. Each frame of such animated displays may amount to a few megabytes, and there may be a few hundred frames to be displayed each second. Further, the animation is also sensitive to inter-frame delay, and the order of frames. Many techniques to retain the integrity of objects have been successfully used in non-multimedia data, such as buffering, reordering of data before display, reconstructing lost data from encoded information, and reissuing request for lost data. These techniques provide new hurdles in case of multimedia data, and methods are being sought to overcome these hurdles. Another characteristic of multimedia objects is that they often occur *concurrently* with other multimedia objects. For example, animation objects are often accompanied with concurrent voice annotations. Or, two animated streams are displayed together.

On the other hand, there are some characteristics of multimedia data which hint towards optimization methodologies which might not be applicable otherwise. Multimedia data tends to very often accessed in the *read* mode. This means that modifications of multimedia data objects, in many applications, are relatively few. This allows designers to *read-optimize* the data. Multimedia data also tends to show strong temporal locality. This allows easier management and optimization of cache buffers. These optimizations are not universal, however, and some kinds of applications will not benefit from them. As multimedia technology matures, multimedia objects will become "first-class" objects and users will start expecting same kind of manipulative versatility from them as they do from other objects such as text. At that stage, designers will not, in general, be able to assume multimedia objects to be read-only type.

Overwhelming portion of multimedia system processing consists of storage and display of multimedia objects. This means that most processing is either *output* at the display site or the storage device, or it is *input* from one device to another device. The current speeds of disks used in the storage of multimedia objects are not sufficiently high to handle the extremely high volumes of these objects. As a result, I/O is currently a bottleneck for multimedia systems. For the same reason, I/O is the primary candidate for optimization in the multimedia system for increase in overall performance. In all the solutions proposed for improving I/O of multimedia systems, we must consider the following factors. The data-transfer throughput of the system should be high. Temporal requirements of multimedia data must be met. Anomalies and noise in multimedia displays must be held to acceptable levels, including temporal discontinuities in display (jitter), as well as dropping of parts of data-stream, causing lower display resolutions.

Because of the difficult state of affairs in multimedia I/O systems and its extreme importance in the success of overall system design, considerable amount of research has been directed towards obtaining workable solutions. We identify some of the approaches that can be used to ameliorate or solve the problem of slow disk I/O in multimedia systems. Most of these methods have their counterparts in previous operating system research, but modifications have to be made to incorporate the special characteristics of multimedia data, such as temporal requirements.

Several kinds of *I/O optimizations* can be performed. These improvements or optimizations include *zero latency reads*, where the disk transfer unit is equal to disk track. Thus rotational latency of disk reads is reduced. *Intermediate fast memories*, such as DRAM, may be used between the cache resource and the disk memory. I/O processing can be overlapped with other processing tasks, such as decompression of compressed data. For example, we have opportunity for *pipeline parallelism* by decompressing a chunk of multimedia data, while the I/O subsystem fetches a chunk of temporally latent data for the next step of multimedia data-object retrieval.

8 Conclusion

One of the main requirements of multimedia database systems is that they will need data models more powerful and more versatile than the relational model, without compromising the advantages of the former. The relational data model exhibits limitations in terms of complex object management, indexing and content-based retrieval of video/image data, and facility for handling the spatio-temporal dimensions of objects. To address these issues, we have emphasized two key requirements for multimedia databases: the process of saptio-temporal modeling, and the computational needs for automatic-indexing of spatio-temporal data. We have highlighted various other challenges that need to be tackled before multimedia database management systems become a reality.

References

1. A. Ghafoor, and P.B. Berra, "Multimedia Database Systems," *Advanced Database Systems*, Eds. B. Bhargava and N. Adams, Lecture Notes in Computer Science, Vol. 759, pp: 397-411, Springer-Verlag Publishers, 1993.
2. T. D. C. Little, and A. Ghafoor, "Synchronization and Storage Models for Multimedia Objects," *IEEE Jour. on Sele. Areas in Comm.*, Vol. 8, No. 3, April 1990, pages 413-427.
3. W. Niblack, R. Barber, W. Equitz, M. Flickner, E. Glasman, D. Petkovic, P. Yanker, C. Faloutsos, and G. Taubin, "The QBIC Project: Querying Images by Content using Color, Texture, and Shape,", *Proc. SPIE Storage and Retrieval for Image and Video Databases*, San Josw, CL, February 1995, pp: 173-181.
4. S.W. Smoliar, and H. Zhang, "Content-Based Video Indexing and Retrieval," *IEEE Multimedia*, Vol. 1, No. 2, 1994, pp: 62-72.
5. K. Hirata and T. Kato, "Query by Visual Example," *Advances in Database Technology - EDBT '92*, pages 56-71.
6. S.-K. Chang, Q.-Y. Shi, and C.-W. Yan, "Iconic Indexing by 2-D Strings," *IEEE Trans. on PAMI*, Vol. PAMI-9, No. 3, May 1987, pages 413-427.

7. S.-K. Chang, C.-M. Lee, and C. R. Dow, "A 2-D String Matching Algorithm for Conceptual Pictorial Queries," *Proceeding SPIE, Image Storage and Retrieval Systems*, San Jose, 1992, pages 47-58.
8. T. Arndt and S.-K. Chang, "Image Sequence Compression by Iconic Indexing," *IEEE VL '89 Workshop on Visual Lang.*, Rome, Italy, October 1989, pp. 177-182.
9. D. Swanberg, C.-F. Shu, and R. Jain, "Knowledge Guided Parsing in Video Databases," *Proceeding of SPIE*, San Jose, California, February 1993, pp. 13-24.
10. A. Del Bimbo, M. Campanai, and P. Nesi, "3-D Visual Query Language for Image Databases," *Journal of Visual Languages and Computing*, Vol. 3, 1992, pp. 257-271.
11. M. Campanai, A. Del Bimbo, and P. Nesi, "Using 3D Spatial Relationships for Image Retrieval by Contents," *Proceeding of IEEE VL' 92 Workshop on Visual Languages*, Seattle WA, September 1992, pp. 184-190.
12. A. Del Bimbo, E. Vicario, and D. Zingoni, "A Spatio-Temporal Logic for Image Sequence Coding and Retrieval," *Proceeding of IEEE VL' 92 Workshop on Visual Languages*, Seattle WA, September 1992, pp. 228-230.
13. A. Nagasaka and Y. Tanaka, "Automatic Video Indexing and Full Video Search for Object Appearances," *in 2nd Working Conference on Visual Database Systems*, Budapest, Hungry, October 1991, IFIP WG 2.6., pp. 119-133.
14. E. Oomoto and K. Tanaka, "OVID: Design and Implementation of a Video-Object Database System," *IEEE Transactions on Knowledge and Data Engineering*, Vol. 5, No. 4, August 1993, pp. 629-643.
15. M. Iino, Y. F. Day, A. Ghafoor, "An Object-Oriented Model for Spatio-Temporal Synchronization of Multimedia Information," *Proceeding of First IEEE Int. Conf. on Multimedia Computing and Sys.*, Boston, Mass, May 1994, pp. 110-119.
16. L. D. Harmon, "Some Aspects of Recognition of Human Faces," In O. J. Grusser and R. Klinke (Eds.), *Pattern Recognition in Biological and Technical Systems*, New York, Springer-Verlag, 1971.
17. W. E. L. Grimson, "Object Recognition by Computer," *MIT Press, Cambridge*, MA, 1990.
18. M. Zerroug, and R. Nevatia, "Volumetric Descriptions From a Single Intensity Image," to appear in *International Journal on Computer Vision.*
19. T. Kohonen, "Self-Organization and Associative Memory," Springer-Verlag, 1984.
20. T. J. Stonham, "Practical Face Recognition and Verification with WISARD," In H. Ellis, M. Jeeves, F. Newcombe, and A. Young (Eds.), *Aspects of Face Processing*, Kluwer Boston, 1986.
21. M. Turk and A. Pentland, "Face Recognition Using Eigenfaces," *Proceedings of the 1991 IEEE Computer Society Conference on Computer Vision and Pattern Recognition*, Maui, HI, June 3-6 1991, pp. 586-591.
22. J. A. Marshall and R. K. Alley, "A Self-Organizing Neural Network That Learns to Detect and Represent Visual Depth From Occlusion Events," *Proceedings of the AAAI Fall Symposium on Machine Learning and Computer Vision*, Research Triangle Park, NC, October 1993, pp. 70-74.
23. A. L. Yuille, D. S. Cohen, and P. W. Hallinan, "Feature Extraction From Faces Using Deformable Templates," *Proceedings of th IEEE Conference on Computer Vision and Pattern Recognition*, Rosemont, IL, June 6-9 1989, pp. 104-109.
24. L. Mohan and R.L. Kashyap, "A Visual Query Language for Graphical Interaction With Schema-Intensive Database," *IEEE Trans. on Data and Knowledge Engineering*, Vol. 5, No. 5, October 1993, pp. 843-858.

Combining Inheritance and Parametric Polymorphism in a Functional Database Language

Simon Courtenage and Alexandra Poulovassilis

Dept. of Computer Science, King's College London
Strand, London WC2R 2LS
{alex,simonc}@dcs.kcl.ac.uk

Abstract. We consider extending a functional database language to support subtyping, inheritance and method overloading. We do so by extending previous work on type inference with subtypes for the pure λ calculus to cater for structured types, ML-style parametric polymorphism and overloaded function definitions. We attach semantics to overloaded functions by developing a generalisation of best-fit pattern-matching. Although developed for a specific language, our approach is applicable to other functional database languages, for example languages with a functional data model.

1 Introduction

Two major trends in recent database research have been deductive databases and object-oriented databases. Deductive databases extend the relational data model with rules that enable the derivation of intentional relations from the stored, extensional, relations. Object-oriented databases typically start off with a semantic data model [HK87] supporting object identity and complex objects, and extend it with features such as inheritance, methods and encapsulation from object-oriented programming. Deductive and object-oriented databases are thus largely complementary and recent research has aimed at integrating them [DOO].

For reasons discussed at length in [PS91], we are interested in *functional programming* as opposed to logic programming as the basis for deductive databases. A database language, PFL [PS91] [SP91], has been developed which exhibits all the desirable features of a functional language (such as higher-order functions, static type checking and lazy evaluation) but which also supports functions that simulate the extensional and intentional relations of logic languages such as Datalog.

In common with many functional programming languages, PFL supports ML-style parametric polymorphism of types and functions. We now show how to incorporate subtyping, inheritance and overloading into PFL, thereby taking a functional programming route to the integration of deductive and object-oriented databases. Two fundamental requirements for this work have been (a) to preserve upwards-compatibility with the current version of PFL, and (b) to avoid "impedance mismatch" problems by maintaining a single semantic and operational framework. Our approach is easily applied to other functional database languages, for example languages with a functional data model such as FDL [Pou92].

We begin the paper with a brief review of the current PFL language in Section 2. We then introduce its new features in Section 3. In particular, we discuss how the type system is enriched by allowing the declaration of subtype relationships between atomic (i.e. non-structured) types, and how subtyping extends to structured types and function types. We describe how function definitions can be overloaded for different subtypes of a type, and we attach semantics to overloaded functions by developing a generalisation of the best-fit pattern-matching of [FH88]. We also briefly consider schema evolution. Type-checking remains static in the extended language but some type inference is also carried out at run time in order to perform run-time binding to overloaded functions. We give the type inference algorithm in Section 4. It is based upon Mitchell's $\mathcal{GA}$ algorithm [Mit91], with additions to infer types for constructors, "let" and "letrec" expressions and overloaded functions. In Section 5 we consider related work in the area of type inference with subtypes. We end the paper in Section 6 with a summary of our contributions and directions of further work

2 Overview of PFL

In this section we give an overview of the current PFL language, covering only aspects of the language that are prerequisites for our discussion of its new features in subsequent sections. More comprehensive accounts of PFL can be found in [PS91], [SP91].

2.1 Types

The syntax of PFL types is as follows, where σ ranges over type expressions, α over type variables and κ^n over n-ary type constructors:

$$\sigma ::= \alpha \mid \sigma_1 \rightarrow \sigma_2 \mid \kappa^n\ \sigma_1\ \ldots\ \sigma_n$$

Types of the form $\sigma_1 \rightarrow \sigma_2$ are *function types*. Types of the form κ^0 are *atomic types* (so the set of 0-ary type constructors and the set of atomic types are identical). Types of the form $\kappa^n\ \sigma_1\ \ldots\ \sigma_n$, where $n > 0$, are *structured types*. Below, we also use the symbols ι, κ to range over atomic types and τ, υ to range over type expressions.

The atomic types *Num*, *Chr*, *Bool* and *Str* are built-in and declared as follows in PFL's standard environment:

_type Num :: *Type*
_type Chr :: *Type*
_type Bool :: *Type*
_type Str :: *Type*

Also built-in are a number of type constructors for structured types:

$\_type\ List\ \ \ \ \ \ \ \ :: Type \rightarrow Type$
$\_type\ Set\ \ \ \ \ \ \ \ \ :: Type \rightarrow Type$
$\_type\ Product2 :: Type \rightarrow Type \rightarrow Type$
$\_type\ Product3 :: Type \rightarrow Type \rightarrow Type \rightarrow Type$
...

These declarations can be read as stating that a type constructor takes one or more types as arguments and constructs a new type. PFL supports some syntactic sugar for structured types: $(\tau_1, \ldots, \tau_n)$ is synonymous with $Product_n\ \tau_1\ \ldots\ \tau_n$ for any types $\tau_1, \ldots, \tau_n$; $[\tau]$ is synonymous with $List\ \tau$ for any type τ; and $\{\tau\}$ is synonymous with $Set\ \tau$. Also, $\rightarrow$ is right-associative, so that $\tau_1 \rightarrow \tau_2 \rightarrow \tau_3$ and $\tau_1 \rightarrow (\tau_2 \rightarrow \tau_3)$ are synonymous.

New constructors for atomic and structured types can be declared at any time during the lifetime of a PFL database e.g.

$\_type\ Person\ \ \ \ :: Type$
$\_type\ Student\ \ \ :: Type$
$\_type\ Employee :: Type$
$\_type\ RA\ \ \ \ \ \ \ \ \ :: Type$
$\_type\ Tree\ \ \ \ \ \ :: Type \rightarrow Type$

We use the notation E :: τ to indicate that an expression E has type τ. We postpone a precise definition of the syntax of expressions to Section 2.4.

2.2 Values

Both structured and atomic types are incrementally populated by declaring *value constructors* which return values of that type when applied to appropriate arguments. The 0-ary value constructors populating the built-in *Num*, *Chr*, *Str* and *Bool* types are predeclared and non-deletable - these are, respectively, integer and real numbers, characters, strings, and *True* and *False*. Also predeclared are constructors for empty lists, lists consisting of a head and tail, and tuples:

$\_value\ [\,]\ \ \ \ \ \ \ \ :: [a]$
$\_value\ (:)\ \ \ \ \ \ \ :: a \rightarrow [a] \rightarrow [a]$
$\_value\ Tuple2 :: a \rightarrow b \rightarrow (a, b)$
$\_value\ Tuple3 :: a \rightarrow b \rightarrow c \rightarrow (a, b, c)$
...

In the above declarations, a, b, and c are type variables that can be instantiated by any type. Generally, in PFL identifiers starting with a lower-case letter are variables while identifiers starting with an upper-case letter are type or value constructors.

Some syntactic sugar is supported for structured values in that, for any expressions $E_1, \ldots, E_n$, an n-tuple $(E_1, \ldots, E_n)$ is synonymous with $Tuple_n\ E_1\ \ldots$

E_n and an enumerated list $[E_1, \ldots, E_n]$ is synonymous with $E_1 : (\ldots : (E_n : [])\ldots)$.

New value constructors can be declared at any time during the lifetime of a PFL database e.g.

$$
\begin{array}{llll}
\_value\ E1 & :: Employee & \_value\ E2 & :: Employee \\
\_value\ S1 & :: Student & \_value\ R1 & :: RA \\
\_value\ Leaf & :: a \rightarrow (Tree\ a) & \_value\ Node & :: (Tree\ a) \rightarrow (Tree\ a) \rightarrow (Tree\ a)
\end{array}
$$

0-ary constructors such as $E1$, $E2$, $S1$, $R1$ above serve as *object identifiers* in PFL. User-declared atomic types are analogous to the non-lexical types of languages such as FDL and 0-ary constructors are analogous to non-lexical entities.

2.3 Functions

The usual arithmetic, comparison and boolean operators are built-in. Also built-in are several operators over sets, including set union, $\cup :: \{a\} \rightarrow \{a\} \rightarrow \{a\}$, and *setmap* $:: (a \rightarrow \{b\}) \rightarrow \{a\} \rightarrow \{b\}$. The latter distributes a function of type $a \rightarrow \{b\}$ over a set of type $\{a\}$ and returns the union of the results. Binary operators may be written either infix or prefix, and in the latter case they must be enclosed within brackets.

The user can define new functions by means of one or more equations. Equations use pattern-matching to deconstruct their arguments, where a *pattern* is either a variable or an application of an n-ary constructor to n patterns. For example, the following PFL commands specify two equations for the *foldr* function and one equation for the *sum* function (note that in PFL the symbol $==$ is used for equational definitions while $=$ is the equality operator):

$$
\begin{array}{ll}
\_define\ foldr\ op\ e\ [\,] & == e \\
\_define\ foldr\ op\ e\ (x : xs) & == op\ x\ (foldr\ op\ e\ xs) \\
\_define\ sum\ xs & == foldr\ (+)\ 0\ xs
\end{array}
$$

Single-equation definitions are simply syntactic sugar for named λ- abstractions e.g. the definition for *sum* above states that $sum = \lambda xs.foldr\ (+)\ 0\ xs$.

Multi-equation definitions also translate into a single expression - the reader is referred to [PJ87], [FH88] for a detailed description of the process. For example, the single expression that defines *foldr* above is

$$
\begin{array}{lll}
foldr & = \lambda op.\lambda e.\lambda l. & (\lambda op.\lambda e.\lambda[\,].e)\ op\ e\ l\ \| \\
& & (\lambda op.\lambda e.\lambda(x : xs).op\ x\ (foldr\ op\ e\ xs))\ op\ e\ l\ \| \\
& & error
\end{array}
$$

where:

- $\| :: a \rightarrow a \rightarrow a$ is a built-in binary infix operator (pronounced "fatbar") which returns its first argument if this is not the value *Fail* and its second argument otherwise;
- *error* $:: a$ is a built-in function which generates a run-time error when invoked; and

– *Fail* :: a is a built-in value of unconstrained type which is used to denote a pattern-matching failure.

Thus, when at run time *foldr* is applied to three arguments *op*, *e* and *l*, if *l* matches the pattern [ ] (i.e. it is the empty list) then the first definition is used, otherwise if *l* matches the pattern $(x : xs)$ the second definition is used, otherwise the third definition is used.

λ-abstractions with patterns as their bound argument, such as $\lambda[\,].e$ and $\lambda(x : xs).op\ x\ (foldr\ op\ e\ xs)$ above, are just syntactic sugar for ordinary λ-abstractions of the form λx.E. In particular, corresponding to each n-ary constructor $c :: \tau_1 \rightarrow \ldots \rightarrow \tau_n \rightarrow \tau$ is a built-in function $unpack\_c :: (\tau_1 \rightarrow \ldots \rightarrow \tau_n \rightarrow a) \rightarrow \tau \rightarrow a$ and λ-abstractions of the form $\lambda(c\ p_1\ \ldots\ p_n)$.E translate into $unpack\_c\ (\lambda p_1 \ldots .\ \lambda p_n.\mathrm{E})$. The semantics of *unpack_c* are

$$\begin{aligned} unpack\_c\ f\ (c\ \mathrm{E}_1\ \ldots\ \mathrm{E}_n) &= f\ \mathrm{E}_1\ \ldots\ \mathrm{E}_n \\ unpack\_c\ f\ (c'\ \mathrm{E}_1\ \ldots\ \mathrm{E}_m) &= Fail \qquad\qquad if\ c' \neq c \\ unpack\_c\ f\ \bot &= \bot \end{aligned}$$

where $\bot$ denotes a non-terminating computation. In other words, when at run time *unpack_c* is applied to two arguments, f and E, E is evaluated as far as is necessary to determine its constructor; if this evaluation fails to terminate, the result is a non-terminating computation; if E evaluates to an expression of the form $c\ \mathrm{E}_1\ \ldots\ \mathrm{E}_n$ the result is $f\ \mathrm{E}_1\ \ldots\ \mathrm{E}_n$; otherwise the result is *Fail*.

The type of any equationally-defined function is inferred automatically by the system and the user is warned if the function is not well-typed.

Bulk data is stored within extensionally defined sets termed *data functions* whose types are explicitly declared by the user [1] e.g.

$$\begin{aligned} &\_datafun\ courses :: \{(Student, Course)\} \\ &\_datafun\ salary\ \ :: \{(Employee, Num)\} \\ &\_datafun\ income :: \{(Person, Source, Num)\} \end{aligned}$$

For example, the following functions return respectively the courses of a student, the salary of an employee, the set of $(source, income)$ tuples for a person, and the total income for a person [2]:

$$\begin{aligned} &\_define\ attends\ s &&== \{c \mid (q, c) \leftarrow courses;\ q = s\} \\ &\_define\ earns\ e &&== one\ \{s \mid (q, s) \leftarrow salary;\ q = e\} \\ &\_define\ incomes\ p &&== \{(s, i) \mid (q, s, i) \leftarrow income;\ q = p\} \\ &\_define\ totalInc\ p &&== sum\ [i \mid (s, i) \leftarrow set\_to\_list\ (incomes\ p)] \end{aligned}$$

[1] This is actually a simplification of how the current implementation of PFL handles bulk data; in particular, data functions cannot be used directly but only via functions termed *selectors* [SP91]. However, in the interests of simplicity, we assume in this paper that data functions are directly usable: the type system with which we are concerned copes equally well with selector functions and data functions.

[2] See [PS94] for a discussion of the function *set_to_list* which deterministically converts a set to a list. The function *one* in *earns* is equal to *head* o *set_to_list*

We note the use of set and list comprehensions in the above definitions. As described at length elsewhere [PJ87] [PS94], these constructs are merely syntactic sugar for applications of *setmap* and *flatmap* (the analogue of *setmap* for lists).

The initial value of any data function is the empty set. This value is updateable by means of two built-in functions which respectively add a value to a data function and delete a value from a data function, returning the updated data function [3]:

$inc :: a \rightarrow \{a\} \rightarrow \{a\}$
$exc :: a \rightarrow \{a\} \rightarrow \{a\}$

2.4 Type-Checking and Evaluation

PFL expressions are translated into the following kernel syntax for the purposes of type-checking and evaluation, where $x \in \mathit{Variables}$, including the names of equationally-defined functions, and $c \in \mathit{Constants}$, including the names of constructors, built-in functions and data functions:

$$\begin{aligned} \mathrm{E} ::= {} & x \mid c \mid \mathrm{E}_1\mathrm{E}_2 \mid \lambda x.\mathrm{E} \mid \\ & \mathit{let}\ x = \mathrm{E}_1\ \mathit{in}\ \mathrm{E} \mid \\ & \mathit{letrec}\ (x_1,\ldots,x_n) = (\mathrm{E}_1,\ldots,\mathrm{E}_n)\ \mathit{in}\ \mathrm{E} \end{aligned}$$

In order to type-check and evaluate a query, E, the *call graph* of E, $CG(\mathrm{E})$, is first constructed i.e. the set of equationally-defined functions that are either directly or indirectly referenced by E. From the discussion in the previous section, $CG(\mathrm{E})$ is a set of definitions $\{f_1 = \mathrm{E}_1, \ldots, f_r = \mathrm{E}_r\}$. This set is next partitioned into strata, $S_1, \ldots, S_m$, such that every function defined in a stratum S_i either directly or indirectly references every other function defined in S_i, and does not reference any function defined in a stratum S_j with $j > i$. Each stratum S_i is finally translated into a "let" or "letrec" clause, L_i, as follows. If S_i consists of just one non-recursively defined function, $S_i = \{f_{i,1} = \mathrm{E}_{i,1}\}$, then L_i is

$$\mathit{let}\ \ f_{i,1} = \mathrm{E}_{i,1}$$

otherwise if S_i consists of one or more mutually recursively defined functions, $S_i = \{f_{i,1} = \mathrm{E}_{i,1}, \ldots, f_{i,r_i} = \mathrm{E}_{i,r_i}\}$ then L_i is

$$\mathit{letrec}\ \ (f_{i,1}, \ldots, f_{i,r_i}) = (\mathrm{E}_{i,1}, \ldots, \mathrm{E}_{i,r_i})$$

---

[3] This is again a simplification of how updates are handled in PFL since, as they stand, *inc* and *exc* have the drawback that loss of referential transparency can occur, and that the evaluation order of expressions must be known to the programmer in order to sequence evaluations of *inc* and *exc*. [SS95] discusses how to overcome these problems. The type system with which we concerned in this paper is largely orthogonal to the way in which updates are accommodated.

The overall expression that will be type-checked and evaluated given a query E is thus

$$L_1 \; in \; L_2 \; in \; \ldots \; L_m \; in \; \mathrm{E}$$

Type inference is performed essentially by means of Milner's W algorithm and query evaluation is performed by means of the standard technique of graph reduction used in many functional programming languages. We refer the reader to [PJ87] and [FH88] for a detailed description of both issues.

3 New Features

We are now ready to introduce the new features of PFL. We begin with a description of how *subtyping* is supported by the, possibly incremental, declaration of an inheritance graph (Section 3.1). We then discuss the implications of subtyping on constructors, built-in functions and equationally-defined functions (Sections 3.2, 3.3 and 3.4). Overloading of function definitions is now supported by allowing variables annotated with atomic types to appear in equation left-hand sides. Overloaded functions are analogous to methods in object-oriented languages and we define their semantics in Section 3.5. In Section 3.6 we describe how the extended language is translated into a kernel syntax for type-checking and evaluation. Finally, in Section 3.7 we discuss the issue of schema evolution.

3.1 Subtypes

The first new feature is that atomic types can participate in an *inheritance graph*. For example, given the atomic types declared in Section 2.1, the usual inheritance graph of $RA < Employee, RA < Student, Employee < Person, Student < Person$ is defined by the following commands:

_type RA < Employee
_type RA < Student
_type Employee < Person
_type Student < Person

Arcs can be added to the inheritance graph at any time during the lifetime of a PFL database. Before proceeding with the insertion of a new arc, $\iota < \kappa$, into the current inheritance graph, G, we:

(i) verify that the subtype relationship $\kappa < \iota$ is not inferable from G, thereby ensuring that no cycles are introduced into G;
(ii) verify that for each arc $\iota' < \kappa' \in G \cup \{\iota < \kappa\}$ the subtype relationship $\iota' < \kappa'$ is not inferable from $(G \cup \{\iota < \kappa\}) - \{\iota' < \kappa'\}$, thereby ensuring that every arc in the new inheritance graph is non-redundant.

The insertion of a new arc $\iota < \kappa$ into the inheritance graph has two effects: it causes the extent of κ to expand to include the extent of ι, and it induces further subtype relationships between types. The inference rules for deducing new subtype relationships from a given set of subtype relationships C are as follows:

$$\frac{}{C \vdash \sigma < \sigma} \text{ Reflexivity}$$

$$\frac{C \vdash \sigma < \tau \quad C \vdash \tau < \upsilon}{C \vdash \sigma < \upsilon} \text{ Transitivity}$$

$$\frac{C \vdash \tau_1 < \sigma_1 \quad C \vdash \sigma_2 < \tau_2}{C \vdash \sigma_1 \rightarrow \sigma_2 < \tau_1 \rightarrow \tau_2} \text{ Function types}$$

$$\frac{C \vdash \sigma_1 < \tau_1, \ldots, \sigma_n < \tau_n}{C \vdash \kappa^n \sigma_1 \ldots \sigma_n < \kappa^n \tau_1 \ldots \tau_n} \text{ Structured types}$$

We notice from these rules that the $\rightarrow$ type constructor is anti-monotonic in its first argument while all other type constructors are monotonic in all arguments. These monotonicity properties ensure the semantic soundness of subtypes - see [CW85] for a discussion.

3.2 Values

In the presence of subtypes, constructors now have richer types than before. We term the declared types of constructors *Curry types* and the enriched types *Mitchell types*, after [Mit91]. In particular, a Mitchell type is a pair (C,τ) where C is a *coercion set* consisting of subtype assertions between atomic types and type variables and where τ is a type expression that references no atomic types. For example, the Mitchell type of the constructor $E1$ of Section 2.2 is $(\{Employee < a\}, a)$, meaning that $E1$ has type *Employee* and also any supertype thereof.

The Curry types declared for constructors are straightforwardly converted into the corresponding Mitchell types. In particular, the Mitchell type corresponding to a Curry type τ is given by EXPAND$(\tau, True)$ where the algorithm EXPAND is defined below over the syntax of type expressions. The second argument to EXPAND indicates whether the current sub-expression appears covariantly in the overall type expression. The definition of EXPAND for a function type negates this value for the argument type:

$$\begin{array}{ll} \text{EXPAND}(\kappa, True) & = (\{\kappa < \beta\}, \beta) \\ \text{EXPAND}(\kappa, False) & = (\{\beta < \kappa\}, \beta) \\ \text{EXPAND}(\alpha, True) & = (\{\alpha < \beta\}, \beta) \\ \text{EXPAND}(\alpha, False) & = (\{\beta < \alpha\}, \beta) \end{array}$$

where β is a new type variable

$$
\begin{array}{l}
\text{EXPAND}(\sigma_1 \rightarrow \sigma_2, \textit{covariant}) \quad = (C_1 \cup C_2, \tau_1 \rightarrow \tau_2) \\
\quad \text{where} \\
\quad (C_1, \tau_1) = \text{EXPAND}(\sigma_1, \textit{not}(\textit{covariant})), \\
\quad (C_2, \tau_2) = \text{EXPAND}(\sigma_2, \textit{covariant}) \\
\text{EXPAND}(\kappa^n\ \sigma_1 \ldots \sigma_n, \textit{covariant}) = (C_1 \cup \ldots \cup C_n, \kappa^n\ \tau_1 \ldots \tau_n) \\
\quad \text{where} \\
\quad (C_1, \tau_1) = \text{EXPAND}(\sigma_1, \textit{covariant}) \\
\quad \ldots \\
\quad (C_n, \tau_n) = \text{EXPAND}(\sigma_n, \textit{covariant})
\end{array}
$$

For example, the type declared for the constructor (:) in Section 2.2 was $a \rightarrow [a] \rightarrow [a]$ and

$$\text{EXPAND}(a \rightarrow [a] \rightarrow [a], \textit{True}) = (\{b < a, c < a, a < d\}, b \rightarrow [c] \rightarrow [d]).$$

Thus whereas before (:) constructed lists of elements all of the same type a, it now constructs lists of elements all with a common supertype a, and the resultant list possesses all types $[d]$ such that $a < d$. For example, $[E1, S1]$ is now a list of type $[Person]$ whereas before it would have been incorrectly typed.

3.3 Built-in functions

In the presence of subtypes, built-in functions generally have richer types than before. Unlike our treatment of constructors above, the Mitchell type of a built-in function cannot in general be determined from its Curry type but instead has to be declared explicitly by the implementor. The following are some of the more interesting changes to the built-in functions:

The *asaκ* family of functions. For every atomic type κ, we now support a new built-in function $as a\kappa :: (\{a < \kappa\}, a \rightarrow \kappa)$ which generalises the type of an expression from a subtype of κ to κ itself. As we will see below, this family of functions is useful for generalising the type of an expression in order to bind at run time to the method definition for a supertype.

The arithmetic operators. We can now refine PFL's built-in Num type with a subtype structure representing different kinds of numbers and we can enrich the built-in arithmetic operators appropriately. For example, if $Int < Real$ and $Real < Num$ we can implement an addition operator $(+) :: (\{a < Num, b < Num, a < c, b < c\}, a \rightarrow b \rightarrow c)$ in which case $1 + 2 :: (\{Int < c, c)$ while $1.5 + 2 :: (\{Real < c\}, c)$.

The *unpack_c* family of functions. Analogously to constructors, the *unpack_c* functions of Section 2.3 now have types obtained by applying EXPAND to their Curry type. For example, the Curry types of *unpack_[ ]*, *unpack_(:)* and *unpack_Tuple2* were

$$\begin{array}{ll} unpack\_[\,] & :: a \rightarrow [b] \rightarrow a \\ unpack\_(:) & :: (a \rightarrow [a] \rightarrow b) \rightarrow [a] \rightarrow b \\ unpack\_Tuple2 & :: (a \rightarrow b \rightarrow c) \rightarrow (a,b) \rightarrow c \end{array}$$

while their Mitchell types (after some simplification of the coercion sets) are

$$\begin{array}{ll} unpack\_[\,] & :: (\{a < c\}, a \rightarrow [b] \rightarrow c) \\ unpack\_(:) & :: (\{f < c, f < d, e < g\}, (c \rightarrow [d] \rightarrow e) \rightarrow [f] \rightarrow g) \\ unpack\_Tuple2 & :: (\{g < d, h < e, f < i\}, (d \rightarrow e \rightarrow f) \rightarrow (g,h) \rightarrow i) \end{array}$$

For example, the expression $\lambda(e,s).(earns\ e, attends\ s)$ translates into
$unpack\_Tuple2\ (\lambda e.\lambda s.(earns\ e, attends\ s))$
and has type $(\{a < Employee, b < Student, Num < c, Course < d\}, (a,b) \rightarrow (c, \{d\}))$, while the expression $\lambda[e,s].(earns\ e, attends\ s)$ translates into
$unpack\_(:)\ (\lambda e.unpack\_(:)\ (\lambda s.unpack\_[\,]\ (earns\ e, attends\ s)))$
and has type $(\{a < RA, Num < b, Course < c\}, [a] \rightarrow (b, \{c\}))$. Notice that this latter expression would not be typable without subtyping.

The *inc* and *exc* functions. These now have type $(\{a < b, b < c\}, a \rightarrow \{b\} \rightarrow \{c\})$, which means that subtype values can now appear within data functions. For example, given the data functions declared in Section 2.3, the following inclusions are now valid:

$$\begin{array}{l} inc\ (E1, PropertyRent, 2000)\ \ income \\ inc\ (S1, Demonstrating, 50)\ \ income \\ inc\ (R1, DepositAccount, 200)\ \ income \\ inc\ (R1, 15000)\ \ salary \end{array}$$

In contrast, without subtyping, if we had wanted to record incomes for employees, students and RAs we could not have used the data function *income* as above but would have required three further data functions: $empIncome :: \{(Employee, Source, Num)\}$, $stuIncome :: \{(Student, Source, Num)\}$ and $raIncome :: \{(RA, Source, Num)\}$. Similarly, we could not have used the data function *salary* for RAs but would have required a further data function $raSalary :: \{(RA, Num)\}$.

3.4 Equationally-defined functions

Just as built-in functions, equationally-defined functions too can have richer types in the presence of subtypes. For example, the functions *incomes* and *totalInc* defined in Section 2.3 can now be used to determine the income of employees, students and RAs, as well as that of persons.

We now also extend the syntax of equation left hand sides to allow variables to be optionally annotated with atomic types. This extension allows functions to be *overloaded* for different subtypes of a type. For example, suppose we wish to define a function which computes the taxable income of a person in terms of their salary, if any, and other sources of income. Without subtyping, we would have had to define four different functions to do this, using the various data functions for persons, employees, students and RAs. With subtyping and overloading we need define only one function:

$$\_define\ taxInc\ p :: Person \quad == totalInc\ p$$
$$\_define\ taxInc\ p :: Employee == (taxInc\ (asaPerson\ p)) + (earns\ p)$$

The type inferred for *taxInc* is $(\{a < Person, Num < b\}, a \rightarrow b)$. If at run time *taxInc* is applied to an argument of type $(\{Employee < a\}, a)$ or $(\{RA < a\}, a)$ the second equation will be selected as a *more specific* match (see below) for the given argument than the first equation. Otherwise if *taxInc* is applied to an argument of type $(\{Student < a\}, a)$ or $(\{Person < a\}, a)$ the first equation will be chosen as the only match. Notice in the second equation the use of *asaPerson* to generalise the type of p to *Person* and thus to pick up the first equation of *taxInc* for p rather than the second equation.

Annotated variables can appear anywhere within patterns. In particular, functions over structured types and multiple arguments can also be overloaded. For example, *countStudents* counts the number of students within a list of persons:

$$\_define\ countStudents\ [\,] \quad == 0$$
$$\_define\ countStudents\ (x :: Student : xs) == 1 + (countStudents\ xs)$$
$$\_define\ countStudents\ (x :: Person : xs) == countStudents\ xs$$

and *same* checks whether two person "objects" have the same "value" over their common attributes:

$$\_define\ same\ x :: Person\ y :: Person \quad == incomes\ x = incomes\ y$$
$$\_define\ same\ x :: Student\ y :: Student \quad ==$$
$$\quad (same\ (asaPerson\ x)\ (asaPerson\ y))\ \&\ (attends\ x = attends\ y)$$
$$\_define\ same\ x :: Employee\ y :: Employee ==$$
$$\quad (same\ (asaPerson\ x)\ (asaPerson\ y))\ \&\ (earns\ x = earns\ y)$$
$$\_define\ same\ x :: RA\ y :: RA ==$$
$$\quad (same\ (asaStudent\ x)\ (asaStudent\ y))\ \&$$
$$\quad (same\ (asaEmployee\ x)\ (asaEmployee\ y))$$

3.5 Semantics of Equationally-defined Functions

As before, multi-equation function definitions must be translated into a single expression. To cater for the presence of annotated variables in equation left hand sides we have developed an extension of the *best-fit pattern-matching* of [FH88] which we now describe. For the purposes of this description, n-ary functions are treated as functions of a single n-tuple. Thus for any function f we have a set of equations

$$f\ p_1 == E_1\ ,\ f\ p_2 == E_2\ ,\ \ldots\ ,\ f\ p_r == E_r$$

which are to be ordered according to some criterion. The criterion we use is that of the relative *specificity* of the patterns $p_1, \ldots, p_r$, defined as follows:

Definition 1. A pattern p_i is *more specific* than a pattern p_j, written $p_i \sqsubset p_j$, or *equally specific* to a pattern p_j, written $p_i \sim p_j$, according to the following criteria:

x	$\sim$	y	for any variables x and y
$x :: \iota$	$\sqsubset$	y	
$x :: \iota$	$\sim$	$y :: \iota$	
$x :: \iota$	$\sqsubset$	$y :: \kappa$	if $\iota \neq \kappa$ and $\iota < \kappa$
$x :: \iota$	$\sim$	$y :: \kappa$	if $\iota \not< \kappa$, $\kappa \not< \iota$ and ι and κ have a common subtype
$c\ p_1 \ldots p_n$	$\sqsubset$	x	for any constructor c and variable x
c	$\sqsubset$	$x :: \kappa$	if the declared type of c is ι and $\iota < \kappa$
$c\ p_1 \ldots p_n$	$\sim$	$c\ q_1 \ldots q_n$	if $p_i \sim q_i$ for all $1 \leq i \leq n$
$c\ p_1 \ldots p_n$	$\sqsubset$	$c\ q_1 \ldots q_n$	if $p_i \sqsubset q_i$ or $p_i \sim q_i$ for all $1 \leq i \leq n$ and $p_i \sqsubset q_i$ for at least one $1 \leq i \leq n$

However, ordering equations by specificity of their left hand sides is not in general sufficient to yield an unambiguous definition. Consider for example the following ordered definition in which neither of the first two equations has a more specific left hand side than the other and yet both equations match arguments of type (RA, RA):

$$
\begin{array}{ll}
f\ (x :: Employee, y :: Employee) & == \ldots \\
f\ (x :: Student, y :: Student) & == \ldots \\
f\ (x :: Person, y :: Person) & == \ldots
\end{array}
$$

Clearly what is needed here is a fourth equation with a left hand side of $(x :: RA, y :: RA)$ which is more specific than both $(x :: Employee, y :: Employee)$ and $(x :: Student, y :: Student)$ c.f. the function *same* of the previous section.

Such ambiguities are of course analogous to multiple inheritance conflicts in object-oriented languages. In our case we verify that all equational definitions are *unambiguous* (see Definition 2 below), notifying the user of any ambiguities and not allowing ambiguous functions to be invoked in queries.

Definition 2. Two patterns p_i and p_j *overlap* if there exists a third pattern p_k that is more specific than either. A set of patterns p_1, p_2, ... p_r is *unambiguous* if for any two overlapping patterns p_i and p_j such that neither is more specific than the other, there exists a set of patterns $p_{k,1}$, $p_{k,2}$, ..., $p_{k,s}$ such that any value which matches p_i and p_j also matches one of $p_{k,1}$, $p_{k,2}$, ..., $p_{k,s}$.

This is a generalisation of ordinary best-fit pattern-matching where a *single* pattern p_k is sufficient to disambiguate two overlapping patterns p_i and p_j. This is not possible in the presence of subtyping. For example, consider the atomic types A, B, C, D such that $C < A, C < B, D < A, D < B$ and the patterns

$x :: A, x :: B$. These patterns are overlapping since expressions of type C and D are matched by both, but the patterns can only be disambiguated by two further patterns $x :: C, x :: D$.

3.6 Type-Checking and Evaluation

As before, given a query to type-check and evaluate, its call graph is constructed and a single expression in the kernel language is derived from it. However, the kernel syntax is now extended to:

$$
\begin{aligned}
\mathrm{E} ::= {} & x \mid c \mid \mathrm{E}_1\mathrm{E}_2 \mid \lambda x.\mathrm{E} \mid \lambda x :: \kappa.\mathrm{E} \mid \\
& \mathit{let}\ x = \mathrm{E}_1\ \mathit{in}\ \mathrm{E} \mid \\
& \mathit{letrec}\ (x_1, \ldots, x_n) = (\mathrm{E}_1, \ldots, \mathrm{E}_n)\ \mathit{in}\ \mathrm{E} \\
& \mathit{method}\ \mathrm{E}_1,\ \ldots,\ \mathrm{E}_n
\end{aligned}
$$

The two additions to the previous kernel syntax of Section 2.4 are λ-abstractions of the form $\lambda x :: \kappa.\mathrm{E}$ and "method" clauses. The former are needed in order to translate patterns containing annotated variables while the latter are needed in order to type-check overloaded functions. In particular, suppose the equations defining an n-ary function f are

$$
\begin{aligned}
& f\ p_{1,1}\ \cdots\ p_{1,n} == rhs_1 \\
& f\ p_{2,1}\ \cdots\ p_{2,n} == rhs_2\ \cdots \\
& f\ p_{r,1}\ \cdots\ p_{r,n} == rhs_r
\end{aligned}
$$

ordered so that if $(p_{i,1}, \ \cdots p_{i,n}) \sqsubset (p_{j,1}, \ \cdots p_{j,n})$ the ith equation precedes the jth one. Then, the single expression defining f is

$$f = \mathit{method}\ \lambda p_{1,1}.\ldots.\lambda p_{1,n}.rhs_1,\ \lambda p_{2,1}.\ldots.\lambda p_{2,n}.rhs_2, \ldots, \lambda p_{r,1}.\ldots.\lambda p_{r,n}.rhs_r$$

Finally, the *unpack_c* functions can be used exactly as before to simplify λ-abstractions.

We discuss the new type inference algorithm in Section 4 below. After a query has been type-checked, and before it is evaluated, all expressions of the form

$$\mathit{method}\ \mathrm{E}_1, \mathrm{E}_2,\ \ldots\ , \mathrm{E}_r$$

are, as before, translated into expressions invoking the $||$ operator, assuming here the function being defined is an n-ary one and that $x_1, \ldots, x_n$ do not occur free in $\mathrm{E}_1, \ldots, \mathrm{E}_r$:

$$\lambda x_1.\ldots.\lambda x_n.\mathrm{E}_1\ x_1\ \ldots\ x_n\ ||\ \mathrm{E}_2\ x_1\ \ldots\ x_n\ ||\ \ldots\ ||\ \mathrm{E}_r\ x_1\ \ldots\ x_n\ ||\ \mathit{error}$$

Thus, for the purposes of evaluating the extended kernel language, it only remains to define the semantics of expressions of the form $\lambda x :: \kappa.\mathrm{E}$. Since these semantics invoke the type inference algorithm in order to perform run-time binding, we postpone this discussion to Section 4.4 below.

3.7 Schema Evolution

We next consider the issue of schema evolution and, in particular, the addition and removal of arcs in the inheritance graph and the specialisation and generalisation of the types of object identifiers (i.e. 0-ary constructors of atomic type). Due to space constraints, we can only give a brief discussion here and postpone a fuller treatment to a future paper.

The addition of a new arc into the inheritance graph requires no special type-checking. This is because it cannot invalidate the current value of any data function, and because equationally-defined functions are type-checked in any case prior to their use in a query.

The removal of an existing arc from the inheritance graph is not so simple since data functions may be rendered type-incorrect (again we do not need to worry about equationally-defined functions since these are typed-checked before they are used in any query). In particular, the removal of an arc $\iota < \kappa$ may invalidate any data function $f :: \sigma$ such that σ references κ or any supertype thereof, so we only allow the deletion of the arc if there are no such data functions. We can determine this by querying the "dependency" information which is maintained in any case by PFL for use in validating the declaration and deletion of type and value constructors. Broadly speaking, this information consists of a set of triples of the form (id_1, id_2, n), meaning that id_1 references id_2 n times, which are stored in a hash file (see [PS91] for details).

As with the insertion of a new arc into the inheritance graph, the specialisation of the type of an object identifier does not require any extra type-checking since its use within any data function remains valid and since equationally-defined functions will be type-checked as needed.

Conversely, if a constructor c currently of (Curry) type ι is generalised to be of type κ (where $\iota < \kappa$), the occurrence of c within a data function may render it type-incorrect. In particular, if the type expected for the occurrence is κ' (i.e. type of the data function is of the form $\{\ldots\kappa'\ldots\}$) then $\kappa < \kappa'$ must hold. One way to support this validation efficiently is to extend the dependency information described above to be quadruples of the form $(id_1, id_2, expected\_type, n)$. We are currently evaluating this, and other, alternatives.

4 Type Checking the Extended Language

In this section we discuss how types are inferred for expressions in the extended kernel syntax of Section 3.6. We first review some preliminary terminology in Section 4.1. We then define our type inference algorithm, $\mathcal{M}$, in Section 4.2, considering in turn each category of expressions in the kernel syntax. $\mathcal{M}$ is based on the $\mathcal{GA}$ algorithm of [Mit91] which performs type inference with atomic subtyping for the pure λ calculus i.e. for expressions of the form $\mathrm{E} ::= x \mid \mathrm{E}_1\mathrm{E}_2 \mid \lambda x.\mathrm{E}$. We thus extend GA to infer types for constants, "let", "letrec" and "method" clauses, and λ-abstractions whose bound variable is annotated with an atomic type. The coercions inferred by $\mathcal{GA}$, and hence by $\mathcal{M}$, may be inconsistent or unsatisfiable with respect to the predeclared inheritance graph. We thus apply a further algorithm COERCE_CHECK, defined in Section 4.3, to verify the consistency and satisfiability of the coercion sets inferred at each step of $\mathcal{M}$. Finally, in Section 4.4 we define the semantics of λ-abstractions whose bound variable is annotated with an atomic type.

4.1 Terminology

We will require the following terminology (mainly taken from [Mit91]):

A *coercion set* C is a set of subtype assertions between arbitrary types. An *atomic coercion set* C is a set of subtype assertions between type variables and atomic types only. A *type environment* A is a set of typing statements of the form $x :: \tau$, where x is a variable and τ a type expression.

A$-\{x_1, \ldots, x_n\}$ denotes the type environment obtained from A by removing the existing typing for each variable $x_1, \ldots, x_n$, if any. A$+\{x_1 :: \tau_1, \ldots, x_n :: \tau_n\}$ denotes the type environment $(\mathrm{A}-\{x_1, \ldots, x_n\}) \cup \{x_1 :: \tau_1, \ldots, x_n :: \tau_n\}$.

A *substitution* is a mapping of type variables $\alpha_1, \ldots, \alpha_n$ to type expressions $\tau_1, \ldots, \tau_n$, respectively, written $[\tau_1/\alpha_1, \ldots, \tau_n/\alpha_n]$. The composition of two substitutions R and S is denoted by $S \circ R$. The type expression resulting from the application of a substitution S to the type variables of a type expression σ is denoted by $S\sigma$. The coercion set resulting from the application of a substitution S to the type variables of a coercion set C is denoted by SC i.e.

$$S\mathrm{C} \equiv \{S\sigma < S\tau \mid \sigma < \tau \in \mathrm{C}\}$$

The *unification* [Rob65] of two type expressions σ and τ is denoted by UNIFY$(\sigma = \tau)$ and returns a most general unifying substitution for σ and τ if one exists, or else fails. More generally, if P is a set of type equations $\{\sigma_1 = \tau_1, \ldots, \sigma_n = \tau_n\}$, then a substitution S *unifies* P if $S\sigma = S\tau$ for all $\sigma = \tau \in$ P, and the unification of P is denoted by UNIFY(P). Unification is extended to type environments by using the notation $\mathrm{A}_1 = \mathrm{A}_2$ for the following set of type equations:

$$\mathrm{A}_1 = \mathrm{A}_2 \equiv \{\sigma = \tau \mid x :: \sigma \in \mathrm{A}_1 \text{ and } x :: \tau \in \mathrm{A}_2\}$$

Two type expressions σ and τ *match* if they differ only in occurrences of type variables and atomic types. Given a coercion $\sigma < \tau$ such that σ and τ match, a semantically equivalent *atomic* coercion set can be computed using the algorithm ATOMIC below. This is as given in [Mit91] but extended to cater for structured types in our case:

$$\begin{aligned}
&\mathrm{ATOMIC}(\iota < \kappa) &&= \{\iota < \kappa\}\\
&\mathrm{ATOMIC}(\alpha < \kappa) &&= \{\alpha < \kappa\}\\
&\mathrm{ATOMIC}(\iota < \beta) &&= \{\iota < \beta\}\\
&\mathrm{ATOMIC}(\alpha < \beta) &&= \{\alpha < \beta\}\\
&\mathrm{ATOMIC}(\sigma_1 \rightarrow \sigma_2 < \tau_1 \rightarrow \tau_2) &&= \mathrm{ATOMIC}(\tau_1 < \sigma_1) \cup \mathrm{ATOMIC}(\sigma_2 < \tau_2)\\
&\mathrm{ATOMIC}(\kappa^n \sigma_1 \ldots \sigma_n < \kappa^n \tau_1 \ldots \tau_n) &&= \textstyle\bigcup_{i=1}^{n} \mathrm{ATOMIC}(\sigma_i < \tau_i)
\end{aligned}$$

Given a substitution S and a coercion $\sigma < \tau$ such that $S\sigma$ and $S\tau$ match,

$$S \cdot \sigma < \tau \equiv \text{ATOMIC}(S\sigma < S\tau)$$

A substitution S is said to *respect* a coercion set C if for all $\sigma < \tau \in$ C, $S\sigma$ and $S\tau$ match. If S respects C, the $\cdot$ notation is extended as follows:

$$S \cdot \text{C} \equiv \{S \cdot \sigma < \tau \mid \sigma < \tau \in \text{C}\}$$

4.2 The $\mathcal{M}$ algorithm

Our type inference algorithm, $\mathcal{M}$, takes a type environment, an atomic coercion set, and an expression E, and returns a triple consisting of a new type environment containing typing statements for any free and let-bound variables in E, an associated atomic coercion set, and a type expression for E. The initial coercion set, C_0, and type environment, A_0, passed to $\mathcal{M}$ are defined as follows.

Let $c_1, \ldots, c_n$ be the names of the built-in functions, current value constructors and current data functions. Let $(\text{C}_1, \tau_1), \ldots, (\text{C}_n, \tau_n)$ be their respective (Mitchell) types, and assume that no type variable appears in more than one of these n types. Then $\text{A}_0 = \{c_1 :: \tau_1, \ldots, c_n :: \tau_n\}$ and $\text{C}_0 = \text{C}_1 \cup \ldots \cup \text{C}_n$.

As in ML, the presence of "let" and "letrec" expressions allows a form of parametric polymorphism where universal quantification of type variables is permitted at the top level of a type expression. In our definition of $\mathcal{M}$ below, the type of a polymorphic function is expressed as $\forall\alpha_1 \ldots \alpha_n.\sigma$ where $\alpha_1 \ldots \alpha_n$ are called *generic* type variables. In order to use a polymorphic function, it is necessary to *specialise* its type i.e. to substitute a type expression for each generic type variable $\alpha_1 \ldots \alpha_n$ in σ. Constructors and built-in functions are also polymorphic i.e. in the initial type environment A_0, all typing statements $c :: \tau$ are actually assumed to be $c :: \forall\alpha_1 \ldots \alpha_n.\tau$ where $n \geq 0$ and $\alpha_1, \ldots, \alpha_n$ are the type variables appearing in τ.

We are now ready to define the type inference algorithm, $\mathcal{M}$, considering in turn each category of expressions in the kernel syntax.

The first case for $\mathcal{M}$ types occurrences of constants i.e. constructors, data functions and built-in functions. The type of the constant c is retrieved from the type environment A and any generic type variables are replaced by fresh type variables so that the type is unique for this occurrence of c:

$\mathcal{M}$ (C,A,c)
  = let $\forall\alpha_1 \ldots \alpha_n.\sigma = \text{A}(c)$
    in $([\beta_1/\alpha_1, \ldots, \beta_n/\alpha_n]\text{C}, \{\}, [\beta_1/\alpha_1 \ldots \beta_n/\alpha_n]\sigma)$
    where $\beta_1 \ldots \beta_n$ are fresh type variables

The next case for $\mathcal{M}$ types occurrences of variables. If a typing for the variable x exists in the type environment A (as a result of x having been introduced by a "let" or "letrec" clause), it is retrieved and any generic type variables are replaced by fresh type variables in order to create a unique type for this occurrence of x. If no typing for x exists in A (i.e. x is a free or λ-bound variable) a new type and coercion set are created for x from fresh type variables:

$\mathcal{M}$ (C,A,x)
  $= ([\beta_1/\alpha_1, \ldots, \beta_n/\alpha_n]\mathrm{C}, \{\}, [\beta_1/\alpha_1 \ldots \beta_n/\alpha_n]\sigma)$, if $x :: \forall\alpha_1 \ldots \alpha_n.\sigma \in \mathrm{A}$
  $= (\mathrm{C} \cup \{\alpha < \beta\}, \{x :: \alpha\}, \beta)$, otherwise
  where $\alpha, \beta, \beta_1 \ldots \beta_n$ are fresh type variables

Applications, $\mathrm{E}_1\mathrm{E}_2$, are typed as in [Mit91]. As Mitchell discusses, the substitution that unifies the types inferred for E_1 and E_2 (R below) may not respect their associated coercion sets (C_1 and C_2 below). Thus, it is necessary to perform a second process of unification over the set of coercions $R\mathrm{C}_1 \cup R\mathrm{C}_2$ which will find a most general substitution that respects this set, if one exists, and which will fail otherwise. This is performed by the algorithm MATCH described in [Mit84], [Mit91]. MATCH is similar to UNIFY except that type expressions are unified only up to their structure. The complexity of MATCH is the same as that of as that of UNIFY, for which a linear implementation exists [PW78]:

$\mathcal{M}$ (C,A,$\mathrm{E}_1\mathrm{E}_2$)
  = let $(\mathrm{C}_1,\mathrm{A}_1,\sigma) = \mathcal{M}(\mathrm{C},\mathrm{A},\mathrm{E}_1)$
    $(\mathrm{C}_2,\mathrm{A}_2,\tau) = \mathcal{M}(\mathrm{C},\mathrm{A},\mathrm{E}_2)$
    $R = \mathrm{UNIFY}(\{\sigma = \tau \rightarrow \alpha\} \cup \mathrm{A}_1 = \mathrm{A}_2)$
    $S = \mathrm{MATCH}(R\mathrm{C}_1 \cup R\mathrm{C}_2) \circ R$
  in
    $(S \cdot (\mathrm{C}_1 \cup \mathrm{C}_2), S\mathrm{A}_1 \cup S\mathrm{A}_2, S\alpha)$
  where α is a fresh type variable

Ordinary λ-abstractions, λx.E, are also typed as in [Mit91] by first typing the body E and then for the argument type using the type inferred for x if x is appears free in E, otherwise using a new type variable:

$\mathcal{M}$ (C,A,λx.E)
  $= (\mathrm{C}_1, \mathrm{A}_1 - \{x\}, \sigma \rightarrow \tau)$, if $x :: \sigma \in \mathrm{A}_1$
  $= (\mathrm{C}_1, \mathrm{A}_1, \alpha \rightarrow \tau)$, otherwise
  where $(\mathrm{C}_1,\mathrm{A}_1,\tau) = \mathcal{M}(\mathrm{C},\mathrm{A},\mathrm{E})$ and α is a fresh type variable

λ-abstractions whose argument is annotated with an atomic type, $\lambda x :: \kappa$.E, are typed by independently typing $x :: \kappa$ and E. Unification and matching then bring the two typings into line with each other:

$\mathcal{M}$ (C,A,$\lambda x :: \kappa$.E)
  = let $(\mathrm{C}_1,\mathrm{A}_1,\tau) = \mathcal{M}(\mathrm{C},\mathrm{A},\mathrm{E})$
    $(\mathrm{C}_2,\mathrm{A}_2) = (\{\alpha < \kappa\}, \{x :: \alpha\})$
    $R = \mathrm{UNIFY}(\mathrm{A}_1 = \mathrm{A}_2)$
    $S = \mathrm{MATCH}(R\mathrm{C}_1 \cup R\mathrm{C}_2) \circ R$
  in
    $(S \cdot (\mathrm{C}_1 \cup \mathrm{C}_2), S(\mathrm{A}_1 - \{x\}), S(\alpha \rightarrow \tau))$
  where α is a fresh type variable

For expressions of the form *let* x = E_1 *in* E, we first infer a type for E_1 and then infer a type for E with respect to a type environment updated with the typing for x. The process is similar to typing an application $(\lambda x.E)E_1$ except that a let-bound variable x can have a different specialisation of its type at each occurrence in E whereas a λ-bound x cannot:

$$
\begin{aligned}
&\mathcal{M}\ (C,A,\mathit{let}\ x = E_1\ \mathit{in}\ E)\\
&\quad = \text{let} \quad (C_1,A_1,\sigma) = \mathcal{M}(C,A,E_1)\\
&\qquad\qquad (C_2,A_2,\tau) = \mathcal{M}(C_1,A+\{x :: \forall\bar{\alpha}.\sigma\},E)\\
&\qquad\qquad R = \text{UNIFY}(A_1 = A_2)\\
&\qquad\qquad S = \text{MATCH}(RC_1 \cup RC_2) \circ R\\
&\qquad \text{in}\\
&\qquad\qquad (S \cdot (C_1 \cup C_2), SA_1 \cup SA_2, S\tau)\\
&\qquad \text{where } \bar{\alpha} \text{ is the list of type variables in } \sigma \text{ which do not appear in } A_1
\end{aligned}
$$

Typing expressions of the form *letrec* $(x_1, \ldots, x_n) = (E_1, \ldots, E_n)$ *in* E is complicated by the need to unify the types of recursive expressions. We first infer types for $E_1, \ldots, E_n$. We then unify the type of each E_i with the type inferred for x_i in the returned type environment A_i. In addition, since any of $E_1, \ldots, E_n$ may reference x_i (due to mutual recursion), we need to also unify the type for x_i in their returned type environments. We achieve this by unifying over the type environments $A_1, \ldots, A_n$. As usual, unification is followed by matching, to give a substitution S that respects all the coercion sets. We are now in a position to type E with respect to the updated coercion set and type environment, obtaining the typing (C',A',τ) below. Finally, as for "let" expressions, we need to unify and match again for free variables occurring in the whole "letrec" expression:

$$
\begin{aligned}
&\mathcal{M}\ (C,A,\mathit{letrec}\ \ (x_1,\ldots,x_n) = (E_1,\ldots,E_n)\ \ \mathit{in}\ \ E)\\
&\quad = \text{let} \quad (C_i,A_i,\sigma_i) = \mathcal{M}(C,A,E_i) \quad \text{for all } 1 \leq i \leq n\\
&\qquad\qquad \tau_i = \tau_i',\ \ \text{if } x :: \tau_i' \in A_i\\
&\qquad\qquad\quad = \beta_i,\ \ \text{otherwise} \qquad \text{for all } 1 \leq i \leq n\\
&\qquad\qquad R = \text{UNIFY}(\{\sigma_1 = \tau_1, \ldots, \sigma_n = \tau_n, A_1 = \ldots = A_n)\\
&\qquad\qquad S = \text{MATCH}(RC_1 \cup \ldots \cup RC_n) \circ R\\
&\qquad\qquad (C',A',\tau) = \mathcal{M}(S \cdot (C \cup C_1 \cup \ldots \cup C_n),\\
&\qquad\qquad\qquad\qquad SA+\{x_1 :: \forall\bar{\alpha}_1.S\sigma_1, \ldots, x_n :: \forall\bar{\alpha}_n.S\sigma_n\},E)\\
&\qquad\qquad T = \text{UNIFY}(\{SA_1 \cup \ldots \cup SA_n = A'\}) \circ S\\
&\qquad\qquad U = \text{MATCH}(T \cdot (C_1 \cup \ldots \cup C_n) \cup TC') \circ T\\
&\qquad \text{in}\\
&\qquad\qquad (U \cdot (C_1 \cup \ldots \cup C_n \cup C'),\ UA_1 \cup \ldots \cup UA_n \cup UA', U\tau)\\
&\qquad \text{where } \bar{\alpha}_i \text{ is a list of the free variables in } S\sigma_i \text{ which do not appear in}\\
&\qquad\qquad SA_1 \cup \ldots \cup SA_n \text{ and } \beta_1, \ldots, \beta_n \text{ are fresh type variables}
\end{aligned}
$$

Lastly, expressions of the form *method* $E_1, \ldots, E_n$ are typed by first inferring a type for each E_i independently, obtaining the typing (C_i, A_i, σ_i). These typings are then unified and matched, giving the typing $(S \cdot (C_1 \cup \ldots \cup C_n), SA_1 \cup \ldots \cup SA_n, S\alpha)$ below. The algorithm LUB is next applied to the coercion set $S \cdot (C_1 \cup \ldots \cup C_n)$. For all type variables β that appear in $S\alpha$ and correspond to an annotated variable in one or more of $E_1, \ldots, E_n$, LUB replaces a set of coercions of the form $\beta < \kappa_1, \ldots, \beta < \kappa_r$ by a single coercion $\beta < \kappa$, where κ is the least upper bound of $\kappa_1, \ldots, \kappa_r$. If the least upper bound does not exist, or is not unique, then LUB fails. For example, the argument type of a function defined by two equations $f\ x :: Employee == E', f\ x :: Student == E''$ is $a < Person$ whereas a function defined by two equations $f\ x :: Employee == E', f\ x :: Num == E''$ is not well typed.

$$
\begin{aligned}
&\mathcal{M}\ (C, A, \mathit{method}\ E_1, \ldots, E_n)\\
&\quad = \text{let} \quad (C_i, A_i, \sigma_i) = \mathcal{M}(C, A, E_i) \quad \text{for all } 1 \le i \le n\\
&\qquad\qquad R = \text{UNIFY}\ (\{\alpha = \sigma_1 = \ldots = \sigma_n\} \cup A_1 = \ldots = A_n)\\
&\qquad\qquad S = \text{MATCH}\ (RC_1 \cup \ldots \cup RC_n) \circ R\\
&\qquad \text{in}\\
&\qquad\qquad (\text{LUB}\ (S \cdot (C_1 \cup \ldots \cup C_n)), SA_1 \cup \ldots \cup SA_n, S\alpha)\\
&\qquad \text{where } \alpha \text{ is a fresh type variable}
\end{aligned}
$$

4.3 The COERCE_CHECK algorithm

It is possible that $\mathcal{M}$ succeeds but that the coercion set it returns is inconsistent with respect to the inheritance graph. For example, given a predeclared subtype relationship $Int < Real$, the coercion set $\{Real < \alpha, \alpha < Int\}$ is inconsistent. Following Fuh and Mishra [FM89], we therefore verify for each new coercion set C inferred during $\mathcal{M}$ that every subtype relationship derivable from C is also derivable from the inheritance graph. In addition to this check, we verify that each type variable in C can be substituted by an atomic type and still yield a consistent coercion set. This means that for inheritance graphs which are not complete lattices, pairs of coercions $\alpha < \iota, \alpha < \kappa$ such that ι and κ have no common subtype are considered invalid, as are pairs of coercions $\iota < \alpha, \kappa < \alpha$ such that ι and κ have no common supertype. The overall verification of a coercion set C is thus captured by the following recursive algorithm, where G is the predeclared inheritance graph:

$$
\begin{aligned}
&\text{COERCE\_CHECK(C)} =\\
&\quad \forall \iota, \kappa \in \mathit{AtomicTypes}.\ C \vdash \iota < \kappa \ \Rightarrow\ G \vdash \iota < \kappa\\
&\quad \text{and}\\
&\quad \forall \alpha \in \mathit{TypeVars}(C).\ \exists \kappa \in \mathit{AtomicTypes}.\text{COERCE\_CHECK}([\kappa/\alpha]C)
\end{aligned}
$$

4.4 Semantics of $\lambda x :: \kappa.E$

When during the evaluation of a query an expression of the form $\lambda x :: \kappa.E$ is applied to an expression E_1, the application $(\lambda x :: \kappa.E)E_1$ rewrites to the following expression:

$$\begin{array}{ll} \text{let} & (\mathrm{C},\mathrm{A},\tau) = \mathcal{M}(\mathrm{C}_0,\mathrm{A}_0,\mathrm{E}_1) \\ \text{in} & \text{if } \mathrm{C} \vdash \tau < \kappa \\ & \text{then } (\lambda x.\mathrm{E})\mathrm{E}_1 \\ & \text{else } \mathit{Fail} \end{array}$$

Notice that $\mathcal{M}$ cannot fail at this stage, since the overall query has already been type-checked.

5 Related work

Type inference for the λ calculus with subtypes was first studied by Mitchell [Mit84], with later work in [Mit91]. Two algorithms, $\mathcal{G}$ and $\mathcal{GA}$, are described in [Mit91]: $\mathcal{G}$ performs type inference in the presence of unrestricted subtype relationships while $\mathcal{GA}$ performs type inference in the presence of subtype relationships between atomic types only. $\mathcal{G}$ is able to type *all* expressions in the pure λ-calculus since it permits subtype relationships such as $\alpha < \alpha \rightarrow \alpha$. $\mathcal{GA}$ however types only those expressions which possess a Curry type. Our $\mathcal{M}$ algorithm is an extension of $\mathcal{GA}$ to perform type inference for the kernel language of Section 3.6.

Further work on type inference with subtypes appears in [FM89], [FM90] which give heuristics for the simplification of a coercion set and an algorithm to check the consistency of a coercion set. We have extended this in our own COERCE_CHECK algorithm to detect cases where a coercion set is unsatisfiable with respect to the inheritance graph.

Lincoln and Mitchell have analysed the complexity of Mitchell's type inference algorithms in [LM92]. Their main result is that the problem of deciding whether a term has a type, given a set of subtyping relations between atomic types, has a lower bound in NP. Moreover, they report that since the size of a most general typing for a term may be exponentially larger than the term itself, any type inference algorithm which prints the type must take exponential time.

Cardelli has used subtyping over record types to provide a semantics and type inference algorithm in a simple applicative language with classes, objects and (multiple) inheritance [Car88]. Classes are represented by record types, with possibly functional components to represent methods. Objects are represented by instances of such types. Although a formal equivalence has yet to be defined, it is easy to see that our approach possesses similar expressiveness. We can define atomic types whose constructors act as object identifiers and can appear within data functions. The values associated with these constructors correspond to the data components of Cardelli's objects. Functions over atomic types correspond to the functional components of Cardelli's objects, in our case abstracted out of the object as global functions. One advantage of our approach is that functions over structured types and multiple arguments can be inherited and overloaded in just the same way as functions over atomic types. Also, the declaration of subtype relationships between atomic types seems more in tune with PFL's semantic data model than Cardelli's structural approach to subtyping.

Cardelli and Wegner have also formalised subtyping as *inclusion polymorphism* [CW85]. Independently, Girard [Gir71] formulated the second-order λ-calculus, or System F, in which polymorphism is treated by creating parameter bindings for type variables and passing type expressions as arguments in order to specialise a function to a specific type. This form of polymorphism is known as *universal quantification*. Inclusion polymorphism arises as a special case, in the form of *bounded quantification*, in which the type variable declared in a parameter binding is constrained to be a subtype of a type. This work has been extended to deal with recursive records [CCH+89], to integrate existential types with bounded quantification in order to support both encapsulation and (record-based) inheritance [Ghe90], and to support method overloading [Cas93].

An alternative record-based approach to inheritance is that of Jategaonkar and Mitchell [JM88] which extends the language of [Mit84] with functions that allow pattern-matching over record arguments. Types are inferred for record patterns by *reversing* the coercions associated with identifiers: this is the same effect that our *unpack_c* functions have on the type of the constructor c in Section 3.3. The precise relationship between Mitchell's approach to subtyping and F-bounded quantification is an open issue, although superficially the types of the former are more general than those of the latter since more than one subtype assertion can be associated with a type variable.

6 Concluding Remarks

We have shown how the functional database language PFL can be extended to support inheritance and overloading of functions. The resulting language has a single semantic and operational framework and does not suffer from "impedance mismatch" problems. Our approach is easily applied to other functional database languages.

The specific contributions of this paper are firstly an extension of Mitchell's $\mathcal{GA}$ algorithm [Mit91] to infer types for constructors, "let" and "letrec" expressions, λ-abstractions whose bound variable is annotated with an atomic type, and overloaded functions; and secondly an extension of the best-fit pattern-matching of [FH88] to cater for overloaded functions.

With an empty inheritance graph, our $\mathcal{M}$ algorithm types precisely those expressions that are typable by the original W algorithm and our pattern-matching algorithm reduces to ordinary best-fit pattern-matching. Thus, the new version of PFL is upwards compatible with the old, and existing PFL programs need not be rewritten.

There are several directions for further work. On the implementation side, experience has shown that the size of the coercion sets can be large even for simple functions. We are thus developing heuristics to simplify the coercion sets inferred at each step of the algorithm. On the theoretical side, Mitchell has shown the soundness of the $\mathcal{GA}$ algorithm and it remains to formally show the soundness of our extensions to it. Finally, on the language side we are investigating further extensions to the type system in order to support abstraction, encapsulation and modularisation.

Acknowledgements

This work has been carried out under EPSRC grant no. GR/J 48818. We are grateful for many fruitful discussions with our collaborators on this project, Carol Small, Swarup Reddi, David Sutton, Ben Heydecker and Jiashu Wu, and also to Spyros Soukeras for his comments on this paper.

References

[Car88] L. Cardelli. A semantics of multiple inheritance. *Information and Computation*, 76:138–164, 1988.

[Cas93] G. Castagna. $F_{\leq}^{\&}$: integrating parametric and "ad hoc" second order polymorphism. In *Proc. 4th International Workshop on Database Programming Languages (DBPL-4), New York*, pages 338–358. Springer-Verlag, 1993.

[CCH+89] P. Canning, W. Cook, W. Hill, W. Olthoff, and J. C. Mitchell. F-bounded polymorphism for object-oriented programming. In *Proc. 1989 ACM Conference on Functional Programming Languages and Computer Architecture*, pages 273–280, 1989.

[CW85] L. Cardelli and P. Wegner. On understanding types, data abstraction, and polymorphism. *ACM Computing Surveys*, 17(4):471–522, 1985.

[DOO] DOOD. *Proceedings of the International Conferences on Deductive and Object-Oriented Databases.* 1989 (Kyoto), 1991 (Munich), 1993 (Phoenix, Arizona).

[FH88] A.J. Field and P.G. Harrison. *Functional Programming.* Addison Wesley, 1988.

[FM89] Y.-C. Fuh and P. Mishra. Polymorphic subtype inference: Closing the theory-practice gap. In *TAPSOFT'89 - Proc. International Joint Conference on Theory and Practice of Software Development*, pages 167–183, 1989. Springer-Verlag LNCS 352.

[FM90] Y.-C. Fuh and P. Mishra. Type inference with subtypes. *Theoretical Computer Science*, 70:155–175, 1990.

[Ghe90] G. Ghelli. Modelling features of object-oriented languages in second order functional languages with subtypes. Technical Report FIDE/90/3, Dept. of Computing Science, Glasgow University, 1990.

[Gir71] J.-Y. Girard. Une extension de l'interpretation de Gödel à l'analyse, et son application à l'èlimination des coupres dans l'analyse et la thèorie des types. In J. E. Fenstad, editor, *2nd. Scandanavian Logic Symposium*, pages 63–92. North-Holland, 1971.

[HK87] R. Hull and R. King. Semantic database modelling : Survey, applications, and research issues. *ACM Computing Surveys*, 19(3):201–260, 1987.

[JM88] L.A. Jategaonkar and J.C. Mitchell. ML with extended pattern matching and subtypes (preliminary version). In *Proc. 1988 ACM Conf. on LISP and Functional Programming*, pages 198–211, 1988.

[LM92] P. Lincoln and J. C. Mitchell. Algorithmic aspects of type inference with subtypes. In *19th ACM Symposium on Principles of Programming Languages*, pages 293–304, 1992.

[Mit84] J. C. Mitchell. Coercion and type inference (summary). In *Proc. 11th ACM Symposium on Principles of Programming Languages*, pages 175–185, 1984.

[Mit91] J. C. Mitchell. Type inference with simple subtypes. *Journal of Functional Programming*, 1(3):245–285, 1991.

[PJ87] S. Peyton-Jones. *The Implementation of Functional Programming Languages*. Morgan Kaufmann, 1987.

[Pou92] A. Poulovassilis. The implementation of FDL, a functional database language. *The Computer Journal*, 35(2):119–128, 1992.

[PS91] A. Poulovassilis and C. Small. A functional programming approach to deductive databases. In *Proc. 17th International Conference on Very Large Data Bases, (VLDB 91), Barcelonà*, pages 491–500, 1991.

[PS94] A. Poulovassilis and C. Small. Investigation of algebraic query optimisation for database programming languages. In *Proc. 20th International Conference on Very Large Data Bases (VLDB 94) Santiago, Chile*, pages 415–426, 1994.

[PW78] Paterson and Wegman. Linear unification. *JCSS*, pages 158–167, 1978.

[Rob65] J. A. Robinson. A machine orientated logic based on the resolution principle. *Journal of the ACM*, 12(1):23–41, 1965.

[SP91] C. Small and A. Poulovassilis. An overview of PFL. In *Proc. 3rd International Workshop on Database Programming Languages (DBPL-3), Nafplion*, pages 96–110, 1991.

[SS95] D. Sutton and C. Small. Extending functional database languages to update completeness. In *Proc. BNCOD-13 (these proceedings), Manchester*, July 1995.

Extending Functional Database Languages to Update Completeness

David Sutton and Carol Small

Dept. of Computer Science
Birkbeck College
Malet St., London WC1E 7HX
{davids,carol}@dcs.bbk.ac.uk

Abstract. This paper discusses the update operators currently implemented in the functional database programming language PFL and the linear type system which regulates their use.
Updates in functional database programming languages pose a problem because if update operations are expressed as functions from an original database relation to a new updated relation then they are potentially inefficient. However destructive updates may compromise the confluence of the language, with the result that the meaning of an expression is ambiguous.
The update operators discussed here allow relations to be updated destructively but their use is constrained by a linear type system. The purpose of the linearity constraints is to ensure that at all stages in the evaluation of an expression intended to effect an update there is exactly one reference to each relation being updated. This means that the order in which updates are applied to each relation is always clear, and consequently that the meaning of every expression is unambiguous.

1 Introduction

The "impedance mismatch problem" is the name given to a collection of problems which arise when programming languages are used to access database systems. The most important of these problems are the following. First, the programming language and database system often support different data structures (e.g. lists vs sets) and type systems (e.g. records vs tuples), leading to a loss of information at the programming language / database interface. Second, the computational models of the programming language and database system may differ (e.g. record- vs set- at-a-time processing), leading to inefficiency and a loss of opportunities for optimisation. Third, the data pertaining to an application is not to be found solely in the database, but is also "embedded" within the application programs which access the database. Of course, there is the additional problem that applications developers need to be multi-lingual!

In recent years much energy has been devoted to the development of database programming languages (or DBPLs). Since DBPLs provide the features expected of programming languages they are computationally complete; and since they also provide the features expected of database systems their type systems support bulk data types. The important point is that they have a single type system and a single computational model integrating facilities for data manipulation, data update, and general-purpose programming.

One particular class of DBPLs uses a functional computation model [Ban87, Oho89, Erw91], in which both data and computation are specified in the form of functions which are defined equationally. The arguments in favour of functional DBPLs have been presented elsewhere. In summary, however, they are that functional DBPLs: support lazy evaluation of expressions, and allow the specification of higher-order functions which abstract out patterns of recursion [Hug89]; support the specification of datalog rules (including those with function symbols and negation) [Pou93]; and allow the development of integrated optimisation strategies for both "computational" and "data manipulation" functions [Pou94]. A final important advantage of functional languages is that they are confluent, by which we mean that the value of any expression is independent of the evaluation order of the language.

However, it has proved difficult to add update facilities to functional DBPLs that are efficient, easy to use and do not compromise confluence. In this paper we describe the update facilities currently implemented in PFL (Persistent Functional Language) [Pou91, Sma91]. Updates are efficient since they are destructive (ie. updates occur in-place, rather than by copying). We believe the language to be easy to use, since there is no difference between those expressions which update the database and those which query the database. We share the view of Abiteboul and Vianu in that we too:

> "take the position that the difference between updates and queries concerns primarily the interpretation of the results, rather than the computation involved." [Abi90]

Finally, we preserve confluence by adopting a linear type system similar to those described by Wadler in [Wad91].

The remainder of the paper is structured as follows. Section 2 gives an overview of PFL without considering the linear aspects of its type system. In §3 we demonstrate that, without the restrictions imposed by a linear type system, expressions that update relations can be ambiguous. Section 4 introduces the linear type system and §5 gives examples of its use. Section 6 outlines a way in which the restrictions imposed by linear type system may be relaxed for expressions which read but do not update relations. Section 8 outlines some related work and §9 gives our conclusions.

The purpose of this paper is to give an informal account of the language and its update facilities. A formal description of our work will be presented in a subsequent publication.

2 Overview of PFL

PFL is a persistent functional database language in which bulk data are stored as relations. These relations can contain tuples of arbitrarily nested structure.

It has a static polymorphic type inference system which allows new types and value constructors to be defined. New functions can also be added incrementally to the database. The database is queried by entering a PFL expression whose value is the answer to the query. Any expression can be used as a query so long as its type is first-order (i.e. it does not contain the function space constructor introduced below). In the sections that follow we present an informal description of the syntax and type system.

2.1 The type system

In this section we outline PFL's type system without the "linearity" restrictions which are explained in §4. The base types are `Num`, `Chr`, `Bool`, and `Str`. The first of these contains both integers and floating point numbers, `Chr` contains single characters, `Str` contains strings of characters, and `Bool` contains the constants `True` and `False`. List types, function types, and tuple types may be (recursively) constructed. The type expression `T1` → `T2` denotes the type of functions from `T1` to `T2`. The function space constructor → is right associative, e.g. `T1`→`T2`→`T3` is read as `T1`→`(T2`→`T3)`. Functions of more than one argument are curried [Pey87], hence if a function takes `n` arguments of types `T1` to `Tn` and returns a result of type `U` then its type is denoted by `T1`→`T2`→ ⋯ →`Tn`→`U`. The type expression `[T]` denotes the type of lists whose elements are of type `T`. A list is a sequence of zero or more elements and may be expressed either by enclosing those elements in square brackets e.g `[4,5,6,7]` or using the infix constructor ":" where `h:t` denotes the list whose head (i.e. first element) is `h` and whose tail (i.e the rest of the list) is `t`. The empty list is denoted by `[]`. The type expression `(T1,T2,...,Tn)` denotes the type of n-tuples whose elements are respectively of types `T1` to `Tn`. Tuples themselves are written using a similar syntax, e.g. `(1,'a',"hello")` is a tuple of type `(Num,Chr,Str)`.

Polymorphic types are defined using type variables which are denoted by alphanumeric strings beginning with a lower case letter. For instance the type declaration

```
f :: a->[a]
```

indicates that `f` is a function which takes an argument of any type `a` and returns a list whose elements are of type `a`.

The user may define their own type constructors and value constructors. An n-ary type constructor, when applied to n types, denotes a type, whereas an n-ary value constructor, when applied to n values denotes a value. The term *constant* will be used to mean a 0-ary value constructor. As an example

```
Vehicle :: Type
Accident :: Type
```

introduces two types which are denoted by the 0-ary type constructors `Vehicle` and `Accident`. These types may then be incrementally populated. For example

```
G37VMG :: Vehicle
H373CTA :: Vehicle
Acc1 :: Accident
Acc2 :: Accident
```

introduces two constants of type **Vehicle** and two of type **Accident**. The identifiers both of type constructors and value constructors are alphanumeric strings beginning with an uppercase letter.

2.2 Function definitions

We distinguish between system-defined, pre-defined and user-defined functions. System-defined functions are not defined textually, but are implemented internally by the system. Examples of system-defined functions are the arithmetic functions `+`,`-` etc. and the comparison operators `>`,`<`,`<=` etc. In addition, for every user defined type `T`, there is a system-defined function `allT` which evaluates to a list containing all the constants of that type. For instance if **Vehicle** is defined as shown above then **allVehicle** evaluates to `[G37VMG, H373CTA]`.

Pre-defined and user-defined functions are specified by means of equations involving pattern matching, in a style similar to that employed in Miranda, Hope and ML. The difference between pre-defined and user-defined functions is a matter of when and by whom they are written, rather than how they are written. Pre-defined functions are read into a database from a "standard environment" text file at creation time whereas user-defined ones are defined by the user after the database has been created. We now give some examples of function definitions and declarations. These functions could be either pre-defined or user-defined depending on whether the implementor includes them in the standard environment or leaves them for the user to define.

```
if :: Bool->a->a->a
if True x y    == x
if False x y   == y

factorial :: Num->Num
factorial 0 == 1
factorial x == x * (factorial (x - 1))

map :: (a->b)->[a]->[b]
map f []     == []
map f (h:t) == (f h):(map f t)

fold :: (a->b->b)->b->[a]->b
fold op e []      == e
fold op e (x:xs) == op x (fold op e xs)
```

The type of the function is automatically inferred when its definition is given. Type declarations are optional but recommended. If a function has a type declaration then the compiler will check that the type inferred for that function is consistent with its declared type.

Note that the first argument of **map** is itself a function, as is the first argument of **fold**.

2.3 Expressions

Expressions are built up from functions, value constructors, variables, and relation names. The use of relation names is explained §2.4. We adopt the convention that variables start with a lower case letter and that relation names start with a lower case letter and end with the character "!".

Function application is denoted simply by juxtaposition of functions with their arguments. For instance `foo 1 2` denotes the application of the function `foo` to the arguments 1 and 2. We allow "dot-dot" notation, whereby $[n..n+m]$ denotes the list of numbers $[n, n+1, \ldots, n+(m-1), n+m]$, and list comprehensions (or abstractions). The latter take the form $[e \mid q_1;\ q_2;\ \ldots;\ q_n]$ and may be read as "the list of e such that q_1 and ... and q_n". Each q_i is a qualifier, which may be either a filter or a generator. A filter is simply a boolean valued expression. A generator takes the form p ← e where e is a list valued expression, and is read as stating that p iterates over the elements of the list e. For example, the following comprehensions (i) give all accidents occurring in December; and (ii) partition accidents by the month of their occurrence:

```
[a | a <- allAccident ; monthOf a = 12]
[(m,[a |a<-allAccident; monthOf a = m]) | m<-[1..12]]
```

Expressions using "dot-dot" notation or list comprehensions can be translated into expressions that do not use these features (see Peyton-Jones for details on the translation of the latter [Pey87]).

2.4 Relations

Bulk data are stored in relations. As in the relational model, each relation has a *name* and an associated *extent*. In PFL the extent of a relation is a list of values of homogeneous type. If a relation contains tuples of type `T` then its name is of type `Rel! T` (the significance of the ! will become apparent in §4) and its extent is of type `[T]`. A relation, with an initially empty extent, is declared by specifying the type of its name. For example:

```
dateOfAcc! :: Rel! (Accident,(Num,Num,Num))
```

It is important to distinguish between the name of a relation and its extent. In the example above `dateOfAcc!` is a relation *name* and should *not* be thought of as being synonymous with the extent of its associated relation. The expression `dateOfAcc!` evaluates to `dateOfAcc!` rather than to the extent of the relation named by `dateOfAcc!`. Furthermore if `r1!` and `r2!` are two different relation names then they cannot be considered equal, or interchangeable, even if the *extents* of `r1!` and `r2!` are identical.

Three system-defined functions `inc!`, `exc!`, and `look!` are provided to read and update the extents of relations. We give the types of these functions in §4.1 below. The first two update the extent of a relation destructively. Write `ext(r)` for the extent of the relation whose name is `r`, write `ext(r) := xs` to show that `xs` is assigned to be the new extent of `r`, and write `xs-[x]` for the list identical to `xs` less any occurrences of `x`. Then the relation manipulation functions behave as follows:

```
inc! x r == r,              and ext(r) := x:(ext(r)-[x])
exc! x r == r,              and ext(r) := ext(r)-[x]
look! r  == (ext(r),r)
```

For example, if the extent of the relation `dateOfAcc!` is initially

```
[(Acc2,(21,3,85)),(Acc3,(21,3,85))]
```

then the expression `inc! (Acc1,(19,3,85)) dateOfAcc!` returns the relation name `dateOfAcc!` and updates its extent to include the tuple `(Acc1,(19,3,85))`. The query `look! dateOfAcc!` then returns
`([(Acc1,(19,3,85)),(Acc2,(21,3,85)),(Acc3,(21,3,85))],dateOfAcc!)`

The definition of `look!` has been simplified for reasons of clarity. In practice `look!` takes two arguments, the second being the relation name and the first an expression which may contain a "wildcard" constant `Any`. Rather than returning the complete extent of the relation, which would obviously be inefficient, `look!` then returns only those tuples which "match" its first argument in a sense which is explained in [Sma91].

With one exception, which will be introduced in §6, the three functions outlined above are the only ones which can directly access the extent of a relation.

In §5 we demonstrate that "bulk" inclusion and exclusion functions can be defined in terms of the primitive functions `inc!`, `exc!` and `look!`. In §3 we demonstrate that restrictions must be placed on the use of `inc!`, `exc!` and `look!` in order to guarantee that the meanings of PFL expressions are unambiguous. We shall also explain, in §4.1, why it is necessary for `look!` to return a pair containing the name of the relation inspected rather than simply returning the extent of that relation.

2.5 Confluence and ambiguity

A claim made in favour of functional languages is that they are *confluent*. This means that the value of an expression does not depend on the evaluation order of the language. For instance evaluation of an expression $E_1 + E_2$ clearly requires that both E_1 and E_2 be evaluated, but in a confluent language it should not matter which is evaluated first. Since we intend here to give an informal presentation of our work we shall sometimes use the word "unambigous" in preference to "confluent". For the purposes of this paper the two terms should be taken as synonymous. Similarly "ambiguous" should be taken as meaning "not confluent".

Functional languages are also described as *referentially transparent* [Søn90]. We shall not use this term in this paper. We introduce it here in order to forestall any confusion with the related, but different, concept of confluence.

3 The problem: confluence lost

Unfortunately, if we do not restrict the use of the update operators, then PFL is no longer confluent as the following examples show.

Example 1. Suppose that the extent of `r!` is empty and that we evaluate

```
(look! r!, inc! 1 r!)
```

If the subexpression `look! r!` is evaluated first then the result is `(([],r!),r!)`. However if the subexpression `inc! 1 r!` is evaluated first then the result is `(([1],r!),r!)`. The problem arises because the expression contains *two* occurrences of `r!`. Since the second occurrence is within a sub-expression whose evaluation updates the database the user needs to know whether this sub-expression gets evaluated first or second. Note that the same problem can occur as a result of the simplification of some other expression, e.g. if `f` is defined by

```
f x == (look! x, inc! 1 x)
```

and `f r!` is evaluated. Thus expressions can be ambiguous if they contain duplicate occurrences of relation names or if they contain functions which can create duplicate occurrences of a relation name.

Example 2. A similar ambiguity arises if a function can "discard" an expression containing a relation name. For example if `first` is defined by

```
first (x,y) == x
```

then evaluating `first (1,inc! 2 r!)` discards `inc! 2 r!` and gives `1`. However whether the extent of `r!` gets updated or not will depend on whether `inc! 2 r!` is or is not evaluated before being discarded.

The problems that arise from duplication and discarding of relation names cannot be ignored for a number of reasons: They mean that the user must know the evaluation order of the language in order to know the meaning of an expression, this requirement becoming progressively more onerous as the complexity of the expressions being considered increases. The number of equivalences that hold between expressions is reduced and consequently potential for optimisation, for instance by factoring out common subexpressions [Pou94], is lost. Potential for parallelisation is also lost, and it is harder to prove equivalences between expressions.

4 The solution: linear types

To ensure that our language is confluent in the presence of update operators we place restrictions on expressions which are intended to guarantee that no expression can contain two occurrences of the same relation name, and that relation names cannot be duplicated or discarded in the course of evaluation. Thus if an expression `E` contains a relation name `r!` then it must contain exactly one occurrence of `r!` and, furthermore, any expression to which `E` can be reduced must also contain exactly one occurrence of `r!`.

To this end we adopt a type system similar to those described by Wadler in [Wad91]. The type system extends the Hindley-Milner system [Mil78] by establishing a distinction between values of *linear* type which should not be duplicated or discarded in the course of evaluation and values of ***nonlinear type*** which may be duplicated or discarded at will. The syntax of the complete type system is described in figure 1. Type expressions in this system are a superset of those introduced in §2.1. The type system allows us to draw a distinction between three sorts of type expression:

$$
\begin{array}{lll}
T & \in & \textit{Types} \\
K & \in & \textit{Type Constructors} \\
a & \in & \textit{Type Variables} \\
i,j,k,l & \in & \textit{Use Variables} \\
C & \in & \textit{Contexts} \\
\mathbf{T} & \in & \textit{Sequences of zero or more types} \\
T & = & (T \rightarrow T) \mid a \mid (K\ \mathbf{T}) \mid (T,\ldots,T) \mid [T] \\
 & \mid & (T \Rightarrow T) \mid a! \mid (K!\ \mathbf{T}) \mid (T,\ldots,T)! \mid [T]! \\
 & \mid & (T - i \rightarrow T) \mid a!i \mid (K!i\ \mathbf{T}) \mid (T,\ldots,T)!i \mid [T]!i \\
 & & \\
C & = & \{i \Rightarrow j, \ldots, k \Rightarrow l\}
\end{array}
$$

Fig. 1. Abstract syntax of types in PFL

(1) Type expressions denoting non-linear types. These are effectively those introduced in §2.1. A type variable `a` should now be read as meaning "any type so as it is nonlinear". We will show below how type variables of a more general nature are denoted. A type expression `T1->T2` denotes the type of a non-linear function from `T1` to `T2`. Note that this means that the *function* may be duplicated or discarded, not necessarily its argument or result. Type expressions `(T1,...,Tn)` and `[T]` respectively denote nonlinear tuple and list types. The types `Num`, `Chr`, `Bool` and `Str` are all non-linear.

(2) Type expressions denoting linear types. Type variables of the form `a!`, `b!` etc. mean "any type so long as it is linear". Type constructors whose name ends with a ! construct linear types. Hence an object of type `(Rel! Num)` is linear.

Type expressions of the form `(T1,...,Tn)!` denote linear tuple types, which are required because a tuple may have a linear element. For instance suppose that the relation name `r!` is of type `Rel! Num` and consider the tuple `(1,r!)`. Any function that duplicates or discards this tuple will discard or duplicate `r!` and hence the tuple must be given the linear type `(Num,Rel! Num)!`. Similarly expressions of the form `[T]!` denote linear list types.

A type expression of the form `T1=>T2` denotes the type of a linear function from `T1` to `T2`. The reason why a function may have to be assigned a linear type may be understood by considering that defined by

```
f x == r!
```

Since any application of `f` can be evaluated to yield a reference to `r!`, we must avoid duplicating or discarding references to `f`. Note however that the *argument* of `f` is discarded and therefore must be *nonlinear*.

Note that in other work, e.g. [Wad91], the symbol `!` is used to indicate that a type is *non-linear*. We have inverted this convention because we feel that non-linear types will be more common in practice than linear ones.

(3) Type expressions of variable linearity. These contain *use variables* which allow us to express the fact that a particular value may have either a linear or a non-linear type. Use variables are character strings beginning with a lower case character and are used to qualify type expressions as follows: if `i` is a use variable then a type variable ending in `!i` means "any linear or non-linear type", a type expression of the form `(T1,...,Tn)!i` denotes the type of a tuple which may be either linear or non-linear and whose elements are of types `T1 ...Tn`, and a type expression of the form `[T]!i` denotes the type of a list of variable linearity whose elements are of type `T`. Type constructors whose names end in `!i` construct types of variable linearity. The type expression `T1-i->T2` denotes a function from `T1` to `T2` where the function itself may be either linear or non-linear.

As an example of the use of type variables of variable linearity consider the identity function

```
identity :: a!i -> a!i
identity x == x
```

whose type declaration states that it is a non-linear function whose argument may be of any (linear or non-linear) type and which returns a result of the same type. If we did not allow types of variable linearity then we would need to define two versions of `identity`, one of which took a linear argument and the other a non-linear one, and the polymorphism of our type system would be compromised.

We may wish to express relationships between use variables. For instance suppose `tag` is defined by

```
tag x == (1,x)
```

We may wish the argument of **tag** to be either linear or non-linear. However if it is linear then **tag** must return a linear tuple, otherwise the expression **tag r!** would have a non-linear type and hence could be duplicated, resulting in duplication of r!. We may express the type of tag as

```
tag :: a!i -> (Num,a!i)!j    {i=>j}
```

in which {i=>j} (read as "linear i implies linear j") is a *context*, and expresses the fact that if types with use variable i are linear then so are those with use variable j.
Note that if the argument of **tag** was non-linear then it could return either a linear or a non-linear value. It is for this reason that **tag** can be given the type declaration shown above rather than the more restrictive declaration

```
tag :: a!i -> (Num,a!i)!i
```

4.1 Types for the update operators

We now specify the types of PFL's update and lookup operators as[1]

```
inc!  :: a->(Rel! a)->(Rel! a)
exc!  :: a->(Rel! a)->(Rel! a)
look! :: (Rel! a)->([a],(Rel! a)!
```

The reason why **look!** returns a pair containing the name of the relation being queried, as well as its extent, is simple. If we require that an expression never contains more than one occurrence of any given relation name then a sub-expression of the form **look! r!** contains the *only* occurrence of **r!** and must therefore return an expression containing an occurrence of **r!** in order to ensure that it is not discarded and that further updates can be made to it.

In §4.3 we demonstrate how these type declarations, combined with the type inference algorithm, mean that the problematic examples referred to in §3 will be rejected at compile-time as type incorrect.

4.2 Type inference

The type inference mechanism used in PFL is implemented as an algorithm similar to those described by Wadler in [Wad91] with additions to handle system-defined functions, constants, and constructors, as well as recursively defined functions. In addition to checking that functions are passed arguments of the correct type, the algorithm ensures that the following criteria are met:

(a) An expression containing more than one occurrence of the same relation name, e.g. **(r!,r!)** is rejected as type-incorrect.

---

[1] We note that it would be possible to give the operators more general types. For instance we could give **inc!** the type declaration
inc! :: a!i-j->(Rel! a!i)-k->(Rel! a!i) {i=>k}
However for obvious reasons of clarity this will not be done in this paper.

(b) If a function definition contains a formal parameter that does not appear exactly once on the right hand side of the definition, then the argument, or the component of the argument, corresponding to that parameter must be nonlinear. For instance if the function **copy** is defined by

```
copy x == (x,x)
```

then the algorithm will infer that **copy** expects a non-linear argument and will therefore reject a function application such as `copy r!` as type incorrect.

(c) An expression which has a linear sub-expression cannot itself have a non-linear type. For instance the expression `(1,r!)` must not have a non-linear type, because, if it did, then it could be passed as an argument to the function **copy** defined above, resulting in duplicate occurrences of `r!`

(d) The definition of a recursive function may not contain any free identifiers of linear type (e.g. relation names), since these can be duplicated when the function is evaluated. For example, evaluation of **infList**, defined by

```
infList == r!:infList
```

results in `r!` being duplicated ad infinitum.

When applied to expressions containing no relation names or built-in operators that take relation names as arguments, the type inference algorithm behaves in a similar manner to the Hindley-Milner algorithms used in conventional functional programming languages such as Miranda.

4.3 Some examples revisited

We now return to the problematic examples described in §3. It is clear that the expression `(look! r!, inc! 1 r!)` will be rejected as type-incorrect because of consideration (a) above. Furthermore if `f` is defined by

```
f x == (look! x, inc! 1 x)
```

Then `f` will be rejected as type incorrect because of the contradiction between consideration (b), which implies that `x` is non-linear, and the type declarations of `look!` and `inc!` which imply that `x` is linear.

The expression `first (1,inc! 2 r!)` referred to in example 2 is rejected as type-incorrect because the type declaration of `inc!` does not allow us to satisfy consideration (b) which implies that the argument of `first` must be a 2-tuple whose second component is nonlinear.

5 Use of the update operators

We now give some examples to demonstrate how the system-defined update operators may be used to program general updates. We first define functions

incList and **excList** which respectively include and exclude a list of tuples from a selector. [2]

```
incList :: [a]->(Rel! a)->(Rel! a)
incList (h:t) r == incList t (inc! h r)
incList [] r == r

excList :: [a]->(Rel! a) ->(Rel! a)
excList (h:t) r == excList t (exc! h r)
excList [] r == r
```

The function **apply** takes a relation name **rel** of type **(Rel! T)** and a function **fun** of type **[T]->[T]** and performs the update **ext(rel) := fun (ext(rel))**.

```
apply :: ([a]->[a])->(Rel! a)->(Rel! a)
apply fun rel == apply2 fun (look! rel)
    where apply2 f (l,r) == incList (f l) (excList l r)
```

This function allows us to apply any computable transformation to a relation so long as the relation's type is preserved. For example assume that **map** is defined as in §2.2, that **translate** is defined by

```
translate::(Num,Num)->(Accident,(Num,Num))->(Accident,(Num,Num))
translate (a,b) (acc,(x,y)) == (acc, (x-a, y-b))
```

and **coordsAcc!** is a relation of type **(Rel! (Accident,(Num,Num)))** which relates accidents to the grid references at which they occurred. Then evaluating **apply (map (translate (5,10))) coordsAcc!** updates the extent of **coordsAcc!** by taking all its elements and translating each grid reference into a new co-ordinate system whose origin is at (5,10) in the old co-ordinate system. The value returned by this expression is just the relation name **coordsAcc!**.

More generally, it is clear that any computable transformation over an n-tuple of relations can be specified, so long as the type of the n-tuple is preserved.

The function **delete** takes a function **pred** and a relation name **rel** and deletes from the extent of **rel** all tuples **t** for which **pred t** is **True**.

```
delete::(a->Bool)->(Rel! a)->(Rel! a)
    delete pred rel == apply (delete2 pred) rel
        where delete2 p l == [x | x <- l; not (p x) ]
```

The reader will recall from §2.4 that **dateOfAcc!** is a relation name of type **Rel! (Accident,(Num,Num,Num))**. This relation relates accidents to the date at which they occurred. Thus

[2] **incList** and **excList** can also be defined using the higher order function **fold**, that is **incList vals rel == fold inc! rel vals** and **excList vals rel == fold exc! rel vals**, although to do this we would have to change the type declaration for **fold** given in §2.2 so as to allow its second argument to be linear.

```
delete old dateOfAcc!
    where old (a,(d,m,y)) == (y<1990)
```

deletes all accidents occuring before 1990 from the extent of **dateOfAcc!** and returns **dateOfAcc!**.
We can also define a general purpose theta-join function over binary relations. The definition we give below is slightly more cumbersome than necessary. In the next section we shall explain how it can be simplified. First we define a function `join2` as

```
join2 th (l1,r1) (l2,r2) ==
    ([(a,b,c,d)|(a,b)<-l1; (c,d)<-l2; th (a,b) (c,d)],r1,r2)
```

We may then evaluate, for example, the equijoin over the first column of two relations named `bina!` and `binb!` by posing the query

```
join2 eq1 (look!  bina!) (look!  binb!)
    where eq1 (a,b) (c,d) == (a=c);
```

We can then define a function **storeJoin** which materializes the theta-join of two relations **rel1** and **rel2** and stores it in a third relation **rel3** (which is assumed to be initially empty).

```
storeJoin th rel1 rel2 rel3 ==
    storeJoin2 (join2 th (look! rel1) (look! rel2)) rel3
        where storeJoin2 (l,r1,r2) r3 == (r1,r2, incList l r3)
```

Thus the expression

```
storeJoin eq1 dateOfAcc! coordsAcc! timePlaceAcc!
    where eq1 (a,b) (c,d) == (a=c)
```

stores an equijoin of **dateOfAcc!** and **coordsAcc!** in a relation **timePlaceAcc!** which then contains the date and the location of each accident.

6 Non-linear relation names

The type constraints introduced above allow updates to be performed without ambiguity. However they are overly restrictive when applied to the names of relations that are not updated by an expression. Consequently we also allow relations to have non-linear relation names. A relation whose linear relation name is `r!` has a non-linear relation name `r`. If `r!` is of type **(Rel! T)** then `r` is of type **(Rel T)**.

The only system-defined function that may take a non-linear relation name as its argument is the function **look** whose type declaration is

```
look :: (Rel a)->[a]
```

When applied to a non-linear relation name `r`, **look** `r` returns **ext**(`r`). Thus we could simplify `join2` by redefining it as

```
join2 th l1 l2 ==
        [(a,b,c,d)|(a,b)<-l1; (c,d)<-l2; th (a,b) (c,d)]
```

To evaluate the equijoin over the first column of **bina** and **binb** we then pose the query

```
join2 eq1 (look bina) (look binb)
        where eq1 (a,b) (c,d) == (a=c);
```

The use of **look** rather than **look!** overcomes the awkwardness that was caused by the need to preserve references to the relations **bina!** and **binb!**.

To ensure that a relation accessed by **look** cannot be updated we impose the restriction that an expression may refer (directly or indirectly) to a relation either through its linear name or its non-linear name, but not both. Hence if **swAccs** (south-western accidents) is defined by:

```
swAccs  == [a | (a,(x,y)) <- look coordsAcc; x<=0; y<=0]
```

then **excList swAccs coordsAcc!** is type-incorrect because it refers, indirectly, to both **coordsAcc!** and **coordsAcc**.

7 Evaluation

The update facilities described here are currently being used in the context of an investigation into road accidents and have so far been found easy to use and practicable. The compatibility of our type system with conventional Hindley-Milner systems has proved useful as it means that restrictions imposed by the type system to control updates do not hamper the user when they wish only to query the database. The **apply** function allows us to perform any update that can be expressed as a computable function over the extent of a single relation. Since we could define functions similar to **apply** which operate on several relations, it is intuitively clear that PFL is *update complete* in the sense that any update that can be expressed as a computable function over database extents and which does not involve changing the schema can be expressed. We hope to provide a more formal definition, and a proof, of update completeness in a subsequent paper.

However a number of problems remain to be addressed. Firstly the restriction that a relation name must appear only once in an expression limits the extent to which updates can be performed in parallel. This problem could be mitigated by implementing built-in versions of bulk update functions, such as **incList**, in such a way that they effect updates in parallel. However a more general way of performing parallel updates would be desirable. Secondly the restriction that relation names can never be discarded can make programs cumbersome when a large number of relations have to be updated. We are currently investigating ways of discarding relation names in a "safe" manner. Thirdly the type restrictions mean that relation names cannot easily be included in list abstractions. We are currently looking at ways of mitigating this last problem.

8 Related work

A number of other approaches have been adopted to adding updates to database programming languages. The most straightforward approach, adopted by such languages as FAD [Ban87], Napier-88 [Mor89] and our first implementation of PFL [Pou91], is to allow unrestricted use of destructive update functions. However, the resulting language is not confluent and the approach has undesirable consequences, as outlined in Section 3 above.

A different approach is followed by Trinder [Tri89], who proposes that updates be non-destructive, that is to say that an update function is passed a data structure and returns an updated version of that structure whilst leaving the original unaltered. In a naive implementation every update operation would then create a new and completely separate version of the updated data structure. However Trinder demonstrates that by sharing data between the updated and original structures this problem can be mitigated for some data structures. Trinder points out, nonetheless, that there are other data structures which cannot be efficiently modified in the manner he describes. Hash files and graphs where there may be a large number of pointers to the same node are particularly important examples. In contexts where Trinder's approach is practicable it has greater potential for parallelisation than does our system. The functional DBPLs O2FDL [Man90] and Machiavelli [Oho89] follow a similar approach to that advocated by Trinder, as does Manchanda [Man89] in the area of logic languages.

The Glue-Nail [Phi91] and Rock&Roll [Bar94] systems support two languages, a declarative and a procedural one which share, to a greater or lesser extent, a common type system, data model and syntax. The procedural language complements the declarative one by allowing the specification of update procedures which cannot be written in the declarative language. In Rock&Roll the languages are to a degree bi-directional, since side-effect free procedures can be called from the declarative language. Note, however, that although the evaluation strategies of the two languages may in some sense be compatible, a paradigm mismatch clearly remains; and it is an open question whether a parametric polymorphic (as opposed to a monomorphic) type system can be developed for such systems.

The problem of updates in DBPLs is closely related to two problems that have been investigated in the context of non-persistent functional languages, namely the implementation of I/O and the modification of large non-persistent structures such as arrays. The application of linear logic to these problems has been investigated by a number of authors [Wad90, Wad91, Wak90]. Other approaches that have been considered are the use of monads and continuations [Pey93, Sma93].

9 Conclusions and future work

This paper draws on work in the theory and applications of linear logic [Wad91, Wad90, Wak90, Gir87, Gir89]. It demonstrates that, in a database context, linear types can be used to allow destructive update operations to be performed in a simple manner without ambiguity arising through the duplication or discarding of references to bulk data structures.

The update operators and type system described here have been implemented and are being used by the Centre for Transport Studies, University of London, in the context of an analysis of road traffic accidents in Hertfordshire. Our operators are efficient in that they modify relations destructively rather than by copying. However, `look!` may be inefficient since, even with the addition of the "matching" parameter mentioned in §2.4, more tuples may be retrieved than are needed for the evaluation of a query. This problem gets worse as the size of the database relations increases, limiting the scalability of our system. Ideally one would like to allow tuple-by-tuple access to the extent of relations, and this is a subject of current research.

A further problem is the complexity of the types presented to the user, particularly if they involve the "contexts" referred to in §4. This can to some extent be mitigated by presenting to the user a less general type than that returned by the type inference algorithm. Further work is needed to find ways of mitigating this problem and to establish the extent to which it is possible for users to develop an intuitive feel for the type system.

Finally, in a subsequent publication we intend to formalise the type inference rules by which our type system is expressed and prove its correctness.

10 Acknowledgements

We would like to thank our colleagues Simon Courtenage, Alexandra Poulovassilis, Swarup Reddi, Ben Heydecker, Lishan Harbird, and Jiashu Wu for their helpful discussions. We have also had several fruitful discussions with Philip Wadler regarding the formalisation and correctness of our type inference rules. This work has been carried out under EPSRC grant GR/J 49044.

References

[Abi90] Abiteboul, S. and Vianu, V. *Procedural languages for database queries and update*, Journal of Computer and System Sciences, 41, 1990.

[Ban87] Bancilhon, F. et al. *FAD, a powerful and simple database language*, Proc. 13th VLDB Conference, 1991.

[Bar94] Barja, M.L. et al. *An effective deductive object-oriented database through language integration*, Proc. 20th VLDB, 1994.

[Erw91] Erwig, M. and Lipeck, U. *A functional DBPL revealing high level optimizations*, Proc. 3rd DBPL, Morgan-Kaufman, 1991.

[Gir87] Girard, J-Y. *Linear logic*, Theoretical Computer Science, 50, 1987.

[Gir89] Girard, J-Y., Lafont, Y. and Taylor, P. *Proofs and types*, Cambridge University Press, 1989.

[Hug89] Hughes, J. *Why functional programming matters*, The Computer Journal, 32(2), 1989.

[Man89] Manchanda, S. *Declarative expression of deductive database updates*, Proc. ACM PODS, 1989.

[Man90] Manino, M.V. Choi, I.J. and Batory, D.S. *The Object-Oriented Functional Data Language*, IEEE Trans. on Software Engineering, 16(11), 1990.

[Mil78] Milner, R. *A theory of type polymorphism in programming*, Journal of Computer and System Sciences, 17, 1978.

[Mor89] Morrison, R., Brown, F., Connor, R. and Dearle, A. *The Napier-88 reference manual*, Universities of Glasgow and St Andrews, PPRR-77-89, 1989.

[Oho89] Ohori, A., Buneman, P. and Breazu-Tannen, V. *Database programming in Machiavelli - a polymorphic language with static type inference*, Proc. ACM SIGMOD, 1989.

[Pey87] Peyton-Jones, S.L. *The Implementation of Functional Programming Languages*, Prentice Hall, 1987.

[Pey93] Peyton-Jones, S.L. and Wadler, P. *Imperative functional programming*, Proc. 20th ACM Symposium on Principles of Programming Languages, 1993.

[Phi91] Phipps, G., Derr, M.A. and Ross, K.A. *Glue-Nail: A deductive database system*, Proc. ACM SIGMOD Conference, 1991.

[Pou91] Poulovassilis, A. and Small, C. *A functional programming approach to deductive databases*, Proc. 17th VLDB Conference, 1991.

[Pou93] Poulovassilis, A. and Small, C. *A domain-theoretic approach to integrating functional and logic databases*, Proc. 19th VLDB, 1993.

[Pou94] Poulovassilis, A. and Small, C. *Investigation of algebraic query optimisation techniques for database programming languages*, Proc. 20th VLDB Conference, 1994.

[Sma91] Small, C. and Poulovassilis, A. *An overview of PFL*, Proc. 3rd DBPL, Morgan-Kaufman, 1991.

[Sma93] Small, C. *A functional approach to database updates*, Information Systems, 18(8), 1993.

[Søn90] Søndergaard, H. and Sestoft, P. *Referential Transparency, Definiteness and Unfoldability*, Acta Informatica, 27, 1990.

[Tri89] Trinder, P. *Referentially transparent database languages*, Proc. 1989 Glasgow Workshop on Functional Programming, 1989.

[Wad90] Wadler, P. *Linear types can change the world!* In M. Broy and C. Jones (eds.) *Programming Concepts and Methods*, North Holland, 1990.

[Wad91] Wadler, P. *Is there a use for linear logic?* In *Conference on partial evaluation and Semantics Based Program Manipulation (PEPM)*, ACM Press, June 1991.

[Wak90] Wakeling, D. *Linearity and laziness*, PhD dissertation, University of York, November 1990.

Recognizing Graphic Detail
An Experiment in User Interpretation of Data Models

J.C.Nordbotten

Dept. of Information Science, University of Bergen
N-5020 Bergen, Norway.
joan@ifi.uib.no

M.E.Crosby

Dept. of Information and Computer Science, University of Hawaii at Manoa
Honolulu, HI 96822, USA.
crosby@ics.uhics.hawaii.no

Abstract. Graphic data models are used as a communication tool between system users and a system analyst to support database design. It is a tacit assumption that users understand graphic models and can confirm that the model correctly depicts important requirements for the system. For this, the data model syntax and style must facilitate understanding of the information elements, interrelationships, and constraints represented. Unfortunately, little is known about how users read and interpret data models, what level of detail is seen, or how model type or graphic style influences model comprehension. Our observations, from a pilot study in graphic data model perception, indicate that many graph details are seen by less than half of the readers and that graphic style influences both the ease with which the models are read and model comprehension.

Keywords. graphic model perception, data models, database design

1. Reading Graphic Models

Data models, specifying the entity types (objects), attributes, domain types and value sets, classification and associative relationships, constraints, and behaviour (methods) for a DB, are used as a communication tool between system users and a system analyst, a CASE tool, or the DBMS to support database design, distributed DB integration, and query formulation toward both central and distributed systems. Graphic models are assumed to be superior to tabular or text models for enhancing user understanding.

Though many graphic model styles are used in sales, research, and educational literature, little research has addressed how these models are read, how much of their content is seen and understood, or how *graphic style* (the icons, line annotation, and layout used) influences model comprehension. Research on programmer interpretation of system specifications has concentrated on flow chart, tree, or decision table resentations of processes, under the hypothesis that presentation formats effect comprehension [13, 1]. An experiment which presented programmers with design specifications in three spatial formats: sequential, hierarchical, and branching flow charts, indicates that the combined use of the succinct program design language and branching spatial arrangement significantly facilitated design interpretation [11]. An empirical study using a computer program to simulate underlying perceptual and cognitive processes non-programmers use to decode information from graphs showed up to 37% variation in interpretation times for the average subject [5]. Although this research provides an insight into interpretation of graphic presentation of processes, the combined results have yet to explain how information system users view and interpret the more static, structural information of data models.

One method for studying these questions is to track eye movements while subjects interpret models presented in various graphic styles. Eye movement registrations consist of fixations and saccades (movement between fixations). Fixations are defined as the length of time the eye remains focused on one area before moving to another area. Processing information occurs only during the fixations [12]. A minimum of 100 to 125 milliseconds of fixation duration is needed to view an item and transmit that information to the brain [7]. According to a reading model based on immediacy and eye-mind assumptions, text is interpreted immediately during an eye fixation, the fixated word is available for cognitive processing within a few tens of milliseconds, and the eye stays fixated on a word as long as necessary to process it [4]. Although the immediacy theory is sometimes challenged, researchers agree that there is a relation between fixation duration and subjects attention to a specific area.

In the following, we present an analysis of reader interpretation of data models presented in three different graphic styles (see examples in the Appendix):

1) *highly iconized* used in the NIAM model presented in [8],
2) *embedded list* used in an object-oriented model, OODM, [2],
3) *external list* used in an EER based model [3], SSM, [9].

The analysis is based on the eye movement and audio data taken while each subject interpreted a set of models expressed in the above data model types. The model types were modified slightly to emphasize their basic graphic style. A fourth model type, IDEF1X [7], which was familiar to the experiment subjects, was included and used to determine the general data model interpretation ability of the subjects.

2. An Experiment[1] in Graphic Model Perception

Simplified graphic data models were designed for eight information systems chosen for applications in: *travel information, education, project-management, library, sports, concerts, sales, and purchasing.* It was assumed that these were common application areas which would be familiar to any reader of the models. Each model contains equivalent concepts and structure and consists of: 2 independent interrelated entities, a classification structure with 2 subentities, 24 attributes including atomic, composite, derived, and multivalued attributes, domain specifications with data value constraints, primary key specifications, relationship cardinalities, and participation constraints. Six of the systems were modelled using comparable versions of the NIAM, OODM, and SSM model types. (See the models for the project application given in the Appendix.) The tourist and sports applications were modelled using the IDEF1X model type. Six experiment sequences were defined as shown in Table 1.

Immediately preceding each experiment, the subject was given an example data model and verbal explanations of the terminology used. The subject was informed that the experiment consisted of 8 models, 2 each of 4 different data model types, and instructed to give a complete, oral interpretation including the entities, attributes, relationships, and constraints specified in each model. The subject was also instructed to indicate when each interpretation was finished. Maximum interpretation time allowed per model was 4 minutes. Average modell interpretation time was 2 minutes 15 seconds.

1) The Experiment Is Described In More Detail In [10].

Seq.	*Tourist*	*Student*	*Project*	*Library*	*Sport*	*Music*	*Sales*	*Parts*
1	IDEF	SSM	NIAM	OODM	IDEF	SSM	NIAM	OODM
2	IDEF	SSM	OODM	NIAM	IDEF	SSM	OODM	NIAM
3	IDEF	NIAM	SSM	OODM	IDEF	NIAM	SSM	OODM
4	IDEF	NIAM	OODM	SSM	IDEF	NIAM	OODM	SSM
5	IDEF	OODM	SSM	NIAM	IDEF	OODM	SSM	NIAM
6	IDEF	OODM	NIAM	SSM	IDEF	OODM	NIAM	SSM

Table 1. Experiment Sequences

Audio tapes were used to collect the verbal protocols for the subjects. Eye movement data was collected using an Applied Sciences Laboratory Eye Movement Monitor which was connected to a Macintosh II computer. An infrared beam projected at one of the subject's eyes was used to compute the location coordinates of the eye, 60 times a second as the subject viewed each graphic model on a large video monitor. A fixation was defined when at least 10 consecutive points were within a 10 by 18 pixel area, giving a fixation duration of 167 msecs. An area was defined for each component in each data model, such that all concepts and constraints had identifiable graph area.

2.1 The Subjects

System users who are expected to design their own DB or to read and confirm the correctness of data models created by a system analyst, can be expected to have good knowledge of their application area (the topic area for the data model) and some familiarity with the types of models used with computer applications. However, it is not reasonable to expect them to have training in a particular data model type. Ideally, the subjects for an experiment to test data model legibility should represent this user group.

The subjects in this experiment were 17 volunteer students from the Dept. of Information and Computer Science at the University of Hawaii at Manoa (ICS/UH): 12 senior-level undergraduates from a course in systems analysis and design, and 5 graduate students. Though they had training in the development of system design models, and in particular in the use of the IDEF1X model which is taught and used at ICS/UH, none were familiar with the other models used in the experiment. While students do not represent system users, it was assumed that their strategies for reading data models of familiar applications would be similar to those utilized by system users when reading a model of their application domain.

2.2 Data Model Comprehension

Each model contained 21 components, containing an entity, relationship, attribute set, or constraint specification. A *comprehension score* (Q-score) was calculated for each model interpretation as the percent of *correctly identified* model components. Comprehension scores varied greatly within the subject group and within the models read by a single subject. The Q-scores for the 136 model interpretations varied from 27-91. Average scores, Q", were calculated from the Q-scores for each reader (variation from 34 to 77) and for each model-type (variations 52-71). The OODM models contained method sets for selected object (entity) types. To facilitate comparison, the OODM Q-scores were calculated without credit for method recognition.

The readers were grouped into two skill levels; *skilled and non-skilled* graphic model interpreters, according to their Q" score for the IDEF1X models. Skilled IDEF1X model interpreters also demonstrated above average Q" scores for their NIAM, OODM, and SSM (NOS) model interpretations, while the nonskilled readers had below average NOS Q" scores. Table 2 shows the average Q"-scores for the interpretations of each model type for all readers, and for the skilled and nonskilled reader groups.

Level	*# readers*	*IDEF1X*	*NIAM*	*OODM*	*SSM*
Total	17	71	52	59	58
Skilled	9	80	58	68	67
Nonskilled	8	61	46	49	48

Table 2. Average Comprehension scores for each Model Type for All Readers and Skilled and Nonskilled Groups

As noted above, the readers were unfamiliar with the NOS model types but had some training in the use of IDEF1X models which are also less detailed in that neither domain nor data value specifications are included. As shown in Table 3, the nonskilled readers were less familiar with data modelling concepts than the skilled reader group. Their interpretations consisted of the basic entity-attribute sets, with errors identifying the associative relationships and omission of the constraints. The skilled readers recognized 17% more components in the list model types than the icon based models.

2.3 Reader Familiarity with Data Model Concepts

The data models used in the experiment contained the 4 most basic data modelling concepts: *entities (objects), attributes, relationships, and domains (data-types)*, and the 4 constraint types: *primary keys, relationship cardinality, subclass participation, and data-value sets.* In addition, the OODM model contained names of *methods* associated with selected objects. Table 3 shows the percentage of readers who recognized each concept and constraint in at least 1 model interpretation.

	Concept					**Constraint**			
	Ent	***Atr***	***Rel***	***Dom***	***Meth***	***Key***	***Car***	***Par***	***Val***
Total	100	100	100	76	88	76	94	100	41
Skilled	100	100	100	89	100	100	100	100	78
Nonskilled	100	100	100	63	75	50	88	100	0

Table 3. Concept Recognition by Reading Skill Level, percent

Clearly, entities, attribute/methods, and interentity structures are familiar concepts for this group of subjects. More curious is the low recognition of data domain specifications, since all of these readers have had several courses in programming.

Table 4 shows the percentage of models of each type in which the concepts and constraints were correctly identified. Note particularly that recognition of the interentity relationships and their constraints is quite poor in the OODM and NIAM models, considering that these are known concepts.

	Concept					**Constraint**			
	Ent	***Atr***	***Rel***	***Dom***	***Meth***	***Key***	***Car***	***Par***	***Val***
IDEF1X	100	100	93	-[2]	-	53	57	80	-
NIAM	100	100	70	60	-	13	17	13	17
OODM	100	97	63	23	77	3	3	3	20
SSM	100	100	90	40	-	10	30	67	30

Table 4. Concept Recognition by DM Type, percent

2) The '-' indicates that the concept or constraint is not included in the model type.

3. Attention to Graphic Detail

Graph syntax, defined as the icons, symbols, line notations, and layout used should enhance a readers understanding of the concepts included in the graphic model. Entities, attributes, and relationships provide the general structure in a data model. As shown in Table 4, the choice of entity icon and placement of the attribute list did not effect entity and attribute recognition for readers familiar with these concepts. Figure 1 shows the icons used by the four model types in this experiment to represent these concepts, as well as the placement of the primary key attributes. (See also example in the Appendix.) The relationship icons used in the NIAM and OODM models do not appear to be as distinguishable as those used in the IDEF1X and SSM models.

Constraint specification is vital to specification of a consistent database for a given application. These are commonly given in graph details as annotations and/or special symbols placed in, on, or adjacent to the connection lines or the entity/attribute icons. Domain specifications are given in a *programming language style* in the OODM and SSM model types as an extension to the attribute list entries with domain specifications given, while the NIAM model type utilizes pairs of attribute and domain icons. While icon usage appears to be somewhat successful for domain specifications, the other annotation types were far less readily recognized. One possible explanation is that they literally were not seen. A second explanation is that they were seen but not understood.

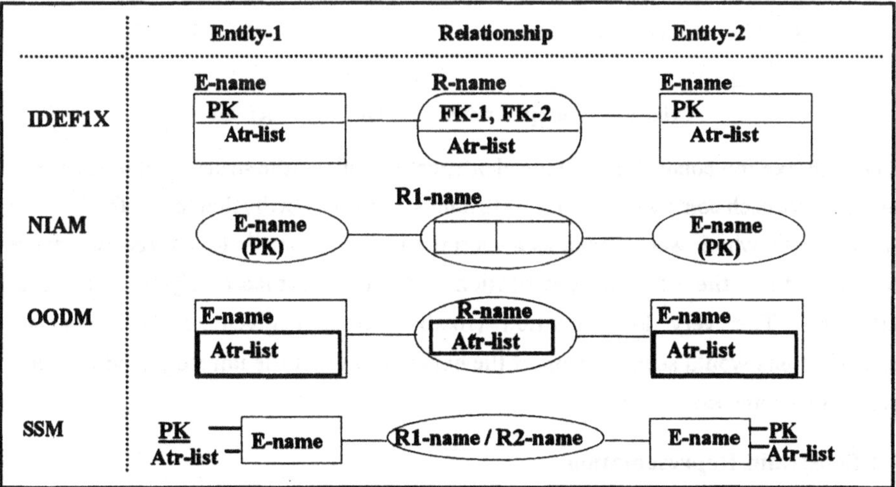

Figure 1: Concept Representations

3.1 Fixation Counts and Attention to Detail

Eye movements used during scene interpretation give data about how a scene is read, which areas are studied, and which areas are not seen. Studies have shown that the number of eye fixations used during scene interpretation is influenced by the complexity of the scene, in our case the data model. Fixations were counted for each concept and constraint area in each model interpretation in the 17 complete experiments, giving fixation counts for 136 model readings, 34 for each model type. The ordered average count for each model type was: IDEF1X: 187, SSM: 232, OODM: 234, and NIAM: 284. As anticipated, the familiar IDEF1X model was the 'easiest' to read, requiring the least number of fixations, while the NIAM model was the most complex, requiring 33% more fixations (or effort).

Table 5 shows the average percent of fixations used in each concept/constraint area in each model type. Note that the basic entity-relationship structure was relatively quickly identified in all model types, requiring between 20-35% of the total fixation counts. Another 39-57% was used to identify the attributes, domains, and methods. Relatively little attention, 9-28% vs 40%, was given to identification of the constraints in the NIAM, OODM, and SSM models, compared to the familiar IDEF1X models.

	Concept					**Constraint**			
	Ent	***Atr***	***Rel***	***Dom***	***Meth***	***Key***	***Car***	***Par***	***Val***
IDEF1X	9	41	11	-	-	24	5	11	-
NIAM	17	49	18	8	-	2	1	5	1
OODM	16	29	13	6	19	6	1	8	3
SSM	16	36	17	3	-	4	4	15	5

Table 5. Concept Fixations per DM Type, percent

The high fixation counts for attribute identification reflects the structure of the attribute areas where each contains a list of 3-6 attributes. It is noteworthy that the method lists in the OODM, which were placed as a continuation of the attribute list, received more attention than the domain specifications which were placed adjacent to 'their' attributes. The very low attention (fixation counts) given to the constraint specifications would seem to support the explanation that the unrecognized concepts were simply 'not seen'.

3.2 Constraint Representation

Though relatively little effort was spent interpreting the constraints, there are differences between the model types which may indicate which graphic forms attract attention, and thereafter recognition.

Key Identification. The primary key attributes in the experiment models were all named *Id.* They were recognized in the familiar IDEF1X model by all of the skilled readers and half of the nonskilled readers. Only 2 of the 9 skilled readers recognized key attributes in the other model types, and only one of these in all model types.

Both primary and foreign key specifications in the IDEF1X model are given in a separate area within the entity icon. OODM models have no graphic specification of key attributes since identifiers are assumed to be generated by the system. Key attributes are placed in parenthesis in the entity icon in the NIAM model, while they are underlined in the SSM model. Neither of these graphic strategies appears to support key recognition.

Domains and Data Value Specification. Both the OODM and SSM models use a programming style for domain and data-value specification:

OODM: Attribute-name : data-type (length | value list | value-range)
SSM: Attribute-name <data-type (length | value list | value-range)>

which was described by 5 of the 9 skilled readers. Two of the nonskilled readers recognized these specifications in the SSM model while none of this group articulated domains in the OODM models. This is interesting considering that all readers have had training and were expected to have some proficiency in programming and this form for data specification.

A domain is considered an object type in NIAM and is modelled with an icon with a named relationship (attribute) connected to the entity icon as shown in the appendix. This graphic strategy is successful in that 2/3 of the skilled readers and 50% of the nonskilled readers articulated domain specifications. The attention given to domain and data-value specifications was very low, < 10%. It could be speculated that these readers, who were somewhat familiar with a data model type without domains, did not expect to 'find' domain specifications in other data model types.

Relationship Specification. The concept of interrelated entities, both associations between separate entity types and classification hierarchies with cardinality and participation constraints was known to all readers (Table 3). However relationship interpretation for the different model types varied considerably (Table 4) as did the effort used for interpretation (Table 5). Figure 2 shows the graphic representation of a 1:10 cardinality for the relationships between E1 and E2 and total, disjoint participation specifications for the subentities SE1 and SE2. Note that the cardinality for the relationship between E2 and E1 is not defined in this figure.

All model types use line annotation, though varying symbol definitions are used. Neither type of cardinality symbol; the *mandatory 'dot'* notation used in NIAM and IDEF1X or the *arrow head* notation used in NIAM and OODM models, was seen, causing partial identification of cardinality constraints in these models. The *(min:max)* notation for cardinality specification was recognized by only 1/3 of the readers. The separate structures used for classification participation in the IDEF1X and SSM models were relatively effortlessly recognized, 11% & 15% of the fixations to interpret 80% and 67% of the structures respectively.

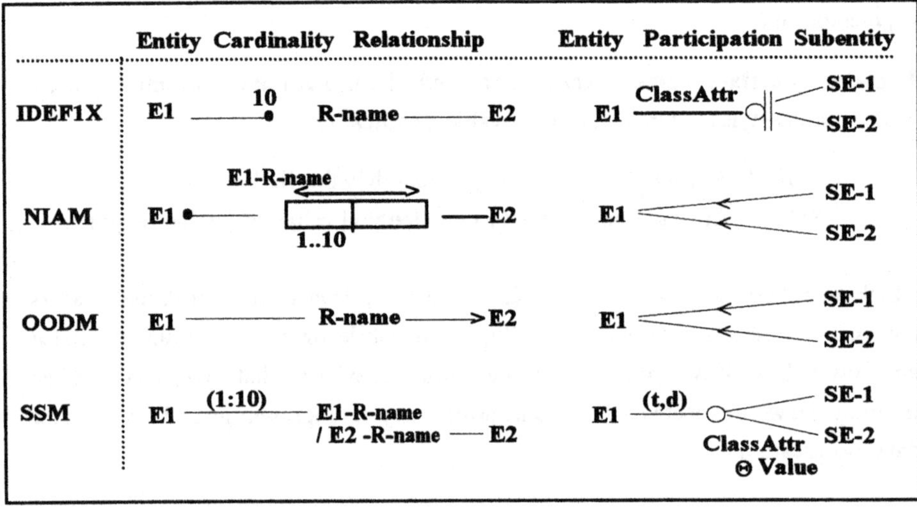

Figure 2. Relationship Constraint Annotations

4. Conclusions & Further Analysis

Graphic data models are intended to support user-designer communication during planning and specification of an information system. Usually, a system analyst is expected to develop a data model which the user confirms as correct with respect to the system requirements. A data model typically presents several aspects of the information system, including:

1) the information or data types which are to be included in the system,
2) the structural relationships, associations and classification structures which are to exist between these information/data types, and
3) the information system constraints which specify valid values and relationships.

The central question addressed in this study has been how graphic syntax influences user interpretation of data models, ie identification of the information/data types, relationships, and constraints represented in a data model. Our data indicate that graphic syntax variation, as used in the data model types studied, appears to influence both the effort a user needs for model interpretation and model comprehension, it does not appear to effect identification of the general system structure; ie the information/ data types and their interrelationships.

However, this experiment indicates that constraint specifications, when given as end-line annotation, are not seen and therefore can not be included in the users' interpretation of the model. Constraint specifications given as distinct icons in clearly distinct graph areas, as used for the IDEF1X-key and IDEF1X & SSM participation constraints, seem to attract attention and were more frequently included in the model interpretation.

Our reader sample was both too small (17 persons) and too homogeneous (CS students) to give certain knowledge about how graph syntax would effect model understanding of 'real' system users. None the less, we believe the observations summarized below, which are based on an analysis of both audio and visual data collected for 136 data model interpretations, are worth confirming.

- Icon rich model types, illustrated here by the NIAM model type, appear to make a model more difficult to interpret than models with fewer icon types supplemented by list structures.
- Center line annotation and/or clearly separate icons in distinct graph areas, appear more visible than end line annotation and/or embedded symbols.

It is disturbing that so many model interpretations omitted descriptive details, particularly the constraint specifications, which were given in the models and with which the interpreters were familiar. Why didn't they attract attention? Were they not understood? Were they considered unimportant? Supplementary experiments are planned to address these questions.

Acknowledgments

A special thank you for help and advice in preparation of the experiment, its execution, preparation of the data, and its analysis is extended to Professors W. Wesley Peterson and Svein Nordbotten. Also appreciated, is the interest and cooperation of Asst. Professor Donald DeRyke and the students of his systems analysis class.

References

1. Brooke, J. and Duncan, K. An Experimental Study of Flowcharts as an Aid to the Identification of Procedural Faults. Ergonomics, 23, 1980, 387-399.
2. Cattel,R.G.G. Object Data Management Object-oriented and Extended RDBS. Addison Wesley, 1991.
3. ElMasri,R. and S.B.Navathe, Fundamentals of Database Systems,2.ed. Benjamin Cummings 1994.
4. Just, M., Carpenter, P., A theory of reading: From eye fixation to comprehension. Psychological Review, 87, 1980, pp 329 -354.
5. Lohse,G., A Cognitive Model for Understanding Graphical Perception. Human-Computer Interaction, 8, 1993, pp.353-388.
6. Loomis,M. Data Modeling - the IDEF1X Technique. Proc. IEEE Conf. on Computers and Communications. pp 146-151. March 1986.
7. McConkie, G. Eye Movements and Perception During Reading. In K. Rayner (Ed.) Eye Movements in Reading: In Eye Movements in Reading: Perceptual and Language Processes, Academic Press, NY, NY. 1983.
8. Nijssen, G.M. and T.A. Halpin. Conceptual Schema And Relational Database Design - A fact oriented approach. Prentice Hall 1989.
9. Nordbotten, J.C. Modelling Relationships And Constraints In SSM - A Structural Semantic Data Model. Report no.14, ISSN 0803-6489. Information Science, Univ.of Bergen. 1993.
10. Nordbotten,J.C. & M.E.Crosby. Graphic Model Legibility - An Experiment. Report no.14, ISSN 0803-6489. Information Science, Univ.of Bergen. 1995.
11. Sheppard, S.B., Kruisi, E., Bailey, J. W. An Empirical Evaluation of Software Documentation Formats. Proceedings Human Factors in Computer Systems, 1982, 121-124.
12. Wolverton, G.& Zola, D. The Temporal Characteristics of Visual Information Extraction During Reading. In K. Rayner (Ed.) Eye Movements in Reading: In Eye Movements in Reading: Perceptual and Language Processes, 1983, New York NY: Academic Press.
13. Wright, P. & Reid, F. Written Information: Some Alternatives to Prose for Expressing the Outcome of Complex Contingencies. Journal of Applied Psychology 57, 1973, pp. 160-166.

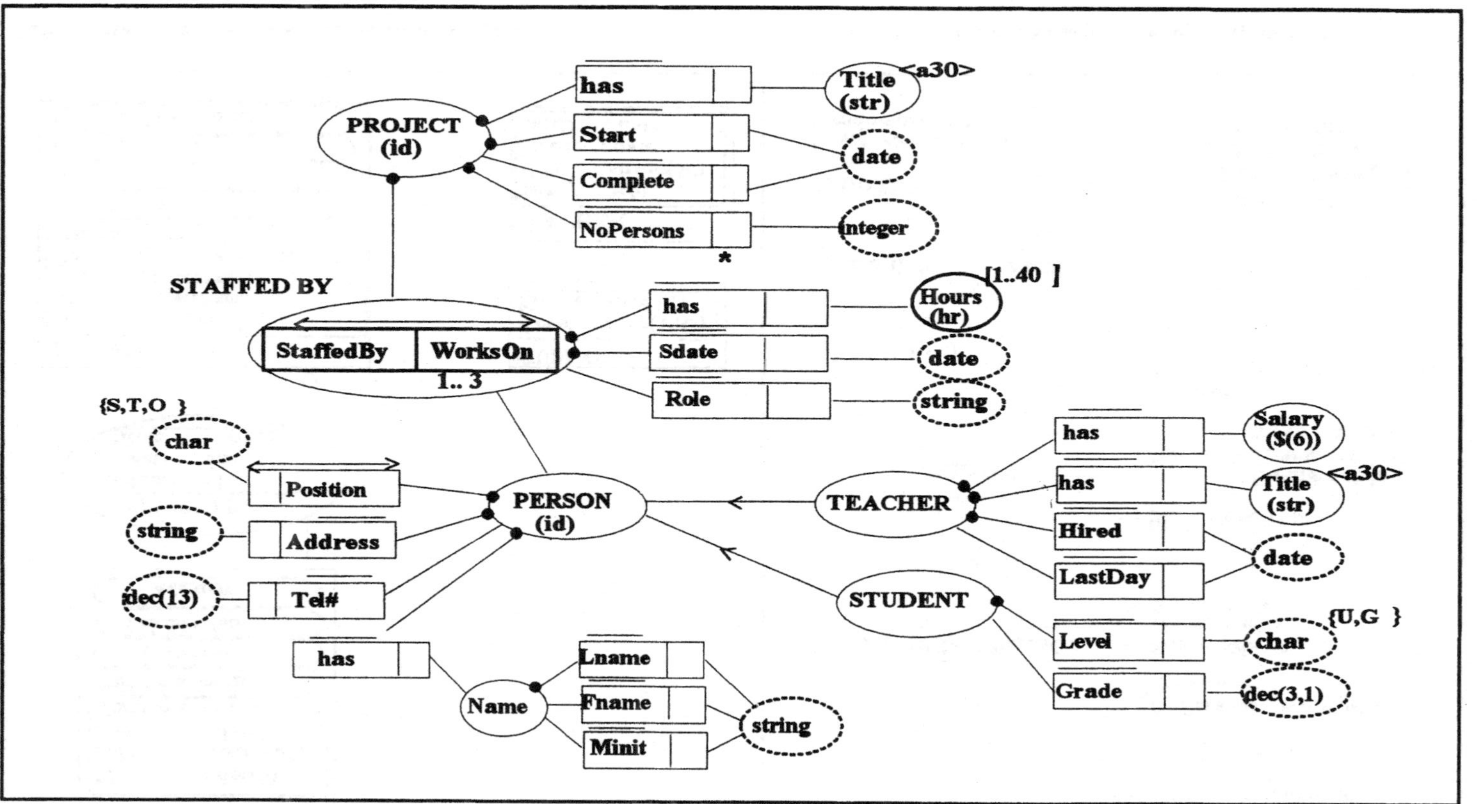

APPENDIX - Fig. A.a: NIAM model of Project application

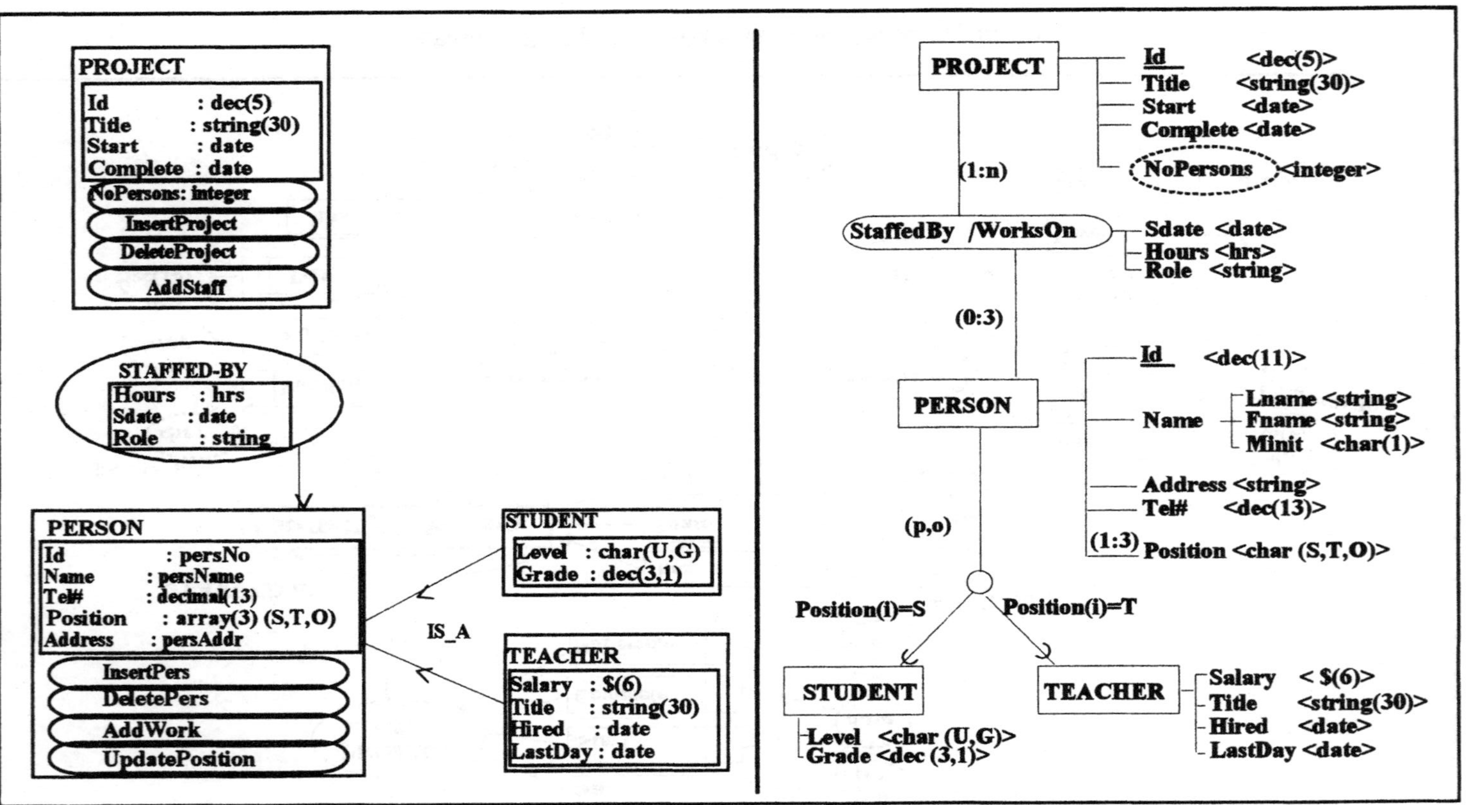

APPENDIX - Fig. A.b: OODM model of Project application

Fig. A.c: SSM model of Project application

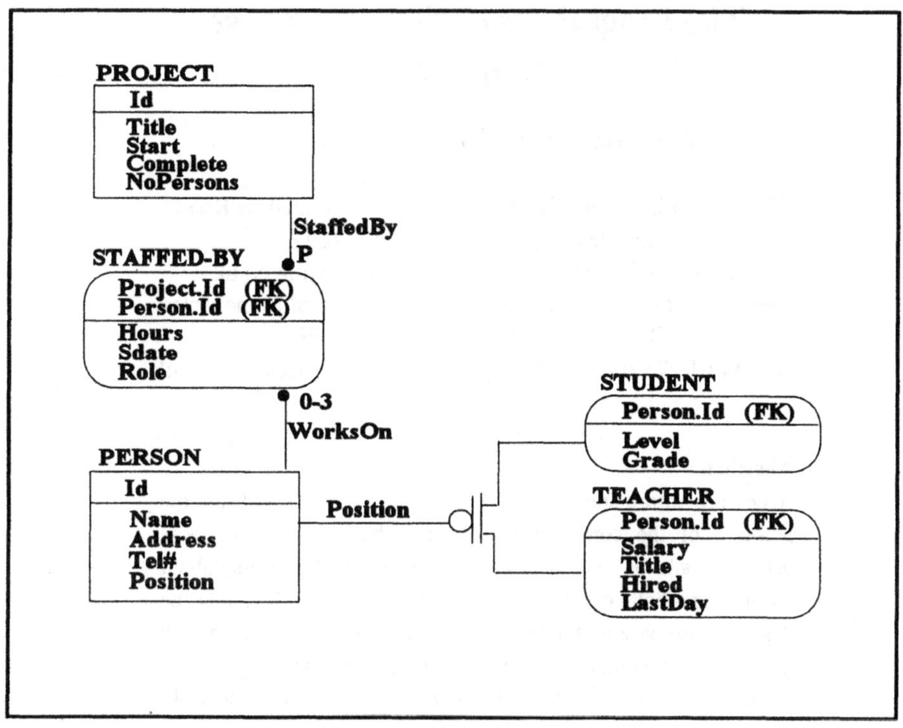

APPENDIX - Fig. A.d: IDEF1X model of Project application

The Pragmatics of Naive Database Enquiry.

David Haw[1], Carole Goble[2], Alan Rector[2]

[1]Harlequin Ltd, 2nd Floor, Queens Court, Wilmslow Road, Alderley Edge, Cheshire, SK9 7QD.
tel: +44 625 588019; internet: dh@harlequin.co.uk
[2]Department of Computer Science, University of Manchester, Oxford Road, Manchester M13 9PL.
tel: +44 61 275 6195/6188; internet: <cag, alr>@cs.man.ac.uk

Abstract.
Accessing information in databases has traditionally been the preserve of the computer professional, but as new interfaces become available, new users need to be less knowledgeable about the nuts and bolts of computing. It is the contention here that the designers of systems for these 'naive' users need to examine the model of the communicative process used in everyday life to support a co-operative dialogue between human and machine. In this paper we investigate at the pragmatics of the communicative process and how it relates to recent interface development, and present GUIDANCE, a system that implements some of its conclusions

"'Forty-two!' yelled Loonqual. 'Is that all you've got to show for seven and a half million years work?'

'I checked it quite thoroughly,' said the computer, 'and that is quite definitely the answer. I think the problem, to be honest with you, is that you've never really known what the question is.' [1]

1 Introduction

Deep Thought, the computer concerned, was designed to provide an answer to the great question of Life the Universe and Everything. The answer of 42 was a little disappointing. They even had to build another computer to find out what the question was. What they hadn't realised is that finding the answer is the easy part and that the really difficult part is working out the right questions to ask.

A similar state of affairs can exist when naive users of database systems[1], who may be experts in their own field, approach the interface with the same idea in mind - "What's the answer to MY great question?". The answer will turn up in a lot less time, but may be of equal use, and engender a similar amount of frustration.

In this paper we present an analysis of the communicative process of enquiry, and go on to discuss two existing interfaces to databases with reference to this. We then describe the GUIDANCE system which is based on ideas derived from the human communicative practices and conventions. The users of GUIDANCE are encouraged to follow a more human model of enquiry - a pro-active and informed search for information - rather than a prescribed and technologically driven path dominated by simple query question-answer pairs. If the human model had been implemented in Deep Thought, perhaps it would have replied "Well, this is what I know about Life the Universe and Everything, which bit would you like to ask me about?"

2 The Communicative Processes.

Norman [19] suggests that many problems that are encountered by users of computer systems are to do with mismatches between a user's intention and the task variables, and that effective human computer interaction occurs when it is possible for a user to easily map their intentions onto actions on the screen, and that these actions produce the desired results. A discussion of the issues raised due to the structural, naming and phrasing problems with regard to relational database navigation are discussed at length in Haw, Goble and Rector [12]. This paper discussed the syntax and semantics of interaction, and we wish here to investigate the *pragmatics* of the process - as semantics is defined as the study of the literal meanings of a symbol or symbols, pragmatics is the study of the meanings of a symbol or symbols to the situated communicative parties, both human and machine, with regard to the context and state of the interaction.

---

[1]The target user group are those who are experts in their own domain , but have no knowledge of the database apart from that it contains information that they may find useful. They have no wish or permission to alter values or set up tables. They have no particular technical expertise, but are computer literate to the extent that they know what a mouse is and how to use it.

We intend here to utilise ideas from cognitive science and linguistics to provide pointers to how an interface to a database may support the communicative process of enquiry. The assumption being made here is that when faced with a computer, the casual user will 'suspend disbelief' and imagine that the communication is taking place with a human [25]. This being the case, we can infer that the model for the pragmatics of human-computer interaction is based on that of human-human conversation or dialogue. If designers of systems built to interface to humans disregard this when their target user group are 'computer illiterate', then they are implicitly attempting an imposition of an alien and unrecognised mode of communication which may break normal conversational convention, and they must not feign surprise if frustration and dissatisfaction result.

2.1. The Nature of Enquiry

The term 'dialogue' in HCI is often considered synonymous with the term 'interface' [5][2], but this point of view implicitly excludes any investigation of interaction from the perspective of pragmatics . We follow Baker's [2] more linguistically based definitions which state that:

- conversation is a free sequence of exchanges with no topic or goals.
- dialogue is a conversation in a specific setting with goals and objectives.

The goals and objectives in a dialogue may be of any level of abstraction, but the intention of the involved parties is to come to a negotiated solution. It is this richer definition of dialogue that we are interested in here when we consider the interaction between a user and a system that can access information in a database.

Clearly human-computer dialogue is severely restricted in comparison to human-human - no intonation, emotion or any non-verbal channels are open. But it is apparent that even with limited channels of communication, human dialogue (such as by telephone) still proceeds according to general communicative practices and conventions. However important the style,

---

[2]For example, Shneiderman's 'Eight Golden Rules of Dialogue Design' [26] could be paraphrased as 'Eight Golden Rules of Interface Design'.

structure and content of human-computer interaction and its consequent limitations may be, these factors are not considered to be the predominant ones for successful interaction [3]. Users bring other related general knowledge and information[3] to bear depending on the task in hand. One of these sources of knowledge will be a model of the human communicative process. We therefore prefer to take an abstracted view of these pragmatics before discussing the specifics of particular interfaces. To that end, our examples are verbalisations - purely semantic interpretations of the presentations at the interface - so that their value in context can be assessed without reference to the stylistic preferences of the system designer.

Here we define an *enquiry dialogue* as a human-machine interaction that starts with an intention on the part of the user, progresses through several stages, and hopefully but not necessarily results in a satisfactory conclusion. As demonstrated in the introduction, users often need assistance in asking the right question, and a truly co-operative system should aid and guide them in finding and asking the questions that will satisfy their needs just as a human partner would.

Many enquiries from our target user group will be vague, ill-formed and under specified [27], but some may be simple and well specified. A well-specified enquiry[4] to a database may be verbalised as:

"How much did Bill Gates earn last year?"

The question is clearly stated, and a direct answer is possible - it will be a big number in dollars. Something more ill-formed may be:

"Tell me about salaries."

This is a kind of 'knowledge discovery' [20], and there is no particular kind of answer that will necessarily be satisfactory. This is opening gambit of an enquiry dialogue that deserves an appropriate and co-operative response.

---

[3]For instance - problem-solving abilities, knowledge of natural language, knowledge of the domain.

[4]As can be seen here, even well specified enquiries may not be straightforward when it comes to mapping intention to action with an interface.

2.2. Turn Taking

We shall go on now to investigate the rules that determine the procedure and conduct of the human communicative process. A basic pragmatic rule governing a two party dialogue is that one party speaks and then the other does, and then the first does again, and so on, each turn being deemed a 'constructional unit' [24]. This may appear so obvious as to be facile, but the designers of human-machine dialogues do not always take this into account, often relying on a process where the user commands and the machine responds using qualitatively different presentations that define distinct constructional units for questioning and answering. This style of single question-answer pair types ('one-shot' query) does not allow the option to take the next communicative 'turn' within the context of the last. For example, SQL uses a command line as a 'questioning presentation' and returns a value which may be a table or a string. This does not allow another 'turn' to be taken by the user who must restart this restrictive process from the beginning in order to query some more.

In the case of the well-specified enquiry above, a presentation as a simple question-answer pair is probably acceptable because if the answer is the one that was expected (big number in dollars) it implies no more turns need be taken. In the case of our more fuzzy discovery based enquiry, it would be more like the human communicative process to offer an opportunity to continue. A technique to enable this is to present the interface constructional unit such that a question may be asked within the context of the previous answer. Early examples of this are QBE [30] and RABBIT [27]. In the former the user is presented with example values inside a representation of a database table and the user can alter the values to investigate the relation. In the latter, example values are also employed and the system explicitly implements turn taking to facilitate the iterative refinement of the example instance presented. Visual query systems and direct manipulation systems [4, 15, 23] because of the fact that they offer question and answer presented in the same form implicitly implement turn taking, and this may account for their popularity, but it does not necessarily mean that they also mimic other human communicative practices and conventions.

2.3. The Co-operative Principle

The linguist Grice put forward four basic maxims of conversation [10], which are simple and straightforward statements of the 'rules' guiding the conduct of the communicative process. They jointly express a general 'co-operative principle'. It is worth stating all of them in full here:

The Co-operative Principle.
Make your contribution such as is required, at the stage at which it occurs, by the accepted purpose or direction of the talk exchange in which you are engaged.

The maxim of Quality
try to make your contribution one that is true, specifically:
(i) do not say what you believe to be false.
(ii) do not say that for which you lack adequate evidence.

The maxim of Quantity
(i) make your contribution as informative as is required for the current purposes of the exchange.
(ii) do not make your contribution more informative than is required.

The maxim of Relevance
make your contributions relevant.

The maxim of Manner
be perspicuous, and specifically:
(i) avoid obscurity
(ii) avoid ambiguity
(iii) be brief
(iv) be orderly

Grice's insight was that in the event that one or more of the maxims being superficially broken by a speaker, the listener will still *assume* that they stand, and will attempt to make inferences to interpret the utterance as if it conformed on some other deeper level, for instance[5]:

A: Where's Bill?
B: There's a yellow VW outside Sue's house.

[5]This example was taken from [16].

B's reply is superficially not co-operative, but at a deeper level A, wishing not to believe that B is being unco-operative, may infer from personal knowledge about Bill and his yellow VW car that actually it is.

The point with reference to human-machine dialogue is that it is the *user* that is normally the initial co-operating system in the exchange - "...making the contribution as required." - as it is they who take the first turn. In doing this the user has made an implicit contract with the system that it should be co-operative on its turn. But it is perfectly possible for the following scenario to take place:

Human: How much did Bill Gates earn last year?
System: NIL

The contract of co-operation commits the user to make inferences to try and interpret this response as co-operative, but these attempts will be fruitless - it is simply not acceptable - and there are two courses of action open. Firstly, accept that the system is not co-operating, and treat it as you would a human that ignores convention - become frustrated and unco-operative, or secondly, reject the human-human conversational process as the model of communication and begin to build a new one. Neither option is acceptable with regard to our target user group.

2.4. Mutual Knowledge

It is the contention here that a foundation for constructing a co-operative system is to give the system knowledge of the terms of reference used in the domain - as mutual understanding appears to be a basic requirement for meaningful dialogue [7, 17]. The role of the system, as a co-operating entity, can then be viewed as an assistant who knows more about the details of data instances existing in that domain than the user, but that shares common knowledge about how it is structured [21]. The structure of the knowledge as embedded in the system must therefore be as close as possible to the structure of the users own knowledge. The mere utilisation of a domain modelling technique does not, unfortunately, imply that the system containing it will be co-operative, and it is the use of this knowledge in the communicative process that is the key factor.

2.5. Description

The maxim of Quantity dictates that the contribution by each party on its turn should be "...as informative as required." This is a fuzzy notion, but can be illustrated by an example. If A asks "Tell me about salaries", B may reply:

> "I know about salaries."

or

> "I know about salaries, I know when they are paid, who they are paid to, and what amounts are paid."

or

> "I know about salaries, and as a for instance Joe Bloggs gets paid £16000 a year and on the first of each month."

We would consider the first reply to break the maxim of Quantity, and the second and third to be co-operative in different degrees. The latter replies open the option for A to take another turn in questioning B with regard to the description. In database terms, the second reply discloses schema-level information, and the third discloses data-level information embedded in schema-level information. The first reply, however, may make A make the inference that B knows something about salaries but is unwilling to respond for some unexplained reason. In human-human conversation this may lead to A taking a turn with:

> "Is there some reason you don't want to tell me about salaries?"

and this may progress to be a healthy conversation, but when B is a machine, this is not the kind of turn we wish to encourage.

It is the contention here that one way of successfully co-operating with a human user is to present at the interface a constructional unit that is a descriptive representation where extra relevant information is available [18]. This description should offer opportunities for discovery by enabling the user to continue turn taking with the interface presentation.

In terms of turn taking, a *prescriptive* approach to query or enquiry obliges the user to formulate their turn in a specific and controlled way. Not proceeding so is a breach of the co-operative principle on the part of the user and results in the breaking of that same principle on the part of the machine. The *descriptive* approach may not be infallible but it implies co-operation on the part of the machine, offers information, and allows the user to discover more information by taking another turn.

3 Interfaces to Databases

We will now go on to look at two different interface styles - visual and form-based - and briefly critique an example of each taken from recent research. In the terms of the discussion so far, the interface to a co-operative system should be interpretable by the user as a constructional unit within which the system and user can take a sequence of turns which adhere to the rules of conduct of the communicative process[6].

3.1. Visual Interfaces

Visual interfaces to databases have a distinct advantage present in all direct manipulation interfaces [13] which is that the presentation of the constructional unit is the same for input as it is for output. The basic manipulation is done on a diagrammatic representation, and when the object is manipulated, it stays where it has been put. When drawing tools are being considered this is clearly appropriate, but when the task is to support the communicative process of enquiry dialogue, the picture is less clear. It has been claimed that visual interfaces are *by definition* easier to use merely because the information is immediately perceptually available [4], but we contend here that there are other communicative issues that must also be addressed.

GLAD

The GLAD system [29] visually displays the entities and their links (and therefore potentially the schema), and it is possible to carry out various operations - 'describe' and 'list members' for example - on the objects displayed. The description windows are colour-coded so that linking references can be made from one description window to another (Figure 1.):

---

[6] Simple command line styles will not be discussed as it is clear that they do not generally support turn taking.

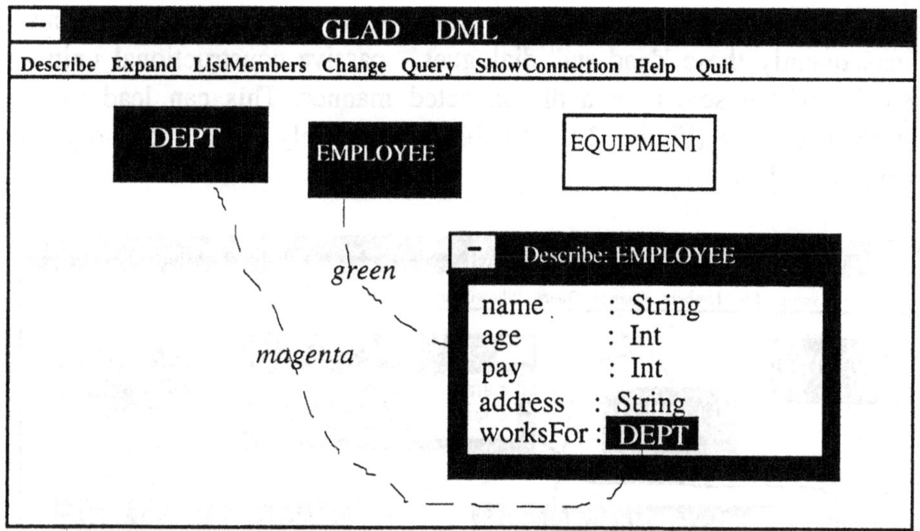

Fig. 1. The Describe window (adapted from [29]).

There appear to be a number of potential problems for the interface as shown in Figure 1. Firstly, that the referential use of colour may break the maxim of Manner in that it is 'obscure', and secondly that the description in the Describe window is at the schema level only, and the inclusion of type information breaks the maxim of Relevance for our user group[7]. Most importantly though, the only interaction allowed with the original interface constructional unit is to spawn another window. So by performing a Describe we are adding another constructional unit in which no more interaction is possible - this dialogue has reached a dead end. In terms of the communicative process, it is as if the system responds to "Tell me about Employees" by:

> "Employees have names, ages, pay, addresses and they work for Departments"

But no further turns may be taken within this context. The user may further query employees by returning to the original interface and performing the ListMembers function, but being able to do this through

[7]It is stated that "...end-user participation is indispensible because otherwise we must rely on data-processing professionals..." (p 106, [29]) - it does appear that this interface is applicable to our taget user group.

the context of the Describe window would be more perspicuous. Consequently these 'dead-end' dialogues - passive constructional units - remain on the screen in a disconnected manner. This can lead to an anarchic display (Figure 2.), and this is with only three entity objects being described.

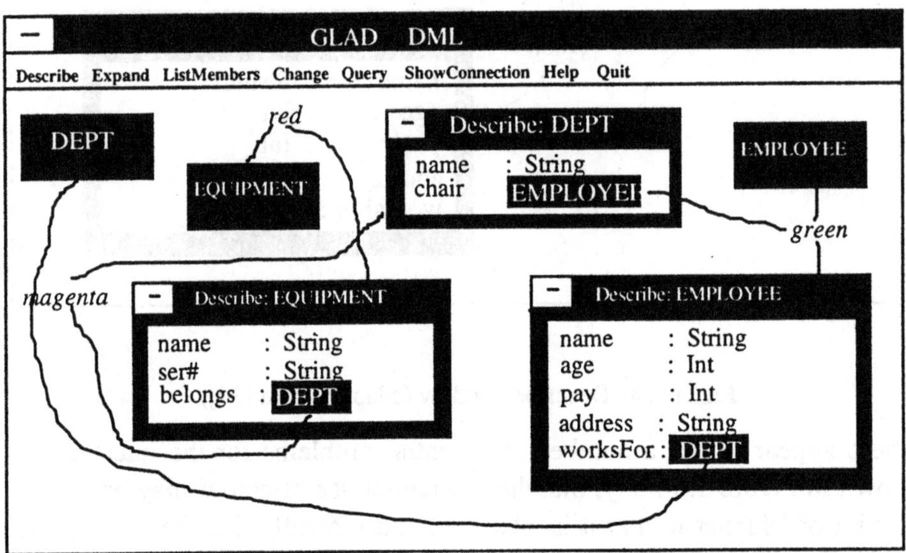

Fig. 2. Describe windows for three entity objects. (Adapted from [29].

Some of the GLAD functionality allows for more levels of dialogue, but still with the approach that windows are spawned off rather than changing to represent the changing state of the enquiry.

In terms of turn taking, what this interface is doing on *its* turn is not only responding to the user request but is also displaying all the previous turns as windows within the main window. This is analogous to a conversational partner repeating all previous utterances from this and other dialogues before the required response. This can lead to information overload and a thoroughly disconnected dialogue, as none of the results of previous turns are displayed in context or ordered in any way[8]. In terms of the communicative process much of the information available will have been produced at a previous turn, breaking the maxims of Quantity and Relevance.

[8]A discussion of a display manager approach to user-machine communication which is relevant to this particular problem in this situation can be found in [8]

3.2. Form-Based Interfaces

The temptation to retain as much information on the screen as possible, whether it be currently contextually relevant or not, can be a problem with database interfaces, as we have seen in the previous example. A slightly different example of this kind of behaviour is apparent in the Visualiser system [23].

Visualiser

This system has been classified as a form based interface, but it is actually more of a visual hybrid, using a dynamic form-based approach to query and implementing a semantic model (an ER model) as layer above the logical structure of the database through which the data is accessed. As such this system shares a basic 'mutual knowledge' of the domain with the user.

Visualiser presents a schema-level view with data compacted to remove redundancy, and the example instances embedded in this view are read across the form, left to right (Figure 3.):

City	University	Department	Class
New York	Columbia	Science	Arithmetic
Cambridge	MIT	Science	Physics

Fig. 3. A Visualiser representation (taken from [23]).

The descriptive representation shown in Figure 3. could be verbalised as:

> "New York city has, for instance, a University called Columbia which has a Science department which has a class in Arithmetic
> and
> Cambridge has, for instance, a University called MIT which has a Science department which has a class in Physics."

Selections can then be made left to right across the form to access more specific information. This system thus implements turn taking as the representation provides the user with the opportunity of asking questions like:

> "Tell me about Universities in New York city."

by selecting the New York cell and 'expanding' it (Figure 4.):

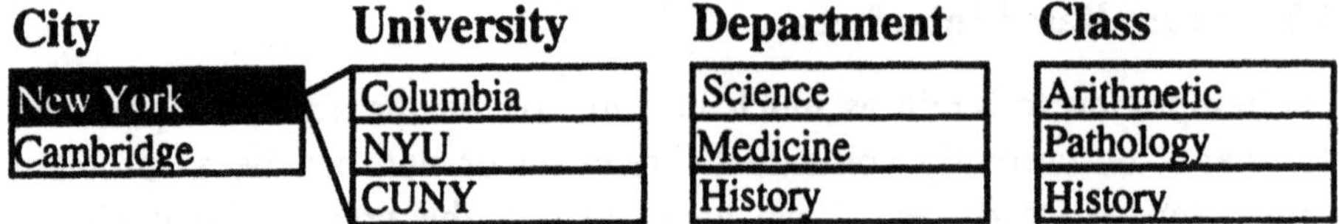

Fig. 4. The representation after expansion (taken from [23]).

Figure 4. may be verbalised as:

> "In New York there are three universities, and Columbia has, for instance a department of Science which has an Arithmetic class...etc."

There are clear problems with this representation, however. The first is that redundant information continues to be displayed - the city Cambridge is not a part of this enquiry - and this leads to the maxim of Quality is being broken. Also, as the metaphor being used to interpret the representation is one of reading left to right along the row, it is possible for a user to read that Cambridge city has a University NYU. Because of this confusion, we also suggest that the maxim of Manner is being broken - the representation is ambiguous and not orderly. As a further example of this (Figure 5.):

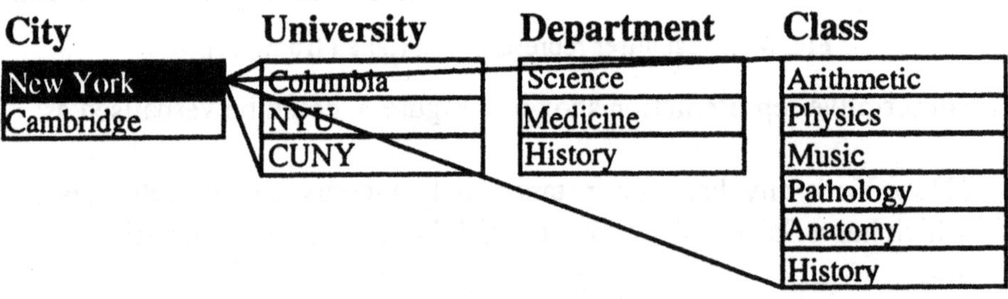

Fig. 5. Multiple expansion based on a single selection (taken from [23]).

Figure 5. is a response to a turn:

> "Tell me about Universities in New York and the classes that they teach."

But this visualisation clearly breaks the maxims of Manner and Relevance - the department examples are relevant to the Universities on their left, and not to the Classes on their right. Music classes are not taught, I believe, in the history department of CUNY.

The Visualiser system is good in so far as it includes domain knowledge, implements turn taking and produces schema-level descriptions with embedded examples, but it breaks conversational convention when viewed in terms of the communicative process.

4 The GUIDANCE RDMS Interface

The strategy behind GUIDANCE design was to provide a 'walk up and use' system that provided access to a relational database [11]. User end issues were paramount and were investigated in a human factors analysis leading to a set of requirements and utilising a number of tactical approaches synthesised from other usable systems. At issue was the investigation of the human-machine communicative process, and its syntax and semantics with regard to database navigational strategies, and the pragmatics as regards the nature of enquiry and user perspective.

Broadly[9], the system uses two models as a knowledge base, one that models the domain (and therefore the user's knowledge of the domain) and one that models the database. The models are written in GRAIL [22, 9] which is a member of the KL-ONE family of knowledge representation formalisms [28]. GRAIL is a descriptive classification-based formalism developed by the University of Manchester for modelling medical terminology, and is used to generate full descriptions of complex entities in the domain, and to provide information that allows the system to map classified composite concepts to the database. A layered approach allows the user to interact and navigate using recognisable domain concepts on a model world interface and not to be bothered with the structural complexities and idiosyncrasies of the database itself.

---

[9] A fuller description of the system can be found in [12].

4.1. Interaction as Communication

Following the command to start the system, GUIDANCE offers a pick list with the singular concepts about which it knows (Figure 6.).

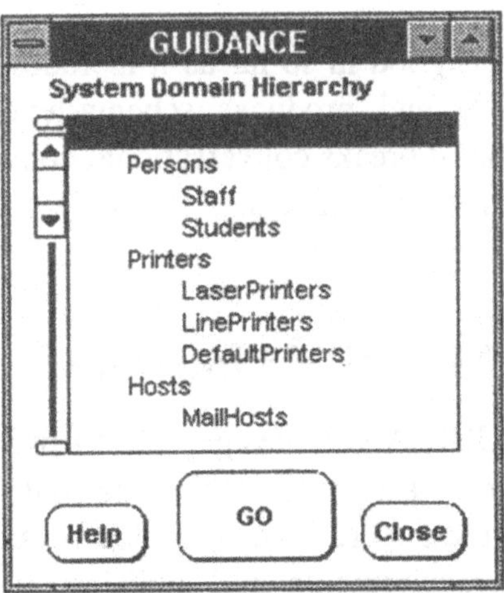

Fig. 6. The opening list box.

This is the systems turn, and can be paraphrased as "What do you wish to know about?". The user can co-operatively respond to this by selecting a single item as his turn, and pressing the GO button[10]. The pick list then disappears to be replaced by the main style of interface (Figure 7.):

The interface depicted in Figure 7. is generated by an enquiry on Person, and the description and the descriptive values within it represent an instance of the class Person. As a constructional unit, the system's turn could be paraphrased as:

> "This is what I know about Persons, and here, as an example, is an instance of a Person."

There are a number of possible turns that the user may now take, and all of those turns can be manifested by pressing a button on the interface:

1. Start again.

---

[10]Errors such as the selection of two items are handled by the system, and any selected help screen is context-sensitive.

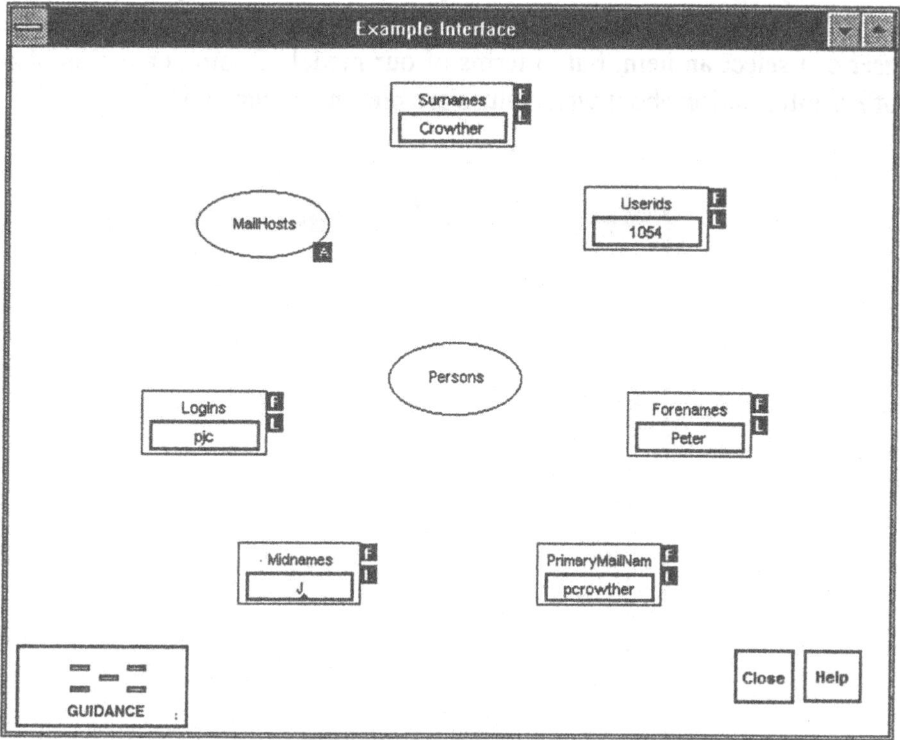

Fig. 7. An Example Interface for a query on Persons.

2. Request a list of values (by pressing the L for List button) for one or more of the descriptive attributes. For example "Tell me about Forenames."

3. Constrain one or more of the descriptive attributes (by pressing the F for Fix button) - "Tell me about Persons whose Forename is Peter.".

4. Navigate conceptually (by pressing the A for Add Focus button) to produce a description that includes another concept - "Tell me about Persons who have MailHosts.".

Turn types 2 and 3 being data-level enquiries, turn type 4 being a schema level enquiry. All these turns (except the first) take place within the confines of the context within which the enquiry was first made. Examples are always given within the description, and the example values are coherent. Requesting a list of values produces a pick-list from which the user can select an item, but in terms of our model of communication also offers information about what values are present (Figure 8.).

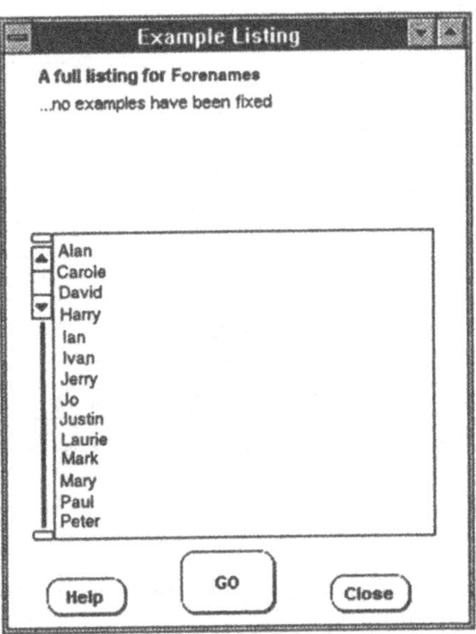

Fig. 8. The listing produced by pressing 'L' on the Forenames attribute.

Picking an item and pressing the GO button on Figure 8. completes the users turn and for its turn GUIDANCE re-populates the interface with an example instance and the pick-list disappears.

In this way GUIDANCE always displays the current state of the communicative process within user context. Ideally, though not yet implemented, it would also retain a history of previous turns such that the user could return to any previous one, and the context within which the turn was originally elicited restored[11]. A user request for a previous turn could be paraphrased:

---

[11]This would be trivial to implement as the context of enquiry is stored in the lower level object that generates the interface object.

"Tell me what you said about People with Peter as their forename"

The interface then displayed would be replaced by the requested one, fulfilling the maxim of Quantity, and the history mechanism thus implemented would be a display manager solution [8] to the kind of problems associated with the GLAD interface.

5 Related Work

As counterpoint to the discussion above, it is worth briefly considering the IMACS system [6]. IMACS is a system that interfaces to multiple databases, typically relational databases, and supports *data archaeology*, this being a skilled user task of piecing together fragments of information to form a coherent and useful knowledge 'find'. This system is related to GUIDANCE in so far as it is a classifier-based system implementing mutual knowledge, it is co-operative and it supports discovery. However, the means by which it co-operates reveals interesting distinctions between systems we have so far described which are targeted at casual users and those targeted at more expert users - which in the case of IMACS are analysts who require training to use the system.

It could be inferred from the previous discussion that attention to the pragmatics of the communicative process is only important if the intended users of a particular system are naive users. We believe that this is not the case and that tuition is a process of learning a new set of rules that *describe* interaction with a system, but do not *redefine* communicative practices and conventions.

For instance, IMACS uses a small set of forms, the style and content of these forms being derived from task analysis. These forms, in terms of the communicative process, can be seen as new and novel types of constructional units that the user can take turns with and which have different ideas about what the Co-operative Principle means. These forms each have a specific role and function in the task and it is as if communication occurs on a number of levels at once with a series of differently biased 'expert assistants' who are aware of the context of the enquiry. For example, one type of constructional unit may consider that '...as informative as required.' means an overview of the enquiry dialogue as a whole, whilst another that listing the contents of a table is appropriate. Tuition to use such a system should outline how each unit will respond to the users turn, and how it will proceed with regard to the communicative process, but internally the conduct of the units must be consistent with the general principles described here.

It is not necessary that interaction should only take place 'one to one' with the same type of constructional unit on every turn, but if different units are to be used, then different interpretations of the maxims of Quantity, Relevance and Manner are likely to be employed in the different presentations. This needs to be recognised when designing a system to support a human-computer dialogue.

6 Conclusion

We have attempted here to consider enquiries to databases as a *communicative process*, on the assumption that our target user group will use the human communicative process as a model for their communication with the interface to a database system. The pragmatics of the human model using the notions of turn-taking, mutual knowledge and co-operation and their implications for enquiry dialogue have been discussed.

We believe that we have come some way to addressing a number of problems that the database community at large needs to face, namely the technologically driven assumptions that:

- *Enquiry* (as defined here) can be immediately satisfied by *query* - that the intention of the user can be directly mapped in advance to a single or a set of single isolated queries obtained by some minor mental effort on the part of the user.

- Dialogue design is equivalent to interface design.

- Context, perspective and communication are side issues that can be dealt with 'later' once the technical issues are sorted out.

We do not believe that to make enquiries of a database it is essential to code explicitly into queries, or into discrete symbols that represent queries. Perspectives represent a major part of user enquiry and emerge from the context in which the information is sought, and can be used. Principles derived from the conduct of the human communicative process must, to a greater or a lesser extent, be implemented in systems that attempt to address the aspirations of the enquiring user. As well as providing systems to answer our queries, we must begin to provide systems that co-operate with users and assist them in asking the right questions.

References

1. D. Adams: *The Hitchhikers Guide to the Galaxy.* London: Pan (1979)

2. M. Baker: Modelling Negotiation in Intelligent Teaching Dialogues. In: R. Moyse and M.T. Elsom-Cook (Eds.) *Knowledge Negotiation.* Academic Press: London (1992) pp. 199-240

3. P.J. Barnard and N.V. Hammond: Usability and its Multiple Determination for the Casual User. In: S. Williams (Ed.) *Pathways to the Information Society: Proc. 6th International Conference on Computer Communication, London.* Amsterdam: North Holland.

4. C. Batini, T. Catarci, M.F. Costabile, S. Levialdi. Visual Query Systems: A Taxonomy. In E. Knuth and L.M. Wegner (Eds.) *Visual Database Systems II.* Elsevier: Amsterdam.(1992) pp 153-168.

5 P. Booth: *An Introduction to Human-Computer Interaction.* LEA: London (1992)

6. R.J. Brachman, P.G. Selfridge, L.G. Terveen, B. Altman, A. Borgida, F. Halper, T. Kirk, A. Lazar, D.L. McGuiness, L.A. Resnick: Integrated Support for Data Archaeology. In: *Int. Journal of Intelligent and Cooperative Information Systems.* **2(2)** (1993). pp. 159-185.

7 I. Clowes, I. Cole, F. Arsted: User Modelling Techniques for Interactive Systems. In P. Johnson and S. Cook (Eds.) *People and Computers: Designing the Interface.* Cambridge: CUP (1985) pp. 35-45.

8. S.W. Draper: Display Managers as the Basis for User-Machine Communication. In: D.A. Norman and S. Draper (eds.): *User-centered system design: New perspectives on HCI.* Hillsdale, NJ: LEA Inc. (1986). pp. 339-360.

9. C.A. Goble, A.J. Glowinski, W.A. Nowlan, and A.L. Rector: A Descriptive Semantic Formalism for Medicine. In *Proc. Ninth International Conference on Data Engineering*. (1992) pp. 624-632.

10. H.P. Grice: Logic and Conversation. In P. Cole (Ed.) *Syntax and Semantics 9: Pragmatics.* NY: Academic Press. (1978)

11. D.C. Haw: *Communicating with the User: An Intelligent System to Enable Relational Database Mediation.* M.Sc. Thesis, University of Manchester. (1993)

12. D.C. Haw, C.A. Goble, and A.L. Rector: GUIDANCE: Making it Easy for the User to be an Expert. In: P. Sawyer (ed.) *Interfaces to Database Systems*. London: Springer-Verlag (1994) pp 25-48.

13. E.L. Hutchins, J.D. Hollan, and D.A. Norman: Direct Manipulation Interfaces. In: D.A. Norman and S. Draper (eds.): *User-centered system design: New perspectives on HCI.* Hillsdale, NJ: LEA Inc. (1986). pp.87-124.

14. E. Knuth and L.M. Wegner (Eds.): *Visual Database Systems II* Elsevier: Amsterdam. (1992).

15. T.L Kunii (Ed.): *Visual Database Systems.* Elsevier Science Publishers: Amsterdam (1989).

16. S.C. Levinson: *Pragmatics*. (1983). CUP: Cambridge.

17. W. Mark: Knowledge-Based Interface Design. In: D.A. Norman and S. Draper (eds.): *User-centered system design: New perspectives on HCI.* Hillsdale, NJ: LEA Inc. (1986) pp.219-238.

18. A. Motro: Annotating Answers with their Properties. In: *SIGMOD record,* **21(4)**. (1992) pp.54-57.

19. D.A. Norman: Cognitive Engineering. In Norman, D.A. and Draper, S (Eds.) *User-centered system design: New perspectives on HCI*. Hillsdale, NJ: LEA Inc. (1986) pp.31-62.

20. G. Piatetsky-Shapiro and W.J. Frawley (Eds.): *Knowledge Discovery in Databases.* AAAI Press, Menlo Park: California. (1991).

21. A.L. Rector, P.D. Newton and P.H. Marsden: What Kind of System does an Expert need? In: P. Johnson and S. Cook (Eds.) *People and Computers: Designing the Interface.* Cambridge: CUP (1985) pp. 239-247.

22. A.L. Rector, W.A. Nowlan, and S. Kay: Conceptual Knowledge: The Core of Medical Information Systems, In Lun, K.C., Degoulet, P., Pierre, T.E., Reinhof, (eds.) *MEDINFO 92 Proc. of the Seventh World Congress on Medical Informatics,* Geneva, North-Holland. (1992) pp.1420-1426.

23. G. Santucci and F. Palmisano: A Dynamic Form-based Visualiser for Semantic Query Languages. In P. Sawyer *Interfaces to Database Systems*. London: Springer-Verlag (1994) pp. 249-265

24. E.A. Schegloff and H. Sacks: Opening up Closings. In *Semiotica* **8(4)**, (1973) pp. 289-327.

25. N.P. Sheehy: Nonverbal Behaviour in Dialogue. In R.G. Reilly (Ed.) *Communication Failure in Dialogue and Discourse.* Amsterdam: Elsevier (1987)

26. B. Shneiderman: *Designing the User Interface—Strategies for Effective Human-Computer Interaction*. Reading, Mass: Addison-Wesley (1992)

27. F.N. Tou, M.D. Williams, R. Filkes, A. Henderson, and T. Malone: RABBIT: an Intelligent Database Assistant. In *Proc. AAAI 1982* pp. 314-318.

28. W.A. Woods: The KL-ONE family. In: *Computers and Mathematics Applications*. **23** (1992) pp.133-177.

29. C.T. Wu and D.K. Hsiao: Implementation of Visual Database Interface Using an Object-Oriented Language. In T.L Kunii (Ed.) *Visual Database Systems*. Elsevier: Amsterdam. (1989). pp.105-125.

30. M.M. Zloof: Query-by-Example: *Proc. of the National Computer Conference*, Montvale, NJ: AFIPS Press (1975). pp.431-438.

Using a Conceptual Data Language to Describe a Database and its Interface

Kenneth J. Mitchell, Jessie B. Kennedy and Peter J. Barclay

Computer Studies Department, Napier University
Canal Court, 42 Craiglockhart Avenue, Edinburgh EH14 1LT, Scotland, UK
e-mail: <kenny,jessie,pete>@dcs.napier.ac.uk

Abstract. We propose a conceptual approach to defining interfaces to databases which uses the features of a fully object oriented data language to specify interface objects combined with database objects. This achieves a uniform, natural way of describing databases and their interfaces. It is shown how this language can be used in the role of data definition and, when combined with interface classes, in the definition of database interfaces. A prototype developed to test this approach is presented.

1 Introduction

The presentation and manipulation of information are central to interacting with database systems. The efficacy of this interaction is determined by the interface to the database and therefore the design and usability of such interfaces requires investigation to ensure optimal facilitation.

The traditional approach to providing interfaces to databases is through a variety of textual language interfaces, such as SQL [17] and DAPLEX [43]. However, as these interfaces rely heavily on the user to retain knowledge of the structure of the database together with the syntax of commands, they are difficult to use without being accomplished in this style of interaction.

In an attempt to improve the interaction with databases, forms based interfaces were developed. A few notable results have been found on providing graphical interfaces to relational databases, covering specific applications, HIBROWSE [20], Office-By-Example [49][56], FORMANAGER [53] and general applications, Query-By-Example [55], TIMBER [46], GUIDE [52], Santucci and Palmisano's Visualiser [42].

Graphical interfaces that support complex models of information have flourished in recent years, with the application visualisation system (AVS) [48], and application visualisation environment (AVE) [19], for dataflow visualisation. Surveys on complex graphical interfaces provided by Pickover [37], and Wolfe et al [51] provide insights into their potential.

With the development of object oriented databases systems, the variety and complexity of information modelled has increased. Two dimensional graphical interfaces to object oriented databases have been developed for specific applications, e.g. in EcoSystem [5] and the Banksia geographical information system [54], as well as general applications, such as schema designers and browsers, e.g. Almarode's Schema Designer [1], the O2 browser [18], the CLOSQL interface [32], and Kirby and Dearle's Napier88 browser [28].

Recently, software and hardware technology has improved to the point where the practical use of applications with interactive three dimensional graphics is a viable prospect [41]. With this enabling technology and the promise of improved interaction, 3D interfaces to databases are beginning to emerge, e.g. WINONA [38][39], AMAZE [12][13], PIT [9], Bead [14], GRADE-3D [45], and LyberWorld [24].

Many languages exist for the specification of graphical interfaces, from interface programming languages, OWL [35], OSF/Motif [34], and graphics languages GKS [2], PHIGS [3], to state-transition notations, such as the Storrs-Windsor notation [50], which are surveyed by Green [22]. Higher level abstractions are found in languages for user-interface management systems (UIMS), such as, COUSIN [23] and MIKE [33] based on interaction sequence specification, and HIGGINS [25] and the UIDE [21], which are based on data models. However these languages are designed purely for interface design independent of database interface requirements.

An interface is a rather elusive entity. One interface style may be preferable to another rather different one depending on the particular user's requirements. Considerable effort has been directed towards the customisation of interfaces to databases, eg. EVE [36], CDMS [15], Dbface [26][27], and NIOME [30]. Attention to this concern has been realised in the method of integration between data and interface languages, i.e. by the close coupling, but ultimate separation of data and interface objects. This permits the replacement of one set of interface objects for another to support alternative interfaces to the same data.

Given this accumulation of many diverse interfaces to databases there is an identifiable need for a concise language for database interface description. The language would expect to achieve the same degree of specification which exists for the description of data, in that interface objects may be defined with various properties and behaviour. For this reason the authors believe that an interface to a database should be specified in part of the database's schema definition and must be able to specify any level of interface or data visualisation sophistication.

This broadly applicable approach enables the definition of database interfaces from simple command line textual interfaces to 3D interfaces. However, our work is currently focusing on investigating the potential of 3D interfaces to databases [39]. The work presented in this paper describes a prototype 3D interface to an object oriented database in which both the interface and the database is described using NOODL [7], a simple data language intended to allow object oriented modelling of data at a conceptual level.

The following section introduces NOODL by showing an example schema definition. Section 3 continues this example with the introduction of interface classes for the combined definition of a database and its interface. Section 4 presents the prototype interface and how the language description may be mapped to an implementation. Finally, conclusions and further work are discussed.

2 NOODL as a Data Language

The Napier Object Oriented Data Language (NOODL) is a simple language which allows object oriented modelling of data at a conceptual level; it is introduced in [4], described fully in [7] and most recently in [8] in its role as a query language. A NOODL schema contains a list of class definitions, which show the name and ancestors of each class. A class definition also includes a set of properties, operations, constraints and triggers. Some of the details of this language are exemplified in a NOODL schema describing a company database which holds information about the departments in which employees are located (figure 1).

Departments and people have names and each employee has a job title; all of these are represented by text strings. A person's age is represented by a number. Every department has a set of employees and every employee is associated with a department. This is represented by the pair of obverted properties, *employees* and *department*. A department can perform a query through its *list_mature_employees* operation to return the set of all employees associated with that department, who are older than 25. An employee may be transferred to any department, achieved by simply changing the value of their department property through its transfer operation. The fact that this is an obverted property implies this change will also result in removing the employee from the current department's employee set and adding them to the new department's employee set. The *person's age constraint* (PAC) defines the permitted limits for a valid age. This constraint is overridden in the employee class, in order to disallow employees with an age of less than 18. An employee may retire through object migration to person status. This happens automatically once they reach the age of 65, through the use of the *retiral* trigger. Employees may be promoted to managers and managers may be demoted to employees through their *promote* and *demote* operations, respectively. Triggers and constraints are detailed in [6].

```
schema Company

class Department
properties
  name      : Text ;;
  employees : # Employee \ department
operation
  list_mature_employees : # Employee is
    Employee where self.employees.age>25

class Person
properties
  name : Text ;;
  age  : Number
constraint
  PAC is 0<self.age and self.age<120

class Employee
ISA Person
properties
  job_title   : Text ;;
  department  : Department \ employees
operation
  transfer Department d is self.department(d) ;;
  retire    is self.goto(Person) ;;
  promote   is self.goto(Manager)
constraint
  override PAC is 18<self.age
trigger
  retiral is self.age>65 :: self.retire

class Manager
ISA Employee
operation
  demote is self.goto(Employee)

end_schema { Company }
```

Fig. 1. A company schema definition

3 NOODL as a Database Interface Language

In order to provide an interface for the data described in figure 1 it is necessary to describe how the data should be visually represented in the interface. The authors believe that a set of objects in an interface should be described conceptually in a similar manner to the objects contained in a database, therefore NOODL has been adopted as a possible language with which to describe the database interface.

An interface object contains only those features pertaining to the behaviour and visual representation of the database object in the interface. Using NOODL, an interface object can be represented by a set of properties describing its visual appearance, a set of operations describing its interaction with the user and other objects, a set of constraints describing how an object's behaviour or properties may be constrained in the visualisation and a set of triggers which respond to 'events' in the interface. Therefore, any interface should be able to be described by a NOODL schema thereby allowing the interface objects to be stored in the database along with the database objects. This provides a unified model of the data and interface (figure 2). This model states that each database object with a set of data related features has an associated interface object with a set of interface related features.

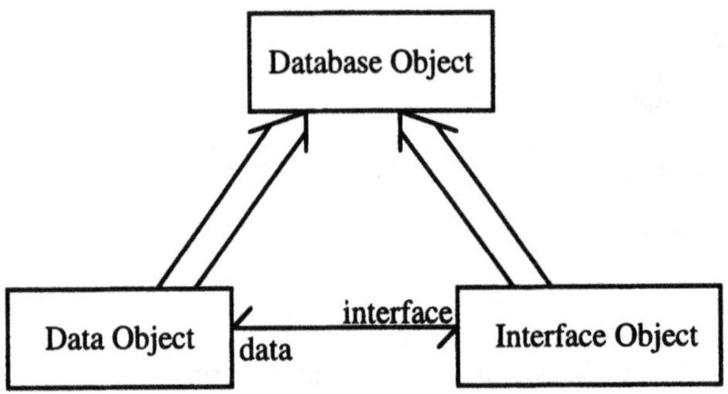

Fig. 2. Unifying Model of Data/Interface Objects

In using NOODL to describe data objects the properties and operations of the object are entirely free and dependent only on the semantics of the equivalent real world object being modelled. However, when defining interface objects there exists a 'well defined set' of interface properties and operations which may be used to describe interface objects, the subset used determining the sophistication of the visualisation. The values for these properties define the representation of the objects in the interface. The properties used in the prototype described here include:

- The shape of an object as it appears in the interface. This may be a 2/3D object, a dialog form, or simply refer to a textual description.

- The position of the object in 2/3D space (which may be translated).

- The size of the object (which may be scaled).

- The orientation of the object relative to interface space (which may be rotated).

- The colour of the object.

- The extent of the object which defines the bounding volume of the object in the interface.

This by no means defines the full range of interface properties which may be of use in a conceptual description, e.g. ambient, diffuse and specular coefficients, texture and properties of animated objects, such as, path, spin speed and velocity.

The properties of interface objects may be defined as part of the schema (see Appendix for example definition of position, shape, size, orientation and colour used in the prototype) or may be pre-defined in the language.

Interface object operations are those which either manipulate the interface object in some way or describe interface actions performed by the user to which the object will respond. Interface object manipulation operations are defined in the same way as data object operations, except that they manipulate some aspect of the interface. An interface action is described as a sequence of primitive interface actions. The actions in this example are move and select (see Appendix for definitions of these). To describe that a promotion operation requires the user to select an object (a mouse-click in a WIMP interface) the following might be written,

```
promote is self.select
```

An initial set of primitive actions identified are select, pick_up, drop, move, turn, time_click. With drop, move, turn, and time_click interface actions a value is associated. For example, if an object is moved to a position this may be described by,

```
self.move.position
```

Constraints on interface objects are merely the same as constraints on data objects, but are particular to interface object properties as opposed to data object properties. Examples of these have been shown in the definition of *Colour* and *Position* (Appendix).

In common with interface object operations and constraints, triggers may pertain to the values of interface object properties. In addition, triggers are used to respond to interface actions described in the operations section. For example, if the user performs a promote action on an employee, i.e. selecting it, the corresponding data operation may be triggered with the following,

```
PET is self.promote :: self.data.promote
```

This method of representing interface actions is similar to the approach used in many user interface programming languages [35], i.e. the event is declared for the operating system's event handler as an undefined operation which is defined in an event response operation. The code which states how an event will be recognised is hidden. This allows the designer to specify exactly what sequence of interface actions are required to perform an operation at an abstract level. This exemplifies the integration of data language and interface language. Once the concept of a trigger is understood the modeller has knowledge to apply this to both responding to integrity violations in the data as well as responding to interface actions.

An Example Company Database Interface

This example (figure 3) defines a 3D interface with direct representations of departments and employees.

The data classes have been omitted for brevity, but are identical to those in figure 1 with the exception that each data class has an obverted property, *interface*, which couples a data object to its interface object. The obverted pair of *interface* and *data* is the first property in each interface class.

When referencing a data object's properties from its interface object via the *data* property, this data property may be omitted, i.e.

```
self.data.department.interface.extent
```

can be expressed in short-hand as,

```
self.department.extent
```

As every interface object has a data object and vice-versa, their associated properties may be referenced directly.

Departments are represented by a department shape positioned on the 'ground' in the interface and is constant for all departments. The colour and size are not specified thereby allowing different departments to take on different appearances in the interface. The *move department trigger* (MDT) states that when a department object is moved then the employees belonging to that department are triggered to move to a new relative position inside the extent of the department's new position.

Persons do not have a representation in the interface as we are only interested in employees. Employees are represented by blue human shapes with a vertical orientation. Therefore all employees look the same in this interface only their position may vary. The *in department constraint* (IDC) specifies the position of the employee inside the spatial extent of a department. The *promote employee trigger* (PET) states that on execution of the promote operation in the interface object the promote operation of the data object is triggered. Similarly the *transfer employee trigger* (TET) triggers the equivalent data operation, passing a parameter defining the new department to which the employee has been transferred. Manager objects are specialised kinds of employees shown by the ISA reserved word. This demonstrates that interface objects may be inherited and that their properties, operations, etc. may be overridden. For example, the manager's inherited colour property is overridden from blue to white.

```
schema Company

{ Data Classes }
...
{ Interface Classes }

class Department_Interface
properties
   data      : Department \ interface ;;
   shape     : Shape is "department" ;;        { constant }
   position  : Position is "on ground" ;;      { constant }
   size      : Size ;;
   colour    : Colour
trigger
   MDT is not self.extent.holds(self.employees.position)::
     self.employees.position.put_inside(self.extent)

class Person_Interface
property
   data : Person \ interface

class Employee_Interface
ISA Person_Interface
properties
   data        : Employee \ interface ;;
   shape       : Shape is "human" ;;           { constant }
   position    : Position ;;
   orientation : Orientation is "vertical" ;; { constant }
   colour      : Colour is "blue"             { constant }
operations
   promote is self.select ;;
   transfer is not self.move.position.is_inside
     (self.department.extent)
constraint
   IDC is
     self.position.is_inside(Department_Interface.extent)
trigger
   PET is self.promote :: self.data.promote ;;
   TET is self.transfer :: self.data.transfer
     (Department where its.extent.holds(self.position))

class Manager_Interface
ISA Employee_Interface
properties
   data : Manager \ interface ;;
   override colour : Colour is "white"   { constant }
operation
   demote is self.select
trigger
   DMT is self.demote :: self.data.demote

end_schema { Company }
```

Fig. 3. A combined company database interface definition

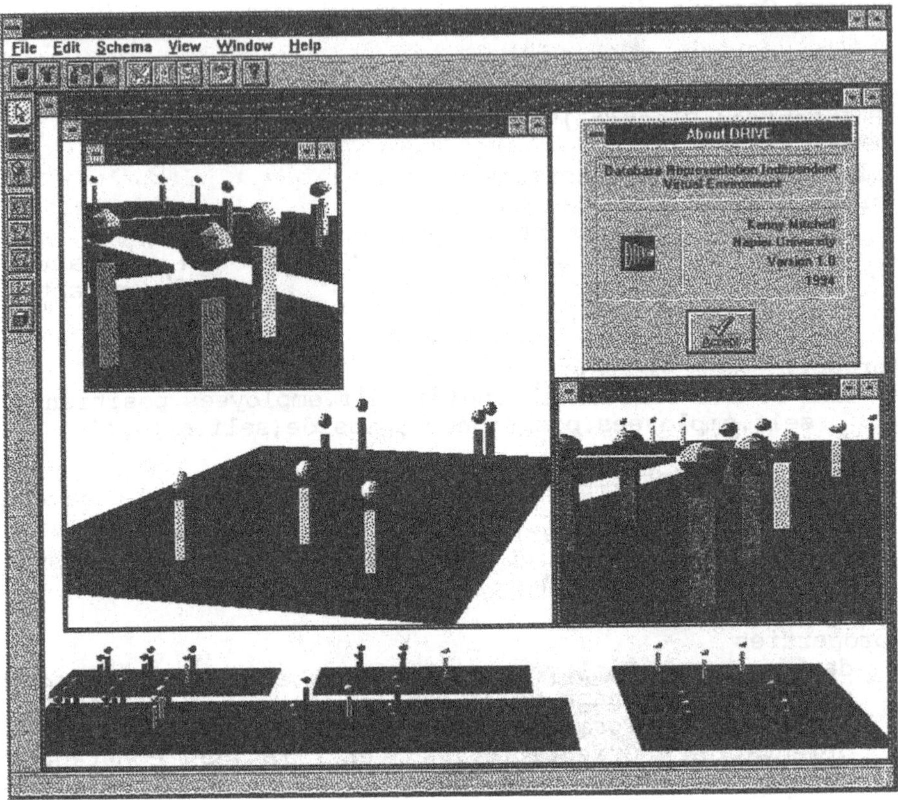

Fig. 4. Prototype company database interface

4 Prototype Interface

A prototype has been developed to test and evaluate the use of NOODL as a database interface language. It has been implemented on a PC-platform under Microsoft Windows in C++ [47], using the Borland's ObjectWindows Library [11] [35] and the RenderWare [40] graphics dynamic link library for the 3D representation of interface objects. A NOODL data model layer (similar to ObjectStore's Meta Object Protocol [29]) implemented with the POET [10] persistent C++ extension provides a means of dynamically creating persistent database interface schemata together with their data.

The prototype system allows the user to specify NOODL schemata for database interfaces interactively and automatically generates the resulting 3D representation from instances created by the user. Currently, this implementation supports only the structural aspects of NOODL. Therefore, for both data and interface schemata only the properties and inheritance semantics can be realised in the prototype without behavioural aspects, such as operations, constraints and triggers. There are two modes of operation in the system, *designer mode* which allows the user to manipulate the database interface schema and instances and *interface mode* which simulates the specified database interface.

Figure 4 shows a display from the prototype for the schema described. The display shows several windows each depicting a different viewpoint of the interface. The main window shows all the departments in the database with their associated employees, the medium sized window shows a close up of one department while the smallest windows show close-ups of some employees. Any number of windows of different database interfaces are permitted and the user is free to navigate anywhere in the 3D space. The representation for the employees and departments in figure 4 are purposely simple; however a more sophisticated visualisation of the interface to the Company database is possible.

Figure 5 displays an interface where the employees and departments can be represented by more sophisticated shapes. Selecting an object in designer mode shows its instance details. The dialog box in the top right of the display shows an Employee data instance and provides access to its properties and associated interface instance through the middle-right dialog box. The dialog box on the bottom right of the display shows a preview facility in which the shapes available for assigning to objects may be viewed.

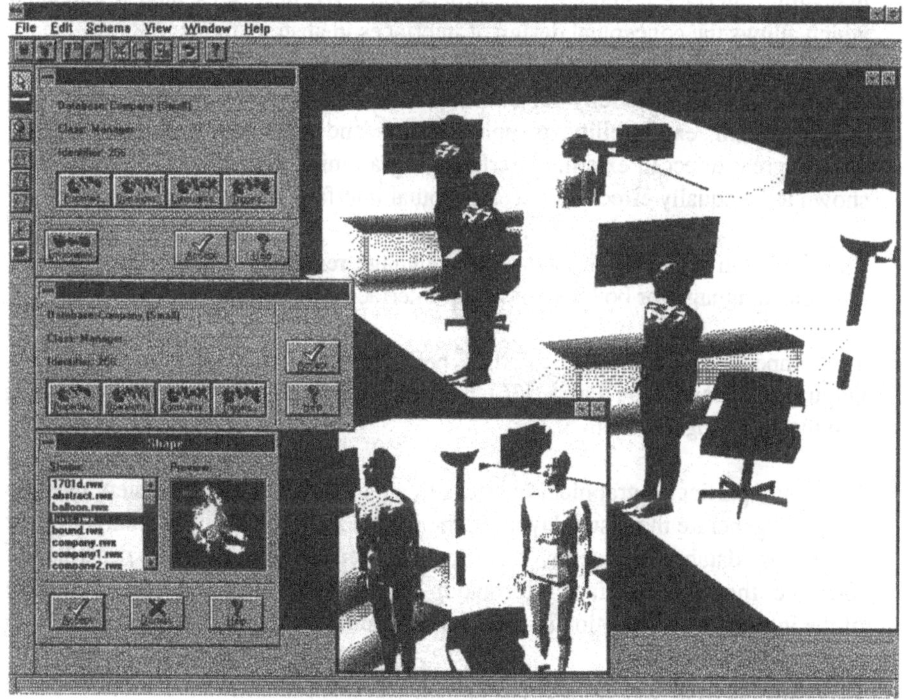

Fig. 5. Alternative company database interface

The performance of this software for interacting with large scale complex collections of data is determined by the efficiency of both hardware and software architectures supporting graphical and database system components. With a high-specification system sophisticated interfaces (such as figure 5) may be used whilst maintaining a practical level of interactivity.

5 Conclusion

We have presented a unified model for the conceptual design of databases and their interfaces. In considering a language suitable for the description of interfaces to databases, we chose to investigate the use of NOODL. The authors believe that the following benefits have been gained from such an approach:-

- An integrated data and interface language provides a much tighter coupling between the data and interface components of a database system. This facilitates the construction of direct manipulation interfaces [44] as shown in the prototype presented.

- Cooper [16], states that the provision of interfaces requires considerable '*intricate low-level programming*' *e.g.* event handling, drawing graphical primitives, managing interface component identifiers, *etc.*. We have presented a language which allows the conceptual design of interfaces in abstract terms.

- NOODL provides a fully object oriented data model. Features such as, polymorphism, extensibility, complex objects and behaviour which have been used to great effect in existing interface programming languages [35], have been shown to be equally effective in a conceptual interface language.

- The provision of a unified model and language results in the necessity to learn only one language for both database and interface description.

- The impedance mismatch existing between data languages and interface languages observed by Paton [36] has been eliminated through the use of a common language for both.

- Given any particular graphical interface to a database, a database system must be able to regenerate the visual layout of the interface. As NOODL is a language for describing database contents, this implies that if it is used to describe an interface, then this interface information may be stored in the database. Storage of the interface's description in the database facilitates this regeneration.

6 Further Work

Further work to be undertaken includes the development of both NOODL as a language for the specification of database interface descriptions and further experimentation of the interface styles for databases using the prototype software already developed. In addition the prototype will be enhanced to support the behaviour of operations, constraints and triggers on the data. The architecture which fully supports the genericity and configurability of this prototype requires further development for these enhancements.

The presentation of NOODL as an interface description language shows how we suggest the language be used. It does not show exactly how certain conceptual interface features map to their implementation. There are several ways in which this may be done and although we have mapped our example to an implementation we intend to investigate alternative mechanisms before committing to a particular specification.

As NOODL is a general purpose conceptual modelling language we feel that there is enormous potential for the variety of features that may be described in an interface using this language. We plan to investigate the full power of NOODL is this way and evaluate NOODL as an interface description language in comparison to existing purpose-built user interface languages.

In providing an interface to a database it is possible to view the database in many different ways. Possible interfaces to databases include ones based on a schema visualisation, a schema visualisation combined with some instance representation or a representation of all the instances in the databases. In addition to this, different users of the same database may have differing preferences for how they wish to visualise and interact with the data. Therefore, besides developing a more sophisticated or realistic example interface using the prototype, it is planned to experiment with interfaces based on these different views of a database and the ability to switch between them.

It is important that in providing an interface to a database for end-users that the layout of the objects in the interface be 'meaningful'. We plan to investigate the possibility of defining layouts of interfaces and the automatic generation of the layouts from its definition. This investigation includes the generation of visualisations for the results and construction of database queries.

Addressing these issues requires an inter-disciplinary approach. The results of research on both databases and human-computer interaction require integration in a framework to promote organised mutual exploitation. In satisfying this need a conceptual framework for user-interfaces to databases has been developed [31].

References

1. J. Almarode (1991) Issues in the Design and Implementation of a Schema Designer for an OODBMS, *ECOOP'91*.

2. A.N.S.I. (1985) *American National Standard for Factors Engineering of Visual Display Terminal Workstations - Graphics Kernal System (GKS).* American National Standards Institute.

3. A.N.S.I. (1988) *American National Standard for Information Processing Systems - Programmer's Hierarchical Interactive Grahpics System (PHIGS).* American National Standards Institute.

4. P.J. Barclay & J. Kennedy (1991) Regaining the conceptual level in object oriented data modelling. *BNCOD,* 9, 269-305.

5. P.J. Barclay & J.B. Kennedy (1992) Using a Persistent System to Construct a Customised Interface to an Ecological Database, *1st International Workshop on Interfaces to Database Systems,* 1:14.

6. P.J. Barclay & J.B. Kennedy (1992) Semantic Integrity for Persistent Objects, *Information and Software Technology,* 34:8, 533-541.

7. P.J. Barclay (1993) *Object oriented modelling of complex data with automatic generation of a persistent representation.* Phd Thesis. Edinburgh: Napier University.

8. P.J. Barclay & J.B. Kennedy (1994) A conceptual language for querying object-oriented data, *Proceedings of BNCOD,* 12:13, 187-204.

9. S. Benford & J. Mariani (1994) Populated Information Terrains, *2nd International Workshop on Interfaces to Databases,* 2:9, 159-169.

10. B.K.S. Software (1994) *POET (Version 2.1) - Programmer's & Reference Guide.* B.K.S. Software.

11. Borland (1995) *Borland C++ compiler (version 4.0) - user manual.* Borland International Inc.

12. J. Boyle, J.E. Fothergill & P.M.D. Gray (1993) Design of a 3D user interface to a database, *Database Issues for Data Visualisation Workshop.*

13. J. Boyle, J.E. Fothergill & P.M.D. Gray (1994) Amaze: a three dimensional graphical user interface for an object oriented database, *2nd International Workshop on Interfaces to Databases,* 2:7,117-131.

14. M. Chalmers (1994) Design Perspectives in Visualising Complex Information, *FADIVA Workshop,* 1:4.

15. R. Cooper (1991) Configurable data modelling systems, *Entity-Relationship Conference,* 9,35-52.

16. R. Cooper (1994) Configuring Database Query Languages, *2nd International Workshop on Interfaces to Databases,* 2:1, 1-17.

17. C.J. Date (1987) *A Guide to the SQL Standard,* Addison-Wesley.

18. O. Deux, *et al* (1991) The O2 System, *Communications of the ACM,* 34:10, 34-48.

19. D.S. Dyer (1990) A Dataflow Tookit for Visualisation, *IEEE Computer Graphics and Applications*, 10:4, 60-69.

20. G.P. Ellis, J.E. Finlay, A.S.Pollitt (1994) HIBROWSE, *2nd International Workshop on Interfaces to Databases,* 2:3,45-58.

21. J. Foley, W. Kim, S. Kovacevic, & K. Murray (1989) Defining Interfaces at a High Level of Abstraction, *IEEE Software*, 6:1, 25-32.

22. M. Green (1987) A Survey of Three Dialog Models, *ACM Transactions on Computer Graphics,* 5:3, 244-275.

23. P. Hayes & P. Szekely (1983) Graceful Interaction Through the COUSIN Command Interface, *International Journal of Man-Machine Studies,* 19:3, 285-305.

24. M. Hemmje (1994) LyberWorld - A 3D Graphical User Interface for Fulltext Retrieval, *FADIVA Workshop,* 1:5.

25. S. Hudson & R. King (1988) Semantic Feedback in the Higgens UIMS, *IEEE Transactions on Software Engineering*, 14:8, 1188-1206.

26. R. King & M. Novak (1993) Designing Database Interfaces with Dbface, *ACM Transactions on Information Systems,* 11, 105-132.

27. R. King & M. Novak (1989) FaceKit: A Database Interface Design Toolkit, *Proceedings of VLDB,* 15.

28. G.N.C. Kirby, & A. Dearle (1990) An Adaptive Graphical Browser for Napier88, *Technical Report, University of St.Andrews.*

29. M.O.P. (1994) *ObjectStore - Language Interface Users Guide (Release 3.0),* Object Design Ltd, 249-326.

30. K.J. Mitchell (1994) *Schema visualisation.* MSc Thesis. Edinburgh: Napier University.

31. K.J. Mitchell, J.B. Kennedy, & P.J. Barclay (1995) A Framework for Interfaces to Databases, *Technical Report, Napier University (submitted to VLDB'95).*

32. S. Monk (1994) A Graphical User Interface for Schema Evolution in an Object Oriented Database, *2nd International Workshop on Interfaces to Databases,* 2:9, 171-184.

33. D. Olsen (1989) MIKE: The Menu Interaction Kontrol Environment, *ACM Transactions on Graphics,* 5:4, 318-344.

34. O.S.F. (1989) *OSF/MOTIF - Manual,* Open Software Foundation.

35. O.W.L. (1994) *ObjectWindows (Version 2.0) for C++ - Programmer's Guide.* Borland International Inc.

36. N. Paton, G. al-Qaimari & K. Doan (1994) On Interface Objects In Object-Oriented Databases, *BNCOD,* 12:11, 153-169.

37. C.A. Pickover (1991) *Visualisation, Computers and the Imagination,* Alan Sutton Publishing.

38. M.H. Rapley (1994) *Three dimensional interface for an object oriented database.* MSc Thesis. Edinburgh: Napier University.

39. M.H. Rapley (1994) Three dimensional interface for an object oriented database, *2nd International Workshop on Interfaces to Databases,* 2:8, 133-158.

40. RenderWare (1994) The RenderWare API Reference (Version 1.4), *Criterion Software Ltd.*

41. G. Robertson, S. Card & J.Mackinlay (1993) Information Visualisation Using 3D Interactive Animation, *Communications of the ACM* 36, 57-71.

42. G. Santucci & F. Palmisano (1994) A Dynamic Form Based Visualiser for Semantic Query Languages, *2nd International Workshop on Interfaces to Databases,* 2:14, 235-250.

43. D.W. Shipman (1980) The Functional Data Model and the Data Language DAPLEX, *ACM Transactions on Database Systems,* 6:1.

44. B. Shneiderman (1983) Direct Manipulation: a Step Beyond Programming Languages, *IEEE Computer,* 16, 57-69.

45. F. Steinfath, K. Bohm & B. Lange (1994) Evaluation of Complex Information Processing Systems in 3D-Space, *FADIVA Workshop*, 1:2.

46. M. Stonebraker & J. Kalash (1982) TIMBER: A Sophisticated Relational Browser, *Proceedings of VLDB*, 8.

47. B. Stroustrup (1982) *The C++ programming language*. Addison-Wesley.

48. C. Upson, T. Faulhaber, D. Kamlins, D. Laidlaw, D. Schlegel, J. Vroom, R. Gurwitz & A. van Dam (1989) The Application Visualisation System: A Computational Environment for Scientific Visualisation, *IEEE Computer Graphics and Applications,* 9:4, 30-42.

49. K.Y. Whang et al (1987) Office-by-Example: An Intergrated Office System and Database Manager, *ACM Transactions on Office Information Systems,* 5:4, 393-427.

50. P. Windsor & G. Storrs (1993) Practical User Interface Design Notation, *Interacting with Computers,* 5:4, 423-438.

51. R.H. Wolfe, M. Needels, T. Arias & J.D. Joannopoulos (1992) Visual revelations from Silicon Ab Initio Calculations, *IEEE Computer Graphics and Applications,* 12:4.

52. H.K.T Wong & I. Kuo (1982) GUIDE: Graphical User Interface for Database Exploration. *Proceedings of VLDB,* 8, 22-32.

53. S.B. Yao, A.R. Hevner, Z. Shi, & D. Luo (1984) FORMANAGER : An office forms management system, *ACM Transactions on Office Information Systems,* 2:3, 235-262.

54. K.Yap & G.Walker (1992) The Object User Interface to the Banksia Geographical Information System, *1st International Workshop on Interfaces to Databases,* 1:13.

55. M.M. Zloof (1975) Query by Example, *Proceedings of the National Computer Conference*, 431-437.

56. M.M Zloof (1982) Office-by-example: A business language that unifies data and word processing and electronic mail. *IBM Systems Journal,* 21:3, 272-304.

Appendix

Interface Class Definition

```
class Interface_Class
properties
  shape       : Shape ;;
  position    : Position ;;
  size        : Size ;;
  orientation : Orientation ;;
  colour      : Colour ;;
  extent      : Extent
operations
  move    : Move ;;
  select  : Select
```

The above class definition shows the initial set of interface properties and operations considered. These are available to all interface classes in a NOODL database interface description. A brief description of each is given below.

Interface Class Properties and Operations

- **Shape** -

```
class Shape
property
  name : Text ;;
```

The shape of an object as it appears in the interface. A simple text string is used to refer to a shape. Alternatives include 2/3D objects, dialog forms, or simple textual descriptions. In the case of a dialog forms interface the Shape representation may include properties itself referring to fields in the form, *e.g.* shape.field.name="Fred".

- **Position** -

```
class Vector_3d
properties
  x : Real ;; y : Real ;; z : Real

class Position
ISA Vector_3d
operations
  translate Real x, Real y, Real z ;;
  is_inside Extent e : Boolean ;;
  put_inside Extent e
constraint
  PLC is -1.0 >= self.x >= 1.0 and
         -1.0 >= self.y >= 1.0 and
         -1.0 >= self.z >= 1.0
```

This represents the position of the object relative to the interface space. This definition is for a position in a 3D Cartesian coordinate interface space with real numbers holding the x, y and z coordinates. Positions in other interface spaces follow a similar definition. The *position limit constraint* (PLC) defines the bounds of coordinate values permitted. *Is_inside* tests whether or not the position is within the bounds of an extent and *Put_inside* sets the position to a point within an extent.

- **Size** -
```
class Size
properties
  width : Real ;; height : Real ;; depth : Real
operation
  scale Real w, Real h, Real d
```

The size of the object relative to interface space. Again for the purposes of our example, this is particular to a 3D interface space. The size of the object made be scaled through its *scale* operation.

- **Orientation** -
```
class Orientation
ISA Vector_3d
operations
  rotate Real d ;;
  rotate Real x, Real y, Real z, Real d
```

The orientation of the object relative to interface space. The object may be rotated through *d* degrees, about either its own orientation or a specified axis of rotation.

- **Colour** -
```
class Colour
properties
  name : Text ;;
  red  : Real ;; green : Real ;; blue : Real
constraint
  CLC is 0.0 >= self.red    >= 1.0 and
         0.0 >= self.green  >= 1.0 and
         0.0 >= self.blue   >= 1.0
```

The colour of the object specified by red, green, blue intensity components. As with position vectors, a set of constraints defines the limits for these values. This may be specified by for example red, green, blue intensity components. or a textual colour name, e.g. “dark blue”, or through an alternative colour model, e.g. the hue, saturation, value (HSV) model. The choice of colour representation is entirely dependent on the modeller’s preferred colour model.

- **Extent** -
```
class Extent
properties
  lower_back_left : Position ;;
  upper_front_right : Position
operation
  holds Position p : Boolean
```

The bounding box which completely encloses the object, consisting of properties to define the lower back left and upper front right limits of the extent. *Holds* returns a boolean value depending on whether or not a given position lies within the extent.

- **Move** -
```
move : Move
class Move
properties
   event : Boolean ;;
   position : Position
```

This operation describes a response to the user moving the object in the interface. The position property represents the point to which the interface object has been moved. It is intended that a system interpreting this language is able to handle the operating system's events in order to recognise that the user has moved the object.

- **Select** -
```
select : Select
class Select
property
   event : Boolean
```

Select describes a response to the user selecting the object in the interface.

Scheduling Query Plans with Buffer-Requirement Estimates *

John C. Sieg, Jr.[1], David Pinkney[1], and James Lamoureaux[2]

[1] Computer Science Department, University of Massachusetts Lowell, Lowell, MA 01854, USA
[2] GTE Government Systems, Needham, MA 02192, USA

Abstract. The cost of a database query plan can often be drastically reduced by allocating more buffers to it. But allocating an optimal number of buffers may be infeasible when there is high contention for the buffer space. Previous research has explored the idea that query plans have multiple *hot points*, which yield local minima of buffer consumption. We describe and analyze query-scheduling strategies that use knowledge of the hot points of each query and actual buffer availability when a query is about to be scheduled.

1 Introduction

This paper explores one dimension along which buffer managers and database-system load controllers can collaborate to more efficiently process queries. While conventional database-system load controllers may use a single estimate of buffer usage of a query, techniques described in [21, 22] assign to a query multiple *hot points* or buffer allocations likely to yield good combinations of buffer usage and disk I/O. We describe and evaluate scheduling policies that use knowledge of the number of available system buffers and the various hotpoints of the queries awaiting database-system service.

2 Background

2.1 Buffer Management

Database systems typically store their data on secondary-storage devices such as magnetic disks. Before queries access storage objects, the objects must be brought into main memory. Storage objects are brought into memory in fixed-sized pages. The database-system *buffer manager* brings referenced pages into slots of memory called buffer frames or buffers. If no buffers are empty, the buffer manager chooses a victim page from a set of *look-aside buffers*. Look-aside buffers contain database pages that have been recently referenced. If the victim was updated while in the buffer, its new value is written back to secondary storage. The newly referenced page is copied over the buffer version of the victim, and a pointer to the buffer is passed back to the calling program.

* This research was supported by the National Science Foundation under Grant No. IRI-9211060.

2.2 Scheduling Queries

Scheduling of queries is typically done at several levels, e.g., (1) scheduling a query's code to be loaded in memory; (2) scheduling a query to compete for buffers, processors, and I/O bandwidth; (3) scheduling requests to read or write data items; and (4) scheduling I/O requests. In this paper we consider only the second of these levels.

Motivating factors in the design of query schedulers include fairness and high throughput. Fairness is usually achieved by scheduling using a first-in-first-out discipline. The key factor in maintaining high throughput is load control, i.e., avoiding thrashing [9, 10] in the buffer space by not always allowing every submitted query to be active.

Conventional query schedulers are naive about resource usage [17]. IBM's Database 2 is typical: demand on resources is constrained only by multiprogramming level (mpl) set at installation time [5]. The scheduler does not match query resource demands to resource availability. If too many queries contend for a finite number of buffer frames and if the replacement policy is global, processes waste their time stealing pages from each other. This phenomenon is called external thrashing. If the replacement policy is local to each query, a query can victimize pages likely to be re-referenced, resulting in internal thrashing. Either kind of thrashing can easily occur in a system constrained only by mpl-scheduling, if queries make unpredictable demands on the buffer pool. The problem is that the buffer space becomes overcommited. The solution is to refrain from scheduling new queries unless there are enough buffers to handle their predicted demands. Various models based on this idea have been explored [6, 21, 22], which are variations on Denning's working-set model [9, 10] for scheduling processes in virtual-memory environments. Schedulers derived from these models consider the buffer demand of a process before scheduling it.

2.3 Hot Sets

Our research is derived from Sacco and Schkolnick's notion of *hot sets* [21, 22]. A hot set of a query is a collection of pages that the query repeatedly accesses.

Sacco and Schkolnick's hot-set scheduler postpones the execution of new queries when buffer availability is less than a particular *hot point*, i.e., the size of one of the hot-sets.

The buffer pool is partitioned. Each partition element is owned by an active query. No query triggers the victimization of another query's hot-set pages. Partitioning by query does not preclude sharing data pages. Shared pages are charged to one query that most recently referenced the page.

A query can have more than one hot point. For example, a query implemented as multiple nested loops scanning relations r_1 (innermost), $r_2, \ldots, r_k$ (outermost) has hot points 1, k, $size(r_1) + k - 1$, and $size(r_1) + size(r_2) + k - 2$ among others, where $size(rel)$ is the number of pages in rel. Hot point 1 is enough to get the query evaluated, hot point $size(r_1) + k - 1$ is enough to keep the innermost relation resident, and hot point $size(r_1) + size(r_2) + k - 2$ is enough to keep the innermost two relations resident.

3 Scheduling Policies

3.1 Policy Quadruples

Conceptually, a query plan with a set of hot points is a multiple-implementation package. Each implementation corresponds to allocating a different hot set to the plan. (Thus an implementation is a <plan, hot point> pair.) We approach the problem of scheduling queries with multiple hot points as an instance of a more general problem: scheduling multiple-implementation packages.

Having multiple implementations of a query to choose from adds a level of complexity to the problem of scheduling queries in a database management system. One approach is to apply scheduling algorithms at two levels. The first level is package-level scheduling and the second level is implementation-level scheduling.

Queries await scheduling in the ready queue in the form of packages of plans (implementations). It is the scheduler's task to first select a package among those waiting in the ready queue. The schedulers we consider also act as load controllers: they usually consider the plans contained in the package currently at the head of the ready queue as long as the package contains at least one plan having an estimated buffer demand that is less than or equal to current buffer availability.

We characterize the policies by a quadruple containing the following components:

package-ordering policy. What is the queuing discipline for packages?

package-admission policy. When does the scheduler (i.e., load controller) allow a query package to compete for system resources? The package-admission policy is intended to prevent thrashing in the buffer pool. Because most package admission policies are based on the choice to wait for the availability of h buffers for a particular hotpoint h, the package admission policy implicitly chooses an implementation (<plan, hot set> pair).

plan-selection policy. Of the plans in a package, which one will be executed?

reservation policy. Does a query reserve its buffers, disallowing them to be victimized by other queries?

In the next section we list options for each component of a policy quadruple.

3.2 Package-Ordering Policy

FIFO. Queries enter the system in the same order as they enter the load controller.

min-minimal-weighted-sum, min-minimal-weighted-product, min-buffers-for-innermost-loop-resident. These package-ordering policies are variations on shortest-job-first. They all are based on measures of expected resource-usage of a query, where the relevant resources are the I/O bandwidth used for data retrieval and the buffers. The query with the smallest expected resource-usage is admitted first. These measures are related to package admission policy, soon to be discussed. For example, the min-minimal-weighted-sum policy computes the minimal-weighted-sum over the hotpoints of each query. The query with the smallest value for this measure is admitted first.

3.3 Package Admission Policy

mpl. This is a conventional policy that uses no knowledge of estimated cost or estimated buffer demand. Thrashing is avoided – or so system designers hope — by limiting the multiprogramming level (mpl), i.e., the number of queries that are allowed to contend for system resources.

working-set. This policy ignores the optimizer's prediction of buffer demand. Instead the policy depends on a run-time estimate (the working-set size), analogous to the working-set technique for estimating a process's use of virtual memory [9, 10].

innermost-loop-resident. For any pure nested-loops plan, there is always a hot point h such that, if h buffers — but no fewer — are made available to the plan, the pages of the relation scanned in the innermost loop are guaranteed to stay resident after initially retrieved until the plan is completely executed. The hot point h is the sum of the size of the relation scanned in the innermost loop and the number of other loops in the plan. For example, for a three-way join

r join s join t

implemented as a pure-nested-loops plan with t scanned in the innermost loop, h is

number_of_pages(t) + 2

For join plans whose innermost loop involves a clustered index lookup of a relation, the analogous hotpoint h is the number of pages of that relation that satisfy the join clause. For other types of plans, h is defined similarly.

The load controller/scheduler does not allow a query package into the system until h buffers are available to it. Each query Q_i has its own value h_i of h. Buffer availability is computed as the total number of buffers minus the sum of the h_i's for the active queries.

minimal-consumption. The package is scheduled when its minimal-consumption hotset [21, 22]. is available.

minimal weighted-sum. The scheduler has no knowledge of methods used by the optimizer in calculating the cost factor of each of the plans generated for a query. This is in keeping with the goal of modularity.

The scheduler does, however, have knowledge of both the estimated buffer demand for each plan, and the run-time buffer availability. In the weighted-sum policy, the scheduler selects (for the package admitted by the package-admission policy) the implementation that has the smallest sum of the estimated cost and the buffer demand:

$$P = C + B \cdot w \ . \tag{1}$$

where C is the estimated cost, B is the estimated buffer demand, and w is a weight assigned by the scheduler. Furthermore, the scheduler does not admit the package until buffers equal to the hotpoint (B) for the selected implementation are available. The weight reflects the criticality of the buffer space and other system resources (typically, processors and I/O bandwidth). If the system load is heavy, and buffer availability is low, then the value assigned to w will be relatively large. On the other hand if buffer availability is high, the scheduler has the option of reducing the value of w, thereby decreasing the importance of buffer demand when assessing the attributes of a candidate plan for initiation.

minimal weighted-product. This admission policy is similar to the previous one, but it chooses the plan that has the smallest weighted product of the estimated cost and the buffer demand:

$$P = C \cdot B^w \ . \tag{2}$$

This expression is intended to model overall buffer consumption [20] of a plan.

3.4 Plan-Selection Strategy

NOP. There is only one plan (possibly with multiple hotpoints) in each package. Choose this plan.

greedy. Choose the plan that uses as many of the available buffers as possible.

minimal weighted-sum. Among the plans of a given package, the one with the minimal weighted sum is chosen.

minimal weighted-product. Among the plans of a given package, the one with the minimal weighted product is chosen.

3.5 Reservation Policy

nonreservable. With a nonreservable pool, a query can access any buffer that the replacement policy allows it to, including those other queries have recently used.

reservable. A buffer pool is reservable if a query can (and must) reserve a set of buffers before it starts. We assume a query does not increase the size of its reserved set after its first reservation. Nor does a query decrease the size of its reserved set until it releases all its buffers.

4 The Experiments

4.1 Experimental Design

We used an event-based database-system simulator to evaluate the scheduling policies. The simulator was built using MacDougall's set of tools called *smpl* [14]. The simulator model is diagrammed in Fig. 1. The circles in the figure represent servers,

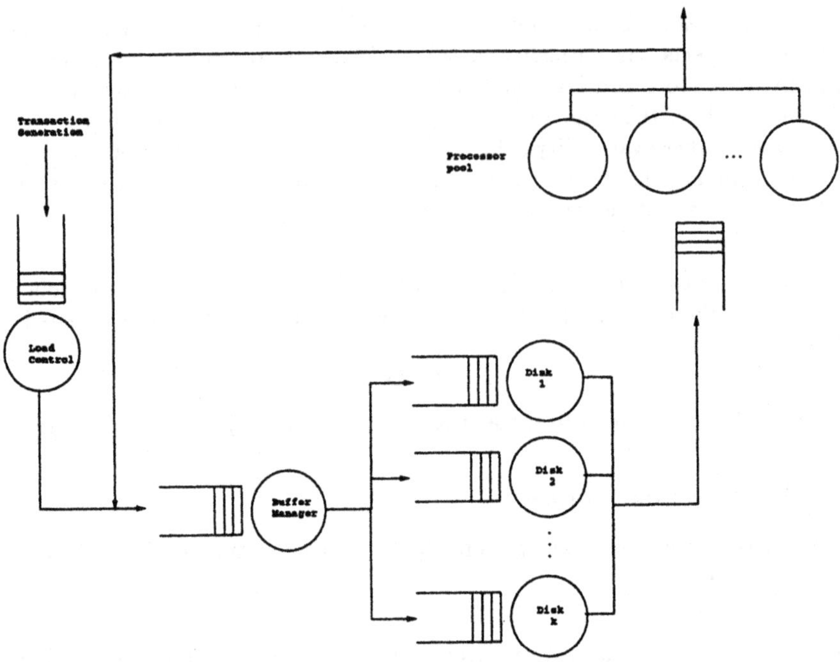

Fig. 1. Simulation model

which are depicted with their queues. The processor pool shares a single queue while each disk has its own queue. The arrows represent the paths of queries through the simulated database system.

The load-control server decides when to schedule a query. It also designates a hotpoint for the query. If appropriate, the load-control server reserves buffers for the query. When a query is scheduled, it is sent to the buffer manager.

The simulator supports two kinds of buffering, as determined by the simulation parameter BUFFER_POOL. If the buffer pool is nonreservable, queries vie for all the buffer frames. If the buffer pool is reservable, each query must reserve a set of buffers (typically equal in size to one of the hot points). Only one query contends for the buffer frames reserved to it.

If the buffers are not reservable, the query makes a data-request of the buffer manager. If the buffers are reservable, the query requests that the buffer manager reserve a hot-set worth of pages. The query makes a new request — a data request — of the buffer manager when the buffers are reserved to the query.

The buffer manager determines whether the requested page is already in a buffer. If so, the query is sent to the processor queue. Otherwise, the query is sent to the appropriate disk queue (for the page to be fetched). After disk service, the query is sent to the processor queue.

After processor service, the query is sent to back to the buffer manager for the next data request (and so on).

Not all policy quadruples make sense. For example, the package-ordering policy *min-minimal-weighted-sum* makes sense only if the package-admission policy is *minimal-weighted-sum*. The policy quadruples we evaluated are

1. FIFO/mpl/NOP/nonreservable
2. min-minimal-weighted-sum/minimal-weighted-sum/NOP/nonreservable
3. FIFO/minimal-weighted-sum/NOP/nonreservable
4. min-minimal-weighted-product/minimal-weighted-product/NOP/nonreservable
5. FIFO/minimal-weighted-product/NOP/nonreservable
6. FIFO/innermost-loop-resident/NOP/nonreservable
7. min-minimal-weighted-sum/minimal-weighted-sum/NOP/reservable
8. FIFO/minimal-weighted-sum/NOP/reservable
9. min-minimal-weighted-product/minimal-weighted-product/NOP/reservable
10. FIFO/minimal-weighted-product/NOP/reservable
11. FIFO/innermost-loop-resident/NOP/reservable
12. FIFO/minimal-consumption/hotset/reservable

4.2 Assumptions

Query plans are modeled as external (merge-)sorts and as left-deep multiple-join trees, where all joins are equijoins. Joins are implemented as nested loops. Each loop either iterates across an entire relation in sequence or accesses tuples satisfying a join predicate via a b+ tree index. Database systems offer other, sometimes more efficient, ways of performing joins, but we chose the implementation for which conventional buffer-management policies are most problematic.

To capture the inaccuracy of optimizer estimates, hot points are perturbed from their exact values. The required buffer availability (hotpoint) is chosen to be in the range

$$((1 - delta) \times h, (1 + delta) \times h) \ . \tag{3}$$

where delta is a parameter of the simulation. The perturbation captures the non-exactness of optimizer estimates.

The number of available buffers is computed by subtracting the hotpoint corresponding to each selected implementation of an active query from the total number of buffers.

Buffers can be shared among queries. The degree of sharing is controlled by a simulation parameter.

The I/O cost of a plan depends on physical-level implementation code — the access methods and operator implementations. Consider, for example, a nested loops implementation of

r join s on predicate p

This request can be implemented by the following code:

```
for each tuple tr of r
   for each tuple ts of s
      if concatenation(tr, ts) satisfies predicate p
            then output concatenation(r, s)
```

This plan often does not effectively use the available buffers. A nested-blocks implementation is better:

```
for each block br of r
   for each block bs of s
      for each tuple tr of br
         for each tuple ts of bs
            if concatenation(tr, ts) satisfies predicate p
               then output concatenation(r, s)
```

If there are fewer buffers than the size of s in pages, the first implementation retrieves each page of s once for each tuple in r, while the second implementation retrieves each page of s once for each page in r. The hot-set papers [21, 22], because they dealt with System R and its access methods, assumed that nested-loops plans were implemented using the first technique. In generating reference strings and in making cost estimates, we have assumed the latter implementation.

Modeling systems is an abstraction process. We have abstracted out of our model many costs that we suspect to be policy-neutral, e.g., scheduling cost, the processor cost of executing buffer management code, the cost of contending for system resources with non-database processes, concurrency-control overhead, etc.

4.3 Results

In order to fairly compare the various policy quadruples, we tried to find good values of parameters for the parameterized policies under the range of system parameters (number of joins, relation sizes, buffer space sizes, etc.) that we investigated. The parameters are maximum mpl for the the mpl package-admission policy and weight for the weighted-sum and weighted-product package-admission and package-ordering policies.

When we evaluated various weighted-product policies for differing weights, we found that the varying the weight yielded only two hotpoints: the smallest (one buffer) and the largest.[3] Because under the ranges of system parameters that we examined, scheduling according to the biggest hotpoint always worked better than scheduling according the smallest hotpoint, the weighted-product policy devolved into scheduling into the biggest-hotpoint strategy, which did not perform well compared to the non-weighted product policies. For this reason, we did not perform extensive experimentation with the weighted-product policies.

Effect of Buffer Perturbation. For all transactions other than sorts, buffer sizes were perturbed by plus or minus 20%. The perturbations tended to favor the nonreservable policies, because the average amount of buffer perturbation is zero. If buffers are nonreservable, transactions that were allocated less buffers than the original desired amount victimize the pages of other transactions; since there is approximately an equal amount of transactions with an excess buffer allocation, the victimization effects are minimal.

[3] The scheduler only examines hotpoints whose buffer requirements do not exceed the total system buffer space; since a hotpoint with a buffer size of 1 is always present, if all other hotpoints are too large for the system, this hotpoint is selected.

With a reservable policy, a transaction can only use the buffers that were allocated to it, and hence either suffers internal thrashing (if it was allocated too little buffers), or runs correctly but gains nothing from the excess buffers (which cannot be used by other transactions).

Effect of Transaction Ordering Policies. Interestingly, policies that ordered waiting transactions by a method other than FIFO generally performed worse than their FIFO counterparts, as can be seen in Fig. 2 and Fig. 3, which represent the throughputs of the weighted-sum reservable policies, and in Fig. 4 and Fig. 5, which represent the throughputs of the weighted-sum nonreservable policies. In general, the non-FIFO transaction ordering policies placed smaller, quicker transactions first (via minimum consumption or minimum weighted product), and these transactions tended to have smaller buffer requirements than later transactions. This implies that more transactions were active simultaneously and that fewer free buffers were available. The interactions of many small transactions tended to overload the system resources. The fact that smaller transactions are scheduled first is not taken into account by the transaction admission policies; as the number of active transactions increases, resource utilization increases and transactions may have to wait longer before gaining access to the disks or processors.

In addition, the nonreservable policies perform worse when there are fewer free buffers, since transactions under these policies can use free buffers before victimizing buffers that are about to be reused. This is especially true when considering the effects of buffer perturbation, as free buffers can also reduce these effects.

The Weighted-Sum Policy. The weights that were tested for the weighted-sum policy did not provide sufficient variation in plan selection. The majority of transactions simulated selected one of two hotpoints, either the largest hotpoint or the smallest non-trivial hotpoint, under all weighting schemes; the optimal choice of weight, similar to the choice of mpl, depends on knowledge of the query load.

As mentioned, the policies that scheduled transactions on a FIFO basis performed better then those scheduling via minimum weighted sum. The FIFO/weighted-sum/nonres policy had the best performance for a weighted sum policy, followed by the FIFO/weighted-sum/res policy. The minimum-weighted-sum/weighted-sum/nonres policy was the next best, performing slightly better then the minimum-weighted-sum/weighted-sum/res policy.

The Inner-Loop-Resident Policy. The results for the inner-loop-resident policy are presented in Fig. 6. As can be seen from the graph, both reservable and nonreservable versions of the policy show increased throughput with increased buffer size until some peak is reached, and then throughput performance drops. Because this policy requests the minimal non-trivial hotpoint, it results in many transactions running with small buffer requirements. As the buffer size increases, the concurrency level also grows, resulting in increased competition for system resources. We conjecture that the increased contention for resources results in the throughput drop that is evident in Fig. 6. We believe the non-reservable version of the policy performs best because it is less adversely affected by the buffer perturbation.

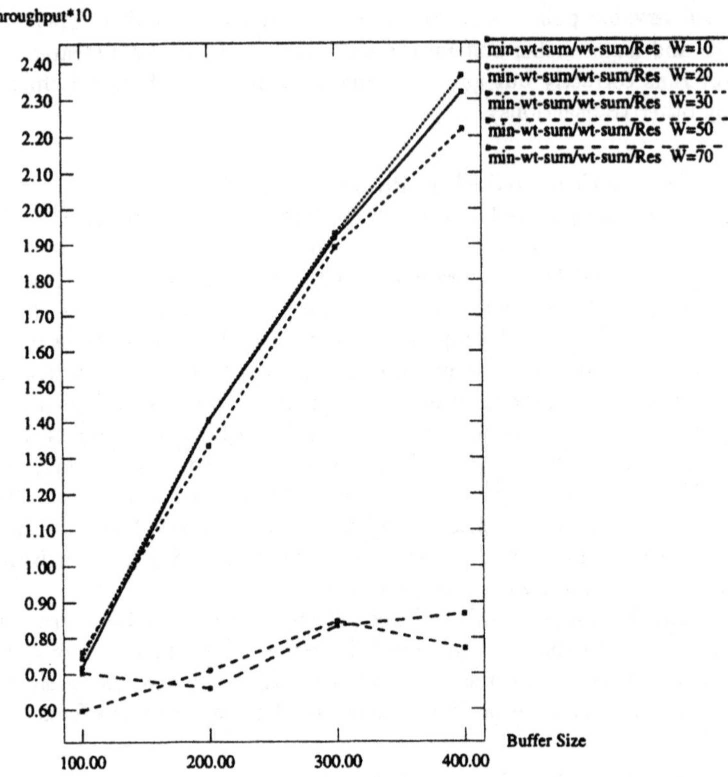

Fig. 2. The effect of weight on throughput for the min-wt-sum/wt-sum/NOP/Res policy

Which Policies Are Best? Of the policies tested, the FIFO/minimal-weighted-sum/NOP/nonreservable policy had the best overall throughput performance. Examining Fig. 7, the throughput graph of the 5 best policies, it can be seen that all of these policies were relatively close; these policies were (in order of best performance): FIFO/weighted-sum/nonres with a weight of 20, FIFO/weighted-sum/res with a weight of 10, min-minimal-weighted-sum/minimal-weighted-sum/NOP/nonreservable with a weight of 30, min-consumption/hotset/Res, and min-minimal-weighted-sum/minimal-weighted-sum/NOP/reservable with a weight of 20.

Maximum throughput was attained by the FIFO/weighted-sum policies; this suggests that executing a variety of hotpoints yields better throughput results then scheduling either small or large hotpoints only. We conjecture that a system that schedules small hotpoints will eventually suffer adverse resource contention, while a system only scheduling large hotpoints yields too low a concurrency level. Thus, we conjecture a balanced load containing both small and large hotpoints will yield the maximal throughput.

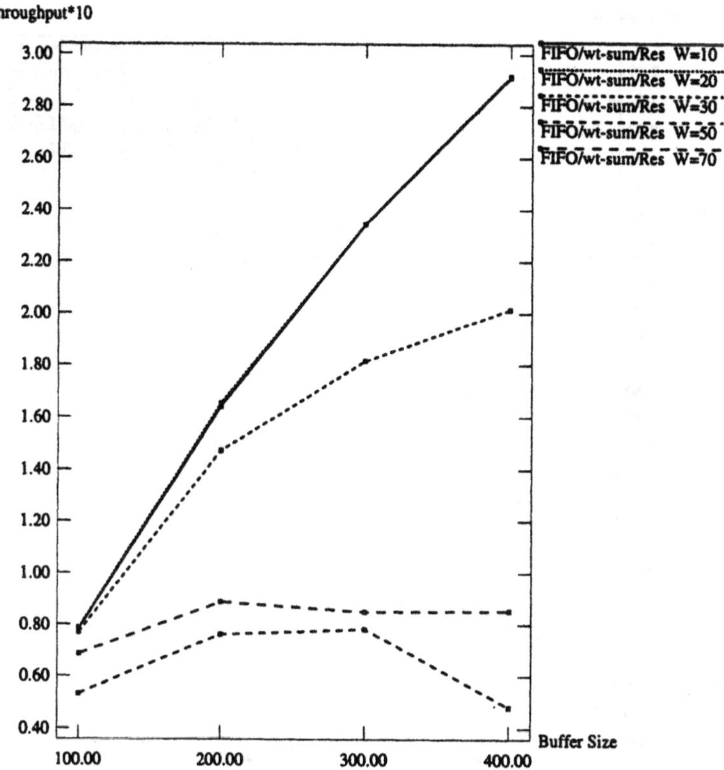

Fig. 3. The effect of weight on throughput for the FIFO/wt-sum/NOP/Res policy

5 Related Research

Effelsberg and Haerder [11] survey strategies to search the buffers for a referenced block, to allocate buffers for concurrent queries, and to select victims.

Stonebraker reveals what's wrong with operating systems support for buffer management and other database-system services in [23]. His observations about the failings of LRU replacement when the number of buffers is too low motivated considerable research into buffer management. Stonebraker also proposes a scheduling solution to buffer management problems in [24].

The hot-set approach to buffer management is due to Sacco and Schkolnick [21, 22]. Chou and DeWitt present DBMIN, a variation of the hot-set technique, in [6]. Ng, Faloutsos, and Sellis describe a variation on DBMIN that uses *marginal gains* analysis to decide how many buffers to allocate to a query [16]. The same authors describe in [12] a technique to predict the effect on system performance of activating a new query.

In [8] is a proposal for non-modular query optimization and buffer management. Cornell and Yu describe an "integrated" strategy in which multiple query optimiza-

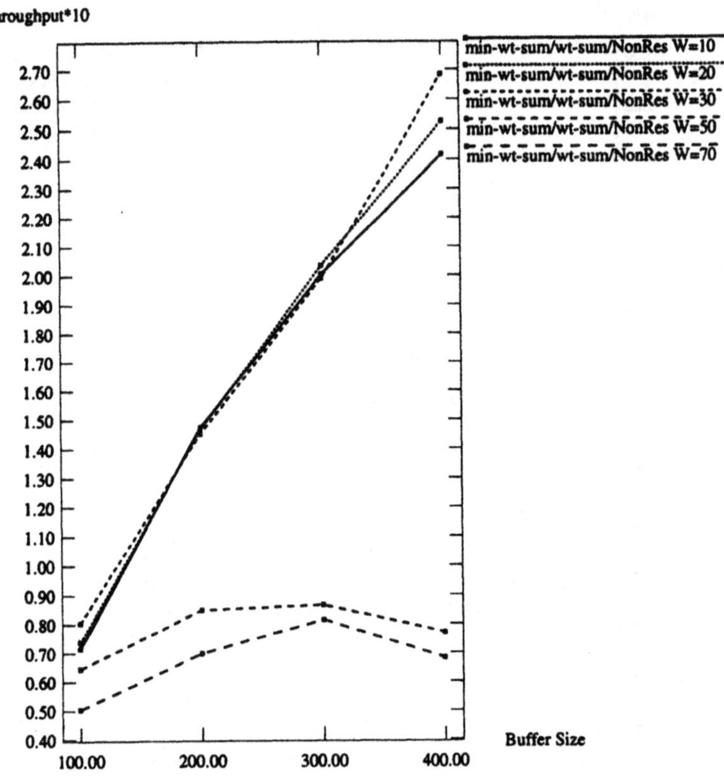

Fig. 4. The effect of weight on throughput for the min-wt-sum/wt-sum/NOP/NonRes policy

tion is done for all query types an installation will handle. The optimizer attaches to each query type a buffer requirement that the scheduler will use to determine when the corresponding plan can be scheduled. Cornell and Yu's scheme assumes optimizer knowledge of the query load, including yet-to-be-submitted queries. Yu and Cornell present a different perfect-knowledge strategy in [25]. They define and use return-on-consumption, which measures the the improvement in response time as buffer consumption increases. They found an admission policy based on return-on-consumption, and a heuristic version of this policy, to be more efficient than conventional policies.

Chen and Roussopoulos describe a technique in [4] that allocates buffers to a query on the basis of system feedback about the query's reference string.

Like our research, the work of Mehta and DeWitt [15] seeks to allocate buffers and schedule transactions so to avoid overcommitment of the buffer space. Their approach, unlike ours, does not take advantage of the existence of multiple hot points for a plan.

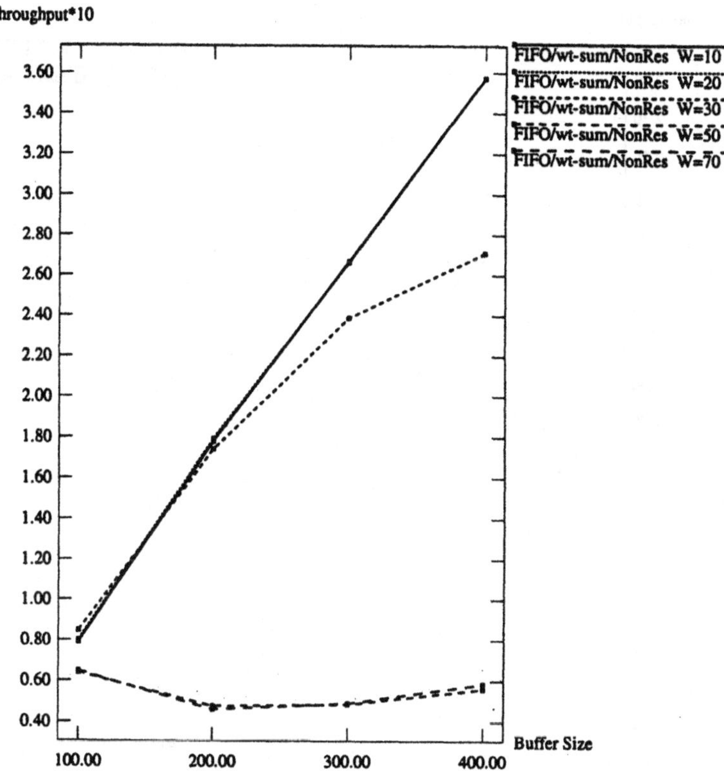

Fig. 5. The effect of weight on throughput for the FIFO/wt-sum/NOP/NonRes policy

Our simulator resembles in many respects the simulators developed by Drs. R. Agrawal, M. Carey, M. Livny, D. Ries, and M. Stonebraker [1, 2, 3, 18, 19].

6 Conclusions and Directions for Future Research

We have shown that the best scheduling policies are weighted-sum policies. The weighted-sum policies require the optimizer to communicate multiple hotpoints per query. These policies also must be tuned by selecting an appropriate weight. How to do this is an open question.

We intend to generalize our method in two phases. First, we shall model packages that contain different plans. Our current packages contain different implementations (<plan, hot set> pairs) by varying the hot-set coordinate, not the plan coordinate, of an implementation. An optimizer can collaborate with a query-plan evaluator by producing more than one plan, among which the evaluator can schedule one. The evaluator matches the available system resources (e.g., buffers) against each plan's estimated demand for those resources. The resulting scheduling problem is a

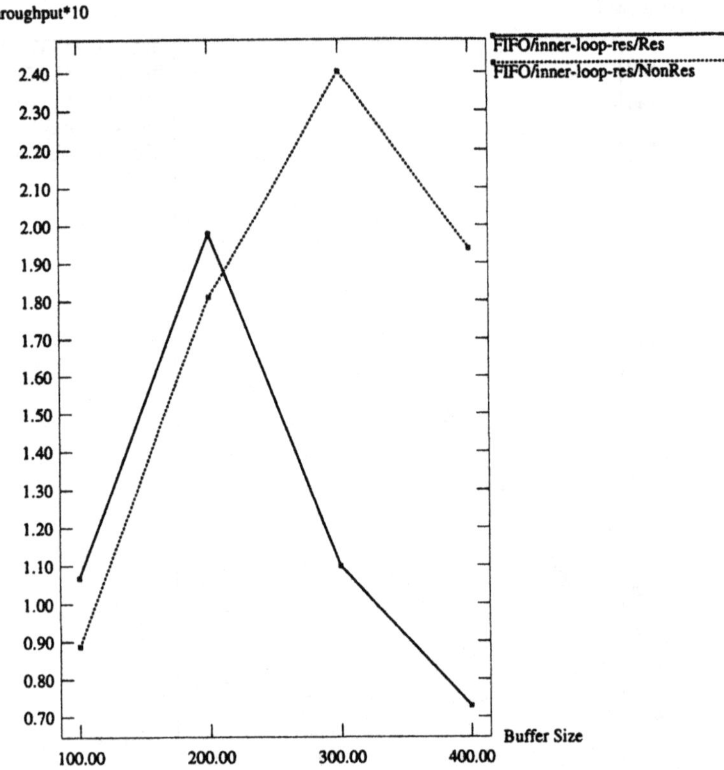

Fig. 6. The effect of buffer availability on throughput for the FIFO/innermost-loop-resident policies

generalization of the one we tackled in this paper: how does one intelligently schedule plans that have more than one implementation? The scheduling problem is also a nontrivial generalization of job scheduling [7, 13]. We hope to report results on the generalized problem in the near future.

The research reported in this paper and that of the first phase of future research are based on the assumption that the optimizer can compute relation sizes and thus hotpoints. In the second phase, we do not make this assumption. Data objects for applications built in extensible database systems can be expected to be heterogeneous and often very large. For example, when a conventional optimizer generates a plan part of which is to retrieve a tuple from relation r satisfying selection predicate c, the optimizer can reliably guess the number of pages containing r tuples satisfying c. Replace "relation r" with a sequence r of text documents, and it becomes likely that buffer requirements for the subplan cannot be reliably known to the query scheduler. In the second phase of future research we shall explore techniques for handling this problem.

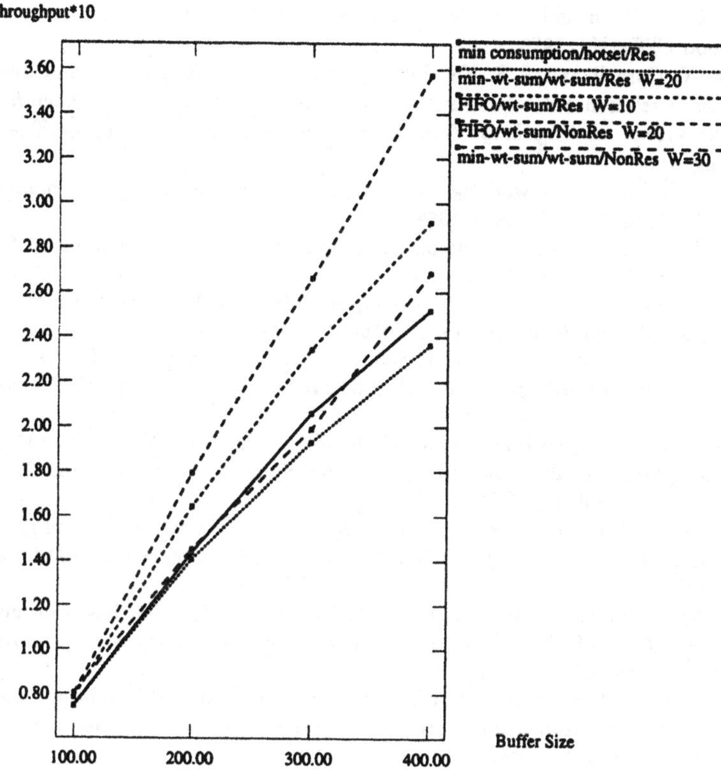

Fig. 7. Policies that achieved the best overall throughput performance

References

1. R. Agrawal, M. J. Carey, and M. Livny. Models for studying concurrency control performance: Alternatives and implications. In *Proceedings of the SIGMOD International Conference on the Management of Data*, pages 108–121, Austin, TX, May 1985.
2. M. J. Carey. *Ph.D. Thesis: Modeling and Evaluation of Database Concurrency Control Algorithms.* University of California - Berkeley, 1983.
3. M. J. Carey and M. R. Stonebraker. The performance of concurrency control algorithms for DBMSs. In *Proceedings of the 10th International Conference on Very Large Databases*, pages 107–118, Singapore, 1984.
4. C. M. Chen and N. Roussopoulos. Adaptive database buffer allocation using query feedback. In *Proceedings of the 19th International Conference on VLDB*, pages 342–353, 1993.
5. J. M. Cheng, C. R. Loosley, A. Shibamiya, and P. S. Worthington. IBM Database 2 performance: Design, implementation, and tuning. *IBM Systems Journal*, 23(2):189–210, 1984.
6. H.-T. Chou and D. J. Dewitt. An evaluation of buffer management strategies for relational database. In *Proceedings of the International Conference on Very Large Data Bases 1985*, pages 127–141, Stockholm, 1985.

7. E. G. Coffman and P. J. Denning. *Operating Systems Theory.* Prentice-Hall, Englewood Cliffs, NJ, 1973.
8. D. W. Cornell and P. S. Yu. Integration of buffer management and query optimization in relational database environment. In *Proceedings of the Fifteenth International Conference on Very Large Data Bases*, pages 247–256, Amsterdam, The Netherlands, Aug. 1989.
9. P. J. Denning. The working set model for program behavior. *Communications of the ACM*, 11(5):323–333, May 1968.
10. P. J. Denning. Working sets past and present. *IEEE Transactions on Software Engineering*, SE-6(1):64–84, Jan. 1980.
11. W. Effelsberg and T. Haerder. Principles of database buffer management. *ACM Transactions on Database Systems*, 9(4):560–595, Dec. 1984.
12. C. Faloutsos, R. T. Ng, and T. Sellis. Predictive load control for flexible buffer allocation. In *Proceedings of the 17th International Conference on VLDB*, pages 265–274, 1991.
13. L. Kleinrock. *Queueing Systems, Volume 2.* Wiley, New York, NY, 1976.
14. M. H. MacDougall. *Simulating Computer Systems: Techniques and Tools.* The MIT Press, Cambridge, MA, 1987.
15. M. Mehta and D. J. DeWitt. Dynamic memory allocation for multiple-query workloads. In *Proceedings of the 19th International Conference on VLDB*, pages 354–367, 1993.
16. R Ng, C. Faloutsos, and T. Sellis. Flexible buffer allocation based on marginal gains. In *ACM SIGMOD International Conference on the Management of Data*, pages 387–396, Denver, CO, 1991.
17. A. Reuter. Load control and load balancing in a shared database management system. In *Proceedings International Conference on Data Engineering*, pages 188–199, Los Angeles, Feb. 1986.
18. D. Ries and M. Stonebraker. Effects of locking granularity on database management system performance. *ACM Transactions on Database Systems*, 2(3):233–246, Sept. 1977.
19. D. Ries and M. Stonebraker. Locking granularity revisited. *ACM Transactions on Database Systems*, 4(2), June 1979.
20. G. M. Sacco. Fragmentation: A technique for efficient query processing. *ACM Transactions on Database Systems*, 11(2):113–133, June 1986.
21. G. M. Sacco and M. Schkolnick. A mechanism for managing the buffer pool in a relational database system using the hot set model. In *Proceedings of the 8th Conference on Very Large Databases*, pages 257–262, Mexico, 1982.
22. G. M. Sacco and M. Schkolnick. Buffer management in relational database systems. *ACM Transactions on Database Systems*, 11(4):473–498, Dec. 1986.
23. M. R. Stonebraker. Operating systems support for database management systems. *Communications of the ACM*, 24(7):412–418, July 1981.
24. M. R. Stonebraker, R. Katz, D. Patterson, and J. Ousterhout. The design of XPRS. In *Proceedings of the Fourteenth International Conference on Very Large Data Bases*, pages 318–330, Los Angeles, 1988.
25. P. S. Yu and D. W. Cornell. Optimal buffer allocation in a multi-query environment. In *Proceedings of the International Conference on Data Engineering*, pages 622–631, 1991.

Optimization of Spatial Joins Using Filters

Hein M.Veenhof[1], Peter M.G. Apers[1], and Maurice A.W. Houtsma[2]

[1] University of Twente, Department of Computer Science, P.O. Box 217, 7500 AE Enschede, the Netherlands
[2] Telematics Research Centre, P.O. Box 217, 7500 AE Enschede, the Netherlands

Abstract. When viewing present-day technical applications that rely on the use of database systems, one notices that new techniques must be integrated in database management systems to be able to support these applications efficiently. This paper discusses one of these techniques in the context of supporting a Geographic Information System. It is known that the use of filters on geometric objects has a significant impact on the processing of 2-way spatial join queries. For this purpose, filters require approximations of objects. Queries can be optimized by filtering data not with just one but with several filters. Existing join methods are based on a combination of filters and a spatial index. The index is used to reduce the cost of the filter step and to minimize the cost of retrieving geometric objects from disk.

In this paper we examine n-way spatial joins. Complex n-way spatial join queries require solving several 2-way joins of intermediate results. In this case, not only the profit gained from using both filters and spatial indices but also the additional cost due to using these techniques are examined. For 2-way joins of base relations these costs are considered part of physical database design. We focus on the criteria for mutually comparing filters and not on those for spatial indices. Important aspects of a multi-step filter-based n-way spatial join method are described together with performance experiments. The winning join method uses several filters with approximations that are constructed by rotating two parallel lines around the object.

1 Introduction

In the past, a lot of research has been done on query optimization techniques for (relational) databases. A survey is given in [10]. Optimization efforts mainly concentrated on queries stemming from administrative applications. Recently, databases are increasingly used not only for administrative, but also for technical applications. Technical applications, e.g. CAD/CAM, cartographic applications, and applications using multimedia, place a heavy burden upon a database management system. This is caused by aspects such as huge amounts of data,

For more information send an email to one of `veenhof@cs.utwente.nl`, `apers@cs.utwente.nl`, or `houtsma@trc.nl`. Our WWW site can be reached at `http://wwwis.cs.utwente.nl:8080/dolls.html`.

complex data structures, and expensive operations. Because of the different characteristics of technical applications, query optimization techniques need to be reconsidered.

We consider a Geographic Information System (GIS) as a typical technical application. The important operations to be supported differ from those in traditional database systems and some are very expensive (for instance, overlay, and intersection). A GIS typically maintains thematic data (e.g., street names, soil type, area size) and geometric data (e.g., geometry of buildings, of land parcels, of mountains). Thematic data can easily be supported by a database. The advantages of databases, amongst others persistency, efficient retrieval, and recovery, should also be exploited for geometric data.

To reduce the heavy burden that complex operations in GISs place on the database management system, *filters* are used [15]. A filter acts as a preprocessor for a complex operation. The main idea of filters is to reduce the size of the operands. Thus, a filter is used before a complex operation to reduce the size of its operands (just like semi-joins are used to reduce join-operands in relational queries [5]). With smaller operands, the cost of an operation will be smaller; however, the cost of using a filter has to be taken into account. In addition to using one filter, several filters of different type may be combined into a filter sequence. Each filter in such a sequence will reduce the operand in size.

Optimization techniques developed to access huge amounts of geometric data concentrate on spatial indices [8, 9, 18]. Emphasis is on efficient retrieval of sets of geometrical objects. Using a hierarchically organized structure a spatial index tries to retrieve from disk a requested set of disk pages, containing the set of objects, with minimal cost for disk I/O. In [14] an overview and classification is given of spatial indices.

One of the most expensive operations a GIS has to support is the spatial join. Existing methods, for efficiently solving 2-way spatial joins, are based on both filters and spatial indices. In a GIS, spatial queries will usually be composed of many spatial joins. Solving such n-way joins requires solving several 2-way joins for intermediate results. Although, in general, both filters and spatial indices will be available for base relations, we cannot expect them to be present on every intermediate result. Different criteria, for choosing a good or the best combination of both filter and spatial index techniques, are important in this case. So, it is worthwhile studying these criteria again in the context of a n-way join method. We propose a generic model, using both techniques, for optimization of operations on intermediate results. The main focus is, however, on the multi-filter technique.

This paper is organized as follows. In Section 2, we give a characterization of the problem. The importance of n-way joins is shown. Basic concepts of optimizing spatial queries when using one or multiple filters are introduced in Section 3. Section 4 presents some typical filters, and Section 5 discusses important criteria for comparing them. Next, Section 6 deals with the experiments done to evaluate the multi-filter technique; several results are explained. In Section 7, we describe which spatial index to choose with the proposed filter technique. Finally, we draw conclusions and elaborate on future research in Section 8.

2 Problem Definition

Geographic Information Systems handle large amounts of thematic and geometric data that describe spatial objects like roads, buildings, and lakes. Whereas thematic data only occupies relatively small amounts of disk storage, geometric data is often large in size and spans several disk pages. This has a negative effect on the response times for those spatial queries that rely on the transfer of many spatial objects from disk to main memory.

Operations on simple data types (e.g., $\leq, >, +, *$) are not very expensive. These operations are hardly ever a bottleneck in standard query processing. Operations on geometric data, such as *overlay* and *intersection*, are not seldom extremely complex and can therefore become a bottleneck in spatial query processing. Queries that rely on such expensive operations should be optimized to have as few of them as possible actually calculated. When these expensive operations are avoided or replaced by simpler ones, a faster response to queries will be the result.

Although a GIS has to support queries on thematic data efficiently as well, in this article our interest is mainly on spatial queries. Without being complete and without defining each, a list of spatial queries contains at least : *point query*, *region query*, *vacant place query*, *path query*, *nearest neighbor query*, *enclosure query*, *buffer zone query*, and *spatial joins*. In [11] a definition for each of these queries can be found.

An n-way spatial join combines spatial objects from n spatial relations according to their geometric attributes; matching attributes have to fulfill a spatial predicate. An example of a spatial query composed of several spatial joins is the following:

```
Retrieve all rural areas below sea level
         having soil type equal to sand
         within 3 miles of polluted lakes
```

Assuming the base relations *Land_Use(geometry, use)*, *Soil(geometry, type)*, *Pollution(geometry, pollution-code)*, and *Elevation(geometry, height)*, several spatial joins have to be calculated to construct the answer to this query. A spatial join of, e.g., relations *Land_Use* and *Elevation*, gives the intermediate result to the subquery: `rural areas below sea level`.

We focus here on spatial joins, especially on the n-way spatial join. Spatial queries are often based on n-way spatial joins, and the spatial join is one of the most expensive database operations a GIS has to support.

Based on the availability of spatial indices for operands, three types of 2-way spatial joins can be distinguished in a n-way spatial join tree. Figure 1 illustrates these three types assuming that a spatial index exists for each base relation. Especially for bushy join trees, it is often the case that intermediate results must be joined. It are those non-indexed intermediate results, to be used as operands of successive spatial joins, that can effectively be reduced in size by the use of filters. Adding a spatial index reduces CPU-time of filter processing and I/O time of retrieving geometric objects.

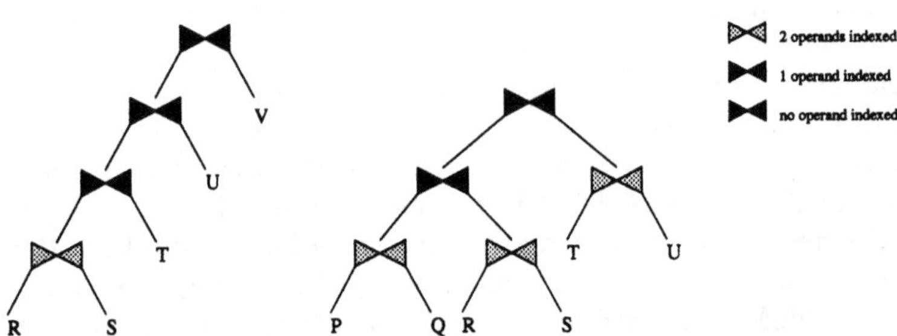

Fig. 1. Illustration of the three 2-way join types within a left-linear and a bushy join tree.

In [2] one a well-known filter and a spatial index, both based on (minimum) bounding boxes, are used to identify pairs of geometric objects that overlap. Algorithms are presented for tuning both CPU- and I/O-time for 2-way spatial joins. CPU-time of the expensive join operation itself is not considered. In [3] research of [2] is extended; several single filter types are examined. Criteria for mutually comparing filters are described and a filter sequence of size two is advised. The first filter is based on minimum bounding boxes, the second filter is based on the n-corner. Again, a spatial index is used in combination with the first filter. In [4], in addition to the results of [3] a third filter and a special algorithm to reduce CPU-time of the identification process are advised. This third filter is based on the maximum enclosed box. Still, only 2-way spatial joins on base relations are considered. Recently, some progress is made for n-way spatial joins. In [13] performance improvements of a n-way spatial join technique are described. For an intermediate result, in a linear join tree, a spatial index is created which adapts to the existing spatial index of the other operand. This technique significantly reduces I/O-time of n-way joins. In their article the main focus is on the spatial index technique.

Both filters and indices are very important for solving n-way spatial joins. Most research concentrates on the 2-way case. Since, criteria for mutually comparing filters in the more general n-way case differ from the ones which are important in the 2-way case, we reexamine those criteria. We do this first for a 2-way join of two non-indexed intermediate results. We make a proposal for the filter technique to use based on experimental results. The spatial index to choose follows immediately from the choice of the filter technique. The proposed method can easily be generalized to an n-way spatial join method.

3 Using Filters in Optimization

Without indices, a spatial join of two relations can be solved by calculating the spatial comparison operation for each pair of spatial objects in a nested-loop strategy. For two spatial relations R and S with cardinality n and m, respectively, the spatial comparison operation Θ is evaluated $n * m$ times. To speed up the evaluation process, a simple test can be performed before evaluating the actual comparison operation. This test indicates if, for a given pair of spatial objects, the comparison operation can be avoided altogether.

An example of such a simple test, in case of e.g. an intersection operation, is whether the minimum bounding boxes of the spatial objects have any overlap at all. The bounding box of a spatial object is an example of a simplification of the spatial object, also called *approximation* [3, 4]. If the bounding boxes of two spatial objects have no overlap, then there is no need to calculate the overlap of the spatial objects themselves.

So, when using a filter, instead of evaluating Θ, a simple test operation f_Θ is performed for each pair of object approximations. Operations on approximations are much cheaper than on the spatial objects themselves. Following a nested-loop strategy, this test is performed $n*m$ times, resulting in a set of k candidate pairs (with $k \leq (n*m)$). After the test has been performed, Θ now has to be evaluated only k times.

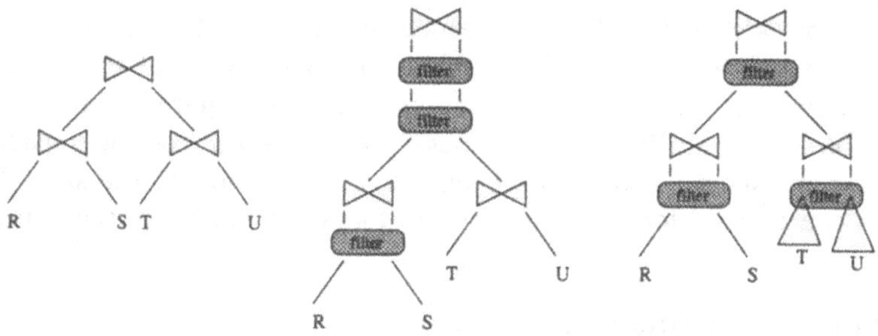

Fig. 2. Query tree and two optimized versions.

We can extend this approach to using a sequence of filters. The query optimizer, based on cost estimations, can decide to use multiple filters in a sequence; each one reducing the set of candidate pairs further. This is shown in Figure 2. The benefit of using such a sequence of filters can be estimated as follows. Assume a sequence of filters $F_1, \ldots, F_p$, with a resulting set of k_p candidate pairs. The cost of the remaining spatial comparison operation is $k_p C_\Theta$ (with C_Θ indicating the cost of the actual spatial operation on two objects), plus the cost of reading the k_p-pairs from disk and writing the output back to disk. Without specifying storage costs, the cost of applying the filters is given by $C_{k_1} + \ldots + C_{k_p}$, where each C_{k_i} is a function of the cost of the test operation and the number of candidate pairs resulting from F_{i-1}.

Not only may the use of filters result in a smaller number of CPU-intensive spatial comparison operations, it may also result in considerable savings on the number of disk accesses, because approximations will occupy considerably less disk space than the spatial objects.

Of course, the query optimizer also has to take into account the availability of spatial indices on approximations. The use of such a spatial index will NOT further reduce the set of candidates. It will reduce the total number of calls of test operations f_Θ. A filter based on minimum bounding boxes can be combined with a spatial index, for example an R-tree [8], which is also based on bounding boxes. The spatial index will considerably reduce the $n*m$ calls of test operation f_Θ needed for the first filter step when a nested loop approach was used. The number of candidate pairs resulting from the first filter step will, however, still be k. The spatial index will also reduce the I/O cost for retrieving objects from disk. A spatial index on approximations can thus be used to speed up filter processing. The right side of Figure 2 also shows an alternative query plan in which the optimizer has chosen to make use of the approximations in the two available spatial indices. Notice the overlap between the pictogram for the indices and for the filter. This has been done to stress the orthogonality of filters and bounding indices.

Computing an n-way join involves computing a number of 2-way joins each using a certain filter sequence; results of joins are used as input for other joins. Such intermediate results are, in fact, new sets of spatial objects, for which no approximation is available. The approximations used by the sequence of filters in the following 2-way join should now be constructed without much cost. For solving n-way joins, we can no longer assume that all required approximations are available (as we do for base relations). Therefore, the cost of constructing approximations should also be taken into account. Although, the same line of argument can be used for spatial indices we focus here on filter techniques.

4 Approximations used by Filters

Several approximations have been described to be used in spatial query processing, see [3]. Among these approximations are: the *minimum bounding box* (MBB), which is the well-known axes-parallel rectangle fitted along the boundary of the object approximated. The *rotated minimum bounding box* (RMBB) this is the non axes-parallel minimum bounding box with minimal area. The orientations of the RMBBs of two different objects are not necessarily the same. The *minimum bounding circle* (MBC) [20], the *minimum bounding ellipse* (MBE) [21], the *convex hull* (CH) [1] [17], and the *n-corner*. An n-corner is defined as the optimal n-sided polygon circumscribing a convex polygon [6].

In addition to these approximations we use a variant of the MBB, derived from ideas in [9], that is very well suited for solving n-way joins. This is the *g-degrees rotated x-range* (gRxR). A gRxR is a pair of two x-values $[x_{min}, x_{max}]$.

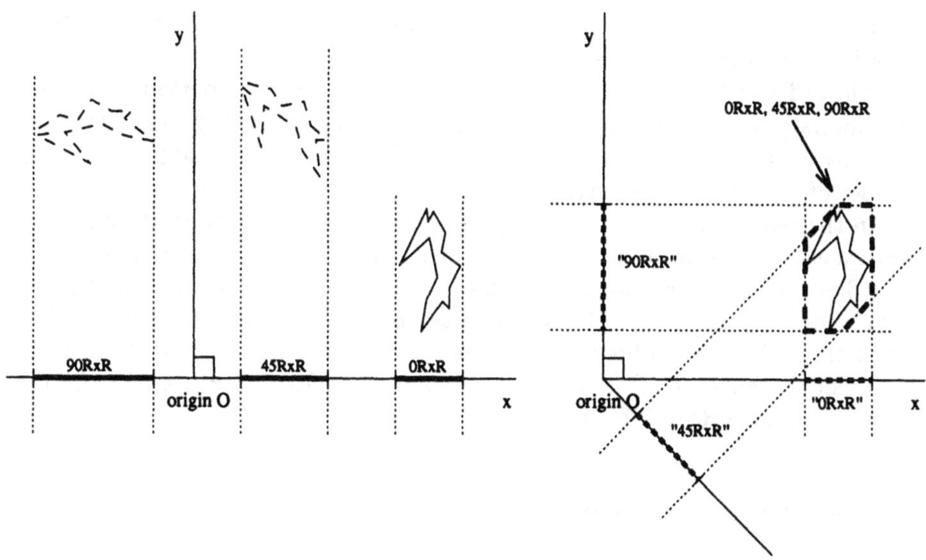

Fig. 3. View of the single filters 0RxR, 45RxR, 90RxR, and their combination.

These two x-values are the minimum and maximum of the g-degrees rotated x-coordinates of an object. The x-range describes the infinite area bounded by the two lines $x = x_{min}$ and $x = x_{max}$. For EACH g-degrees rotated x-range the origin has been chosen as the center of rotation and rotation is counter clockwise. Constructing the gRxR only requires calculating the minimum and maximum values of the new x-coordinates. The *g-degrees rotated y-range* (gRyR) can be defined the same way; moreover, it is the same range as a $(g+90)$RxR. The left side of Figure 3 shows a spatial object with both its 0RxR, 45RxR, and 90RxR. Since, a rotated x-range determines an infinitely sized area perpendicular to the x-axis, drawing its boundary is not practical. Therefore, the rotated x-range is drawn as a line-segment in two dimensions.

Single filters are based on one of the above mentioned approximations. Filter sequences are based on combinations of several such approximations. On the right side of Figure 3 the combination of the single filters 0RxR, a 45RxR, and 90RxR is presented. Although, the three rotated ranges are in fact perpendicular to the x-axis, the figure shows how these three together approximate the object. A filter sequence based on these three rotated ranges first tests intersection of a pair of 0RxRs, then of two 45RxRs, and finally of two 90RxRs. As we can see in Figure 3 the area occupied by this combination is smaller than the area of 0RxR alone (which in fact is infinite) and even smaller than the area of a combination of only a 0RxR and a 45RxR, or the combination of 0RxR and a 90RxR. Note that the area approximated or its border is never constructed explicitly. Only pairs of ranges with the same rotation may be compared. Mutually testing of, for instance, a 0RxR with a 45RxR is not allowed, because x-values of different rotation are incomparable.

The order of the single filters in a filter sequence is very important. If successive filters of a sequence are chosen well—the intersection of the used approximations should fit the object increasingly narrow—it is thus capable of reducing the set of candidate pairs further.

In the remainder of this paper, sequences of filters are identified by the approximations they are based on. Thus, MBB-MBC stands for a filter sequence that first filters with minimum bounding boxes and then with minimum bounding circles. The standard MBB is viewed as the filter sequence 0RxR-0RyR. The notation gBOX is an abbreviation of the filter sequence gRxR-$(g+90)$RxR, or the identical sequence gRxR-gRyR. The notation 10-70-130RxR is short for the filter sequence 10RxR-70RxR-130RxR.

5 Criteria for Comparing Filters

To determine what a good filter sequence is, we need some criteria for comparing them. The following five criteria are important: *approximation quality*, *storage requirement*, *cost of the simple test operation*, *cost of constructing approximations*, and *orientation insensitivity*. The first two criteria have been described in [3] as well, however, they only considered single filters and not sequences.

Approximation quality : Using better fitting approximations within filters results in less candidate pairs for the spatial comparison operation, therefore, a measure for the quality of an approximation should be based on the area of an approximation compared to the object. A general definition of *single approximation quality* taking into account over- and underestimation of the original objects can be found in [3]. For combined use of approximations in a filter sequence F of size p we propose the following measure of *combined approximation quality* :

Definition 1 $$AQ_{combined}(F, O) = \frac{area(\bigcap_{i=1}^{p} Appr(O, F_i))}{area(O)} \times 100\%$$

Where $\bigcap$ denotes geometric intersection, $area()$ is the area function, and $Appr(O, F_i)$ is the approximation of object O needed by the i-th filter of filter sequence F. This definition only takes into account overestimating approximations.

Storage requirements : This criterion concerns the amount of storage occupied by the approximations of a filter sequence. Compared to the spatial objects, their approximations should be described with as few parameters as possible and thus occupy minimal disk space. The storage requirement of convex hulls is very high, since a long list of points is stored for each hull. The other approximations all have small constant storage requirements.

Cost of test operations : The cost of the test operations f_Θ is important, since, as stated before, it must be simple compared to its associated spatial comparison operation Θ. The test operation for the range filter gRxR is the cheapest. At most two floating point comparisons are used for this test. For MBB the test operation is a box intersection test which is at most twice as costly as the test for a gRxR filter. For MBC, the test operation involves calculating a distance in addition to a simple comparison. Intersection tests for the other filters like convex hulls and n-corners are even more expensive.

Construction cost of approximations : For n-way joins, this criterion is particularly important. Constructing approximations like n-corners, convex hulls, minimum bounding circles, and minimum bounding ellipses—for which algorithms exists with good worst-case complexities—is considered too expensive. This is due to high constants associated with these complexity functions. We expect to gain more from a combination of several approximations that can be constructed almost for free, than from one tight fitting approximation that is constructed with huge costs.

Orientation insensitivity : A method for solving spatial queries is *orientation insensitive* if the expected spatial query time is independent of the orientation of the data [16]. Thus, for the filter based 2-way join method an equal rotation of all geometric objects involved should have no impact on its performance. However, the approximation quality of an approximation can vary if the object approximated is rotated. This occurs for example with the MBB. When such an approximation is used in a filter sequence, rotation of the data could influence the size of the set containing candidate pairs for the spatial operation, and thus effect the query response time. A method using at least one of these approximations in a filter sequence could be orientation sensitive. Some approximations (e.g., the MBC) are unique regardless of the orientation of the object. When used in a filter sequence they do not influence the orientation (in)sensitivity of the join method.

6 Experiments

We implemented a prototype of the query optimizer/evaluator in C++, using the Library of Efficient Data Types and Algorithms (LEDA) [12]. It allows us to check the effectiveness of filter techniques, and the usefulness of using several filters instead of just one. A 2-way intersection join was implemented with a simple nested-loop join algorithm adapted to the use of successive filters. The filters we have implemented are: MBB, gRxR, MBC, and CH. Despite the high construction cost involved both MBC and CH have been taken into account to test our premises. Other single filters mentioned before, have not been implemented due to their prohibitively expensive construction costs (little is gained, if we have to construct approximations using costly algorithms, for new spatial objects part of intermediate results).

In the remainder of this section, we will elaborate on the results of several experiments. After giving a description of the test data, we give figures for the approximation quality and storage requirement of some filters. Next, we show that a sequence of filters can successfully be used to reduce the number of expensive spatial operations. This reduction is directly reflected in the amount of CPU-time needed for the intersection operations. We show that the cost for constructing several good fitting approximations is too high. In contrast, the construction of the gRxR is rather cheap. A filter sequence formed by several gRxRs, each with a certain angle of rotation, is shown to be the clear winner with respect to all criteria described before. How to choose the angles of rotation follows from the orientation sensitivity tests.

6.1 Description of test data

The data sets used in our tests concern real world data. These data sets describe regions in Europe on different levels of detail. A characterization of the real world data sets is given in Table 1. N denotes the number of polygons in the data sets, P_{avg} the average number of points per polygon. The polygon described with the fewest (most) points is given by P_{min} (P_{max}).

	europe0	**europe1**	**europe2**	**europe3**	**europe4**
N	337	352	408	515	810
P_{min}	4	4	4	4	4
P_{avg}	78	84	95	94	84
P_{max}	7725	3230	1932	1932	869

Table 1. Characterization of the real world data sets.

In addition to these five sets others can be derived from them by means of two set operators for translation and rotation. See Figure 4 for a part of the test data. With **europe0_t50_r20** a map is denoted derived from real world data set **europe0**, which is first translated in both x- and y-direction over 50 points followed by a counter clockwise rotation round a standard origin over 20 degrees. The data set **europe2_x3** contains three times the objects from the set **europe2**. Each additional set is translated in a certain direction. Thus, set **europe2_x4** contains $4 \times 408 = 1632$ different objects.

6.2 Approximation Quality

The approximation quality of several filters has been calculated for each of the five real world data sets (see Table 2). The convex hull is the best fitting approximation for an object. Results for filters like MBB-45BOX-CH have not been shown because their approximation quality is determined by the final filter in the filter sequence (here CH). Since, no procedure was implemented that determines the intersection of a rotated range and a circle, we did not determine

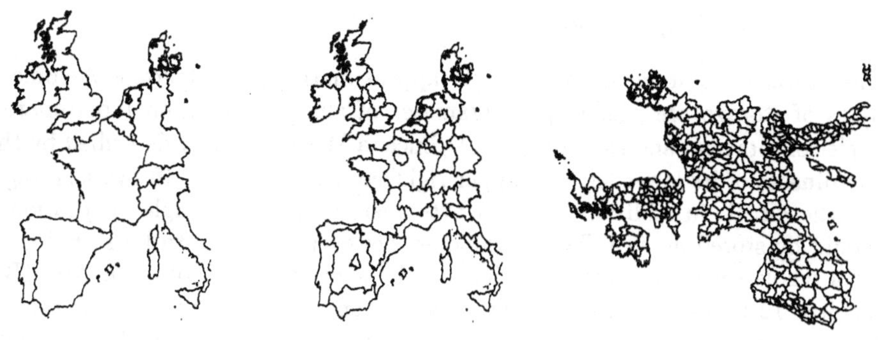

Fig. 4. Several samples of real world test data sets. (From left to right: **europe1**, **europe2**, **europe4_r70**).

the approximation quality of, for example, the filter 30RxR-MBC. Note that approximation quality is a measure which is almost independent of the data it is derived from.

Table 2 also shows that a better approximation quality is obtained by just adding extra gRxRs to a filter sequence. In fact, when more and more gRxRs are added, such a filter will eventually have the same approximation quality as a convex hull filter. A proof is straightforward and based on the definition of both a convex hull and a gRxR as an area bounded by a set of half-spaces. However, the benefit gained from adding an extra gRxR filter will become smaller and smaller.

Filter	europe0	europe1	europe2	europe3	europe4
MBC	336	332	320	299	276
MBB	227	226	222	214	207
45-135RxR (=45BOX)	232	230	227	220	212
10-70-130RxR	180	179	177	174	170
MBB-45BOX	165	164	163	160	157
20-92-164-236-308RxR	155	155	154	152	149
5-45-85-125-165-205-245-285-325RxR	143	143	142	141	139
CH	129	129	129	129	129

Table 2. Approximation quality of several filters shown for various real world data sets. The numbers are percentages: the object approximated is 100%.

6.3 Storage Requirements

The storage requirement for a single approximation is as follows. Assume 4 bytes of storage are needed per parameter of an approximation (coordinates, angles of rotation, and radii of circles). Since, a MBB is usually described by the coordinates of its lower-left and upper-right corner, it requires 16 bytes storage. For the gRxR, in addition to the 8 bytes per x-range, the angle of rotation g should be stored as well. This parameter, however, only has to be stored once for a whole set of x-ranges each having the same angle of rotation. An MBC requires 12 bytes of storage; 8 bytes for its center, and 4 bytes for its radius. For a convex hull the storage required is much higher, since a long list of points must be stored.

Using extra filters in a sequence increases the storage requirements for approximations, however, compared to the storage required for the objects themselves, it is still very little.

6.4 Reduction in Costly Spatial Operations

We performed various intersection tests of real world data combined with other real world data sets. Typical results of these tests are shown in Tables 3 and 4 for intersection of **europe4_t10** and several versions of map **europe2**.

Filter	europe2	europe2_x2	europe2_x3	europe2_x4
none	330480	660960	991440	1321920
10RxR	11983	22010	30408	39562
MBC	1895	2639	3581	4155
30RxR-MBC	1736	2365	3265	3743
0-90RxR (=MBB)	1578	2157	2952	3430
MBB-MBC	1502	2059	2803	3252
10-70-130RxR	1417	1918	2592	3024
MBB-45BOX	1360	1829	2468	2884
20-92-164-236-308RxR	1305	1757	2368	2766
5-45-85-125-165-205-245-285-325RxR	1233	1663	2256	2635
MBB-CH	1189	1595	2145	2500
minimum	1071	1417	1904	2228

Table 3. Result of using (multiple) filters on number of remaining candidate pairs. Intersection of map **europe4_t10** with several versions of map **europe2**. The numbers are calls to the actual intersection function on a pair of spatial objects.

Table 3 gives the number of calls to the actual intersection operation on a pair of spatial objects. Both Table 3 and Figure 5 give an impression of the reduction of candidate pairs. They show that each filter has its own precision; note, e.g., that the minimum bounding box (MBB) filter reduces the number of candidate pairs more than a single 10RxR filter, which was to be expected.

Results also show that a sequence of filters may indeed reduce the number of candidate pairs more than a single filter. For instance, in case of the intersection of data sets **europe4_t10** and **europe2_x4**, the filter MBB-45BOX reduces the number of calls to the spatial operation from 1321920 to 2884, whereas the MBB-filter by itself reduces it to 3430 (see the last column of Table 3). Using more filters is no guarantee for an extra reduction in the number of calls to the actual spatial operation; it very much depends on the approximation the filter is based on. E.g., there is hardly any reduction at all when an extra MBC filter is used after the filters MBB, and 45BOX.

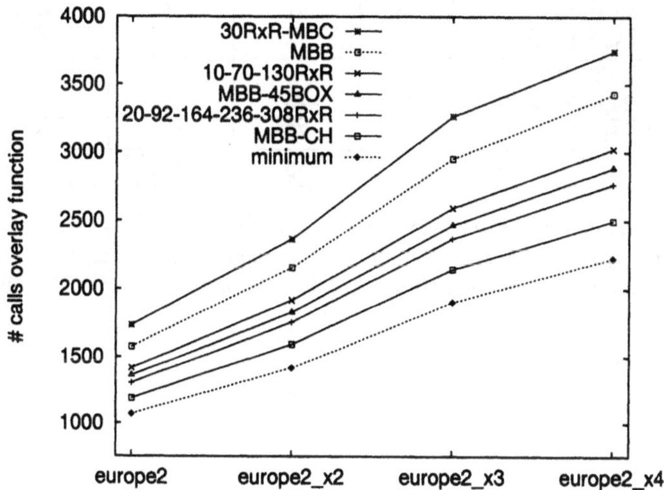

Fig. 5. Reduction of candidate pairs for the intersection of europe4_t10 and the four versions of map europe2.

We also counted all calls of the actual intersection operation which delivered at least one result (calls that were not a false hit). See the last row of Table 3. Of course, this number is exactly equal to the minimal number of candidate pairs which must always pass each filter in a sequence. Using convex hulls as approximations in filters gives almost optimal reduction, at least for the data sets we used. Using a sequence of nine gRxR-based filters comes close to using convex hulls.

Table 4 gives the CPU-time as needed by the actual intersection operation. Each figure is given as a percentage of the intersection time needed when only the MBB filter is used. The numbers for the MBB filter are therefore set at 100%. Table 4 shows the positive effect of our filter technique on the CPU-time of the intersection operation. We see that we can gain about 30% when a convex hull (CH) filter is used in the filter sequence (see the last row but one in Table 4). The x-range based filter sequence in the 20-92-164-236-308RxR version is able to gain about 20% in CPU-time. The last row of Table 4 shows the minimum CPU-time required to calculate the intersection of the pairs given in the corresponding last row of Table 3.

Filter	**europe2**	**europe2_x2**	**europe2_x3**	**europe2_x4**
MBC	123	127	125	124
30RxR-MBC	110	109	107	108
0-90RxR (=MBB)	100	100	100	100
MBB-MBC	95	95	94	94
10-70-130RxR	89	87	85	86
MBB-45BOX	86	81	80	81
20-92-164-236-308RxR	81	78	77	78
5-45-85-125-165-205-245-285-305RxR	76	73	71	73
MBB-CH	73	70	69	68
minimum	64	59	59	58

Table 4. Result of using filter sequences on CPU-time of intersection operation. Intersection of map **europe4_t10** with the four versions of map **europe2**. The numbers are percentages: the intersection time needed while only using an MBB filter is set at 100%.

6.5 Construction cost of Approximations

One may wonder: why not use precisely one filter, based on a convex hull (CH) approximation, which has after all the best approximation quality. This question is answered by showing the cost for constructing approximations. For n-way joins it is necessary to build approximations on the intermediate result, therefore, the cost for constructing approximations should be low.

Computing an MBB takes time $O(n)$, where n is the number of coordinates of the spatial object approximated. All coordinates of the spatial object must be traversed to find the minimum and maximum value of both its x- and y-coordinates. Only low-cost comparisons are needed for such an algorithm. The time complexity of an algorithm for constructing a gRxR approximation is also $O(n)$. Here n is again the number of coordinates of the spatial object approximated. First, for each coordinate pair (X, Y) of the spatial object, a g-degrees rotated x-coordinate X' is calculated as follows: $X' = X * cos(g) + Y * sin(g)$. Hereafter, the minimum and maximum value of the n values for X' are determined. Both $cos(g)$ and $sin(g)$ can be viewed as constants which have to be calculated only once.

The algorithm used for constructing the convex hull of a spatial object takes expected time $O(n \log n)$. Again n is the number of coordinates of the spatial object. The time complexity of this algorithm is not better than the time taken by both algorithms described above. Moreover, the constant associated with the complexity $O(n \log n)$ for computing the convex hull, is much larger. A description of the convex hull algorithm is out of the scope of this paper. Both [1] and [17] give detailed information on algorithms which construct convex hulls.

Table 5 presents the time needed for constructing several approximations. For the union of the five real world data sets, several approximations were constructed. From the measurements shown it is obvious that building approximations based on a convex hull is far too expensive.

Approximation	MBB	30RxR	CH	MBC
Construction time	0.27	0.29	930.4	958.8

Table 5. Construction time in seconds of several approximations for all objects in the union of the five maps.

The cost for constructing approximations of 9 or 10 different gRxR filters is still very much lower than the cost for constructing an approximation based on first constructing a convex hull. In [3] it was proposed to use a MBB-5C filter. This proposal is turned down, since the algorithm for constructing the n-corner is also based on the convex hull. Due to their high construction costs, the convex hull, the minimum bounding circle, the minimum bounding ellipse, and the n-corner should not be constructed for intermediate results. Especially, for intermediate results, it is preferred to use a filter sequence of several gRxRs, which approximates a convex hull and can be constructed much cheaper.

6.6 Orientation Insensitivity

To examine the sensitivity of the multi-filter based join method to rotation of the data a 2-way spatial join of the maps `europe4_t50` and `europe2` was calculated using various filter sequences. Each filter sequence contained one to five gRxR filters. No other single filters were used, since, they do not affect the orientation (in)sensitivity of this join method. Instead of rotating the data we added a constant angle of rotation k to the parameters g in the filter sequences. This has the same effect as rotating the data. The result, see Table 6 for a summary, was examined again with the number of remaining candidate pairs. This criterion will guide us in choosing the best angles of rotation g for the rotated x-ranges part of a filter sequence.

In Table 6, results show that for a filter sequence of size two, such as the kBOX, different values of k result in different sizes of the remaining candidate set. For example, the 0BOX reduces the candidate set to 1105 pairs, while the 50BOX is only capable of reducing it to 1220 pairs. A join method based on the kBOX alone is thus orientation sensitive. There is still too much variation among the reduction capabilities of the various kBOX filters.

k	0	10	20	30	40	50	60	70	80
$(0+k)$-$(90+k)$RxR (=kBOX)	1105	1154	1204	1205	1206	1220	1183	1148	1118

k	0	18	36	54
$(0+k)$-$(72+k)$-$(144+k)$- $(206+k)$-$(288+k)$RxR	906	907	906	906

Table 6. Result of adding a constant k to the degrees of rotation in a gRxR based filter sequence on the number of remaining candidates. Intersection of map **europe_2** with **europe4_t50**. The numbers are calls to the intersection function on a pair of objects.

We then increased the number of gRxRs in the filter sequence. As can be seen in Table 6, for a filter sequence of size five, the variation almost disappeared. Therefore, at least five orientations are required to make the join method orientation insensitive.

A very good gRxR based filter sequence is now constructed as follows. Determine the number of different single gRxRs to be used (at least five). How many exactly, depends on how well the convex hull needs to be approximated, and on the available storage. Spred these in a regular way over the possible range of orientations (0–360 degrees). Choose as the first filter the one which is expected to be the most selective.

7 Combination of Filter and Spatial Index Techniques

In our experiments a nested-loop approach was used for the matching process needed by the first filter. An initial set of candidate pairs is found. This nested-loop approach had the disadvantage that all approximations of the two join operands must be compared with each other. This number of comparisons can significantly be reduced by using a spatial index build for the same approximation.

The most well-known spatial index based on bounding approximations is the R-tree [8]. An R-tree is a hierarchical data structure. A non-leaf node of the R-tree contains entries of the form `(MBB,cp)`, where `cp` points to a child node, and `MBB` is the minimum bounding rectangle of all objects contained in the child node. A leaf node contains entries of the form `(MBB,oid)` where `oid` refers to a spatial object in the database, and `MBB` is the minimum bounding box of that object. In our view, the R-tree is build to improve on the MBB filter step.

As we have seen, the MBB filter is a filter sequence of two g degrees rotated ranges; 0RxR-0RyR. Thus, actually, the non-leaf nodes of the R-tree contain entries of the form (0RxR,0RyR,cp), and the leaf nodes contain entries of the form (0RxR,0RyR,oid). It therefore improves on not one but on two filter steps. Extending this to gRxR-based filter sequences of arbitrary size we get the following definition. A non-leaf node has entries of the form (g_1RxR,g_2RxR,...,g_pRxR,cp), and a leaf node contains entries of the form (g_1RxR,g_2RxR,...,g_pRxR,oid). In fact, this tree is called the P-tree and has been described in [9]. Building and maintaining these P-trees requires almost the same effort as needed for R-trees.

The P-tree as defined above, is an index that improves on p filter steps. To support a gRxR-based filter sequence of size $p+q$, the approximations of the q additional filters can be stored with the p approximations in the leaf-nodes. The two parameters p and q are very important. They determine the size of the tree and the space it will occupy on the disk. Without having done any experiments with the P-tree yet, we propose to set p and q equal to 3 or 4.

8 Conclusions

In this paper, we have shown that using a filter sequence can greatly reduce the number of calls to expensive spatial operations. This is especially important for n-way spatial joins, which frequently occur in Geographical Information Systems. Each filter in a sequence reduces the set of candidates for which the expensive spatial operation must be computed. In the context of solving n-way spatial joins, we have described several criteria for comparing filter sequences.

Test operations of a filter should be very simple in comparison to the spatial operation they replace. To test, for example, the intersection of two approximations should be much cheaper than to calculate the spatial intersection of the objects approximated.

Filters with an inexpensive associated test operation should precede filters with an expensive associated test operation. For example, testing intersection of two minimum bounding boxes (MBB) is cheaper than testing two convex hulls (CH). The cost of test operations for the filter sequence MBB-CH is thus much lower than those for CH-MBB.

For a filter sequence, we have shown that the intersection of approximations of successive filters, should fit the objects increasingly narrow, to avoid that the filters at the end of the sequence have no effect at all. The filter sequence MBB-CH is thus preferred to the sequence CH-MBB.

Approximations, as needed by the test operation of a filter, should be available, or it should be cheap to calculate them on the spot. This is very important when spatial joins of intermediate results must be calculated. Calculating convex hulls, or even bounding circles and n-corners, during the query evaluation process is prohibitively expensive. It is much better to use several inexpensive approximations on intermediate results, instead of one precisely fitting but costly to compute approximation.

We have described such an approximation called the g-degrees rotated x-range (gRxR). Constructing gRxRs as well as testing intersection of two gRxRs is very cheap. A combination of several gRxRs, each having another angle of rotation, is shown to be an approximation for the convex hull of a spatial object. This means that when using several gRxR-based filter steps, a reduction of the candidate set can be obtained, which is almost as good as the reduction of a convex hull based filter. Using at least five gRxR-based filters, also makes the spatial join method orientation insensitive. A method for solving n-way spatial joins should be based on these gRxR-based multi-step filter ideas.

We have described how several gRxR based filter steps can be improved by the P-tree; a spatial index which is as simple as, however, not as well-known as the R-tree.

In addition to the filter techniques described we will, in the near future, examine spatial index techniques. We are currently extending our prototype implementation with the P-tree and will start experimenting with n-way joins. Because disk accesses for objects play a major role in technical applications (due to their large size), we are currently refining our cost model, to better take into account disk-I/O.

9 Acknowledgements

We thank Thomas Brinkhoff at the Department of Computer Science of the Ludwig-Maximilians-Universität Munich for making the geometric data sets of Europe available to us.

References

1. Bradford, C.B., Dobkin, D.P., Huhdanpaa, H.: The Quickhull Algorithm for Convex Hull. Technical Report GCG53, The Geometry Center, University of Minnesota, Minneapolis, USA, July 30, 1993.
2. Brinkhoff, T., Kriegel, H-.P., Seeger, B.: Efficient Processing of Spatial Joins Using R-trees. *Proc. ACM SIGMOD Int. Conf. on Management of Data*, Washington, D.C., USA, 1993.
3. Brinkhoff, T., Kriegel, H-.P., Schneider, R.: Comparison of Approximations of Complex Objects Used for Approximation-based Query Processing in Spatial Database Systems. *Proc. 9th Int. Conf. on Data Engineering*, Vienna, Austria, 1993.
4. Brinkhoff, T., Kriegel, H-.P., Schneider, R., Seeger, B.: Multi-Step Processing of Spatial Joins. *Proc. ACM SIGMOD Int. Conf. on Management of Data*, Minneapolis, Minnesota, USA, 1994.
5. Ceri, S., Pelagatti, G.: Distributed databases. McGrawHill, 1984.
6. Dori, D., Ben–Bassat, M.: Circumscribing a convex polygon by a polygon of fewer sides with minimal area addition. *Computer Vision, Graphics and Image Processing*, 24(1983):131–159, 1983.
7. Frank, A.U.: Properties of Geographic Data: Requirements for Spatial Access Methods. *Proc. Advances in Spatial Databases*, SSD'91, Zürich, Switzerland, 1991.

8. Guttman, A.: R-trees: A dynamic index structure for spatial searching. *Proc. ACM SIGMOD Int. Conf. on Management of Data*, Boston, Massachusetts, USA, 1984.
9. Jagadish, H.V.: Spatial search with Polyhedra. *Proc. 6th. Int Conf. on Data Engineering*, Los Angeles, California, USA, 1990.
10. Jarke, M., Koch, J.: Query optimization in database systems. *Computing Surveys*, 16(2):111–152, June 1984.
11. Laurini, R., Thompson, D.: Fundamentals of spatial information systems. Academic Press, 1992.
12. Näher, S.: LEDA User Manual, version 3.0. Max-Planck-Institut für Informatik, Saarbrücken, Germany.
13. Lo, M.L., Ravishankar C.V.: Spatial joins using seeded trees. *Proc. ACM SIGMOD Int. Conf. on Management of Data*, Mineapolis, Minnesota, USA, 1994.
14. Lu, H., Ooi, B.: Spatial Indexing: Past and Future. *Data Engineering Bulletin*, 16(3):16–21, Sept 1993.
15. Orenstein, J.A.: Redundancy in spatial databases. *Proc. ACM SIGMOD Int. Conf. on Management of Data*, Portland, Oregon, USA, 1989.
16. Oosterom, van P., Claassen, E.: Orientation insensitive indexing methods for Geometric Objects, *4th Int. Symp. on Spatial Data Handling*, Zürich, Switzerland, July 1990.
17. Preparata, F.P., Shamos, M.I.: Computational Geometry; an introduction. Springer–Verlag, 1985.
18. Samet, H.: Spatial Data Structures. To appear in *Database Challenges in the 1990's*, W. Kim, ed., Addison Wesley/ACM Press, Reading, MA, USA, 1994.
19. Seeger, B., Kriegel, H.-P.: Techniques for Design and Implementation of Efficient Spatial Access Methods. *Proc. 14th Int. Conf. on Very Large Data Bases*, Los Angeles, California, USA, 1988.
20. Skyum, S.: A simple algorithm for computing the smallest enclosing circle. *Information Processing Letters*, 37(1991):121–125, February 1991.
21. Welzl, E.: Smallest Enclosing Disks (Balls and Ellipsoids). Paper B91-09, Freie University of Berlin, 1991.

An Efficient Transient Versioning Method

Sreenivas Gukal, Edward Omiecinski, Umakishore Ramachandran

College of Computing, Georgia Institute of Technology, Atlanta GA 30332, USA

Abstract. Transient versioning methods, where prior versions are maintained temporarily, are proposed to execute long-running queries without affecting concurrent transactions. However, transactions in these methods do not exploit the prior versions. This paper presents a transient-versioning method, called *Dynamic Versioning*, which uses the transient versions to not only support queries but also increase concurrency among transactions. Data conflicts due to incompatible requests are resolved by dynamically creating dependence orders among the requesting transactions and queries. These orders help precisely identify the prior versions that have to be kept for the queries. Since only the required versions are stored, the storage overhead for the transient versions is reduced to the minimum possible. We present the results of simulation experiments that show that our method provides high transaction concurrency and supports queries almost as efficiently as the other transient-versioning methods, while incurring only a fraction of the storage overhead.

1 Introduction

One of the important concurrency control problems in high-performance database systems [9] is to prevent the execution of queries (read-only transactions) from affecting concurrent update transactions. Long-running queries lock the data items for a long time and may starve transactions trying to update the same data items. Transient-versioning algorithms have been proposed as an elegant way to support queries without affecting transactions [14]. These algorithms maintain prior versions of updated data items. Queries can read the prior versions, while transactions update the current version. The prior versions are transient; they are removed when the queries no longer need them.

The transient-versioning algorithms proposed (eg., [3, 8, 6, 13]) use the prior versions only to support queries. Transactions see only the current version and execute based on a single-version concurrency control scheme. In this paper, we present a record-level transient-versioning method, called *Dynamic Versioning* (DV), that

- uses the prior versions to increase transaction concurrency besides supporting queries
- minimizes the storage overhead by keeping only the required prior versions.

In the dynamic versioning approach, a conflict between two incompatible requests for a data item is dynamically resolved by creating a dependence order between the requesting transactions. The dynamic ordering of the transactions avoids blocking due to read-write conflicts and hence increases concurrency. A dependence graph stores the dependence orders among the transactions. The dependence graph is kept acyclic to ensure serializability and provide transactions (and queries) a single version view of the database. The dynamic ordering also positions the queries in the transaction serialization order dynamically based on data conflicts. This flexibility enables DV to support queries using a minimum number of prior versions.

We present simulation experiments which compare the performance and overheads of the dynamic versioning method with those of two recent transient versioning methods [6, 13]. The results show that DV reduces the number of transactions blocked due to data contention by 60% to 90%. The higher concurrency results in better resource utilization and higher transaction throughput. DV also supports queries almost as efficiently as the other two methods while reducing the storage overhead by 75% or more.

The rest of the paper is organized as follows. A review of the related work is presented in Sect. 2. Section 3 outlines the dynamic versioning method. We also describe three techniques to efficiently support queries. Section 4 presents the results of the simulation studies which evaluate the performance of dynamic versioning. Here we determine how the data contention and resource contention affect the performance metrics. The last section summarizes our work.

2 Related Work

Multiversioning algorithms have been in existence for more than 15 years. Since it is beyond the scope of this paper to refer to all of them, we mention only the relevant work. A two-version two-phase locking algorithm was proposed by Bayer et al. [4]. The algorithm is based on the observation that in a shadowing environment all updates are done only to the shadow pages. Since the prior copies of the pages are maintained for recovery purposes, this algorithm proposes that the readers be allowed to read the "before" values.

Two-version and multi-version two-phase locking methods are also presented in [5]. The two-version method is similar to that in [4]. The multi-version algorithm assumes that for a data item there is a single committed version used by readers and several uncommitted versions simultaneously being updated by the writers. Allowing multiple writers makes the task of maintaining the dependence graph NP-complete [12]. In addition, keeping only a single committed version blocks the transactions from committing if a query is using the committed version.

Several other approaches for supporting transient versioning have been proposed [15, 3, 13, 8, 6, 7]. Multiversion timestamp ordering was introduced by [15]. Although read requests are never rejected, they may be blocked and may cause update transactions to abort. Another method that uses prior versions to support queries is described in [8]. This method employs page-level versioning and locking. Prior versions are stored in a version pool. Bober and Carey [6] improve this method to support record-level versioning. Queries are synchronized using multi-version timestamp ordering. Since timestamp ordering is used, the versions created after a query is started are maintained until the query completes. A fixed space on each data page is reserved for caching versions. The same method is extended in [7] to support queries of weaker consistencies more efficiently. The method presented in [3] assigns a unique version number to all the versions created by a committed transaction. Each query is provided with a version number which determines which prior versions the query can access. This method is generalized to version periods by Mohan et al. [13]. In this method, queries read the stable version of the database of the previous version period, while update transactions execute in the current version period. Each data item has one stable version in the previous version period and may have at most two additional versions in the current version period. The system periodically switches to a new version period and purges the prior versions.

Previous transient-versioning algorithms assign version numbers to the prior versions. On initiation a query is assigned the version number(s) of the prior versions which it can access. In other words, the position of the query in the transaction serialization order is fixed as soon as the query is started. Since the set of items which the query accesses is not known a priori, this fixed order requires maintaining the prior versions of all the records with the version numbers assigned to the query. Storing all the prior versions results in a huge storage overhead.

The two recent methods described above [6, 13] are good representatives of all the transient versioning methods. They are based on earlier methods but are more efficient and flexible. We consider these two methods as benchmarks to evaluate the performance and overheads of the dynamic versioning method.

3 Dynamic Versioning

The dynamic versioning method *dynamically* orders the transactions based on data conflicts to avoid blocking where possible. Our method builds on the transient versioning ideas proposed by Bober and Carey [6] and Mohan et al. [13], while avoiding the storage overhead inherent in those two schemes. The following subsections describe the design of the dynamic versioning method. A small example sketched in Fig. 1 is used to illustrate various concepts in the following discussion. The example shows four transactions (T_1, T_2, T_3 and T_4) accessing three data items (A, B and C). T_2 created versions A^1 and B^1 and committed. Transactions (T_1, T_3 and T_4) are still active.

3.1 Lock Modes and Dependence Graph

A data conflict between two transactions is resolved by dynamically creating a dependence order (successor / predecessor) between them. In contrast to two-phase locking where the dependence order is the same as the order in which the requests are made, the dynamic versioning method selects the dependence order that avoids blocking if possible.

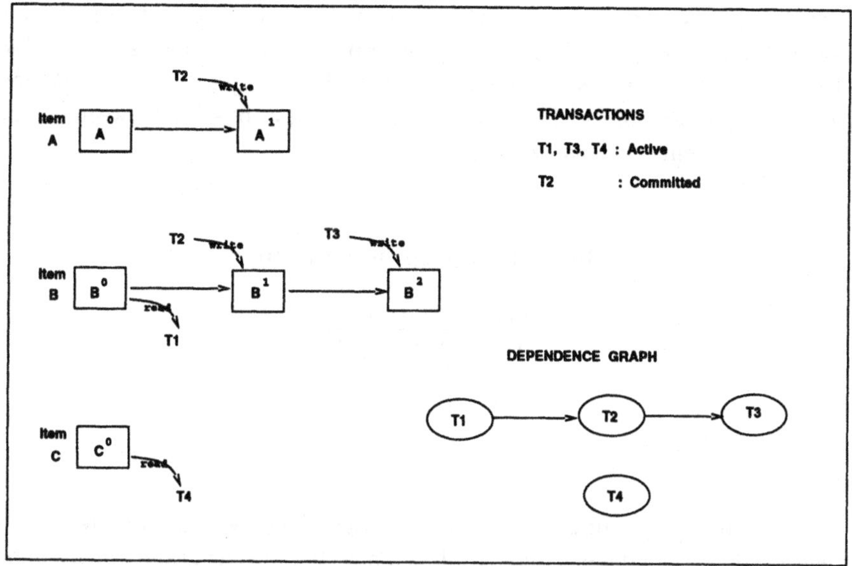

Fig. 1. Versions and the dependence graph

The dynamic versioning method allows each record to have several committed versions and at most one uncommitted version. A conflict between a read request and a write request may be resolved without resorting to blocking, by making the transaction requesting the read, a predecessor to the transaction requesting the write. The reader can access one of the earlier committed versions of the data item, while the writer updates a new version. However, a conflict between two write requests will always result in blocking one of the requests until the other is done.

The *dynamic ordering* of the transactions increases transaction concurrency by allowing several readers and one writer to simultaneously access the same data item. For example, consider Fig. 1. If transaction T_3 requests a write lock for item C, the request can be granted without blocking by making T_3 a successor of transaction T_4. On the other hand, if transaction T_4 requests a read lock for item B, T_4 can be made a predecessor of T_3 and allowed to read the prior version B^1 without waiting.

The lock modes and the lock compatibility matrix that allows the desired combinations are given in Table 1. Here, (+) indicates that the request can be granted immediately and (–) indicates that the requesting transaction has to wait due to incompatible lock modes. We also have (±) to denote conditional compatibility, where the requesting transaction is granted read access without blocking only if it can be made a predecessor to the transaction that has the write lock.

The dynamic ordering also provides the flexibility to never reject a read request. Since multiple versions are maintained, the read request can always be allowed to access the version that satisfies the dependence orders created previously. However, a write request may cause the requesting transaction to be aborted. For example, in Fig. 1, suppose transaction T_1 requests a write-lock on item A. The lock modes (for A) are compatible. Yet, granting the write-lock makes T_1 a successor of T_2. This violates the order established between T_1 and T_2 for item B. Hence T_1 has to be aborted.

Table 1. Lock compatibility matrix

Requested Lock	Current Lock *read*	*write*
read	+	±
write	+	−

The dynamic versioning method uses a dependence graph to store the dependence orders. The dependence graph is a directed acyclic graph, where nodes represent transactions and edges denote the successor/predecessor orders among transactions. Figure 1 shows a dependence graph resulting from resolving conflicts among the four transactions. A topological sort of the acyclic dependence graph generates a serializable order of the transactions.

3.2 Implementation Issues

Maintaining Versions.

All the versions of a data item are placed in the same page as the data item whenever possible. Usually a database page contains some free space to accommodate growing tuples or for inserting new tuples [10]. This space in a data page may be used for holding the transient versions of the records on the same data page. Since the number of versions maintained is small, in most cases this space should be sufficient. To reduce the space requirements, only the incremental difference of a version may be stored.

There are two alternatives in case the free space in a data page is not sufficient. If records can be moved from one page to another, data pages with insufficient free space may be split. Under this method, only those pages that contain frequently updated data records end up with additional free space. Alternatively, a set of overflow pages may be used to hold the transient versions that do not fit in the database pages.

On the data page, all the versions of a data item are linked in the order of creation. Each version also stores the identifier of the transaction that created it. This identifier helps both in retrieving the correct versions and in garbage collection.

Garbage Collection.

A prior version of a data item may be replaced by a later, committed version, as soon as there is no possibility of any other transaction (or query) accessing the earlier version. For example, in Fig. 1, the earlier versions (A^0 and B^0) may be deleted as soon as T_1 (a predecessor of T_2) commits.

Nodes for committed transactions with no predecessors are deleted from the dependence graph, along with all incident edges. Versions created by such transactions (committed, with no predecessors) can replace prior versions for the corresponding data items. The overhead for garbage collection can be reduced using a "lazy" approach: an unnecessary prior version in a page is deleted only when a transaction tries to create a new version in the same page. Such an approach (similar to the method followed in [6]) is inexpensive since creating the new version will in any case dirty the page.

3.3 Supporting Queries

One of the important problems in concurrency control [9] is to prevent the execution of read-only transactions (referred as *queries*) from affecting concurrent update transactions (i.e., transactions which also update some data items, called *transactions* in the rest of the paper). One solution is to violate serializability and run the queries at degree 2 or degree 1 isolation [11]. The problem becomes interesting if the queries wish to see a transaction consistent database. We consider here only the problem of running queries at degree 3 isolation, which requires repeatable reads.

The single-version, two-phase locking method results in poor performance of transactions in the presence of long-running queries. Queries hold read-locks to ensure serializability. Update transactions, which conflict with the queries, could be blocked for inordinate periods. The ensuing waiting causes unacceptable transaction response times, especially in an online transaction processing (OLTP) environment. The dynamic versioning method maintains multiple committed versions. Hence, queries can read the earlier versions without blocking any transactions. We propose three different techniques for executing queries efficiently in DV.

First Technique. Queries can be run the same way as transactions. Queries acquire read-locks before reading any data item. The read-locks ensure degree 3 isolation. The only requirement is that if a query conflicts with an uncommitted transaction for a data item, the query should be made a predecessor of that transaction and allowed to read an earlier committed version of the data item. This design precludes a query ever being involved in a cycle, either with transactions or other queries, which in turn leads to three important properties:

- a request for a read-lock by a query is never blocked,
- queries are never rolled back and
- no transaction is ever aborted because of a query.

These three properties help avoid any interaction between queries and transactions. The disadvantage of this technique is that the queries incur the overhead of acquiring and releasing locks.

Second Technique. Queries can also be executed in DV without incurring the lock overheads. Read locks in the first technique are used only to create dependence orders with conflicting transactions. Alternatively, all uncommitted transactions can be considered as sources of potential conflicts and a query can be made a predecessor to all such transactions. This ensures that the committed state of the database at the start of the query is maintained until the query completes. This technique is specially suitable for long-running queries which access most of the database. Since all uncommitted transactions are made successors of the query, the disadvantage of this technique is that the number of prior versions maintained here is much more than that in the first technique. The idea in the second DV technique is similar to multi-version timestamp ordering (same as the method by Bober and Carey [6]).

Third Technique. The large space overhead in the second technique can be reduced in some cases, without acquiring locks. The reason for the large space overhead in the second technique is that a query is made a predecessor of *all* uncommitted transactions. If it were possible to identify a subset of the transactions that are likely to update some records in the part of the database accessed by the query, then only the transactions in that subset can be made successors of the query. This avoids the necessity of maintaining prior versions created by the other transactions in other parts of the database. For example, consider a database containing a million records. Suppose a long-running query accesses the first 100,000 records. Though the query accesses only 10% of the database, the second technique requires maintaining all the prior versions created even in the remaining 90% of the database until the query completes. This unnecessary overhead can be avoided if only the transactions, which are likely to update any of the first 100,000 records, are made successors of the query. This technique has all the advantages of the second technique, but requires much lower storage space.

The first technique is applicable for queries which access only a small part of the database. The second technique is for long-running queries, accessing a significant portion of the database. The third technique is best suited for long-running queries accessing small and well-defined parts of the database.

4 Simulation Experiments and Results

The simulation experiments evaluate the performance of the DV method compared to the methods of Bober and Carey [6] and Mohan et al. [13], the two recent transient versioning methods described in Sect. 2. This section reports the results of four simulation experiments. The first three experiments compare the three methods in an environment containing only transactions. The fourth experiment evaluates the performance and overheads by considering a mix of queries and transactions. We first present the simulation model and the parameters considered.

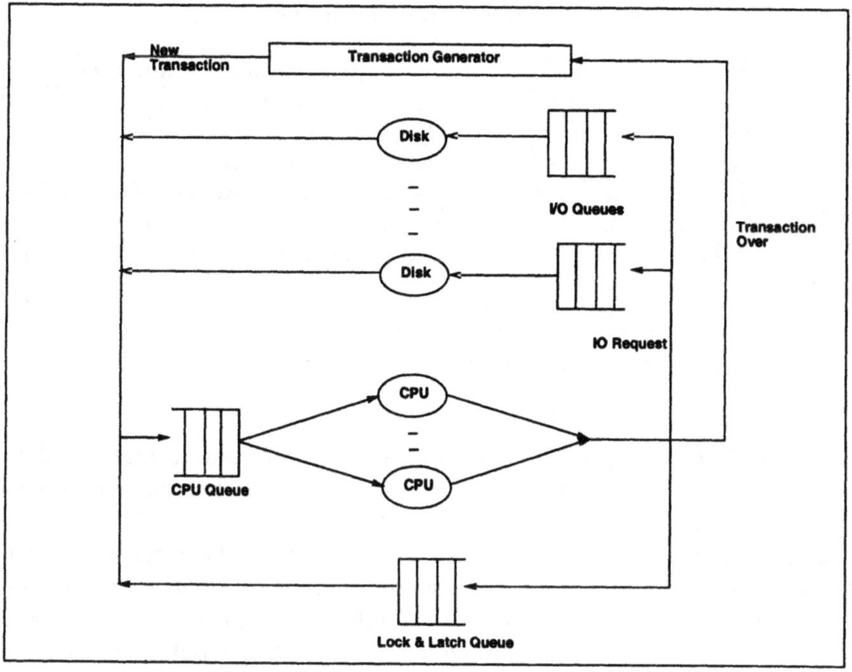

Fig. 2. Closed queuing simulation model

4.1 Simulation Model

The simulation model is shown in Fig. 2. The database is modeled as having a number of data pages, each page containing a fixed number of records. Transactions contain a series of record references. Each reference is made up of a record identifier, the type of access and the amount of operation time the transaction spends in the CPU after accessing the record. The operation time models the time for accessing the data item, performing any computations using the fetched value and determining the new value for the data item in case of updates.

Resources are modeled in terms of resource units (similar to [1, 2]). Each resource unit contains one CPU and two disks. Data pages are uniformly distributed among all the available disks.

Transactions from a common CPU queue are assigned to an available CPU. For each data reference, a transaction first acquires the appropriate lock on the data item and a latch on the corresponding data page. If either one is unavailable, the transaction is blocked. After acquiring both the lock and the latch, the transaction checks if the data page already exists in the main memory. If not, the transaction joins the appropriate I/O queue. Upon I/O completion, the transaction acquires a CPU again. The transaction accesses the record, holds the CPU for the amount of operation time specified in the reference, updates the record if needed and releases the page latch. A transaction releases all the locks it acquired at the commit time. The number of active transactions in the system

Table 2. Simulation parameters

Database Parameters		**Transaction Parameters**	
Data Base Size (in records)	150,000	References per Transaction	
Records per Data Page	10	Percentage of updates	
Page Fill Factor	83%	Data Access Pattern	80-20
Resource Parameters		Lock Acquisition (Release) Time	500 μs
Number of Resource Units†		Latch Acquisition (Release) Time	50μs
Disk Access Time	20ms	Record Modification Time	500 μs
Main Memory Size	2000 pages	Operation Time	5ms
Multi-programming Level	100		

†1 resource unit = 1 CPU & 2 disks

is determined by the degree of multiprogramming. A closed queuing simulation model is followed. When a transaction is completed, the transaction generator creates a new transaction.

Each simulation run uses a set of 1000 transactions. The same sets of transactions are used for all methods. For each set of input parameters, the system is simulated on a number of transaction sets until the 90% confidence interval for the transaction throughput is within a few percent. The simulator is written in CSIM [16], a process-oriented simulation package.

4.2 Simulation Parameters

All the parameters relevant to the simulation are summarized in Table 2. The table also contains the parameter values that remain the same in all the simulations.

We consider a database size that models an average-sized actual database. Each data page contains ten records and free space to accommodate at most two prior versions. Any versions that do not fit in a data page are stored in overflow pages. The times for lock and latch operations and the disk access are constant for all requests. The record modification time and the operation time are exponentially distributed. We assume an 80-20 reference pattern (i.e., 80% of the references go to 20% of the database), since uniform reference pattern does not model hot-spot pages.

4.3 Transaction Concurrency

The methods by [6] and [13] use the standard single version two-phase locking method for concurrency control for transactions. The transactions in these methods do not see the prior versions and are not affected by them. To make the simulations simpler, we consider the single-version two-phase locking method (denoted as 2PL) for comparing transaction concurrency in this section.

The performance of a transaction system depends on the extent of both data contention and resource contention. The first two sets of simulations evaluate

Table 3. Variable parameters for the experiments

Expt. 1 - Data contention		**Expt. 2 - Resource contention**	
References per Transaction	50	References per Transaction	50
Percentage of updates	10% to 50%	Percentage of updates	30%
Number of Resource Units	4	Number of Resource Units	1 to 16
Expt. 3 - Transaction mix		**Expt. 4 - Queries**	
Percentage of Short Transactions	90%	Percentage of Transactions	75%
References - Short Transactions	20	References per Transaction	20
Percentage of Long Transactions	10%	Percentage of updates	30%
References - Long Transaction	100	Percentage of Queries	25%
Percentage of updates	30%	References per Query	100
Number of Resource Units	1 to 16	Number of Resource Units	1 to 16

the DV and the 2PL methods by varying the data and resource contention respectively. The third simulation compares the two methods in the presence of a mix of short and long transactions.

Varying Data Contention.

Data contention in a system depends on a number of factors: multiprogramming level, the size of the database, the number of references per transaction and the percentage of updates. We report the results of varying the percentage of updates from 10% to 50%, while keeping the other values constant[1]. Table 3 shows the values used for the variable parameters. Varying each of the other factors (that lead to data contention) resulted in very similar performance differential between DV and 2PL. These results are not presented here due to space constraints.

Figure 3 shows how the average blocking (i.e., average number of transactions blocked waiting for locks) varies with the percentage of updates. The average blocking in either method increases with the percentage of updates. DV has much lower blocking rates than 2PL. The difference in blocking between the two methods initially increases with the percentage of updates. As the number of transactions blocked reaches the multiprogramming level, the difference starts reducing. When a high percentage of the transactions are already blocked, further increase in data contention results in only a slight increase in the blocking. Note that at zero percent (and hundred percent) updates, the average blocking for both methods would be the same.

Figure 4 gives the number of aborts (due to deadlocks) for the two methods. At low percentage of updates, DV has almost the same number of aborts as 2PL. As the percentage of updates increases, DV results in higher number of

[1] We also used a uniform distribution of +30% to −30% for the number of references per transaction. The results are similar to the case when the number of references is constant. We report the results of having constant number of references, because the variance in the transaction response times makes more sense here.

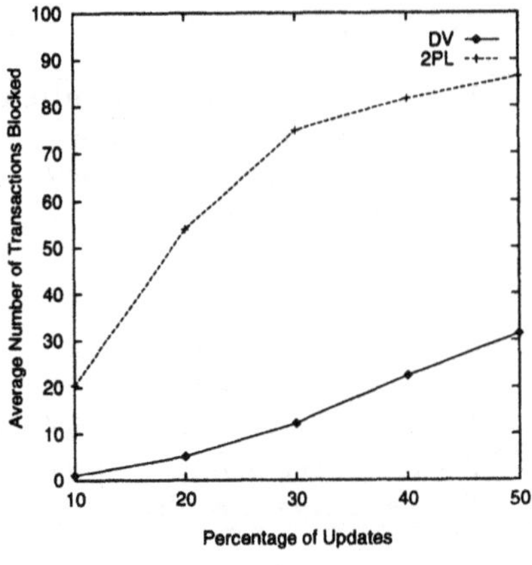

Fig. 3. Blocking rates vs Data contention

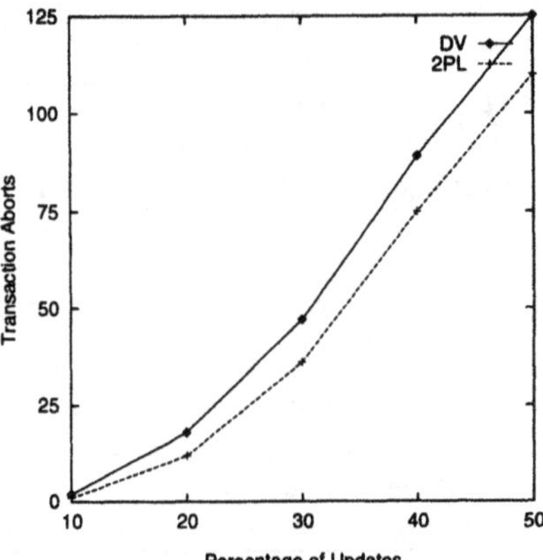

Fig. 4. Aborts vs Data contention

aborts than 2PL. There are two factors which affect the number of aborts in DV as compared to that of 2PL. The latter, being pessimistic, blocks a transaction upon the first read-write, write-read or write-write conflict. DV, on the other hand, tries to resolve the read-write and write-read conflicts, if possible, by dynamically imposing an order on the contending transactions. This sometimes results in avoiding what would be a deadlock in 2PL. For example, suppose transaction T_1 has a w-lock on item A and tries to acquire an r-lock on item B. At the same time transaction T_2, which has a w-lock on B, requests for an r-lock on A. 2PL would abort one of the transactions to maintain serializability. In DV however, it is possible create an order on the two transactions (say T_2 is a successor of T_1). Hence T_1 can read the prior version of B and proceed, while T_2 is blocked. Such a resolution is beneficial if there is very little chance of T_1 and T_2 again entering into a conflict for a different item. If T_1 and T_2 again conflict, one of them may have to be aborted if the earlier order cannot be maintained. Hence at low data contention (which means less chance of repeated conflicts), DV has the same or lower number of aborts than 2PL. At higher data contentions, DV results in more aborts. Note that in an actual system, aborts are rare [10]. In such an environment, DV will have the same or lower number of transaction aborts than 2PL, while reducing the blocking considerably.

Figure 5 presents the transaction throughput for the two methods. As the percentage of updates is increased, the throughput of both the methods reduces. However, the reduction in throughput for DV is much lower than that of 2PL. At 10% updates, DV has almost the same transaction throughput as 2PL. At 50% updates, DV has 22% more transaction throughput than 2PL. Comparing Fig. 5 with Fig. 3 shows that the improvement in the transaction throughput for DV is due to the reduction in blocking. As the percentage of updates is increased beyond 50%, the difference in transaction throughput reduces since DV results in a higher number of aborts.

Smaller blocking rates have an important side-effect; they reduce the variance in the transaction response times. Due to lower blocking rates, the variance in

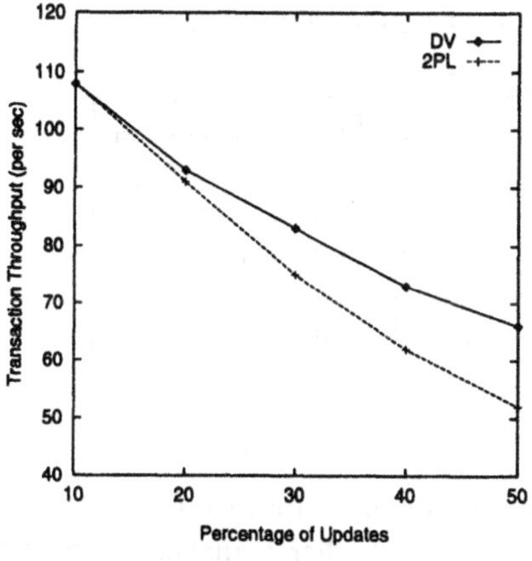

Fig. 5. Throughput vs Data contention

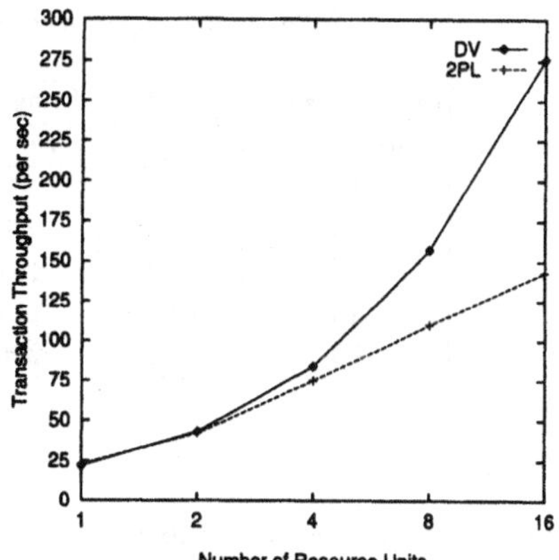

Fig. 6. Throughput vs Res. contention

Table 4. Records with prior versions

Percentage of updates	Number of records with prior versions			Maximum versions (for the entire database)
	1 Version	2 Versions	3 Versions	
10	300	1	0	414
20	772	4	0	1247
30	1342	18	0	2383
40	1728	28	0	2814
50	2143	44	1	3535

DV is much lower than that of 2PL. The reduction in variance is considerable, varying from 85% (for 10% updates) to 70% (for 50% updates).

Tables 4 and 5 summarize the observed number of prior versions. Table 4 lists the average number of records with one, two and three prior versions. The number of records with more than one prior version is very small. There are never more than three prior versions for any record. The last column in Table 4 shows the maximum number of prior versions (for all the records combined) that are stored at any time in the database. The maximum space overhead, even at 50% updates, is about 2% of the database size. Each data page in our simulation contains ten records and has enough free space to accommodate two prior versions. Table 5 gives the number of data pages for which the records in the page have prior versions. Given that there are 15,000 data pages (150,000 records and 10 records per page), the number of pages for which all the records in the page together have more than two prior versions is quite small. At 50% updates, about 7 overflow pages are required to hold the prior versions that do not fit in their respective data pages.

Varying Resource Contention.

In an actual database environment, contention for resources affects the met-

Table 5. Pages whose records have prior versions

Percentage of updates	Number of pages whose records have prior versions				
	1 Version	2 Versions	3 Versions	4 Versions	5 Versions
10	284	8	0	0	0
20	662	53	4	0	0
30	1030	141	18	2	0
40	1239	211	36	4	0
50	1416	296	60	10	1

rics studied in the previous section. Varying data contention, we found that DV has much lower blocking rates than 2PL leading to higher transaction throughput. Here we would like to determine if the lower blocking rates translate into better performance in the presence of resource contention. Table 3 lists the values used for the variable parameters. The resource contention is varied by letting the number of resource units range from 1 to 16. The multiprogramming level used here (100) is such that having only one resource unit models high resource contention, and having sixteen resource units models low resource contention.

Figure 6 shows the transaction throughput of DV and 2PL as the number of resource units is varied. Figure 7 shows the corresponding CPU (DV-cpu, 2PL-cpu) and disk (DV-disk, 2PL-disk) utilizations. For small number of resource units (i.e., high resource contention) both methods perform similarly. As the number of resource units is increased (i.e., as resource contention is reduced), DV starts performing better. At high resource contention, one of the resources is being utilized nearly 100% by both the methods. Lower blocking rates in DV only result in longer queues for the bottleneck resource. Under such circumstances, transactions end up waiting for resources in DV, as opposed to waiting for locks in 2PL. As the resource contention is reduced, data contention becomes the dominant factor. A higher number of active transactions in DV results in better resource utilization and higher transaction throughput. At 16 resource units, the resource utilizations in DV is nearly 100% more than those of 2PL.

The average blocking rates for 2PL increase as the resource contention is reduced (from 69 blocked transactions at 1 resource unit to 78 blocked transactions at 16 resource units). At high resource contention, the transactions wait longer in the resource queues thereby reducing the transactions competing for data. As resource contention is reduced, there are more transactions competing for data and hence higher blocking rates. In DV, there is little increase in the blocking rates.

Transaction Mix.

We consider a a mix of transactions of different lengths in this experiment. When short transactions are run together with relatively long transactions, the short transactions may starve while waiting for locks held by long transactions. In this experiment, 10% of the transactions are long, each with 100 record ref-

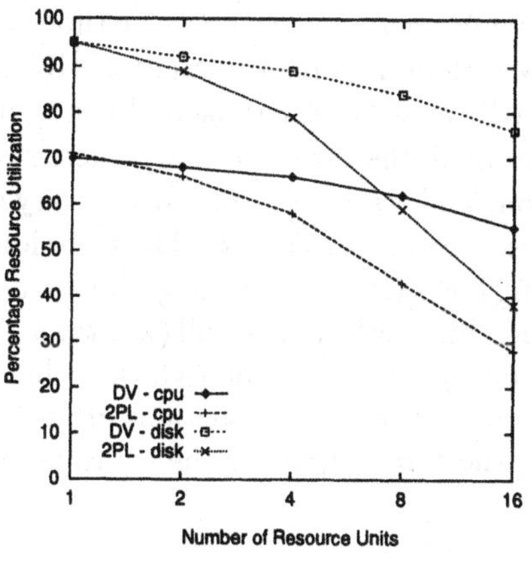

Fig. 7. Res. utilizations vs Res. contention

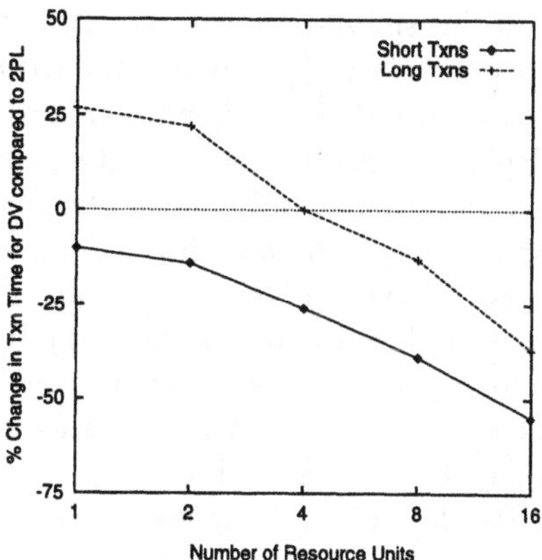

Fig. 8. Transaction mix

erences. The other 90% transactions are short, with 20 record references each. Both types of transactions update 30% of the records accessed. The number of resource units is varied from 1 to 16. Table 3 lists the values used for the variable simulation parameters.

Figure 8 shows the percentage change in the transaction response times for DV, compared to those of 2PL, as a function of resource contention. At high resource contention, the long transactions take more time and the short transactions take less time in DV than in 2PL. In 2PL, most of the short transactions are blocked due to data contention. Since there are smaller number of transactions contending for resources, the waiting times are smaller and hence long transactions execute fast. When a short transaction is blocked by a long transaction, the short transaction has to wait until the long transaction completes. This adds significantly to the response time of the short transaction. Note that giving short transactions higher priority for resource access does not solve the problem, since the cause is the data contention. On the other hand, in DV, there is very little blocking. Hence both short and long transactions compete for the resources, which increases the queue lengths and the waiting times. This results in long transactions taking more time to complete. The short transactions execute faster since now they only have to wait for the resources. As the resource contention is reduced, the transaction response times for both types of transactions become far lower than those of 2PL. The transaction throughput and resource utilization follow the same pattern as in the Fig. 6 and 7.

4.4 Supporting Queries

We consider an OLTP environment to compare the DV method with the other two methods. An OLTP environment has a large number of short transactions and a small number of long queries. We model this environment by considering a mix of 75% transactions, each with 20 data references, and 25% long queries, with 100 references each. The variable parameter values used are listed in Table 3.

In this simulation, we compared the first DV technique with the methods by Bober and Carey [6] (same as the second DV technique) and Mohan et al. [13]. In all the three methods, queries are not affected by the transactions and hence are independent of the extent of data contention. In all the three methods, queries do not wait for locks and have similar throughput and response times, which vary in a predictable fashion with the number of resource units. The first DV technique incurs the overhead of acquiring and releasing locks (the locks, though, are issued immediately without any blocking). However, this overhead is small (less than 2% in our experiments) compared to the total query response time (which includes disk access times and wait times for resources). Since the transactions are never blocked by queries in all the three methods, the throughput for the transactions follows the same pattern as in Fig. 6.

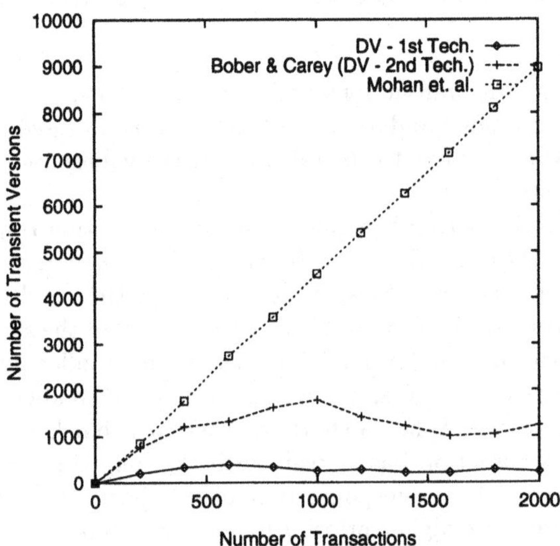

Fig. 9. Space overhead for versions

The more interesting metric to compare the three methods is the amount of additional space required for the prior versions. Figure 9 compares the number of prior versions maintained by the first DV technique with that of the methods of Bober and Carey (second DV technique) and Mohan et al.[2]. The first DV technique has an average of 294 versions (with a maximum of 457 versions). The method of Bober and Carey (second DV technique) has nearly four times more overhead, with an average of 1305 versions and a maximum of 2007 versions. The graph for the method by Mohan et al. shows that the number of versions increases almost linearly with the number of transactions in the version period. For example, if the version period is switched after every 1000 transactions, this

[2] We consider only the two version period algorithm here, since it has less space overhead than the multiple version period algorithm.

method maintains a maximum of 4524 versions. If the version period is switched after 2000 transactions, the number of versions nearly doubles to 8961.

The methods by Bober and Carey [6] and Mohan et al. [13] use the transient versions to both eliminate locking overhead for queries and avoid blocking of transactions by queries. The DV method (first technique) incurs the locking overhead for queries. The locks are used to dynamically position queries in the serialization order so that no transaction is ever blocked by a query. The locks also reduce the storage overhead by identifying the prior versions that a query needs. By incurring a small locking overhead for queries (less than 2% increase in response times), the dynamic versioning method significantly reduces the storage overhead (75% or more).

5 Conclusion

Transient versions have been used to efficiently support queries in high performance transaction processing systems. In this paper, we presented a method that uses the transient versions, that are maintained to support queries, to also increase transaction concurrency. We used a dependence graph to not only maintain serializability, but also to exactly identify the prior versions that may be required by the queries. By keeping only the versions absolutely necessary, the storage overhead for the transient versions is reduced to the minimum. We also developed different techniques for efficiently executing queries based on their lengths and access patterns.

We presented results of simulation experiments that compared the performance and overheads of the dynamic versioning method with those of two other recent transient versioning methods [13, 6]. The following are the main conclusions of our study.

- The DV method significantly reduces the number of transactions blocked due to data contention. For the work loads considered, the reduction varies from 60% to 90%.
- At resource utilizations (60% to 80%) that are typical in actual databases, the higher concurrency in the DV method results in better resource utilization (15% to 20% more) and hence in higher transaction throughput.
- In a mix of short and long transactions, the DV method significantly reduces the starvation of short transactions by long transactions.
- The DV method executes queries almost as efficiently as the other two methods.
- The storage overhead for the transient versions in the DV method is only 25% of that for [6] and significantly lower than that needed by [13].

References

1. Agrawal, R., Carey, M., Livny, M.: Concurrency Control Performance Modeling: Alternatives and Implications. ACM Transactions on Database Systems, December 1987.

2. Agrawal, R., Carey, M., McVoy, L.: The Performance of Alternative Strategies for Dealing with Deadlocks in Database Management Systems. IEEE Transactions on Software Engineering, December 1987.
3. Agrawal, D., Sengupta, S.: Modular Synchronization in Multiversion Databases: Version Control and Concurrency Control. ACM SIGMOD International Conference on Management of Data, May 1989.
4. Bayer, R., Heller, H., Reiser, A.: Parallelism and Recovery in Database Systems. ACM Transactions on Database Systems, June 1980.
5. Bernstein, P.A., Hadzilacos, V., Goodman, N.: Concurrency Control and Recovery in Database Systems. Addison-Wesley Pub. Co., 1987.
6. Bober, P., Carey, M.: On Mixing Queries and Transactions via Multiversion Locking. Proc. 8th International Conference on Data Engineering, February 1992.
7. Bober, P., Carey, M.: Multiversion query locking. Proc. 18th International Conference on Very Large Data Bases, August 1992.
8. Chan, A., et al.: The Implementation of an Integrated Concurrency Control and Recovery Scheme. ACM SIGMOD International Conference on Management of Data, June 1982.
9. DeWitt, D., Gray, J.: Parallel Database Systems: The Future of High Performance Database Systems. Communications of the ACM, June 1992.
10. Gray, J., Reuter, A.: Transaction Processing: Concepts and Techniques. Morgan Kaufmann Publishers, 1993.
11. Gray, J., Lorie, R., Putzolu, F., Traiger, I.: Granularity of Locks and Degrees of Consistency in a Shared Data Base. Modeling in Data Base Systems, North Holland Publishing, 1976.
12. Hadzilacos, T.: Serialization graph algorithms for multiversion concurrency control. ACM SIGMOD International Conference on Management of Data, March 1988.
13. Mohan, C., Pirahesh, H., Lorie, R.: Efficient and Flexible Methods for Transient Versioning of Records to Avoid Locking by Read-Only Transactions. ACM SIGMOD International Conference on Management of Data, June 1992.
14. Pirahesh, H., Mohan, C., Cheng, J., Liu, T.S., Selinger, P.: Parallelism in Relational Database Systems: Architectural Issues and Design Approaches. IEEE 2nd Int'l Symp. on Databases in Parallel and Distributed Systems, July 1990.
15. Reed, D.: Naming and Synchronization in a Decentralized Computer System. PhD Thesis, Technical Report MIT/LCS/TR-205, MIT, September 1978.
16. Schwetman, H.: CSIM Users Guide. March 1990.

Concurrency Control of Tiered Flat Transactions

W. Hussak[1] and J.A. Keane[2]

[1]Deprtment of Computer Studies, University of Loughborough, UK.
[2]Department of Computation, UMIST, Manchester, UK.

Abstract. In some database systems it has become evident that transactions can consist of a succession of 'tiers' where different types of data are being accessed. Despite the different nature of the data accessed by each tier the transactions cannot be split up because of the interdependencies between the albeit different data of the individual tiers. However, the tiered nature of such transactions can offer greater scope for parallel execution and hence more efficient throughput of transactions without breaching data consistency. In this paper, we extend the standard transaction model by defining formally the notion of a *tiered transaction.* We give a concurrency control condition on tiered transactions being executed in parallel which is weaker than the standard serializability condition. We develop the theory in the context of the 'syntactic' methods of classical serializability theory.
A financial database example is used to illustrate the concepts. The concurrency control condition is verified by an algebraic approach.

1 Introduction

The concept of a transaction as a unit of work in database systems is well-known [Dat95]. The perceived restrictions imposed by 'flat' transactions are also well-known [Gra93]. One of the aims of extending the flat transaction model is to increase the potential for parallel execution. However, in moving from a flat transaction model there is extra complexity [LMW94].

Serializability theory has been used as a concurrency control condition, for parallel transactions on databases as for example in [BSW79]. Different forms of serializability are possible depending on whether the values read by the transactions or the value of the final state are required to be as in some serial execution of the transactions. All, these theories work with a traditional transaction model. Changes to this model have been suggested. For example, in [Kai88], an extended transaction model is proposed with a corresponding notion of *commit-serializability*, as being suitable for the transaction-like facilities that concurrent object-oriented applications might require. There, the committed transactions are serializable but may not correspond to the transactions that were initiated. Another model is where the transactions may execute *subtransactions* or *nested transactions* ([Mos85] and [BBG89]). These recognise that real systems are multilevel and that at each level each operation is implemented by a program that uses operations at the next lower level. Such extensions seek to provide serializability analysis tools at several levels of abstraction.

In some database systems, particularly multi-media databases [GhB93], it has become evident that transactions can consist of a succession of 'tiers' where different types of data are being accessed. Such transactions are typically of a longer duration than traditional database transactions. Despite the different nature of the data accessed by each tier the transactions cannot be split up because of the interdependencies between the albeit different data of the individual tiers. However, the tiered nature and long duration of such transactions can offer both greater scope and greater need for parallel execution, and hence more efficient throughput of transactions without breaching data consistency. In this paper, we extend the standard transaction model by defining formally the notion of a *tiered transaction*. We give a concurrency control condition on tiered transactions being executed in parallel which is weaker than the standard serializability condition. We develop the theory in the context of the 'syntactic' methods of classical serializability theory.

The paper is divided as follows: §2 first describes the 'syntactic' framework used in serializability theory before introducing 'tiered transactions' and 'tiered-serializability'; §3 analyses this concurrency control condition and §4 suggests an algebraic approach to proving tier-serializability. The conclusions are in §5.

2 Tiered transactions and tiered-serializability

2.1 Nature of serializability theory

The theory presented in this paper follows traditional serializability theory, such as [Pap79] and [Vid87], in working solely with the *syntactic* information about transactions. Thus, it is concerned with determining which interleaved sequences, called 'histories', of formal reads and writes to variables by the respective transactions are equivalent to histories which are serial executions of the transactions. Consider the following example of a history h:

$$R_1[X];\ R_2[X];\ W_2[X];\ W_1[X] \tag{1}$$

Here, the variable being accessed is given in square brackets and the nature of the access is indicated by a R or a W. The subscript gives the transaction to which the read or write step belongs. A semi-colon separates the steps. The notation will be given formally in section 2.3. Now, it could be argued that h is serializable. For, both *Transaction 1 (T1)* and *Transaction 2 (T2)* perform just the single write to the variable X and so X has the same final value as if *T1* was executed after *T2*.

However, consider the following 'interpretation' of (1):

$$X = 0 \text{ before execution},\ W_1[X] \equiv X := 1,\ W_2[X] \equiv X := 2 \tag{2}$$

in other words, *T1* writes the value 1 to X and *T2* the value 2. The serial execution *T1* followed by *T2* would result in 0 being read by $R_1[X]$ and a final value for X of 2, and the serial execution of *T2* followed by *T1* would result in 2 being read by $R_1[X]$ and a final value for X of 1. This differs from h, where $R_1[X]$ reads 0 and 1 is the final value of X. Here the requirement of serializability has taken into account the values read by transactions as well as the final database state of the variables. This illustrates the distinction between state serializability, where the reads are not important, and view serializability where they are.

Furthermore, there is a sense in which h is not even state serializable. It relates to the extent to which we are allowed to interpret the writes. In an interpretation a write in a transaction may depend upon previous reads in that transaction. We can have the following interpretation:

$$X = 1 \text{ before execution, } W_1[X] \text{ writes the value read by } R_1[X]$$

$$W_2[X] \text{ writes twice the value read by } R_2[X] \quad (3)$$

It can be checked that *T1* followed by *T2* and *T2* followed by *T1* both give a final value of 2 for X, under this interpretation, whereas h gives a final value of 1. This feature of interpretations, where writes depend upon previous reads, will be important when defining the new conditions in section 2.6.

The attraction of such 'syntactic' approaches is that reasoning is straightforward and the problem of serializability is decidable. Such approaches have been used outside of serializability theory, for example in [HuK93] where a formal theory of store coherency classes is developed.

2.2 Data consistency for concurrent transactions

Classical serializability provides data consistency by giving the impression of the whole of transactions being executed atomically and not just their individual steps. In many cases atomicity of the *whole* of the transaction is not necessary to achieve the required data consistency. In such cases, the serializability requirement is too strong and greater parallelism can be achieved with a weaker condition. In this paper, transactions are split into 'tiers'. A history is 'tiered-serializable' if it gives the impression of the constituent tiers of the transaction being executed atomically, though not necessarily the whole transaction. It differs from choosing a transaction model, where the granularity of transactions is smaller and the constituent tiers are deemed to be transactions in their own right, in two respects:

1. There is a pre-existing ordering between the tiers of a transaction, whereas no such ordering exists between transactions
2. In a transaction, writes in a given tier may depend upon reads in a previous tier *as well* as reads in the current tier. This contrasts with treating tiers as whole transactions where writes in a given transaction could only depend upon previous reads in that transaction (by definition of the allowed interpretations of standard transactions systems). That would mean that writes in a tier could only depend upon reads in that and only that tier.

Tiers provide a more general semantics than a corresponding transaction model of smaller granularity. Tiers bear no relation to the nested transactions of [BBG89]. The purpose of nested transactions is to represent an operation at a given level by a sequence of operations at a lower level to be encapsulated in the nested transaction. This permits an analysis of serializability to take place at many levels. However, in such a model, the top-level transactions are still required to be serializable. In contrast, our tiers give a 'flat' model of systems at a single level but enable the serializability requirement to be relaxed.

In the formal definitions that follow V will be some variable set.

2.3 Steps and histories

2.3.1 Definition: *step*

A *step* s is either a *read step* reading a data item in V or a *write step* writing to one data item in V.

2.3.2 Definition: *history*

A *history* h is a sequence of steps. The (total) order of the sequence is denoted $<_h$.

2.4 Tiered transactions

2.4.1 Definition: *transaction*

A *transaction* $(\mathcal{R}_i, \mathcal{W}_i, <_i)$ is a finite (irreflexively) partially ordered set $T_i = \mathcal{R}_i \cup \mathcal{W}_i$ of read and write steps, collectively denoted $\mathcal{R}_i$ and $\mathcal{W}_i$ respectively. Following the database theories in [Pap79] and [Vid87] we restrict the reads to occur before the writes and permit only one read and write to a given variable, in our definition of an ordinary transaction. The steps of T_i will either be denoted

$$s_{i1},\ s_{i2},\ \ldots,\ s_{ik_i}$$

or a step will be given by

$$R_i[X] \text{ or } W_i[Y]$$

indicating whether it is a read or write step and the variable accessed. The subscript indicates a step of the transaction T_i.

2.4.2 Definition: *tiered transaction*

A *tiered transaction* $(\mathcal{R}_{i1}, \mathcal{W}_{i1}, \ldots, \mathcal{R}_{ij}, \mathcal{W}_{ij}, \ldots, \mathcal{R}_{in}, \mathcal{W}_{in}, <_i)$ is a finite (irreflexively) partially ordered set $T_i = \mathcal{R}_{i1} \cup \mathcal{W}_{i1} \cup \ldots \cup \mathcal{R}_{in} \cup \mathcal{W}_{in}$ of read steps $\mathcal{R}_{i1} \cup \ldots \cup \mathcal{R}_{in}$, and write steps $\mathcal{W}_{i1} \cup \ldots \cup \mathcal{W}_{in}$. We assume that the read steps in each $\mathcal{R}_{ij}$ $(1 \leq j \leq n)$ occur before the write steps of the corresponding $\mathcal{W}_{ij}$. Each (ordered) set $\mathcal{R}_{ij} \cup \mathcal{W}_{ij}$ is called a *tier* of T_i and will sometimes be denoted T_{ij}.

2.4.3 Definition: *tiered transaction system*

A *tiered transaction system* T is a finite set of tiered transactions

$$T = \{T_1,\ \ldots,\ T_n\}$$

2.4.4 Definition: *history of tiered transaction system*

A history h is a *history of* T if the steps of h are the steps of all the transactions in T placed in some order such that steps that are ordered in a transaction T_i preserve that order in h, that is

$$s_{ij} <_i s_{ik} \Rightarrow s_{ij} <_h s_{ik}$$

Plainly, a history of T represents some execution of the transactions in T in an interleaved fashion.

2.5 Interpretations

2.5.1 Definition: *previous reads*

Given a write step $W_i[X]$ of a transaction T_i, the *previous reads* is the set

$$previous\_reads(W_i[X]) = \{R_i[Y] : R_i[Y] <_i W_i[X]\}$$

Thus, the previous reads of a write step in T_i are the reads in T_i prior to that write step.

2.5.2 Definition: *interpretation for transaction system*

An *interpretation* for a transaction system T is a triple $I = (dom, init, writes)$, where

- *dom* is a domain of values for the variables V
- *init* is a set of initial values for the variables V
- *writes* is a collection of functions, one for each write step $W_{ij}[X]$ of a transaction T_i

  $$f_i : dom^{|previous\_reads(W_i[X])|} \rightarrow dom,$$

  called the *interpreting function* of the write step $W_i[X]$, each of which writes a value to X which is a function of all the previous reads of $W_i[X]$ in T_i.

The set of interpretations will be denoted $\mathcal{I}_T$.

2.6 Tiered-serializability

2.6.1 Definition: *serial history*

A history is *serial* if given (distinct) transactions T_i, T_j either

$$s_{ik} <_h s_{jl} \text{ for all } s_{ik} \in T_i,\ s_{jl} \in T_j$$

or

$$s_{jl} <_h s_{ik} \text{ for all } s_{ik} \in T_i,\ s_{jl} \in T_j$$

2.6.2 Definition: *tiered serial history*

A history is *tiered-serial* if given (distinct) tiers $T_{i_1 j_1}$, $T_{i_2 j_2}$ either

$$s_{ik} <_h s_{jl} \text{ for all } s_{ik} \in T_{i_1 j_1},\ s_{jl} \in T_{i_2 j_2}$$

or

$$s_{jl} <_h s_{ik} \text{ for all } s_{ik} \in T_{i_1 j_1},\ s_{jl} \in T_{i_2 j_2}$$

2.6.3 Definition: *history equivalence*

Two histories h_1 and h_2 are:

(i) *state-equivalent* if, for every $I \in \mathcal{I}_T$, the "executions" of h_1 and h_2 result in the same final values for the variables in V.
(ii) *τ-equivalent* if, for every $I \in \mathcal{I}_T$, the values read by the individual transactions at their read steps are the same for the "executions" of h_1 and h_2.
(iii) *view-equivalent* if h_1 and h_2 are both *state-equivalent* and *τ-equivalent*.[1]

2.6.4 Definition: *serializability*

A history h is:

(i) *state-serializable* if it is *state-equivalent* to a serial history h';
(ii) *τ-serializable* if it is *τ-equivalent* to a serial history h';
(iii) *view-serializable* if it is *view-equivalent* to a serial history h';

Recall from §2.2, that a history h is to be 'tiered-serializable' if it:

TS1: Behaves as if the tiers were executed atomically;
TS2: Condition TS1 is to hold for all interpretations where writes may be affected by previous reads in other tiers in the parent transaction.

Condition TS1 requires h to be equivalent to a tiered-serial history and condition TS2 states that equivalence is to hold over interpretations of T.

2.6.5 Definition: *tiered-serializability*

A history h is:

(i) *tiered-state-serializable* if it is state-equivalent to a tiered-serial history h' of T;
(ii) *tiered-τ-serializable* if it is τ-equivalent to a tiered-serial history h' of T;
(iii) *tiered-view-serializable* if it is view-equivalent to a tiered-serial history h' of T[2].

3 Tiered-serializability as a concurrency control condition for tiered transactions

In this section we demonstrate by way of an example how tiered serializability is used as a concurrency control condition for parallel tiered transactions.

Aside: *the application of tier-serializability to a multi-media database is perhaps more obvious, however, in order to illustrate the utility of the notion the example used is a financial database transaction.*

[1] The terminology *state-*, *τ-* and *view-equivalence* are as in [Vid87]. In this paper, when we talk of plain history equivalence we shall mean view equivalence.

[2] We shall work with the view version of serializability throughout.

A business has its assets invested with n banks in m countries ($m \times n$ accounts in total). It maintains a database containing the following kinds of data:

- Data on the country in which to access an account.
- Data on which bank from which to access an account.
- For each account, data relating to the amount in the account.

The specific data items are:

D1: C - an integer variable taking one of the values $1, \ldots, m$. It gives the identifier of the country in which an account is to be accessed.
D2: B - an integer variable taking one of the values $1, \ldots, n$. It indicates in which bank an account should be accessed.
D3: A - a data item which is a $m \times n$-matrix of integer variables

$$\begin{pmatrix} a_{11} & \ldots & a_{1n} \\ & \ldots & \\ a_{m1} & \ldots & a_{mn} \end{pmatrix}$$

giving the balance of an account with a particular bank in a given country.

Consider tiered transactions which perform three kinds of task in the following order:

tier1: Access the data giving the country in which an account should be used.
tier2: Access the data supplying the bank that should be used.
tier3: Access the details of a particular account.

We choose a specific case of such tiered transactions. Suppose that it is financially most expedient to have equal access to accounts both nationally and between the banking institutions. Further, suppose that this is achieved by the first tier T_{i1} of a transaction T_i reading C to obtain the identifier of a country and then incrementing C, and after that reading B to obtain the identifier of a bank and incrementing B. If C is m (respectively B is n), then incrementing gives a value of 1 to C (respectively B). Thus,

$$T_{i1} = R_i[C]; W_i[C], \; T_{i2} = R_i[B]; W_i[B]$$

The third tier T_{i3} of T_i accesses an actual account. We assume that this also involves a read and a write access. If the first two tiers produced values x and y for country and bank respectively, then the account represented by the integer variable a_{xy} will be accessed. Formally, this is seen to be an access to the *whole* of the data item A which *depends upon* the previous reads in the transaction. In this case the previous reads determine *which part* of the matrix, that is the data item A, is updated. So,

$$T_{i3} = R_i[A]; W_i[A]$$

and the whole of T_i is

$$R_i[C]; W_i[C]; R_i[B]; W_i[B]; R_i[A]; W_i[A]$$

If there are several transactions of the form T_i, we claim that, for data consistency, the execution of the T_i's should produce an effect equivalent to the aggregate of the tiers of the form T_{i1}, T_{i2} and T_{i3} executing serially. For, consider the case of two transactions

$$T_i = R_i[C]; W_i[C]; R_i[B]; W_i[B]; R_i[A]; W_i[A]$$
$$T_j = R_j[C]; W_j[C]; R_j[B]; W_j[B]; R_j[A]; W_j[A]$$

A history beginning

$$R_i[C]; R_j[C]; W_i[C]; W_j[C]; \ldots$$

would result in T_i and T_j both obtaining the identifier of country 1 leaving country 2 unused. From this, it is clear that the first two tiers should be executed serializably. A similar argument is true for the second tiers. As regards the third tiers which access the actual accounts, it is likely that two transactions will be allocated the same country and account when there are very many transactions. In order to maintain consistency of the account details, the third tiers would also need to be executed serializably. No stronger condition of serializability is necessary. Thus, tier-serializability is the required condition. It is shown in the next section that this is a strictly weaker condition than ordinary serializability and thus efficiency can be improved with the greater scope for parallelism.

Remark 1: *in the above example, it is possible to formulate the first and second tier of the transaction as deductive queries where the country is determined by a rule working on current load balance, or perhaps on total account balance in each country. The selection of a country will obviously update the input data for the rule when it is next applied. A similar type of rule could be used to select the bank within the country.*

Remark 2: *A further example from "traditional" database systems is as follows: a journey is being planned from city* `w` *to city* `z` *in a different country. There is no direct flight from* `w` *to* `z`*, and so the journey must entail a flight from* `w` *to (some intermediate city)* `X`*, a train journey from* `X` *to (some intermediate city)* `Y` *and a bus journey from* `Y` *to* `z`*. The identities of cities* `X` *and* `Y` *will be determined by availability, times etc. The identity of city* `Y` *is of course dependent upon the identity of city* `X`*, determined in an earlier tier of the transaction. The tiered nature of this transaction is obvious as it involves three different sets of data:* **`planes`**, **`trains`** *and* **`buses`** *booking information respectively. In addition, because of availability considerations, reservations, and possible cost for cancellation etc, the transaction cannot be split into three separate transactions. This type of transaction can be handled, in a similar way to the banking example, by tiered serializability in a flat transaction model. In [Gra93] a similar, if slightly less complex, type of transaction is regarded as being too complex for a flat model.*

4 Proofs of tier-serializability

We present a simplified algebraic approach which will be used to prove tier-serializability of a history in the example in section 3. The reason for our approach is that it avoids some of the technicalities of the graph-based approaches that are commonly used for proving serializability, and will provide a clearer illustration of the new concept. In brief, we represent histories as a string of step symbols and apply commutativity to certain adjacent symbols until a tiered serial history is obtained.

4.1 Definition: *step symbol*

A *step symbol* is of the form

$$r_i^x \text{ or } w_j^y$$

where x and y range over some variable set X and i and j range over some (transaction) identifier set I.

The *history algebra* $(H, \equiv)$ is the set H of finite sequences of step symbols

$$s_{i1}^{x_1} \dots s_{in}^{x_n}$$

and a relation $\equiv$ satisfying

HA1: $h \equiv h \ (h \in H)$
HA2: $h_1 \equiv h_2 \ \Rightarrow \ h_2 \equiv h_1 \ (h_1, h_2 \in H)$
HA3: $h_1 \equiv h_2$ and $h_2 \equiv h_3 \ \Rightarrow \ h_1 \equiv h_3 \ (h_1, h_2, h_3 \in H)$
HA4: $r_i^x r_j^y \equiv r_j^y r_i^x \ (x, y \in X, i, j \in I)$
HA5: $r_i^x w_j^y \equiv w_j^y r_i^x \ (x, y \in X, x \neq y, i, j \in I, i \neq j)$
HA6: $w_i^x w_j^y \equiv w_j^y w_i^x \ (x, y \in X, x \neq y, i, j \in I, i \neq j)$
HA7: $h_1 \equiv h_2 \ \Rightarrow \ h_3 h_1 h_4 \equiv h_3 h_2 h_4 \ (h_1, h_2, h_3, h_4 \in H)$

where in HA7 $h_3 h_1 h_4$ and $h_3 h_2 h_4$ denote concatenated histories.

The following theorem is straightforward.

4.2 Theorem (soundness)

For $h_1, h_2 \in H$, if

$$h_1 \equiv h_2$$

then h_1 and h_2 are view equivalent (in the sense of §2.6.3(iii)) if the step symbols of h_1 and h_2 are interpreted as reads and writes by the subscript transactions to the superscript variables, i.e.

$$r_i^x \text{ means } R_i[X], \ w_j^y \text{ means } W_j[Y]$$

A complete algebra of history equivalences is possible though more difficult, and would complicate unnecessarily the discussion here.

4.3 Example proof of tier-serializability

Suppose that in the international banking database example of section 3 there are three transactions T_i, T_j and T_k. Consider the following history h

$$R_i[C]; W_i[C]; R_j[C]; W_j[C]; R_k[C]; R_j[B]; W_j[B]; R_j[A]; W_k[C];$$

$$R_k[B]; W_j[A]; W_k[B]; R_k[A]; R_i[B]; W_i[B]; W_k[A]; R_i[A]; W_i[A]$$

We show that this is equivalent to a tiered-serial-history. Rewriting h in the less cumbersome algebraic notation we have that $h =$

$$r_i^C w_i^C r_j^C w_j^C r_k^C r_j^B w_j^B r_j^A w_k^C r_k^B w_j^A w_k^B r_k^A r_i^B w_i^B w_k^A r_i^A w_i^A$$

$$\equiv$$

$$r_i^C w_i^C r_j^C w_j^C r_k^C r_j^B w_j^B r_j^A w_k^C \underline{w_j^A} \underline{r_k^B} w_k^B r_k^A r_i^B w_i^B w_k^A r_i^A w_i^A$$

$$\equiv$$

$$r_i^C w_i^C r_j^C w_j^C r_k^C r_j^B w_j^B r_j^A w_k^C w_j^A r_k^B w_k^B r_k^A r_i^B \underline{w_k^A} \underline{w_i^B} r_i^A w_i^A$$

$$\equiv$$

$$r_i^C w_i^C r_j^C w_j^C r_k^C r_j^B w_j^B r_j^A w_k^C w_j^A r_k^B w_k^B r_k^A \underline{w_k^A} \underline{r_i^B} w_i^B r_i^A w_i^A$$

$$\equiv$$

$$r_i^C w_i^C r_j^C w_j^C r_k^C r_j^B w_j^B \underline{w_k^C} \underline{r_j^A} w_j^A r_k^B w_k^B r_k^A w_k^A r_i^B w_i^B r_i^A w_i^A$$

$$\equiv$$

$$r_i^C w_i^C r_j^C w_j^C \underline{r_j^B} \underline{r_k^C} w_j^B w_k^C r_j^A w_j^A r_k^B w_k^B r_k^A w_k^A r_i^B w_i^B r_i^A w_i^A$$

$$\equiv$$

$$r_i^C w_i^C r_j^C w_j^C r_j^B \underline{w_j^B} \underline{r_k^C} w_k^C r_j^A w_j^A r_k^B w_k^B r_k^A w_k^A r_i^B w_i^B r_i^A w_i^A$$

In the above, each successive history is equivalent to the previous history by use of one of the laws of commutativity (HA4), (HA5) or (HA6) together with the substitutivity law (HA7). At each stage, the elements switched are underlined. The last history is a tiered-serial-history with respect to the tiers in the example in §3.

The history h is not serializable. For, consider the case $m = n = 3$ (3 countries and 3 banks). In such an interpretation where the country and bank identifiers have an initial value equal to 1, the possible serial executions of T_i, T_j and T_k

$$T_iT_jT_k, T_iT_kT_j, T_jT_iT_k, T_jT_kT_i, T_kT_iT_j, T_kT_jT_i$$

would all result in each transaction accessing an account whose bank identifier was equal to the country identifier. However, we can check that h results in, for example, T_i accessing the account whose country identifier is 1 and whose bank identifier is 3.

5 Conclusions

An important area of research in database theory is how to overcome the constraints imposed by flat transactions. One of these constraints is that parallel activity is restricted by having long duration transactions accessing different types of data. Various extensions to the flat model have been proposed, all increasing the complexity of the model.

In this paper we have extended the standard model by introducing the notion of 'tiers' within a transaction. This extension offers greater scope for parallel execution whilst remaining within the flat transaction world. *tiered transactions* have been defined formally, and a concurrency control condition on tiered transactions given which is weaker than the standard serializability condition. A financial database example has been used to illustrate the concepts, and the concurrency control condition has been verified by an algebraic approach.

Acknowledgements

The authors wish to thank Nic Holt and Tom Thomson of ICL, Manchester, for discussions in the Flagship project on the notion of 'serializability at levels of abstraction' that was a forerunner to this work.

References

[BBG89] C. Beeri, P. A. Bernstein and N. Goodman, A Model of Concurrency in Nested Transactions Systems, *Journal of ACM*, 36 (2), pp.230-269, April 1989.

[BSW79] P. A. Bernstein, D. W. Shipman and W. S. Wong, Formal Aspects of Serializability in Database Concurrency Control, *IEEE Trans. on Software Engineering*, Vol. SE-5, No. 3, pp. 203-216, May 1979.

[Dat95] C.J. Date, *An Introduction to Database Systems*, Addiosn Wesley, Sixth Ed., 1995.

[GhB93] Multimedia Database Systems, A. Ghafoor and P.B. Berra, in *Advanced Database Systems*, N.R. Adam and B.K. Bharagava (Eds), LNCS750, Springer-Verlag, pp. 397-411,1993.

[Gra93] J. Gray and A. Reuter, *Transaction Processing: Concepts and Techniques*, Morgan Kaufman, 1993.

[LMW94] N. Lynch, M. Merritt, W. Weihl and A. Fekete, *Atomic Transactions*, Morgan Kauffman, 1994.

[HuK93] W. Hussak and J. A. Keane, Representation of Coherency Classes for Parallel Systems, *Proc. 5th IEEE Symposium on Parallel and Distributed Processing*, pp. 391-398, Dallas, Texas, December 1993.

[Kai88] G. E. Kaiser, Transactions for Concurrent Object-oriented Programming Systems, *SIGPLAN Notices*, 1988, pp. 136-138.

[Mos85] J. E. B. Moss, *Nested Transactions: An approach to Reliable Distributed Computing*, MIT Press, Cambridge, Mass., March 1985.

[Pap79] C. Papadimitriou, The Serializability of Concurrent Database Updates, *Journal of ACM*, 26 (4), pp. 631-653, 1979.

[Vid87] K. Vidyasankar, Generalized Theory of Serializability, *Acta Informatica*, 24, pp. 105-119, 1987.

Two-Step Pruning : A Distributed Query Optimization Algorithm

Hyeokman Kim[1,2], Sukho Lee[1], Hyoung-Joo Kim[1]

[1] Dept. of Computer Engineering, Seoul National University
Shinrim-Dong, Kwanak-Gu, Seoul, 151-742, Korea
[2] Korea Telecom Research Laboratories
17, Woomyon-Dong, Suhcho-Gu, Seoul, 137-792, Korea
E-mail: {hmkim, shlee}@snucom.snu.ac.kr, hjk@inm4u.snu.ac.kr

Abstract. The problem of finding an optimal global plan for a tree query in a distributed database is studied under the objective of total processing time minimization. A two-step pruning algorithm based on dynamic programming is presented. This algorithm performs a pruning step twice for each subquery by designing two separate equivalence criteria applicable to each subquery. This lessens the search work done by the optimizer considerably. Without losing optimality, the search space for finding the optimum is reduced by aggregating partial plans that always incur the same processing time into a single plan and eliminating partial plans that can never be the optimum.

1 Introduction

The importance of query optimization in centralized and distributed database systems is widely recognized. One of the key components in query optimization is the search strategy. The ability to efficiently find an optimal or best plan among all possible alternatives is indeed essential to performance.

Dynamic programming which is probably the best known standard optimization technique has been employed as a search strategy in query optimization [3, 9, 10, 12, 15]. If dynamic programming is used to solve an optimization problem, the problem must satisfy the *principle of optimality*: in optimal sequence of decisions, each subsequence must be optimal [6]. Thus, the cost function based on dynamic programming is expressed as a recursive form. When building execution plans through dynamic programming, the optimizer systematically builds all possible partial plans and compares them through their cost estimates. It then prunes costly partial plans that are equivalent to a cheaper one. This pruning reduces the optimization cost because partial plans that are not likely to be optimal are pruned as soon as possible. The advantage of dynamic programming stems from the fact that the chosen partial plan with its cost is saved, and reused rather than recomputed when this plan is employed as a subplan of another plan. This means that the saved partial plans are shared by many other subsequent plans built from them.

The pruning is performed based on *equivalence criteria*, that is, the optimal partial plan is chosen among all possible partial plans that are equivalent in some sense. In a centralized environment, equivalent plans are those which capture the same relations. However in a distributed environment, the execution site where the result of a partial plan is materialized and the delivery site where the result is transferred may have impact on the cost of future plans. Thus, the equivalence criteria for distributed plans should consider these sites. In R* optimizer [10, 11] and state transition algorithm [9], their equivalence criteria consider not both but only one of them. Thus, they apply only a single pruning step to each subquery or state.

We propose a query optimization algorithm in distributed database systems. Our objective is to achieve search efficiency without relaxing optimality. We employ dynamic programming as a search strategy. In our approach, both the execution and delivery sites are adopted as equivalence criteria. We apply a pruning step twice to each subquery by carefully designing two equivalence criteria such that the optimal partial plan chosen through the first pruning step is reused when building an optimal partial plan through the second step applied in succession. This reduces the optimization time considerably because the partial plans that are not likely to be optimal are pruned much earlier and there are more chances to share the partial plans.

1.1 Related Work

There have been large volumes of work done regarding optimization for join operations in distributed relational database and surveyed in a number of places, including [5, 13, 16]. Two basic approaches exist to determine an optimal or best join ordering in distributed database systems: join-based [9, 10, 11] and semijoin-based [1, 2, 3, 15]. The main value of a semijoin is to reduce the size of the join operands and then the communication cost. But, using semijoins might increase the local processing cost, since one of the two joining relations must be accessed twice. Furthermore, the join of two intermediate results produced by semijoins cannot exploit the indexes that were available on the base relation. Most of the semijoin approaches assume that communication cost largely dominates local processing cost. This assumption is based on very slow communication networks such as wide area networks with a bandwidth of a few kilobytes per second. However, recent advances on network communications have drastically increased the bandwidth, and distributed database environments now exist where the communication network is much faster, making the cost of local processing no longer negligible. Therefore, using semijoins may not be a good idea and more recent techniques which consider local processing costs as well as communication costs tend not to use semijoins.

R* optimizer is a representative join-based approach [10, 11]. Conceptually, it can be viewed as an exhaustive search among all the enumerated alternative plans. The optimizer reduces the number of alternatives and search work by building partial plans of subquery and pruning them except the cheapest one through dynamic programming. R* optimizer adopts a single equivalence criteria which includes the relations captured by the subquery and the execution site. As a consequence, the optimizer performs a single pruning step for each subquery. We call the optimizer a *one-step pruning (OSP)* algorithm.

In OSP algorithm, a join between relations at different sites is accomplished by transferring one relation to the site of the other or both of them to a third site. In the last case, the subsequent join between the intermediate result of the join executed at this third site and the relation stored here may then be executed without transmissions. We denote T_i to be a subquery of a given query where i represents the number of relations captured by the subquery. A subquery T_i is represented as a set of captured relations. T_1 is a subquery containing only one relation. We denote y to be the resident site of a relation captured by T_1. Let $CostTJ_t(T_i)$ be the minimum cost to execute the join between the results of subquery T_{i-1} and T_1 at site t, $trans_{xt}(T_i)$ be the cost for transferring the result of T_i from site x to site t, and $join_t(T_{i-1}, T_1)$ be the join cost between the results of T_{i-1} and T_1 at site t. $CostTJ_t(T_i)$ is computed according to the following dynamic programming equation.

$$CostTJ_t(T_i) = \min_{\forall pair\ s.t.\ T_i = T_{i-1} \cup T_1\ and\ \forall x \in \{resident\ sites\ of\ relations\ in\ T_i\}} \{CostTJ_x(T_{i-1}) + trans_{xt}(T_{i-1}) + trans_{yt}(T_1) + join_t(T_{i-1}, T_1)\} \quad (1)$$

If $CostTJ_t(T_i)$ is computed for all possible execution site $t \in$ {resident sites of relations in T_i and a third site} and these computations are repeatedly applied to each subquery T_i varying i from 2 to n, the cost of an optimal plan is finally obtained. OSP algorithm uses the heuristic to restrict the search space, that is, either operand of joins must be a base relation. This reduces the optimization overhead. Though the heuristic takes advantages of indexes on base relations, this algorithm does not exploit the huge portion of feasible plans. Thus, OSP algorithm produces a best plan, not an optimal one.

In state transition algorithm [9], the relations and intermediate results are modeled into a state represented as a s-component vector where s is the number of sites related. The state says where the relations and intermediate results are, that is, the delivery sites. When a join is executed (one-step transition), one state transits to another state. The state transitions are equivalent if the resulting states have the same components, that is, the same delivery sites of all subqueries. The algorithm constructs a state space which includes all possible states and their transition relationships. It then chooses an optimal path (trajectory) from the initial state to a final one. The state space X is divided into n disjoint subsets, $X(i)$'s, such that $X = X(0) \cup X(1) \cup \cdots \cup X(n-1)$ where i is the number of joins performed. The initial state x_0 and the final state x_f belong to $X(0)$ and $X(n-1)$ respectively.

When one state $x \in X(i-1)$ transits to another state $y \in X(i)$ by executing a single join, there are at most three alternative strategies which are a sequence of a join operation and additional transmission operations. Let γ be a strategy for doing a one-step transition from state x to state y, Γ be the set of all feasible γ and $cost(x, y)$ be the minimum cost of doing the one-step transition from x to y. Then, the minimum transition cost is

$$cost(x,y) = \min_{\forall\gamma\in\Gamma}\{the\ sum\ of\ the\ costs\ of\ operations\ in\ \gamma\} \qquad (2)$$

The cost of state x means the total join and transmission costs required to go from the initial state to state x. The cost of state y which can be reached from state x in a one-step transition is the sum of the cost of state x and the cost of the transition. Let $CostS_{i-1}(x)$ be the minimum cost to go from the initial state to state x in $X(i-1)$ and $T^{-}(y)$ be the set of states that can reach y in a one-step transition. $CostS_i(y)$ is then computed according to the following dynamic programming equation.

$$CostS_i(y) = \min_{\forall x\in T^{-}(y)}\{CostS_{i-1}(x) + cost(x,y)\} \qquad (3)$$

If $cost(x,y)$ and $CostS_i(y)$ are computed for each state y in $X(i)$ varying i from 1 to $n-1$, the cost of an optimal plan, $CostS_{n-1}(x_f)$, is eventually computed. As opposed to OSP algorithm, the state transition algorithm performs two pruning steps for each state. That is, each of Equations (2) and (3) prunes all feasible transition strategies and trajectories except the optimal ones. However, Equation (2) is not a dynamic programming equation. Thus, we call the state transition algorithm a *semi-two-step pruning (Semi-TSP)* algorithm.

Since semi-TSP algorithm does not employ dynamic programming in the first pruning step, there is no way to reuse the computed results of the first pruning step: if $y \in X(i)$ and $y' \in X(i+1)\cup\cdots\cup X(n-1)$ and the subqueries related with the one-step transitions from x to y and from x' to y' are the same, $cost(x',y')$ must be recomputed though it is equal to $cost(x,y)$. For example, let's consider a chain query with relations A,B,C,D located at sites 1,2,3,4 respectively. A small portion of the state space for the query is given in Figure 1. There are three strategies for one-step transition from state x_0 to x_1, that is, A and B may be joined at one of their resident sites and the result is then transferred to site 3 or both of them may be transferred to site 3 and then joined. Since the transition strategies from x_2 to x_4 are equal to those from x_0 to x_1, $cost(x_0,x_1)$ and $cost(x_2,x_4)$ are the same. Semi-TSP algorithm has to do this redundant computation. Furthermore, the extra work in constructing the state space is too expensive, though the algorithm produces an optimal plan.

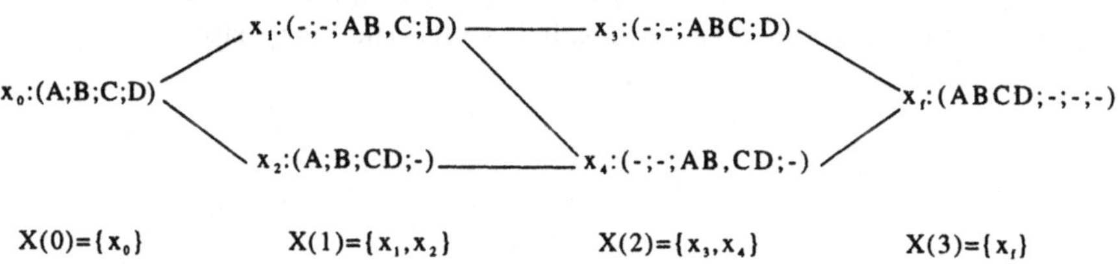

Fig. 1. State space

In a distributed database, both execution and delivery sites have influence on the cost of plan. OSP and semi-TSP algorithms include either execution or delivery site in their equivalence criteria. Our algorithm considers both sites in its criteria. We design two equivalence criteria such that one include an execution site and the other a delivery site, and the pruning steps based on these criteria obey the principle of optimality. Thus, our algorithm applies the pruning step twice to each subquery instead of a single step from the viewpoint of dynamic programming. We call our algorithm a *two-step pruning (TSP)* algorithm. Compared with OSP algorithm, TSP algorithm prunes much earlier the partial plans that are not likely to be optimal. In contrast to semi-TSP algorithm, the costs of partial plans chosen by the first pruning step as well as by the second step are reused every time another partial plan is built from those plan. Our TSP algorithm avoids the redundant computations done in semi-TSP algorithm.

This paper is organized as follows. In Section 2, the problem statement, the global execution plan, and the notion and assumption required are given. In Section 3, we first describe the cost model to compute the cost of execution plan according to the two pruning steps. Then, we show that this cost model obeys the principle of optimality. Based on these, we propose TSP algorithm and compute the complexity of the algorithm. Finally, in Section 4, we draw some conclusions and suggest future research directions.

2 Preliminaries

2.1 Problem Statement

Our goal is to find optimal join and transmission order of a given query under the objective of minimizing total processing time which includes local processing and communication costs. We are given a query T referencing n distinct base relations $R_i^{\prime}s$ distributed among s sites and an *initial distribution* representing the resident sites of n relations in database. We call the *query graph* of T the graph with n nodes, where each join clause in T is indicated as a link between corresponding nodes. Each node has a label which specifies the resident site of the corresponding relation. An example query graph is represented in Figure 2. In this paper, we focus on *tree query* whose query graph is tree. The site where a user gives a query and returns its result is called the query site.

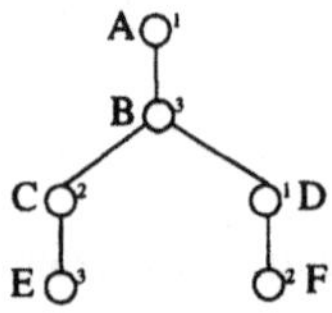

Fig. 2. Query graph

2.2 Global Execution Tree

Distributed query optimizer can be defined as an algorithm to choose an optimal global processing strategy for a given query. The design of such optimizers may be divided into three components: execution space which is the set of the execution plans searched by the optimizer, cost model which predicts the cost of an execution plan, and search strategy to obtain the minimum cost plan. In this subsection, we describe the execution space. The others are described in the following section. Query executions are represented as execution plans which transform a nonprocedural query into a sequence of operations. An execution plan can be syntactically represented as a join processing tree [7] or a dataflow graph [2]. We extend these representations into a *global execution tree (GET)* to express execution plans processed in distributed database environment.

GET is a labelled tree where the indegree of each nodes must not exceed two. It represents the flow of data from leaves to root. The leaf nodes are base relations and each non-leaf node is an intermediate result from joining or transmission: a node with indegree 2 (*join node*) is an intermediate result from joining its children and a node with indegree 1 (*transmission node*) is an intermediate result from the transmission of its child. Each non-leaf node is stored in a temporary file. In GET, the leaf, join and transmission nodes are graphically represented by circle, closed square and open square respectively.

Each node has a site label which represents different meaning according to the kinds of nodes. The site label for a leaf node represents the resident site of its corresponding relation. The site label for a transmission node represents the delivery site to which its child is transferred. If the site labels for a transmission node and its child are the same, no transmission occurs. The site label for a join node represents a join execution site. Relations or intermediate results to be joined must be at the same site. Thus, the site labels for a join node and its children must be the same. We say that GET is *complete* if it captures all the relations of the given query and the site label of the root is equal to the query site. Otherwise, it is said to be *partial.*

GET can be distinguished into *deep* or *bushy* trees [7]. If all join nodes of a GET have as a child at least one leaf node or transmission node which also has a leaf node as a child, the tree is called deep. Otherwise, it is called bushy. Figure 3 gives examples of deep and bushy GETs generated from the query in Figure 2. In Figure 3, the number annotated on each node is the site label. If the execution space does not include all feasible plans for a query, the optimizer may produce a suboptimal plan not an optimal one. For example, OSP algorithm in general produces a suboptimal plan because it has a restricted execution space that includes only deep trees. We do not restrict the execution space of our optimizer. Our optimizer searches execution plans which may be deep or bushy trees.

Execution plans represented by GET specify the order of joins and transmissions to be executed. The order is determined by traversing GET in a postorder sequence. Based on the costs of the individual join and transmission specified in GET, we can estimate the cost of the corresponding execution. This cost is defined as the cost of GET.

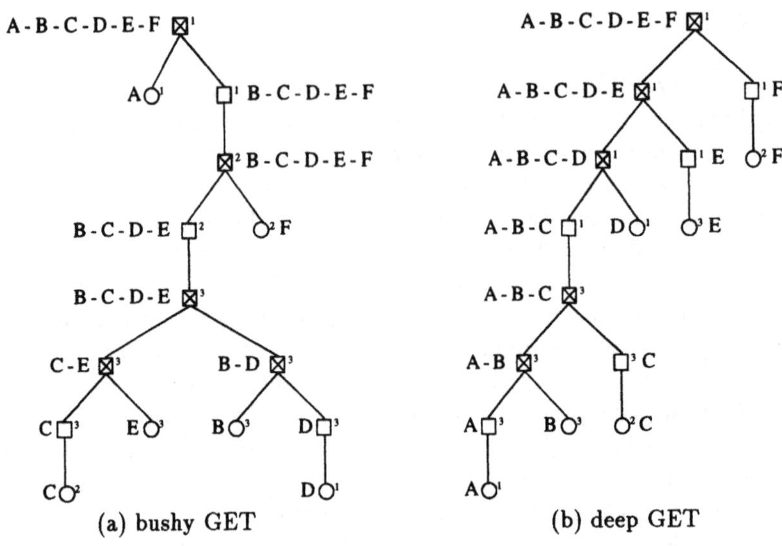

Fig. 3. Global Execution Tree

GET can be expressed as a sequence of operators. Let a, b be subplans of GET and $JN_x(a, b)$ be a join operation between the results of the subplans a and b at site x, $TR_{xt}(a)$ be an operation to transfer the result of the subplan a from site x to site t. The join node with site label x is transformed to $JN_x(-, -)$ operator and its children to operands. Also, the transmission node whose site label is t and has a child with site label x is to $TR_{xt}(-)$ operator and its child to operand. For example, the operator expression for the GET in Figure 3.a is $JN_1(A, TR_{2,1}(JN_2(TR_{3,2}(JN_3(JN_3(TR_{2,3}(C), E), JN_3(B, TR_{1,3}(D)))), F)))$.

2.3 Notions and Assumptions

Let an *i-relation query* $(1 \leq i \leq n)$ be a subquery of a given query T such that the query graph of an i-relation query is a connected subgraph with i nodes constructed from that of a given query. Thus, the given query T becomes an n-relation query. An i-relation query is represented as a node set T_{ij} where i is the number of nodes in T_{ij} and j is a number for distinguishing feasible i-relation queries from one another. By the definition of an i-relation query, T_{ij} can not be null. The number of i-relation queries in T is represented as m_i. Thus, the total number of subqueries is $\sum m_i$. For a query with n relations, there are n 1-relation queries, T_{1j} $(1 \leq j \leq n)$, each of which contains only one relation $(m_1 = n)$. The n-relation query, T_{n1}, is the input query itself $(m_n = 1)$. In addition, we use $RS(T_{ij})$ to denote the set of resident sites of relations captured by T_{ij}. The cardinality of a resident site set, $|RS(T_{ij})|$, depends on the initial distribution. For example, $|RS(T_{n1})| = s$.

An i-relation query may be divided into a pair of subqueries. Let the query graph of an i-relation query be split into two connected subgraphs with r and $i-r$ nodes respectively ($1 \leq r < i$). By the definition of an i-relation query, these subgraphs become the query graphs of r-relation and (i-r)-relation queries. Dividing a query into a pair of subqueries implies that a node set T_{ij} is partitioned into two node sets T_{rp} and $T_{i-r,q}$ such that $T_{ij} = T_{rp} \cup T_{i-r,q}$ when $i \geq 2$. In a tree, the removal of an edge yields two subtrees. Thus, the result of an i-relation query is materialized by joining the results of its r-relation and (i-r)-relation queries. There are $i-1$ ways of dividing an i-relation query into a pair of r-relation and (i-r)-relation subqueries because there are i-1 edges in the corresponding query graph. If r or $i-r$ is always restricted to be 1, the plan produced is a deep GET.

We denote $trans_{xt}(T_{ij})$ to be the cost for transferring the result of T_{ij} from site x to site t. We assume that the communication cost is $trans_{xt}(T_{ij}) = c_1 + c_2 * size(T_{ij})$, where c_1 is the start-up cost of initiating transmission, c_2 is a proportionality constant, and $size(T_{ij})$ is the size of the result of T_{ij} expressed in bytes [16]. If $x = t$, $trans_{tt}(T_{ij}) = 0$. Also, we denote $join_x(T_{rp}, T_{i-r,q})$ to be the join cost between the results of T_{rp} and $T_{i-r,q}$ at site x.

It is assumed that there is no fast access path such as index for all non-leaf nodes and some leaf nodes in GET. This is justified by the observations that in distributed query processing,

- The join node is an intermediate result of a join. The intermediate result is not supported by fast access paths unless some are created dynamically.
- A fast access path is not valid outside the site where it was established. When a relation or intermediate result is sent from one site to another, its fast access path will not be sent. Thus, the transmission node is not supported by fast access paths.
- The operations like selection and projection are executed before joins. Thus, the leaf nodes which are qualified by these operations are also intermediate results.

Besides these, we assume that the usual statistical information for cost estimation is available, even though we have not explicitly expressed it in formalism. When multiple copies of a relation exist, we assume one copy has been preselected.

We make a *uniformity assumption* on a distributed environment, as in [1, 2, 3, 9, 10, 15]. That is, all sites have the same processing capabilities and the communication speeds between any two sites are the same. The assumption is then written formally as follows.

- if $x_1, x_2 \notin RS(T_{ij})$, $join_{x_1}(T_{rp}, T_{i-r,q}) = join_{x_2}(T_{rp}, T_{i-r,q})$.
- if $x_1 \in RS(T_{ij})$ and $x_2 \notin RS(T_{ij})$, $join_{x_1}(T_{rp}, T_{i-r,q}) \leq join_{x_2}(T_{rp}, T_{i-r,q})$.
- if $x_1 \neq t_1$ and $x_2 \neq t_2$, $trans_{x_1,t_1}(T_{ij}) = trans_{x_2,t_2}(T_{ij})$.

If an execution site x is not a site in the resident site set of T_{ij}, $RS(T_{ij})$, the results of subqueries T_{rp} and $T_{i-r,q}$ to be joined may be results materialized at the execution site x or transferred from other sites. In both cases, the intermediate result of join or transmission is stored in a temporary file and there is no index support for the file since we do not create index dynamically. However, if either or both of the subqueries to be joined is a 1-relation query, there may be index. Thus, the cost of join executed at the resident site of the relation captured in the 1-relation query may be lower than the join cost executed at the other site.

3 Two-Step Pruning Algorithm

3.1 Equivalence Criteria

The principle of optimality states that an optimal execution plan (optimal GET) for a query is composed of the optimal plan for its subqueries as subplans. Therefore, in order to produce an optimal plan for a given query through dynamic programming, the optimal plan for its subqueries must be produced in advance. That is, an optimal plan for an i-relation query is built from the optimal plans for its subqueries from 1-relation to (i-1)-relation queries.

If the results of r-relation and (i-r)-relation subqueries to be joined are not at the same site, one of them may be transferred to the site of the other or both of them transferred to a third site where a subsequent join between the i-relation query and another (k-i)-relation query will be executed. The third site can be any resident site of the relations captured in the (k-i)-relation query, since the (k-i)-relation query may materialize its result at this site. Furthermore, the result of the i-relation query materialized at the site where the results of its subqueries are located may be transferred to any resident site of the relations captured in the (k-i)-relation query because of the same reason. Thus, the site at which an i-relation query materializes its result, an *execution site of an i-relation query*, and the site to which an i-relation query delivers its result, a *delivery site of an i-relation query*, can be any resident site of the relations captured in a given query.

When building execution plans through dynamic programming, the optimizer systematically builds and compares equivalent partial plans through their cost estimates. Our optimizer builds the optimal plan of an i-relation query through two separate steps, one for join plan and the other for transmission plan. Let a *join plan of an i-relation query* be a plan which materializes the result of the query at a certain site, and a *transmission plan of an i-relation query* be a plan which transfers the result of the query to a certain site. Our optimizer uses the following *equivalence criteria* for pruning.

- Join plans are equivalent if they capture the same relations and have the same execution site.
- Transmission plans are equivalent if they capture the same relations and have the same delivery site.

For each i-relation query, the optimizer produces the optimal join and transmission plans by applying the pruning step twice based on the two criteria respectively. Thus, our optimizer has two chances to discard costly equivalent plans.

3.2 Principle of Optimality

To help us characterize the principle, we denote $a_x^u(T_{rp})$ to be the u-th transmission plan of T_{rp} at delivery site x among all equivalent transmission plans. The join and transmission plans of T_{ij} are produced by the following functions.

The function $buildJP_x(a_x^u(T_{rp}), a_x^v(T_{i-r,q}))$ combines the plans $a_x^u(T_{rp})$ and $a_x^v(T_{i-r,q})$ into the plan in which the results of T_{rp} and $T_{i-r,q}$ at site x are joined at this site, that is, $buildJP_x(a_x^u(T_{rp}), a_x^v(T_{i-r,q})) = JN_x(a_x^u(T_{rp}), a_x^v(T_{i-r,q}))$. By executing this plan, the result of T_{ij} is materialized at site x. The delivery site of subqueries T_{rp} and $T_{i-r,q}$, site x, becomes the execution site of T_{ij}. We denote $b_x^w(T_{ij})$ to be the plan produced by the function. It means the w-th join plan of T_{ij} at execution site x among all equivalent join plans.

The function $buildTP_{xt}(b_x^w(T_{ij}))$ extends the plan $b_x^w(T_{ij})$ into another plan in which the result of T_{ij} materialized at site x is transferred to site t, namely, $buildTP_{xt}(b_x^w(T_{ij})) = TR_{xt}(b_x^w(T_{ij}))$. The site t is the delivery site of T_{ij}. If sites x and t are equal, no transmission occurs. By executing this plan, we can get the result of T_{ij} at site t. The delivery site of the query T_{ij}, site t, may become the execution site of another query which employs T_{ij} as its subquery.

As the results of T_{rp} and $T_{i-r,q}$ to be joined must be at the same site, the cost of the join plan produced by $buildJP_x(a_x^u(T_{rp}), a_x^v(T_{i-r,q}))$ is the sum of the costs for getting the results of the subqueries T_{rp} and $T_{i-r,q}$ at site x and the cost for joining them at this site. Similarly, the cost of the transmission plan produced by $buildTP_{xt}(b_x^w(T_{ij}))$ is the sum of the cost for materializing the result of the query T_{ij} at site x and the cost for transferring the result from site x to site t. Let $Cost(p)$ be the cost of a plan p. Then, we have

$$Cost(buildJP_x(a_x^u(T_{rp}), a_x^v(T_{i-r,q}))) = Cost(a_x^u(T_{rp})) + Cost(a_x^v(T_{i-r,q})) + join_x(T_{rp}, T_{i-r,q}) \tag{4}$$

$$Cost(buildTP_{xt}(b_x^w(T_{ij}))) = Cost(b_x^w(T_{ij})) + trans_{xt}(T_{ij}) \tag{5}$$

To choose the optimal plans among the plans produced by $buildJP_x(-,-)$ and $buildTP_{xt}(-)$, we use the principle of optimality: If plans differ only in subplans, the plan with optimal subplans is also optimal. This principle can be expressed formally in the following theorem. Proofs for Theorem 1 and the following theorems are given in [8].

Theorem 1. *Let the subplans $a_x^1(T_{rp})$, $a_x^1(T_{i-r,q})$ and $b_x^1(T_{ij})$ be the lowest cost plans among all its equivalent plans $a_x^u(T_{rp})$, $a_x^v(T_{i-r,q})$ and $b_x^w(T_{ij})$ respectively. That is, $Cost(a_x^1(T_{rp})) \leq (\forall u)Cost(a_x^u(T_{rp}))$, $Cost(a_x^1(T_{i-r,q})) \leq (\forall v)Cost(a_x^v(T_{i-r,q}))$, and $Cost(b_x^1(T_{ij})) \leq (\forall w)Cost(b_x^w(T_{ij}))$. Then $Cost(buildJP_x(a_x^1(T_{rp}), a_x^1(T_{i-r,q}))) \leq (\forall u,v)Cost(buildJP_x(a_x^u(T_{rp}), a_x^v(T_{i-r,q})))$ and $Cost(buildTP_{xt}(b_x^1(T_{ij}))) \leq (\forall w)Cost(buildTP_{xt}(b_x^w(T_{ij})))$.*

We call $a_x^1(T_{rp})$ the optimal transmission plan of T_{rp} at site x and $b_x^1(T_{ij})$ the optimal join plan of T_{ij} at site x. According to the theorem, we can get the following equations.

$$Cost(buildJP_x(a_x^1(T_{rp}), a_x^1(T_{i-r,q}))) = \min_{\forall u,v}\{Cost(buildJP_x(a_x^u(T_{rp}), a_x^v(T_{i-r,q})))\} \tag{6}$$

$$Cost(buildTP_{xt}(b_x^1(T_{ij}))) = \min_{\forall w}\{Cost(buildTP_{xt}(b_x^w(T_{ij})))\} \quad (7)$$

Now, let's compute the cost of an optimal join plan of T_{ij} at site x, $Cost(b_x^1(T_{ij}))$. As there are $i-1$ pairs of subqueries T_{rp} and $T_{i-r,q}$ for a query T_{ij}, we must compare $i-1$ costs of all equivalent join plans. For each pair of subqueries, the results of subqueries to be joined must be at site x. Since there are many alternative plans to get the result of subquery at site x, we also compare all equivalent transmission plans of both subqueries at site x and then choose the lowest cost plans. Thus, we have

$$\begin{aligned} Cost(b_x^1(T_{ij})) &= \min_{\forall p,q,r}\{\min_{\forall u,v}\{Cost(buildJP_x(a_x^u(T_{rp}), a_x^v(T_{i-r,q})))\}\} \\ &= \min_{\forall p,q,r}\{Cost(buildJP_x(a_x^1(T_{rp}), a_x^1(T_{i-r,q})))\} \\ &= \min_{\forall p,q,r}\{Cost(a_x^1(T_{rp})) + Cost(a_x^1(T_{i-r,q})) + join_x(T_{rp}, T_{i-r,q})\} \quad (8) \end{aligned}$$

where $\forall p, q, r$ means all pairs of subqueries T_{rp}, $T_{i-r,q}$ such that $T_{ij} = T_{rp} \cup T_{i-r,q}$. This equation is developed from Equations (6) and (4).

Let's compute the cost of an optimal transmission plan of T_{ij} at site t, $Cost(a_t^1(T_{ij}))$. In order to get a result of T_{ij} at site t, the result may be directly materialized at site t or materialized at another site, for example, at site x and then transferred to site t. As the result of T_{ij} may be materialized at any site in the resident site set of the given query, $RS(T_{n1})$, we must compare the costs of all equivalent transmission plans. Before a transmission of a result of T_{ij} occurs, the result must be materialized. Since there are many equivalent join plans to materialize the result of T_{ij} at site x, we also compare them and then choose the lowest cost plan. Thus, we have

$$\begin{aligned} Cost(a_t^1(T_{ij})) &= \min_{\forall x \in RS(T_{n1})}\{\min_{\forall w}\{Cost(buildTP_{xt}(b_x^w(T_{ij})))\}\} \\ &= \min_{\forall x \in RS(T_{n1})}\{Cost(buildTP_{xt}(b_x^1(T_{ij})))\} \\ &= \min_{\forall x \in RS(T_{n1})}\{Cost(b_x^1(T_{ij})) + trans_{xt}(T_{ij})\} \quad (9) \end{aligned}$$

This equation is developed from Equations (7) and (5). In Equation (9), if $x = t$ the result of T_{ij} is directly materialized at site t because of $trans_{tt}(T_{ij}) = 0$. Otherwise, it is materialized at site x and then transferred to site t.

Equations (8) and (9) form an indirect recurrence. Since there is no join plan of 1-relation query, we will initialize the transmission plans of 1-relation query. The initial condition for Equation (8) is $Cost(a_t^1(T_{1j})) = trans_{xt}(R_j)$ where x is the resident site of relation R_j. If $x = t$, $Cost(a_t^1(T_{1j}))$ will be zero. If Equations (8) and (9) are computed for each i-relation query ($2 \leq i \leq n$) varying x and t over all related sites, that is, $\forall x, t \in RS(T_{n1})$, an optimal plan of a given query at a query site can be produced.

Equations (8) and (9) say that the optimal join plan of T_{ij} at site x is constructed by the optimal transmission plans of its subqueries T_{rp} and $T_{i-r,q}$ at this site and the optimal transmission plan of T_{ij} at site t is constructed by the optimal join plan of T_{ij} at site x. That is, the optimal join and transmission plans are constructed recursively using each other.

3.3 Plan Aggregation and Elimination

We will aggregate some plans to avoid redundant computations, and eliminate some plans from the execution space in order to prevent wasteful searches. The optimal plans of an i-relation query are *redundant* if they always have the same cost irrespective of the contents of the relations captured in the query. For example, relation A at site 1 and relation B at site 2 may be joined at site 3 or 4 where a subsequent join will be executed. The costs of the optimal join plans at site 3 and 4 are computed as follows.

$$\begin{aligned} Cost(b_3^1(\{A,B\})) &= Cost(buildJP_3(a_3^1(\{A\}), a_3^1(\{B\}))) \\ &= Cost(a_3^1(\{A\})) + Cost(a_3^1(\{B\})) + join_3(\{A\},\{B\}) \\ &= trans_{13}(\{A\}) + trans_{23}(\{B\}) + join_3(\{A\},\{B\}) \\ Cost(b_4^1(\{A,B\})) &= trans_{14}(\{A\}) + trans_{24}(\{B\}) + join_4(\{A\},\{B\}) \end{aligned}$$

Because of the uniformity assumption, $Cost(b_3^1(\{A,B\}))$ is equal to $Cost(b_4^1(\{A, B\}))$.

Similarly, the join result between A and B may be directly materialized at site 3 or materialized at a site other than site 3 and then be transferred to site 3. This is also true for site 4. Thus, the costs of the optimal transmission plans at site 3 and 4 are

$$\begin{aligned} & Cost(a_3^1(\{A,B\})) \\ &= \min\{\, Cost(buildTP_{13}(b_1^1(\{A,B\}))), Cost(buildTP_{23}(b_2^1(\{A,B\}))), \\ &\qquad Cost(buildTP_{33}(b_3^1(\{A,B\}))), Cost(buildTP_{43}(b_4^1(\{A,B\})))\} \\ &= \min\{\, Cost(b_1^1(\{A,B\})) + trans_{13}(\{A,B\}), Cost(b_2^1(\{A,B\})) + trans_{23}(A,B), \\ &\qquad Cost(b_3^1(\{A,B\})), Cost(b_4^1(\{A,B\})) + trans_{43}(\{A,B\})\} \\ & Cost(a_4^1(\{A,B\})) \\ &= \min\{\, Cost(b_1^1(\{A,B\})) + trans_{14}(\{A,B\}), Cost(b_2^1(\{A,B\})) + trans_{24}(\{A,B\}), \\ &\qquad Cost(b_3^1(\{A,B\})) + trans_{34}(\{A,B\}), Cost(b_4^1(\{A,B\}))\} \end{aligned}$$

Since $Cost(b_3^1(\{A,B\})) = Cost(b_4^1(\{A,B\}))$ and $trans_{x_1,t_1}(\{A,B\}) = trans_{x_2,t_2}(\{A,B\})$ for $x_1 \neq t_1$ and $x_2 \neq t_2$ according to the uniformity assumption, $Cost(a_3^1\ (\{A,B\}))$ is equal to $Cost(a_4^1(\{A,B\}))$. These can be generalized for any i-relation query in the following theorem.

Theorem 2. *Let $x, y, s, t \in RS(T_{n1}) - RS(T_{ij})$. Then $Cost(b_x^1(T_{ij})) = Cost(b_y^1(T_{ij}))$ and $Cost(a_s^1(T_{ij})) = Cost(a_t^1(T_{ij}))$.*

The above theorem states that all optimal join and transmission plans of T_{ij} at a site not in $RS(T_{ij})$ are redundant. The implication of this theorem is that it is unnecessary to compute the cost of an optimal plan of an i-relation query at all resident sites. Therefore, without losing optimality, it is possible to aggregate the redundant join plans into a single plan whose execution site is marked as *undetermined* and also aggregate the redundant transmission plans into a single plan whose delivery site is also marked as undetermined. The undetermined execution and delivery site of an i-relation query T_{ij} can be any site not in $RS(T_{ij})$. An undetermined site is not yet known when the i-relation query is being optimized. It will be determined later when the query employing the i-relation query as a subquery has been optimized.

Since we introduce the concept of an indefinite site, it becomes impossible to compute the transmission cost between the undetermined sites. From the steps of proving Theorem 2, we fortunately know that the only case of any transmission plan from an undetermined site to another undetermined site to be optimal is when both sites are the same. Thus, we can let this transmission cost be zero. By plan aggregation, we can compute Equations (8) and (9) varying execution and delivery site on the restricted set of sites, that is, $\forall x, t \in RS(T_{ij}) \cup$ {undetermined site} instead of $\forall x, t \in RS(T_{n1})$.

A plan of an i-relation query is *inferior* if there is a lower cost equivalent plan irrespective of the contents of the relations involved in the query [15]. Without losing optimality, we can eliminate the inferior plans of an i-relation query when considering the equivalent plans of the query. Let's reconsider the above chain query. The cost of the optimal transmission plan of a subquery A, B at delivery site 3 is computed as follows.

$$
\begin{aligned}
&Cost(a_3^1(\{A,B\}))\\
&= \min\{\, Cost(buildTP_{13}(b_1^1(\{A,B\}))), Cost(buildTP_{23}(b_2^1(\{A,B\}))),\\
&\qquad Cost(buildTP_{33}(b_3^1(\{A,B\}))), Cost(buildTP_{43}(b_4^1(\{A,B\})))\}\\
&= \min\{\, Cost(b_1^1(\{A,B\})) + trans_{13}(\{A,B\}), Cost(b_2^1(\{A,B\})) + trans_{23}(\{A,B\}),\\
&\qquad Cost(b_3^1(\{A,B\})), Cost(b_4^1(\{A,B\})) + trans_{43}(\{A,B\})\}\\
&= \min\{\, trans_{21}(\{B\}) + join_1(\{A\},\{B\}) + trans_{13}(\{A,B\}),\\
&\qquad trans_{12}(\{A\}) + join_2(\{A\},\{B\}) + trans_{23}(\{A,B\}),\\
&\qquad trans_{13}(\{A\}) + trans_{23}(\{B\}) + join_3(\{A\},\{B\}),\\
&\qquad trans_{14}(\{A\}) + trans_{24}(\{B\}) + join_4(\{A\},\{B\}) + trans_{43}(\{A,B\})\}
\end{aligned}
$$

According to the uniformity assumption, the join cost at site 3 is equal to that at site 4 because of $RS(\{A,B\}) = \{1,2\}$. Furthermore, the transmission plan from site 4, that is, $buildTP_{43}(b_4^1(\{A,B\}))$ has an additional transmission cost compared to that from site 3. Thus, the transmission plans from site 4 is inferior to that from site 3. We will show that there may exist inferior transmission plans of an i-relation query in the following theorem.

Theorem 3. *Let* $t \in RS(T_{n1})$, $x \in RS(T_{ij}) \cup \{t\}$, $y \in RS(T_{n1}) - \{RS(T_{ij}) \cup \{t\}\}$. *Then* $Cost(buildTP_{xt}(b_x^1(T_{ij}))) \leq Cost(buildTP_{yt}(b_y^1(T_{ij})))$.

Theorem 3 essentially says that, for any delivery site t, a transmission plan of an i-relation query T_{ij} from a site not in $RS(T_{ij}) \cup \{t\}$ is inferior to that from a site in $RS(T_{ij}) \cup \{t\}$. We can then choose the optimal transmission plan without comparing all equivalent plans. Thus, we have

$$
\begin{aligned}
&min_{\forall x \in RS(T_{n1})}\{Cost(buildTP_{xt}(b_x^1(T_{ij})))\} =\\
&min_{\forall x \in RS(T_{ij}) \cup \{t\}}\{Cost(buildTP_{xt}(b_x^1(T_{ij})))\}
\end{aligned}
\tag{10}
$$

The upshot of Theorem 3 is that we need not search through all the possible transmission plans to find one guaranteed to be optimal. Elimination of inferior plans reduces the execution space That must be searched to find an optimal plans, and thereby makes the process of optimization more efficient.

3.4 Two-Step Pruning

In this subsection, we describe the dynamic programming algorithm to generate an optimal plan of a given query (n-relation query, T_{n1}) at a query site and compute its cost. The optimal cost is obtained by recursively computing the following costs. Let $CostJ_x(T_{ij})$ be the cost of an optimal join plan of T_{ij} at site x and $CostT_t(T_{ij})$ be the cost of an optimal transmission plan of T_{ij} at site t, that is, $CostJ_x(T_{ij}) = Cost(b_x^1(T_{ij}))$ and $CostT_t(T_{ij}) = Cost(a_t^1(T_{ij}))$. By the definition of $CostJ$, $CostT$ and Theorem 2, 3, Equations (8) and (9) are rewritten as follows.

$$CostJ_x(T_{ij}) = min_{\forall p,q,r}\{CostT_{x_1}(T_{rp}) + CostT_{x_2}(T_{i-r,q}) + join_x(T_{rp}, T_{i-r,q})\} \tag{11}$$

$$CostT_t(T_{ij}) = min_{\forall x \in RS(T_{ij}) \cup \{t\}}\{CostJ_x(T_{ij}) + trans_{xt}(T_{ij})\} \tag{12}$$

In Equation (11), if $x \in RS(T_{rp})$, $x_1 = x$. Otherwise, x_1 is an undetermined site. Similarly, if $x \in RS(T_{i-r,q})$, $x_2 = x$. Otherwise, x_2 is an undetermined site. The initial condition for Equation (11) is $CostT_t(T_{1j}) = trans_{xt}(R_j)$ for all $t \in RS(T_{1j}) \cup$ {undetermined site} = {x, undetermined site} where x is the resident site of relation R_j.

If $CostJ_x(T_{ij})$ and $CostT_t(T_{ij})$ are computed for each i-relation query T_{ij} varying x and t over $RS(T_{ij}) \cup$ {undetermined site} and this computations are repeatedly applied for $i = 2, 3, \cdots, n$, $CostT_{query\_site}(T_{n1})$ for n-relation query T_{n1} can be finally obtained. When computing $CostJ_x(T_{ij})$, Equation (11) prunes equivalent join plans except the optimal one. Similarly when computing $CostT_t(T_{ij})$, equivalent transmission plans except the optimal one are pruned by Equation (12). The obtained $CostJ_x(T_{ij})$ and $CostT_t(T_{ij})$ are saved in order to reuse when the query T_{ij} is employed as a subquery of another larger query.

Generating an optimal plan of an i-relation query is the process of constructing feasible optimal subtrees (subplans) of an optimal GET. For each i-relation query, computing the costs $CostJ_x(T_{ij})$ and $CostT_t(T_{ij})$ means computing the costs of optimal subtrees whose roots are the corresponding join and transmission nodes in GET. That is, $CostJ_x(T_{ij})$ is the cost of an optimal subplan whose root is a join node with site label x, and $CostT_t(T_{ij})$ is the cost of an optimal subplan whose root is a transmission node with site label t.

The dynamic programming equations are coded in the algorithm TSP in Figure 4. The algorithm first initializes $CostT_t(T_{1j})$ for each 1-relation query in lines 1-5. In lines 6-23, it then uses Equations (11) and (12) to compute $CostJ_x(T_{ij})$ and $CostT_t(T_{ij})$ for each i-relation query varying x and t over the resident site set of the query and an undetermined site. This process is repeatedly applied in bottom-up fashion, that is, for $i = 2, 3, \cdots, n$.

An optimal GET of a given n-relation query is constructed from that of an i-relation query. For each i-relation query, TSP algorithm maintains not only the optimal join and transmission costs but also additional information such as optimal join pair and execution site in its optimal plan, $OptPlan_t(T_{ij})$. Thus, we can construct an optimal GET of a given query by the postorder traversal from the root node, $OptPlan_{query\_site}(T_{n1})$. The algorithm *Build* in Figure 5 constructs

```
Algorithm TSP
Input: All i-relation query T_ij's (1 ≤ j ≤ m_i) and its resident site set RS(T_ij)'s.
Output: An optimal GET with its cost.
for j:=1 to n do
    let x be the resident site of R_j;
    for all t ∈ {x, undetermined site} do
        CostT_t(T_1j) := trans_xt(T_1j);
        save x into OptPlan_t(T_1j);
for i:=2 to n do
    for j:=1 to m_i do
        /* optimal join plan of T_ij at site x */
        for all x ∈ RS(T_ij)∪ {undetermined site} do  /* execution site */
            CostJ_x(T_ij) := ∞;
            for all pair T_rp,T_i-r,q s.t. T_ij = T_rp ∪ T_i-r,q do
                if x ∈ RS(T_rp) then x1 := x
                    else x1 := undetermined site;
                if x ∈ RS(T_i-r,q) then x2 := x
                    else x2 := undetermined site;
                jc := CostT_x1(T_rp) + CostT_x2(T_i-r,q) + join_x(T_rp, T_i-r,q);
                if CostJ_x(T_ij) > jc then  /* pruning */
                    CostJ_x(T_ij) := jc;
                    save p, q, r and CostJ into OptPlan_x(T_ij);
        /* optimal transmission plan of T_ij at site t */
        for all t ∈ RS(T_ij)∪ {undetermined site} do  /* delivery site */
            CostT_t(T_ij) := ∞;
            for all x ∈ RS(T_ij) ∪ {t} do
                tc := CostJ_x(T_ij) + trans_xt(T_ij);
                if CostT_t(T_ij) > tc then  /* pruning */
                    CostT_t(T_ij) := tc;
                    save x and CostT into OptPlan_t(T_ij);
Plan := OptPlan_query_site(T_n1) with CostT_query_site(T_n1);
```

Fig. 4. Two-step pruning algorithm

an optimal GET from partial plans. The initial call is Build($n, 1, query\_site$, TRANS).

When constructing an optimal GET,the algorithm Build decides the definite sites of the undetermined sites in lines 2-6. Since the decisions are made in a top-down fashion, an undetermined delivery site of an i-relation query T_{ij} is decided before its undetermined execution site. If the delivery site of an i-relation query T_{ij} is in $RS(T_{ij})$, it is not an undetermined site. In this case, the undetermined execution site may be any site not in $RS(T_{ij})$. But if the delivery site of the query is not in $RS(T_{ij})$, it was the undetermined site when the query was being optimized and its definite site has been decided in previous construction stages. In that case, the undetermined execution site is equal to its delivery site, because the only case of any transmission plan from an undetermined site to another undetermined site to be optimal is when both sites are the same.

Algorithm Build($i, j, t, flag$)
Input: Optimal plan of i-relation query T_{ij}, $OptPlant(T_{ij})$. If $flag$ is TRANS, t is the delivery site of T_{ij}. Otherwise, t is the execution site of T_{ij}.
Output: Execution sequence of operations in an optimal GET.

```
if flag = TRANS then
    if OptPlant(T_ij).x = undetermined site then
        /* execution site is undetermined */
        if t ∈ RS(T_ij) then  /* delivery site is not undetermined */
            let OptPlan_t(T_ij).x be any site not in RS(T_ij)
        else  /* delivery site was undetermined */
            OptPlan_t(T_ij).x := t;
    if i ≠ 1 then
        Build(i, j, OptPlan_t(T_ij).x, JOIN);
    if OptPlan_t(T_ij).x ≠ t then
        print "TR_xt(T_ij) : transfer T_ij from site x to t"
else  /* flag = JOIN */
    /* let the execution site of T_ij be the delivery sites of its subqueries */
    Build(OptPlan_t(T_ij).r, OptPlan_t(T_ij).p, t, TRANS);
    Build(i - OptPlan_t(T_ij).r, OptPlan_t(T_ij).q, t, TRANS);
    print "JN_t(T_rp, T_i-r,q) : join between T_rp and T_i-r,q at site t";
```

Fig. 5. Optimal GET construction algorithm

3.5 Complexity of Algorithm

For each site in the resident site set of an i-relation query and an undetermined site, TSP algorithm considers all equivalent join and transmission plans except the inferior plans and chooses the lowest cost join and transmission plans as the optimal ones. Thus, the time complexity of the algorithm is determined by the number of considered plans, which depends on the initial distribution of relations and the number of subqueries.

The number of i-relation queries is determined by the shape of the query graph and the number of relations in the graph. Let's consider the special cases of a tree query, namely, a *chain query* and a *star query* whose corresponding query graphs are chain and star respectively. For a chain query with n relations, an i-relation query is composed of i consecutive relations. Thus, the number of i-relation queries, m_i, is $n - i + 1$. Also, for a star query with n relations, an i-relation query is constructed by choosing $i - 1$ relations from $n - 1$ relations around the root relation. Thus, we have $m_i = \binom{n-1}{i-1}$. It has been shown that, for a tree query, the total number of subqueries, $\sum m_i$, is the largest with a star query and the smallest with a chain query [12]. Thus, if the initial distributions of relations involved in chain and star queries are equal, the algorithm has the worst case complexity with a star query and the best case with a chain query.

For a tree query with n relations distributed over s sites, let's analyze the complexities of TSP algorithm. The time complexity of the algorithm is determined by the number of plans considered in lines 14 and 21. For a chain query, $m_i = n - i + 1$ and there are $i-1$ pairs of subqueries for each i-relation query. The cardinality of the resident site set of an i-relation query varies according to the initial distribution and is no more than s. Thus, the number of join plans considered in line 14 is

$$\sum_{i=2}^{n}\sum_{j=1}^{n-i+1}\sum_{x=1}^{|RS(T_{ij})|+1}\sum_{p=1}^{i-1}1 \leq \sum_{i=2}^{n}\sum_{j=1}^{n-i+1}\sum_{x=1}^{s+1}\sum_{p=1}^{i-1}1 = (s+1)\frac{(n-1)n(n+1)}{6}$$

and the number of transmission plans considered in line 21 is

$$\sum_{i=2}^{n}\sum_{j=1}^{n-i+1}\sum_{t=1}^{|RS(T_{ij})|+1}\sum_{x=1}^{|RS(T_{ij})|+1}1 \leq \sum_{i=2}^{n}\sum_{j=1}^{n-i+1}\sum_{t=1}^{s+1}\sum_{x=1}^{s+1}1 = (s+1)^2\frac{(n-1)n}{2}$$

Clearly, considering join and transmission plans take time $O(sn^3)$ and $O(s^2n^2)$ respectively. Because s is less than or equal to n, the total best case time complexity is less than $O(sn^3)$.

For a star query, the process of complexity computation is the same as that of the chain query except $m_i = \binom{n-1}{i-1}$. Thus, the numbers of join and transmission plans considered in lines 14 and 21 are

$$\sum_{i=2}^{n}\sum_{j=1}^{\binom{n-1}{i-1}}\sum_{x=1}^{|RS(T_{ij})|+1}\sum_{p=1}^{i-1}1 \leq \sum_{i=2}^{n}\sum_{j=1}^{\binom{n-1}{i-1}}\sum_{x=1}^{s+1}\sum_{p=1}^{i-1}1 = (s+1)(n-1)2^{n-2}$$

and

$$\sum_{i=2}^{n}\sum_{j=1}^{\binom{n-1}{i-1}}\sum_{t=1}^{|RS(T_{ij})|+1}\sum_{x=1}^{|RS(T_{ij})|+1}1 \leq \sum_{i=2}^{n}\sum_{j=1}^{\binom{n-1}{i-1}}\sum_{t=1}^{s+1}\sum_{x=1}^{s+1}1 = (s+1)^2(2^{n-1}-1)$$

Therefore, the total worst case time complexity is $O(sn2^{n-1})$ according to the same reason.

The above analysis only shows upper bounds of complexities because we use the maximum upper bound of the cardinality of a resident site set, that is, $|RS(T_{ij})| = s$ instead of a precious bound. Actually, $|RS(T_{ij})|$ is bounded by the following inequalities.

$$\begin{cases} 2 \leq i \leq s, & |RS(T_{ij})| \leq i \\ s < i \leq n, & |RS(T_{ij})| \leq s \end{cases}$$

The complexities are lowered by using these actual upper bounds of the cardinality. For example, the number of join plans considered in the case of a star query is rewritten as follows.

$$\sum_{i=2}^{n}\sum_{j=1}^{\binom{n-1}{i-1}}\sum_{x=1}^{|RS(T_{ij})|+1}\sum_{p=1}^{i-1}1 \leq \sum_{i=2}^{s}\sum_{j=1}^{\binom{n-1}{i-1}}\sum_{x=1}^{i+1}\sum_{p=1}^{i-1}1 + \sum_{i=s+1}^{n}\sum_{j=1}^{\binom{n-1}{i-1}}\sum_{x=1}^{s+1}\sum_{p=1}^{i-1}1$$

$$= \sum_{i=1}^{s-1}\binom{n-1}{i}(i+2)i + (s+1)\sum_{i=1}^{n-s}\binom{n-1}{i+s-1}(i+s-1)$$

Since this equation can not be expressed as a closed form of n and s [4], we can not help using the maximum upper bound of the cardinality. This implies that the above analysis does not reflect the effects of plan aggregation and elimination unfortunately. However, the actual optimization work is considerably smaller compared to the analysis.

Though the number of considered plans is reduced by plan aggregation and elimination, the worst case complexity is still exponential in terms of the number of relations in the query. We do not believe that the exponential complexity at the worst case hinders the practicality of our algorithm. This is because queries with more than 10 joins are rare. In a survey of 30 major DB2 customers [14], for example, the most complex join query involves just 8 relations. Furthermore, a star query is just a hypothetical query that is rarely made by a user.

3.6 Comparison

Though OSP, semi-TSP and our TSP algorithm all employ dynamic programming as a search strategy, their characteristics and search efficiencies are different. The time complexity of OSP algorithm is determined by the number of plans considered in Equation (1). For chain and star queries,these numbers are computed as follows.

$$\sum_{i=3}^{n}\sum_{j=1}^{n-i+1}\sum_{t=1}^{|RS(T_{ij})|+1}\sum_{p=1}^{2}\sum_{x=1}^{|RS(T_{ij})|+1}1 \leq \sum_{i=3}^{s}\sum_{j=1}^{n-i+1}\sum_{t=1}^{i+1}\sum_{p=1}^{2}\sum_{x=1}^{i+1}1 + \sum_{i=s+1}^{n}\sum_{j=1}^{n-i+1}\sum_{t=1}^{s+1}\sum_{p=1}^{2}\sum_{x=1}^{s+1}1$$

$$\sum_{i=3}^{n}\sum_{j=1}^{\binom{n-1}{i-1}}\sum_{t=1}^{|RS(T_{ij})|+1}\sum_{p=1}^{i-1}\sum_{x=1}^{|RS(T_{ij})|+1}1 \leq \sum_{i=3}^{s}\sum_{j=1}^{\binom{n-1}{i-1}}\sum_{t=1}^{i+1}\sum_{p=1}^{i-1}\sum_{x=1}^{i+1}1 + \sum_{i=s+1}^{n}\sum_{j=1}^{\binom{n-1}{i-1}}\sum_{t=1}^{s+1}\sum_{p=1}^{i-1}\sum_{x=1}^{s+1}1$$

In Figure 6, we draw diagrams concerning the number of plans considered in OSP and TSP algorithms varying n and s such that $n \geq 2$ and $n \geq s \geq 2$. In the figure, the bright surface represents the number of plans considered in OSP algorithm and the dark surface, the number of plans considered in TSP algorithm. By comparing the two surfaces, we know that the number of plans considered in TSP algorithm is smaller than that in OSP algorithm when $n \geq 3$ and $s \geq 3$. As OSP algorithm does not search the bushy execution plans, this algorithm produces a suboptimal plan. Therefore, in most cases, our TSP algorithm produces an optimal plan while considering less partial plans than the suboptimal algorithm OSP.

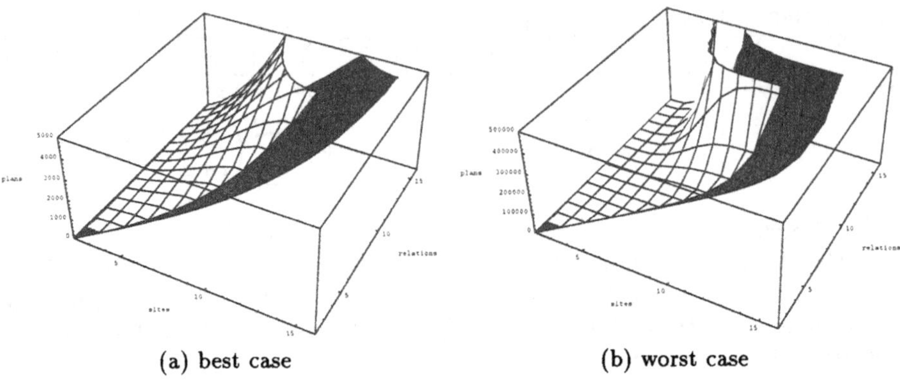

(a) best case (b) worst case

Fig. 6. The number of plans considered in OSP and TSP algorithm

The time complexity of semi-TSP algorithm is determined by the number of trajectories considered in Equation (3) and this number depends on the number of states generated. As in the cases of algorithms OSP and TSP, the number of states generated is determined by the initial distribution and the shape of the query graph. Contrary to these two algorithms, the number is the smallest with a star query because the bushy states like $(-;-;AB,CD;-)$ are not generated with a star query. Thus, semi-TSP algorithm has the best case time complexity with a star query. However, if all n relations are stored at different sites, the number of states generated with a star query is exponential in n (though that number is reduced by the equivalence class technique in [9]). Thus, in case of this initial distribution, the best case time complexity is also exponential in n. Since our TSP algorithm has a polynomial time complexity at the best case with this initial distribution, and its extra work in generating all subqueries is much less than that in constructing a state space of semi-TSP algorithm, our algorithm has computational advantages over semi-TSP algorithm.

4 Conclusion

We have presented an algorithm which determines the optimal global plan for a tree query in a distributed database. The objective function of optimization is the total processing time including not only the communication costs but also the local processing costs. The optimizer we have developed considers the execution plans which may be deep or bushy trees. The search work done by our optimizer is reduced by applying dynamic programming technique. We devise the two-step pruning mechanism to choose an optimal plan among all feasible plans. In the first pruning step, an optimal join plan of a subquery is chosen among all equivalent plans which materialize the result of the subquery at the same site. Then, in the second pruning step, an optimal transmission plan of a subquery is chosen among all equivalent plans which transfer the result of the subquery to the same site. While building an optimal global plan of a given query, we apply the mechanism successively to each subquery so that the plans except the optimal one are pruned efficiently. The algorithm has the polynomial time complexity $O(sn^3)$ at the best case, but the exponential $O(sn2^{n-1})$ at the worst case. Although finding an optimal plan is costly, the optimization overhead is rapidly amortized if the query is executed frequently.

We show that, without losing optimality, it is possible to aggregate some redundant plans into a single plan. Furthermore, we can always guarantee the optimality though we eliminate the inferior plans from the execution space of our optimizer. This means that we can produce the optimal plan without exhaustive search. Clearly, the plan aggregation and elimination significantly reduce the optimization work.

Future work includes: extending the algorithm to minimize the response time of processing a query and to be used in the case of recursive queries, elaborating the cost model to predict the cost of query processing exactly.

Acknowledgement

This work was partially supported by the Korea Science and Engineering Foundation (KOSEF) under Grant No. 931-0900-022-2.

References

1. Apers, P., Hevner, A., and Yao, S.B., "Optimization algorithm for distributed queries", IEEE Trans. Software Engineering, SE-9, No.1, Jan. 1983, pp.57-68.
2. Bernstein, P.A., Goodman, N., Wong, E., Reeve, C.L., and Rothnie, Jr., J.B., "Query Processing in a System for Distributed Databases (SDD-1)", ACM Trans. Database Systems, Vol.6, No.4, Dec. 1981, pp.602-625.
3. Chiu, D-M, Bernstein, P. and Ho, Y-C, "Optimizing chain queries in a distributed database system", SIAM Journal of Computing, Vol.13, No.1, Feb., 1984, pp.116-134.
4. Graham, R.L., Knuth, D.E., and Patashnik, O., *Concrete Mathematics*, Addison-Wesley Publishing Company, Inc., 1989, pp.165-166.
5. Hevner, A.R., and Yao, S.B., "Querying Distributed Databases on Local Area Networks", Proceedings of The IEEE, Vol.75, No.5, May 1987, pp.563-572.
6. Horowitz, E., Sahni, S., *Fundamentals of Computer Algorithms*, Computer Science Press, Inc., 1978, pp.198-202.
7. Ioannidis, Y.E., Kang, Y.C., "Left-deep vs. bushy trees: An analysis of strategy spaces and its implications for query optimization", Proc. ACM SIGMOD, May 1991, pp.168-177.
8. Kim, H., Lee, S., Kim, H.-J., "Two-step pruning algorithm for distributed query optimization", Technical report DBTR-95-1, 1995.

9. Lafortune, S., and Wong, E., "A state transition model for distributed query processing", ACM Transactions on Database Systems, Vol.11, No.3, Sep. 1986, pp.294-322.
10. Lohman, G.M., Mohan, C., Haas, L.M., Lindsay, B.G., Selinger, P.G., Wilms, P.F., "Query processing in R*", IBM Research Report RJ4272, San Jose, Calif., April 1984.
11. Mackert, L.M., Lohman, G.M., "R* optimizer validation and performance evaluation for distributed queries", Proc. VLDB, August 1986, pp.149-159.
12. Ono, K. and Lohman, G.M., "Measuring the complexity of join enumeration in query optimization", Proc. VLDB, August 1990, pp.314-325.
13. Ozsu, M.T., and Valduriez, P., *Principle of Distributed Database Systems*, Prentice-Hall International, Inc., 1991, pp.230-252.
14. Tsang, A., Olschanowsky, M., "A study of Database 2 customer queries", Technical Report 03.413, IBM Santa Teresa Laboratory, April 1991.
15. Yu, C.T., "Optimization of distributed tree query", Journal of Computer and System Science, Academic Press, Inc., Vol.29, 1984, pp.409-445.
16. Yu, C.T. and Chang C.C., "Distributed query processing", ACM Computing Surveys, Vol.16, No.4, Dec., 1984, pp.399-432.

Text Search Using Database Systems Revisited — Some Experiments —

Helmut Kaufmann and Hans-Jörg Schek

Swiss Federal Institute of Technology (ETH Zürich)
Department of Computer Science—Databases
{kaufmann, schek}@inf.ethz.ch

Abstract. With the increasing availability of information in electronic form, the integration of textual data into database systems is becoming more and more important. Motivated by recent technology development, we describe how a preprocessor for simple text retrieval can be realised on top of a relational database system. This approach shows a surprisingly good performance compared to a commercially available information retrieval system and compared to another relational preprocessor product for text search.

1 Introduction and Motivation

In the late seventies and early eighties a considerable amount of research was devoted to the comparison of database systems (DBS) and information retrieval systems (IRS) and to a synthesis of these. Principle differences between both are described in [Rij81]. Specifically, discussions of data model issues are given in, for example, [SP82, DKA+86]; architectural issues in [Bil82, Sch84, LDE+85, LKD+88, Fuh89]. Prototype systems built on top of relational systems are described in [Mac79, SSL+83]. Our own early experience was gained by a prototype system [Pol80] built on top of IBM's SQL/DS by using the reference string indexing method [Sch77]. Although these early attempts showed some promise, the consensus was more or less that relational systems were not really suitable for text retrieval. Many groups started to build new next generation database systems, e.g. [SR86, SW86, SPSW90], rather than putting a document management and search preprocessor on top of existing database systems.

Now, more than ten years later, we believe that this discussion must be resumed for the following reasons:

- **Technology Evolution:** Relational database technology has evolved together with the dramatic changes in hardware and communication technology. Sophisticated client-server architectures and transaction technology provide parallel search and update of many users in a scalable way. They more and more use multi-processor hardware and provide not only inter- but also intra-transaction parallelism.
- **Higher Level of Abstraction:** Increasingly, relational database systems are being used as storage managers upon which sophisticated object managers and application-oriented tools are built. Some consider the relational

interface as a replacement of the file system that, among many advantages, enables parallelisation at the I/O level.
- **More Text:** Many data items in current database systems contain textual attributes. Over eighty percent of the information generated in a business environment is full text, and most of the documents are enriched by structured information such as the type of the documents, their creation dates, authors, keywords, and addressees.

Our general question therefore is whether, and to what extent, we can utilise existing technology and support primitive text search in today's relational databases by building a simple preprocessor on top of these systems. Our initial expectations were the following:

- An information retrieval system should outperform any relational preprocessor solution in the single-user mode.
- A preprocessor solution on top of a relational database system should outperform an information retrieval system in case of multiple parallel users.

In this paper, we will report on our findings but we are far from giving final answers. The contribution of this paper is the presentation of some carefully measured experiments and observations that we made. It shows that our simple preprocessor solution on top of Oracle outperforms a specialised IRS (BASIS-Plus [Inf90]), especially in the case where many parallel searchers have to be supported. We also show that it is necessary to introduce a simple query optimisation by comparing our own preprocessor solution with the commercially available product SQL*TextRetrieval [SQL92]. The test data are taken from a real application. Although we restricted ourselves to a single application, we think that the observations gained there point out that the existing widely-held opinion that it is inappropriate to support an IRS on a DBS should not be taken for granted.

The structure of this paper is as follows: In Sec. 2, we present inverted lists as an access structure for text and show how they can be integrated into a relational database system using a simple preprocessor. In Sec. 3, we introduce BASISPlus and and two preprocessor solutions implemented on top of Oracle. After briefly introducing the real world application *PHONO+* in Sec. 4, we conclude with a presentation and comparison of our measurement results.

2 Simple Access Structures for Relational Database Systems

In order to support full text search in a relational database system efficiently, textual access structures must be introduced. In this section, we present *inverted lists* as a simple access structure for boolean text retrieval and show how they can be included in a relational database system using a simple preprocessor. A *document* — in the context of this paper but without loss of generality — is a tuple of a relation with one full text attribute. By extracting the single words of the full text attribute, we get a number of *descriptors* that approximate the document. The set of all document identifiers which contain a certain descriptor is called an *inverted list* or synonymously a *posting list*. The individual identifiers are called *postings*. The cardinality of a posting list is called the descriptor's *document frequency*. Documents can be retrieved using a *boolean* retrieval method or a *non-boolean* [Sal75]. While the former delivers a set of matching documents, the latter delivers an ordered ranking of documents, from which some prefix must be selected as the query's final result. In the current study, we only address boolean retrieval.

2.1 Indexing Documents using Inverted Lists

Today, inverted lists are the *de facto* standard for word-based indexing of full text documents [Knu73, HFRYL92], which support fast search for individual words in textual documents. In principle, an inverted list works as follows: Assume each document is represented as a tuple of a relation

Document(Document-ID[1], Content)

Each document is assigned a number of keywords (e.g. by extracting the individual words) describing the contents of the document. Hence, a document is approximated by a tuple of a relation with a set-valued attribute *Descriptor*

DocumentApproximation(Document-ID, {Descriptor})

When we are searching for documents, we are interested in all documents containing a certain descriptor. Therefore, we introduce a relation with a set-valued attribute *Document-ID*

InvertedList(Descriptor, {Document-ID})

Here, we store for each descriptor all references to those documents which contain this descriptor, i.e. its posting list.

Below, we present two alternatives for the integration of inverted lists into a relational database system using a simple preprocessor which maps queries involving textual attributes to standard SQL.

2.2 Bitlists

Most database systems, especially relational ones, allow the storage of only well-typed data. However, many contemporary systems offer, in addition to basic types (integer, date, string, ...), a possibility for storing and retrieving uninterpreted objects, often referred to as *BLOBs*[2] or *long fields*. We can make use of this and store an inverted list in a relation

[1] In the following we assume that all documents are identified by a unique number (1, 2, 3, ...)

[2] Binary Large OBject

InvertedListBitlist(Descriptor, Bitlist)

where *Bitlist* is a BLOB interpreted as an array of bits in which we set the i-th bit if the document i contains *Descriptor* (see Fig. 1). By creating an index on

BROWN	0001010000100001000101010000001010
FOX	0011000000000000010000000000000010001
QUICK	1001000000010000000010010001000101
THE	1111011111101111101110000010101110

Fig. 1. Storing inverted lists using bitlists

the first attribute, we can efficiently retrieve the bitlist for a given descriptor.

Whenever we want to retrieve all documents containing a given descriptor *desc*, we proceed as follows:

```
RETRIEVE Bitlist WHERE Descriptor=desc
FOR i=1 TO LENGTH(Bitlist)
  IF IsSet(Bitlist, i) THEN
     RETRIEVE Document WHERE Document-ID=i
  ENDIF
ENDFOR
```

In the case of a more general query of the form $desc_1 \wedge desc_2 \wedge \ldots \wedge desc_n$, the first line of the above algorithm is replaced by

```
RETRIEVE Bitlist1 WHERE Descriptor=desc1
RETRIEVE Bitlist2 WHERE Descriptor=desc2
:
RETRIEVE Bitlistn WHERE Descriptor=descn
Bitlist=Bitlist1 INTERSECT Bitlist2 ... INTERSECT Bitlistn
```

Both of the algorithms can be implemented using embedded SQL and must be run in the client process: Most contemporary database systems neither allow the integration of user-written code into the database server nor do they offer low level functions such as the intersection of bitlists. Therefore, we cannot evaluate the above queries on the server. This results in less workload for the server but more for the client plus higher network traffic because of the transfer of the potentially large bitlists from the server to the client.

2.3 Physical Relations

As an alternative to representing the inverted lists as bitlists, we can model them as a binary relation

InvertedListRelation(Descriptor, Document-ID)

Here, we do not store one tuple per descriptor in the *document collection* (as in the approach with bitlists), but one tuple for *each document* in which the descriptor occurs.

Retrieving all documents of the relation *Document* that have something to do with the *quick brown fox* is formulated in standard SQL as

```
SELECT *
FROM   Document
WHERE  Document-ID IN (
   SELECT Document-ID
   FROM   InvertedListRelation
   WHERE  Descriptor='quick'
   INTERSECT
   SELECT Document-ID
   FROM   InvertedListRelation
   WHERE  Descriptor='brown'
   INTERSECT
   SELECT Document-ID
   FROM   InvertedListRelation
   WHERE  Descriptor='fox')
```

Contrary to the bitlists approach, this query can be completely evaluated on the server side because only standard data types and operations are used.

In the subqueries, we are always interested in retrieving all postings for a given descriptor. This implies a clustering of the postings according to the descriptor in order to minimise I/O for the retrieval of the posting lists. In a relational database system, this clustering can be accomplished in several ways:

1. Physically clustered storage Figure 2 shows the physical layout of some data pages for the relation *InvertedListRelation* physically clustered according to *Descriptor*.

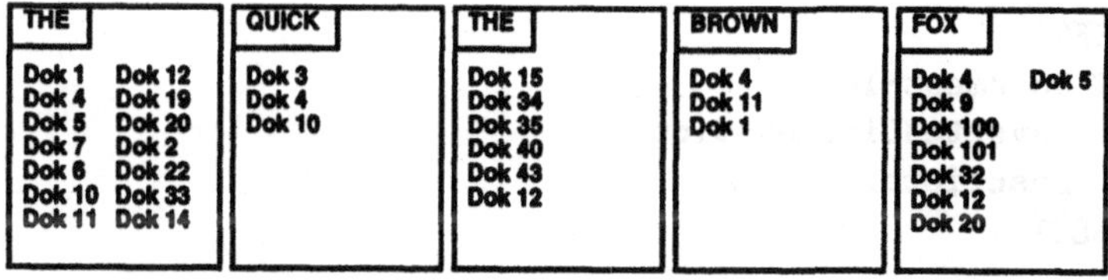

Fig. 2. Storing inverted lists using physically clustered relations

A query of the form

```
SELECT Document-ID
FROM   InvertedListRelation
WHERE  Descriptor='desc'
```

is answered by accessing the (few) pages containing *desc*. Fast access to the qualifying pages is guaranteed by creating an index — often called a *cluster index* — on the cluster attribute (here: *Descriptor*).

This physical storage structure has basically two disadvantages: Firstly, most commercially available database systems do not offer support for variable length clusters. Determining an ideal but *fixed* cluster size is not possible due to the Zipfian distribution [Zip49] of the descriptors: A lot of descriptors only occur once or twice, others very often. Hence, a big cluster size results in a waste of space in the case of infrequent descriptors, whereas, a small cluster size results in a distribution of frequent descriptors over many pages. Often, the system chooses a physical page as the "ideal", and often only, cluster size. Given a 4 kilobyte page and an attribute length of five bytes for a posting — this is the size of a datum of type `NUMBER(8)` in Oracle — approximately 700 postings can be placed on a page. Using a fast (10 ms) disc, at least 70,000 postings/second can be transferred from secondary to primary storage[3] for further processing.

The second negative aspect is that postings are returned unordered, i.e. not with ascending document IDs. This is disadvantageous if more than one descriptor is used in the query: For determining the qualifying document identifiers, the posting lists must be intersected. As the intersection can only be carried out efficiently for ordered posting lists, sorting (in $O(n \log(n)$ steps) is necessary which cannot be accomplished in user-acceptable time in the case of large posting lists.

Hence, physical clustering is not an ideal storage structure, especially when posting lists become large.

2. Physically unclustered storage with a combined index and simple optimisation
In this option, we create a combined index on the relation *InvertedListRelation* over both attributes[4].

Given this storage structure, the query

```
SELECT Document-ID
FROM   InvertedListRelation
WHERE  Descriptor='desc1'
INTERSECT
SELECT Document-ID
FROM   InvertedListRelation
WHERE  Descriptor='desc2'
INTERSECT ...
```

can be answered by accessing the index only (i.e. without accessing the relation) by projecting the second attribute in the index for a given (fixed) value of the first attribute. Hence, we also get a clustering of the data, but on the level of the secondary (index) rather than that of the primary data (relation).

[3] In a worst case scenario, approximately 100 random I/Os can be executed per second.

[4] A combined index on two attributes orders the data according to the first attribute and within one value of the first attribute according to the second.

Note, that the information stored in the combined index is exactly the same as that in the relation *InvertedListRelation.* From a retrieval point of view, the relation *InvertedListRelation* itself is obsolete as it is not accessed when a query is evaluated. Unfortunately, most commercial database systems do not allow the storage of relations using B-trees as secondary (physical) storage structure, as what would be required here.

Contrary to the first storage structure, the postings retrieved are already ordered and need not be sorted before an intersection in the case of queries with more than one descriptor.

Under the assumption that an index entry is 24 bytes long, and index pages are 90 percent full, approximately 140 entries can be stored on a single data page. This results in a transfer rate of 14'000 postings per second from secondary to primary memory, which is not a lot. However, because of prefetching operations, the number of transferred postings/second will be significantly higher.

In experimenting with this storage structure, we recognised that the number of descriptors used for searching the inverted list significantly effected performance. In our experiments, we did not use a fixed number of descriptors for searching the index, but only those which appeared in less than 0.1 percent of all documents. The remaining keywords were incorporated by adding a `LIKE` clause for every keyword not used for the inverted list search. Therefore, in our final physical design, we added an additional relation

InvertedListStatistic(Descriptor, Frequency)

in which we stored the document frequencies of the descriptors. The algorithm to retrieve the qualifying documents reads now as follows:

```
order wi according to their selectivity
use all terms that occur in less than 0.1 percent of all
   documents (at least one) for the search in the inverted list
add the rest of the keywords to the query by means
   of LIKE-statements
display the qualifying documents
```

Example: Consider the query about the *quick brown fox.* In a first step, we retrieve the document frequencies of the descriptors 'quick', 'brown', and 'fox':

```
SELECT Frequency
FROM   InvertedListStatistic
WHERE  Descriptor='quick'

SELECT Frequency
FROM   InvertedListStatistic
WHERE  Descriptor='brown'

SELECT Frequency
FROM   InvertedListStatistic
WHERE  Descriptor='fox'
```

Assume we retrieve *100, 6000, 255*, then we have to pose the following query in order to get the final result from a database containing 500'000 documents:

```
SELECT *
FROM   Document
WHERE  Document-ID IN
 (SELECT Document-ID
  FROM   InvertedListRelation
  WHERE  Descriptor='fox'
  INTERSECT
  SELECT Document-ID
  FROM   InvertedListRelation
  WHERE  Descriptor='quick')
AND Content LIKE '%brown%'
```

Note, that there are some documents qualifying in the subselect clause that contain *fox* and *quick* but not *brown*. These documents are eliminated by sequentially searching them using the LIKE operator.

3 Experimental Systems

Our experiments are based on contemporary information systems: An information retrieval system (BASISPlus) on the one hand, and a relational database system (Oracle) on the other. Below, we briefly introduce these systems and describe their support for text retrieval.

3.1 BASISPlus

We chose BASISPlus [Inf90] as a our reference system on the information retrieval side as it was used in a former project [HKS93] and hence available and familiar to us.

BASISPlus is a hybrid information retrieval and database system with a relational data model and set-valued attributes. BASISPlus allows index structures on standard data types (integer, date, ...) as well as on single words of texts. The boolean model is used for retrieving information.

BASISPlus is implemented in a client–server fashion with a monolithic server, called the *kernel*. For performance reasons, BASISPlus can be run with more than one kernel and an asymmetric assignments of client processes to kernels. Here, the user has to decide to which kernel he wants to connect. Load balancing between kernels — by automatically migrating user requests from one kernel to another — is not supported.

As in many IRS, retrieval is performed in two steps, which are illustrated by the query "retrieve the tuples of the relation *Document* containing the words 'quick', 'brown', and 'fox'":
First, the system retrieves the identifiers of all documents that contain the above keywords using internal access structures:

```
FIND  Document
WHERE Content INC 'quick' & 'brown' & 'fox'
```

If too many documents qualify, the user can refine and re-evaluate the query. In this case, the system makes use of the previously retrieved result set in order to retrieve as little data from secondary memory as is necessary. Alternatively, the user can display the qualifying documents:

```
TYPE *
```

3.2 Preprocessor Solutions

The intention of our experiments was to compare an information retrieval system to a commercially available relational database system. We decided to use Oracle as this system offers its own textual preprocessor. However, we also implemented our own preprocessor and this could have been done equally well on other relational systems.

SQL*TextRetrieval A preprocessor called *SQL*TextRetrieval (SQL*TR)* to manage textual data in Oracle was introduced by Oracle itself some years ago [SQL92]. Unlike "Standard Oracle", SQL*TR allows not only the storage of texts, but also their word-based indexing using inverted lists with a bitlist representation as described in Sec. 2.2. SQL*TR is implemented on top of Oracle and consists of a collection of procedures, which translate high-level user queries to low-level database operations. These procedures can either be called as user-exits from SQL*Forms, or by an embedded SQL program using procedure calls. With the *RTR Command Line Interface*, Oracle provides an interactive query front-end like SQL*Plus.

Querying the database using RTR is performed in two steps (as in BASIS-Plus) and is illustrated using the relation *Documents* and the query "retrieve all documents about the 'quick', 'brown', 'fox'":

1. *Computation of the result set:*

   ```
   CREATE QUERY
   SELECT *
   FROM   Document
   WHERE  Content CONTAINS 'quick' & 'brown' & 'fox'

   RUN QUERY
   ```

   After a syntactic and semantic analysis, the posting lists (bitlists) of the keywords ('quick', 'brown', and 'fox') are retrieved, intersected and stored in a temporary table (the so called *hitlist table*) for further processing.
   Until now, only index structures have been accessed, but not the tuples of the relation *Document*. If the user thinks that the computed result set is

too large, he can refine the query and have it re-evaluated. In this case, the system makes use of the previously computed result set stored in the *hitlist table*.

SQL*Plus' only text search capability is the sequential scan of all tuples of a relation using the LIKE operator. However, as opposed to SQL*Plus, where a query is executed completely on the server side, most of the work in SQL*TR is carried out on the client side: The database system is only used as a repository for storing bitlists and the processing (intersection) is done by the client. As already mentioned in Sec. 2.2, this means less resource consumption on the server side, but more on the client as well as higher network activities.

2. *Display of the result set:*

   ```
   DISPLAY TEXT
   ```

   SQL*TR fetches the identifiers of the qualifying tuples from the *hitlist table*, accesses the user relation (*Documents*) and displays the result.

   Access to the user relation is performed on a "one tuple at-the-time" basis and is therefore resource-intensive and slow. Direct access to the *hitlist table* followed by an array fetch of the qualifying tuples is not supported by SQL*TR.

Oracle plans to extend its activities in the field of text management by releasing a new product, *SQL*TextServer* [Ora94], in the near future. SQL*TextServer will make use of the *Application Programmers Interface*, which allows a tighter coupling of the text retrieval component with the server and therefore will increase retrieval efficiency.

SQL*InvertedList In order to support our own experiments, we implemented a simple textual extension to Oracle called *SQL*InvertedList* (short form: *SQL*-InvList*). Our approach is based on inverted lists stored in an unclustered relation with a combined index and a simple optimisation as described in Sec. 2.3.

We used the following physical relations to store the inverted lists for the attribute *Content* of the relation *Document(Document-ID, Content)*:

```
InvertedListRelation(Descriptor VARCHAR(15) NOT NULL,
                     Document-ID ROWID NOT NULL)

InvertedListStatistic(Descriptor VARCHAR(15) NOT NULL,
                      DocumentFrequency NUMBER NOT NULL)
```

In addition, we created the following unique index in order to achieve clustering of the posting lists as described in Sec. 2.3:

```
CREATE UNIQUE INDEX InvertedListRelationIdx
ON InvertedListRelation(Descriptor, Document-ID)
```

We mentioned earlier — and as can be seen from Oracle's query execution plan — that queries of the form

```
SELECT Document-ID
FROM   InvertedListRelation
WHERE  Descriptor='desc1'
INTERSECT
SELECT Document-ID
FROM   InvertedListRelation
WHERE  Descriptor='desc2'
INTERSECT ...
```

are answered using the index *(InvertedListRelationIdx)* only. The posting lists (document identifiers) of each SELECT statement are already ordered and do not require sorting before the intersection. Unfortunately, Oracle's query optimiser does not make use of this and sorts the (already sorted) data before intersecting the document identifiers. Hence, we basically get the same poor performance as with physical clustering. However, it is possible to make use of the ordered posting lists by performing the INTERSECT operation on the client side. Therefore, we used the following algorithm for answering a query of the form $desc_1 \wedge desc_2 \wedge \ldots \wedge desc_n$:

```
SELECT Descriptor, DocumentFrequency
INTO   :descriptor, :frequency
FROM   InvertedListStatistic
WHERE  Descriptor IN (desc1, ..., descn)
ORDER  BY DocumentFrequency

i=0
DO

   i=i+1

   SELECT Document-ID
   INTO   :invListi
   FROM   InvertedListRelation
   WHERE  Descriptor=:descriptori

WHILE (:frequencyi/NumberOfDocuments<0.1 AND i<n)

inter=invList1
FOR j=2 TO i
   inter=inter INTERSECT invListj
ENDFOR

SELECT Content
FROM   Document
```

```
WHERE  ROWID IN (:inter)
AND    Content LIKE '%:descriptor_{i+1}%'
AND    Content LIKE '%:descriptor_{i+2}%'
  ⋮
AND    Content LIKE '%:descriptor_n%'
```

4 PHONO+: A Music Information System

To evaluate the three approaches (BASISPlus, SQL*TR, SQL*InvList), we performed benchmarks based on an existing application, *PHONO+*, the information system of the Swiss Broadcasting Corporation (SRG[5]) used for the compilation of radio transmissions [HKS93].

Besides logistic data (e.g. place of compact discs in the archives, acquisition mode of the disc (e.g. bought, promotion), ...), all data that appears on the cover of a compact disc is stored in PHONO+, especially:

- Information about the compact disc (title, overall runtime, ...).
- Information about the individual tracks of a compact disc (title, runtime, names of the composers, lyricists, performers, place of recording, ...).
- Information about the above mentioned persons and places.

Most of the data is highly structured and encoded using standard data types, such as *integer* or *date*. It should therefore be easy to manage this data with a contemporary database system. However, the titles of discs and tracks are short texts which are not suitable for storage in a contemporary database system as they do not support indexing of single words which is essential for fast query processing.

PHONO+ holds information about more than 100'000 compact discs, a million tracks and some 100'000 persons. Currently, information grows by approximately 10'000 discs every year, but is likely to increase faster with the constant growth of the compact disc market.

Persons compiling a transmission use basically three different types of queries:

- Queries, that only use standard data types in the selection criterion, e.g. "retrieve the location of a disc with specific EAN[6]–code in the Zurich archive".
- Queries that only have non-standard data types in the selection criterion, e.g. "retrieve all tracks which contain a number of keywords in the title".
- Queries that use standard as well as non-standard data types in the selection criterion, e.g. "retrieve all variations of a song containing the keyword 'love' in the title where 'Sinatra' was playing the 'guitar'".

[5] Schweizerische Rundfunk Gesellschaft

[6] European Article Number, i.e. the barcode identifying a compact disc

An analysis of the queries processed by PHONO+ shows that the title of a disc or a track, i.e. full text, is almost always used as part of the query. As full text retrieval is not well-supported by commercial database systems, SRG decided several years ago to use the information retrieval system BASISPlus to store and process their data. For various reasons, SRG evaluated the possibility of setting up a new information system using relational database technology. Internal experiments showed clearly that a relational system is well-suited to the management of the structured data, but not to the disc and track titles due to the previously mentioned absence of textual indexes. These index structures are vital in an environment of more than one million entities (tracks) as a sequential search of the tracks takes too much time and is not acceptable to the end-user of the system.

5 Measurements

All experiments were run on SPARC 10 with 96 megabytes of real memory under SunOS 4.1. User data was not partitioned across several discs. The machine used for the measurements was not accessed by other users while measurements took place.

We used Oracle 7.0.15, SQL*TextRetrieval 2.0, and BASISPlus release L1. In both systems, data pages were sized two kilobytes with a shared buffer size of eight megabytes. BASISPlus was run with one kernel.

5.1 Data and Index Structures

The schemas used in our three approaches are described below. In each system, we modelled *discs, tracks* and the *persons* that were involved in the production of the tracks. Figure 3 shows the size of the basic data set used in all three systems.

Relation	Number of tuples
Disc	28,000
Track	260,000
Person	125,000
Inverted list (SQL*InvList only)	850,000

Fig. 3. Amount of data loaded

BASISPlus In BASISPlus, we modelled part of the PHONO+ database as

```
Disc(EAN_CODE, Title)
Track(ID, EAN_Code, Title, {PersonName}, {PersonFunction})
```

The *Title* of *Disc* and *Track* are full text attributes with a textual index created on them. *PersonName* and *PersonFunction* are set-valued attributes holding information about the persons involved in producing the track.

Oracle In SQL*TR and SQL*InvList, four relations were required to model the above information:

```
Disc(Disc-Identifier, EAN-Code, Title)
Track(Disc-Identifier, Side, Track, Title)
Person(Person-Identifier, Name)
Track-Person(Disc-Identifier, Side, Track,
             Person-Identifier, Function)
```

Note that four relations are necessary because Oracle does not offer support for set-valued attributes.

*Special index structures for SQL*TR* In order to use SQL*TR efficiently, indices were created on the attribute *Title* of the relations *Disc* and *Track*. The length of the individual bitlists in the *bit location table* was limited to 64 kilobits.

*Special index structures for SQL*InvList* For efficiently answering queries in SQL*InvList, we created inverted lists on the *Title* attributes of the relations *Disc* and *Track*. The inverted lists were stored physically unclustered but with a combined index as described in Sec. 3.2.

5.2 Queries

To compare Oracle with BASISPlus, it is necessary to use two different query sets:

1. Queries that are typical for a database system, i.e. Oracle.
2. Queries that are typical for an information retrieval system, i.e. BASISPlus.

In an earlier report, we investigated the former query set [HKS93]. In this study, we focused on the latter as we were especially interested in whether relational database systems can be used for primitive information retrieval operations. Specifically, we looked at the retrieval of information about tracks with the number of descriptors given that must be contained in the title of the track.

For each query q_i there is given a number n_i of descriptors w_j ($1 \leq j \leq n_i$, $n_i < 10$). The descriptors for the queries had been generated beforehand by extracting words from randomly chosen track titles. The users asked queries independently from each other. Caching of results (from queries asked by other users) did not take place.

The query set of each simulated user consisted of 50 queries. The queries posed by the user, for whom we present the results, were selected by hand and some are shown below:

```
Ain't no mountain high enough      Sunshine life
American trilogy                   Master Blaster
Belinda                            Devil disguise
Never gonna cry again              Playing games
```

```
Telepathy                          Marche militaire
Walk wilde side                    Elusive butterfly
Distant lover                      Impossible
```

A user asked a query approximately every 120 ± 20 seconds. This is about the frequency found in PHONO+.

For each query, we measured the number of logical and physical reads as well as the response time. Results are presented for the single-user as well as for the parallel mode with twenty concurrent users.

5.3 Query Formulation

In the systems used, queries were formulated as follows:

BASISPlus

```
FIND  TRACK
WHERE TITLE INC 'w1' & ... & 'wn'

TYPE  *
```

*SQL*TextRetrieval*

```
CREATE QUERY
SELECT *
FROM   TRACK
WHERE  TITLE CONTAINS 'w1' & ... & 'wn'

RUN QUERY

DISPLAY TEXT
```

*SQL*InvertedList* The retrieval algorithm used for SQL*InvertedList is described in Sec. 3.2.

5.4 Measurement Results

BASISPlus Figure 4 shows the measurement results for BASISPlus. The average response time in the single-user mode (Fig. 4(a)) is 0.49 seconds. Some of the queries (e.g. number 16) take much longer to be answered. This is due to a large result set rather than temporary I/O or CPU contention, i.e. not only one or two tuples qualify, but twenty or even more. The actual fetching of documents is time-consuming and not implemented as efficiently as the searching of the textual index.

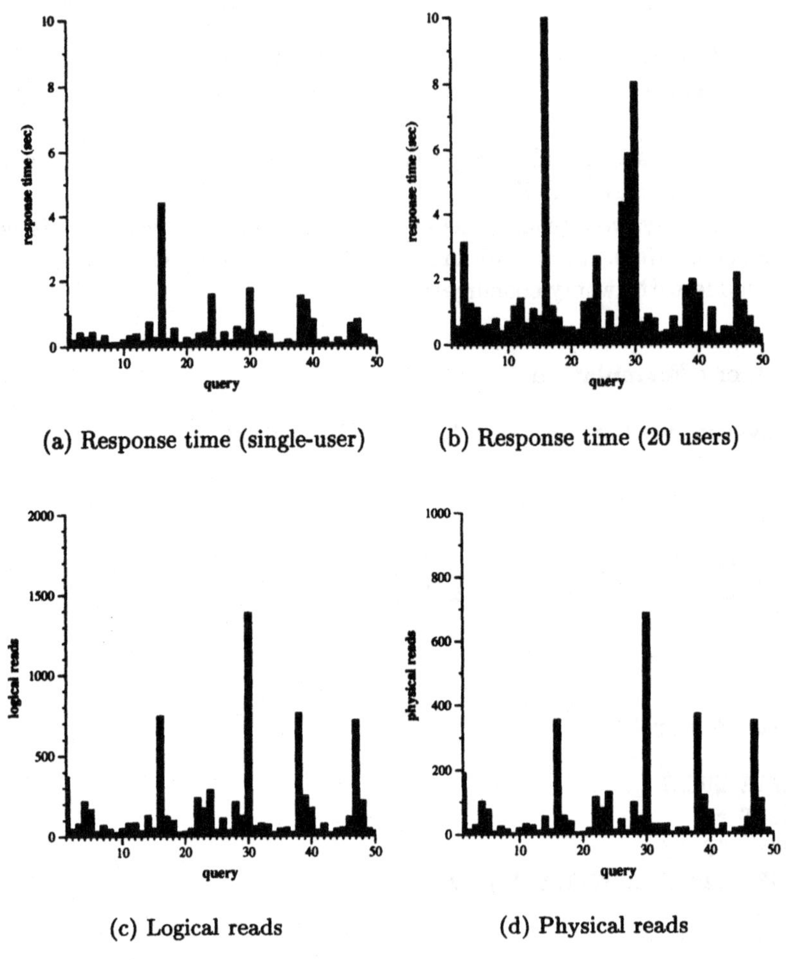

(a) Response time (single-user)

(b) Response time (20 users)

(c) Logical reads

(d) Physical reads

Fig. 4. BASISPlus

In the concurrent environment with 20 users (Fig. 4(b)), response times increase by a factor of three. For some queries, response times become unacceptable. The reason for this is, that in the average case, a new query is processed every six seconds. From time to time, three or more queries arrive in this period causing I/O contention.

The number of logical read operations (Fig. 4(c)) is varying and, basically, correlates with the number of qualifying documents. The number of physical I/Os is always half of the logical ones. It seems that no caching is taking place; this is perfectly reasonable in an information retrieval system because (1) it is unnecessary to cache documents as it is unlikely that a document is accessed more than once in a short period of time, and, (2) caching of indexing structures does not provide huge performance benefits as they are rather large (i.e. not fitting in the database cache) and, in the case of a user refining a query previously accessed, index structures do not have to be accessed again.

SQL*TextRetrieval Figure 5 shows the measurement results for SQL*Text-Retrieval. Comparing the response times in the single-user (Fig. 5(a)) as well

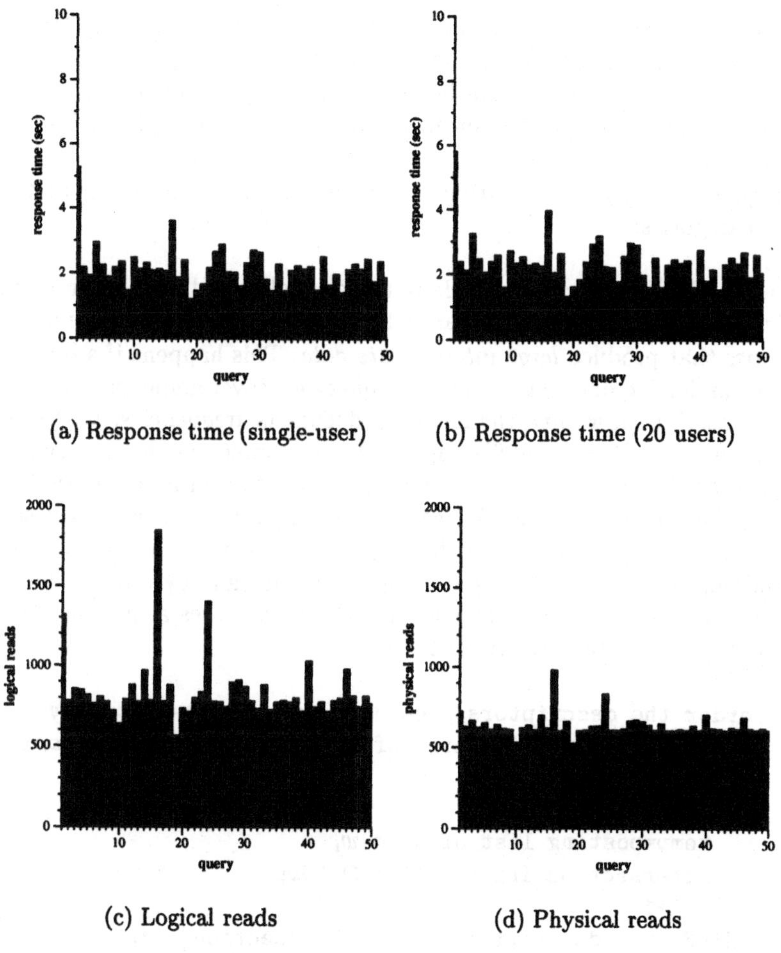

(a) Response time (single-user)

(b) Response time (20 users)

(c) Logical reads

(d) Physical reads

Fig. 5. SQL*TextRetrieval

as in the multi-user mode (Fig. 5(b)) to BASISPlus (Fig. 4(a) and 4(b)), we find that SQL*TR requires approximately four, respectively two times longer to answer a query. This slowdown is to be accepted and followed our expectations.

Also, fetching the qualifying documents on a record–at–a–time basis is time consuming. It is remarkable that neither I/O, nor CPU contention arises when the number of users is increased. The response times remain stable.

We cannot properly explain the number of the physical I/Os (Fig. 5(d)) measured. We would expect at most 20 logical reads[7] per descriptor. With four descriptors and ten qualifying tuples, we expect a maximum of $4 * 20 + 10 = 90$ physical I/Os, which is a lot less than 500. We can only explain this by assuming an inefficient implementation of SQL*TR.

SQL*InvertedList Figure 6 shows the measurement results for SQL*Inverted-List. The average response time in the single-user mode (Fig. 6(a)) is 0.18 seconds. 90 percent of all queries can be answered in less than 0.4 seconds. When increasing the degree of parallelism to twenty, response times (Fig. 6(b)) show not a significant increase.

The queries with a response time well above the average can be subdivided into two categories:

- Queries with *large result sets*: Many tuples qualify and have to be retrieved from disc. In these cases, I/O can only be reduced by refining the query.
- Queries that produce *large intermediate data*: This happens if a query contains unselective descriptors only, e.g. query 4 "never gonna cry again". For these descriptors, we find the following document frequencies: 1031 (never), 736 (gonna), 550 (cry) and 974 (again). In our simple search strategy (use all descriptors for the search in the inverted list that occur in less than 0.1 percent of all documents (=300)), we only use *cry* for the inverted list search. Consequently, 550 tuples must be retrieved from disc and checked for the remaining keywords. As only two tuples contain all keywords, a more sophisticated search strategy should be utilised that uses a dynamic number of descriptors for the inverted list search:

```
order the descriptors according to their selectivity → w_i
intersection=posting list of the most selective descriptor
i=1
DO
   temp=posting list of term w_i
   intersection=intersection ∩ temp
   i=i+1
WHILE (i <| descriptors | AND | intersection |> MAX)
fetch the tuples identified by intersection and
   apply a LIKE query with the rest of the descriptors
```

[7] An uncompressed bitlist of length 15,000 can be stored in a 2 kbyte page. With roughly 300,000 tracks, we expect $\frac{300,000}{15,000} = 20$ logical page reads in the case that bitlists are not compressed.

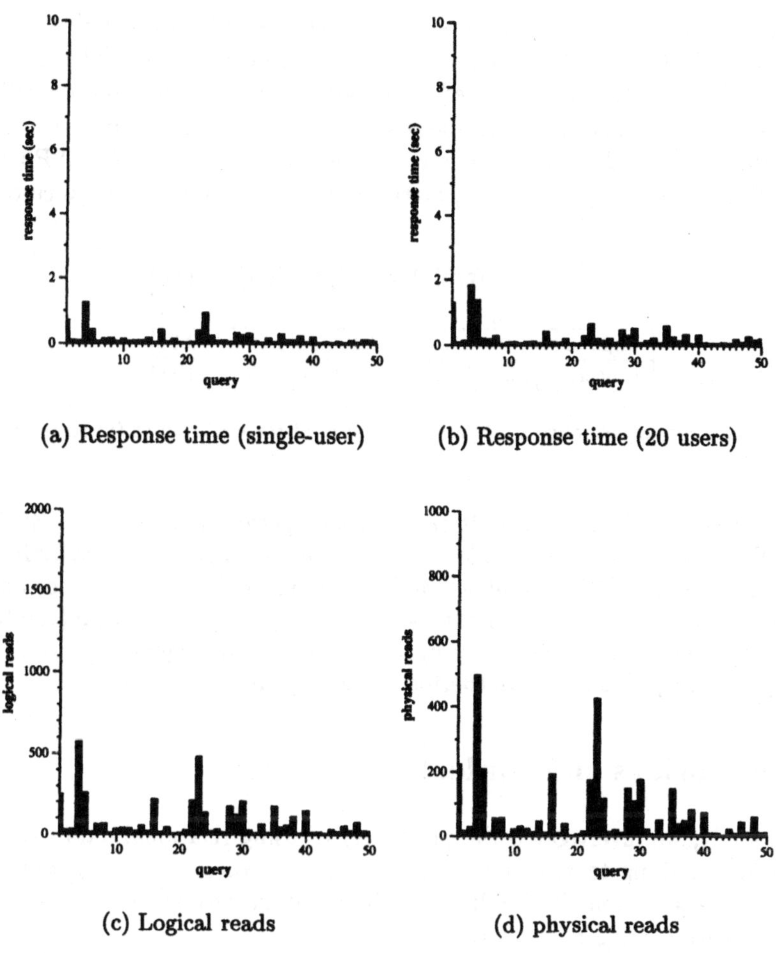

(a) Response time (single-user) (b) Response time (20 users)

(c) Logical reads (d) physical reads

Fig. 6. SQL*InvertedList

Note, that this algorithm cannot be processed using *one* SQL-Statement because of its iterative nature. It can be executed either on the server side using PL/SQL [Ora92] or as an embedded SQL program on the client side. Measurements (with embedded SQL) using this method with MAX = 50 showed performance benefits for both I/O and response times (less tuples have to be fetched for execution of the `LIKE` part) for all cases with previously poor performance.

Comparison Table 7 contains the result of all measurements. As we expected, the stability of the response time against the number of users can be observed by looking at both relational preprocessor solutions. A significant slow-down is visible with the IRS BASISPlus when 20 users have to be supported. This expected result stems from the sophisticated client-server support of today's relational database systems. The difference between the SQL*TR preprocessor and the BASISPlus system also corresponds to the initial expectation. BASISPlus is a factor of 4 faster. A real surprise, however, was the good performance of our

	BASISPlus		SQL*TR		SQL*InvList	
	avg	tot	avg	tot	avg	tot
single-user	0.49	25.13	2.13	106.15	0.18	9.21
20 users	1.54	78.81	2.33	116.76	0.26	13.18

Fig. 7. Average response times and total sum of response times (in seconds)

own preprocessor SQL*InvList. It shows better performance than BASISPlus, especially in the multi-user mode. But, even more importantly, SQL*InvList compared to SQL*TR has similar functionality but a clear performance advantage of almost a factor of 10! This shows that a clever physical design (combined index) together with simple query optimisation (avoid frequent descriptors in query processing) drastically outperforms the commercial product.

6 Conclusions and Outlook

In this study, we investigated the possibility of using relational database technology for handling textual data. We carried out experiments with the information retrieval system BASISPlus and the database system Oracle, which was enhanced with textual access structures.

The experiments showed that a special — but common — class of textual data (short texts) can be retrieved efficiently by using inverted lists that are stored on top of Oracle as "pure" relations (SQL*InvList).

Inverted lists offer indexing support for queries seeking whole or postfix-truncated words, which is sufficient for most applications. Additional functionality (as in BASISPlus) can be achieved by using more complex data structures, but this increase in functionality must be traded against higher resource usage (secondary memory as well as CPU). It must be mentioned that BASISPlus' index structures do not only support the primitive search for keywords as shown in our measurements. For example, they also allow the definition of relationships between keywords such as *X before Y* or *X and Y in the same sentence* and is, consequently, more powerful than SQL*TR and, especially, SQL*InvList. However, BASISPlus offers only one complex type of index structure and does not allow the user to choose between complex structures for sophisticated queries (e.g. "adjacent") and simple index structures for simple queries (e.g. "contains" operator only) in order to speed up retrieval where the extra functionality is not required.

A bitlist representation of posting list, as used in SQL*TR, does not yield good results whenever selective terms are used. Such terms should be stored in user-defined relations as proposed with SQL*InvList. On the other hand, SQL*InvList does not show good results for unselective terms: their posting lists should be stored in bitlists. From these observations, a hybrid approach as implemented in [Pol80] could be taken and relations as well as bitlists could be used.

The results presented for SQL*InvList could give the impression that this approach can be used for any kind of text problem. We think this is not the case. SQL*InvList is a good solution for a lot of applications with highly structured and some textual data. In the case of many long full text documents, specialised systems like BASISPlus should be used. However, this study shows that information retrieval systems are not always the best solution for all textual problems.

Most information retrieval systems — including SQL*TR as well as BASISPlus — show performance problems in the case of online updates. In our future work, we will focus on index structures for highly dynamic data, i.e. data that is changing online. We will also look at weighted information retrieval which is becoming increasingly important with the growth of online-available information.

Acknowledgements The authors would like to thank Moira Norrie, Lukas Relly and Stephen Blott for their helpful comments to this paper.

References

[Bil82] H. Biller. On the architecture of a system integrating data base management and information retrieval. In G. Goos and H. Hartmanis, editors, *Research and Development in Information Retrieval*, volume 146 of *Lecture Notes in Computer Science*, pages 80–97. Springer, May 1982.

[DKA+86] P. Dadam, K. Küspert, F. Andersen, H. Blanken, R. Erbe, J. Günauer, V. Lum, P. Pistor, and G. Walch. A DBMS prototype to support extended NF^2 relations: An integrated view on flat tables and hierarchies. In *Proc. ACM SIGMOD Conf. on Management of Data*, 1986.

[Fuh89] N. Fuhr. Models for retrieval with probabilistic indexing. *Information Processing & Management*, 25(1):55–72, 1989.

[HFRYL92] D. Harman, E. Fox, R.Baeza-Yates, and W. Lee. Inverted files. In W. B. Frakes and R. Baeza-Yates, editors, *Information Retrieval (Data Structures and Algorithms)*, chapter 3, pages 28–43. Prentice Hall, 1992.

[HKS93] R. Hüppin, H. Kaufmann, and H.-J. Schek. MUSE—Ein Musikarchiv für die SRG. MUSE project report, ETH Zürich, Inst. for Information Systems—Database Research Group, April 1993.

[Inf90] Information Dimension Inc., 655 Metro Place South, Dublin, Ohio 43017-1396. *BASISPlus Database Administration Guide*, June 1990. Release L.

[Knu73] D. E. Knuth. *The Art of Computer Programming*. Addison-Wesley, Reading, 1973.

[LDE+85] V. Lum, P. Dadam, R. Erbe, J. Günauer, P. Pistor, G. Walch, H. Werner, and J. Woodfill. Design of an integrated DBMS to support advanced applications. In *International Conference on Foundations of Data Organization*, Kyoto, 1985.

[LKD+88] V. Linnemann, K. Küspert, P. Dadam, P. Pistor, R. Erbe, A. Kemper, N. Südkamp, G. Walch, and M. Wallrath. Design and implementation of extensible database management system supporting user defined data types and furnctions. In *Proceedings International Conference on Very Large Databases*, Los Angeles, California, 1988.

[Mac79] I.A. Macleod. SEQUEL as a language for document retrieval. *Journal of the American Society for Information Science*, 30(5):243–249, September 1979.

[Ora92] Oracle Corporation, 500 Oracle Parkway, Redwood City, CA 94065. *PL/SQL User's Guide and References (Version 2.0)*, December 1992.

[Ora94] Oracle TextServer. White Paper A17283, Oracle Corporation, March 1994. Servers to Manage Very Large Document Databases.

[Pol80] R. Poloczek. SQL Text Retrieval in SQL/DS. Confidential technical report, IBM Scientific Center, Heidelberg, 1980.

[Rij81] C.J. van Rijsbergen. *Information Retrieval.* Butterworth, 1981.

[Sal75] G. Salton. *Dynamic Information and Library Processing.* Prentice Hall, 1975.

[Sch77] H.-J. Schek. The reference string access method and partial match retrieval. Technical Report TR 77.12.008, IBM Germany, Heidelberg Scientific Center, December 1977.

[Sch84] H.-J. Schek. Nested Transactions in a Combined IR–DBMS Architecture. In C.J. van Rijsbergen, editor, *Proceeding of the 3rd BCS/ACM Symposium on Research and Development in Information Retrieval*, The British Computer Society Workshop Series, pages 55–70, Cambridge, July 1984. British Computer Society, Cambridge University Press.

[SP82] H.-J. Schek and P. Pistor. Data structures for an integrated database management and information retrieval system. In *Proceedings International Conference on Very Large Databases*, pages 197–207, Mexico, 1982.

[SPSW90] H.-J. Schek, H.-B. Paul, M.H. Scholl, and G. Weikum. The DASDBS project: Objectives, experiences and future prospects. *IEEE Trans. on Knowledge and Data Engineering*, 2(1):25–43, March 1990. Special Issue on Database Prototype Systems.

[SQL92] SQL*TextRetrieval. Technical overview, Oracle Corporation, 1992. Version 2.

[SR86] M.R. Stonebraker and L.A. Rowe. The design of POSTGRES. In *Proc. ACM SIGMOD Conf. on Management of Data*, pages 340–355, Washington, D.C., May 1986. ACM.

[SSL+83] M. Stonebraker, H. Stettner, N. Lynn, J. Kalash, and A. Guttmann. Document processing in a relational database system. *ACM Transactions on Office Informations Systems*, 1(2):143–158, April 1983.

[SW86] H.-J. Schek and G. Weikum. DASDBS: Concepts and architecture of a database system for advanced applications. Technical Report DVSI-1986-T1, TU Darmstadt, 1986. German Version in: Informatik Forschung und Entwicklung, 1987.

[Zip49] G.K. Zipf. *Human Behaviour and the Principle of Least Effort.* Addison-Wesley Press, 1949.

Integrity Merging in an Object-Oriented Federated Database Environment

R. M. Alzahrani, M. A. Qutaishat[*]*, N. J. Fiddian and W. A. Gray*

Department of Computing Mathematics, UWCC, Cardiff, UK.
[*] Department of Computer Science, University of Jordan, Amman, Jordan
scmrma@cm.cf.ac.uk

Abstract: The process of resolving conflicts between local integrity specifications is an important part of heterogeneous database schema integration. However, previous research in this area has not addressed this problem. The aim of this paper is to present the work undertaken in extending a software tool that integrates heterogeneous schemas to cater for heterogeneity in integrity specifications, while producing a single homogeneous federated schema. Our prototype system is being used as a testbed for the development of a more generic tool to integrate different types of integrity rules and to investigate a wider range of related problems, such as integrity rule context. The novelty of our approach lies in its practicality and extensibility to incorporate various types of constraints. So far as we know, the taxonomy we have developed as a basis for the merging process is the first comprehensive taxonomy in the literature. The result of this work will be used to assist the operation of a global query processor which is being developed for an Object-Oriented multidatabase environment.

1 Introduction

A database must serve as a faithful and incorruptible repository of data. Many techniques and tools have been devised to fulfil this requirement in many inter-related research areas, such as concurrency management, database security and secrecy, and database integrity. Database integrity is concerned with whether or not the state of a database obeys the rules of the organisation it models. These rules take the form of generic statements that govern the way the organisation works. In the database literature, these rules are usually referred to as integrity rules, or integrity constraints (ICs), because they constrain modification processes on data to *legitimate* values only. In addition to the other methods of data protection provided by security systems, the integrity system offers extra guarantees against data corruption [15].

Over the last decade much attention has been paid to the maintenance of integrity in relational databases. This research effort has yielded fruitful results that have given relational systems a substantial level of reliability and robustness. Techniques and methods developed in centralised relational systems constitute an adequate infrastructure for further investigation of integrity in other models and architectures.

1.1 Multidatabase Integrity

Although centralised database integrity has received considerable attention, very little research has been carried out on integrity issues for distributed databases [6]. In a homogeneous distributed database, integrity rules can be defined at distributed database (DDB) design time and incorporated into integrity subsystems at local nodes in a consistent manner. This is generally a straightforward task, since homogeneous environments are mostly designed top-down. However, the heterogeneity of federated[1] DDBs makes consistent support of integrity between global and local levels much more difficult, as they are designed independently and then linked together. Nodal autonomy of local database management systems (DBMSs) requires that local integrity constraints should be preserved when these nodes participate in the federation. Processing of global queries, on the other hand, should not be affected by inconsistencies between local integrity rules. For example, in a country which employs more than one type of calendar, one local node could be using one such calendar while other nodes insist on a different calendar. Integrity constraints on legal date-of-birth values at local nodes will depend on the calendar in use at these sites; this requires a context-based integration process. From this example, it is possible to envisage the need for global integrity management to resolve these inconsistencies and maintain their consistency when local schemas evolve.

The example given above is a relatively simple one in that the local integrity constraints, apart from differences in representation, are probably reasonably close semantically. In more complex situations, the local integrity constraints may display a greater semantic variation. The implementation of an integrity management tool will depend on the architecture adopted in designing the federation.

In [30, 29, 5], global integrity management is regarded as a schema integration issue. Consequently, global integrity is established and inconsistencies are resolved in parallel with handling other types of heterogeneity among local schemas. None of the previous methodologies for schema integration model integrity specifications fully [5], since they fail to handle the possibility that local constraints may be different.

In a distributed environment, pre-existing heterogeneous databases, which may play critical roles, often have to be incorporated into any new system. Interoperability between heterogeneous databases requires a semantically-rich canonical model to fully capture the semantics of local data representations and their associated integrity rules. Many authors have observed that Object-Oriented (OO) techniques could provide a powerful *glue* for integrations within such a context [7, 13, 30, 6, 2]. Section 4 discusses the application of OO concepts in this

---

[1] We use the term *federated* here, as used in [34], to refer to a collection of cooperating autonomous and heterogeneous databases. Our approach is equally applicable to tightly-coupled (single schema) and loosely-coupled (multiple schema) environments.

environment. In the following sub-section and section 2, we explain how the OO data model can support integrity integration in multidatabase environments.

1.2 Object-Oriented Integrity

The semantics of the Object-Oriented (OO) data model provide extra advantages for integrity management in these systems. For instance, the constraint "every car is a vehicle" is inherently supported by the OO model *per se*. The notion of inheritance (and thus class hierarchy) in this model offers an excellent natural basis for implementing this type of integrity constraint. Many types of integrity constraint that relational systems had to specify explicitly are directly captured by the type system and the object class hierarchy in OODBs. Also, given the flexibility and power of OO systems, it should be possible to capture within them other kinds of integrity constraints that have not traditionally been part of the database itself.

[17] describes a proposed model for incorporating declarative integrity constructs in an Object-Oriented database management system (OODBMS). Object-Oriented databases (OODBs) are rapidly gaining in popularity, although they have not yet achieved the maturity level of relational systems [19]. OODB integrity is almost an unresearched area.

In this paper, we will be concentrating on the integration of integrity constraints in a heterogeneous multidatabase (MDB) environment. The approach taken to create and utilise global integrity rules ensures that local autonomy is preserved for the participating databases. As will become clear in the paper, this is especially important in a multidatabase environment. Our prototype can be used, in conjunction with the federated schema generator, to support transparent access to discrepant dispersed data. This is important as this integrated information can be used to improve user understanding as well as query processing in such an environment [4]. We strongly believe that processing MDB queries (as well as transactions) by using integrated semantics is more practical (and promising!) than traditional approaches based on statistics and cost models, which both cannot be completely computed without relaxing autonomy requirements of local databases.

The paper is divided into seven sections. Section 2 classifies integrity semantics in OODBs. In section 3, an integrity specification language is described. Also, various mergeability cases between integrity constraint types are illustrated. The approach adopted in designing and developing our integration system is explained in section 4. Section 5 provides a detailed analysis for the operation of the merging system in deriving global integrity from two selected integrity groups. In section 6, we explain why our approach to global integrity does not violate local autonomy of participating DBMSs. The utilisation of global integrity is summarised in section 7 and the paper is completed by mentioning proposed future extensions of our work as well as the major conclusions derived.

2 A Taxonomy of OO Integrity Semantics

The taxonomy discussed below groups integrity rules according to the semantics of the OO model regardless of whether they are state (i.e. describing the current state of the database) or transition (i.e. constraining future update processes) constraints. Integrity constraint categories that have been introduced in the relational model represent only part of our taxonomy. Furthermore, as we noted above, some relational integrity rules are inherent in the OO context. Our taxonomy is based on whether a constraint spans more than one class or is just for constraining instances of a single class of objects. Currently, only a very few OODBMSs support the first category. In our taxonomy, we do not consider other possible classifications of integrity constraints; for instance, hard constraints (those that must be satisfied immediately before an update) and soft constraints are outside the scope of this paper.

2.1 Intra-class Integrity Rules

These are integrity rules that restrict instances of individual classes. They can be referred to as object constraints or local constraints. These rules can be further sub-divided into intra-instance rules and inter-instance rules, as follows.

2.1.1 Intra-instance Integrity Rules

Integrity constraints that involve the monitoring of user updates on data items in a single object are referred to as intra-instance integrity constraints. Examples of these rules are:

- *Domain Constraints*: these specify legal values in a particular domain. Examples are: *network_type in [ethernet, arpanet]; age > 21; sex in [m,f]*.

- *Implication Constraints*: these specify interdependencies between data values. For example, the rule: all top-secret items are stored in Plymouth, is interpreted as: *status = 'top-secret' ⇒ storage_city = 'Plymouth'*. [2]

- *Inter-property Constraints*: these restrict property values of an object. For instance, the natural constraint: an employee cannot be the manager of himself, is specified as: *employee.name ≠ employee.manager_name*. [3]

- *Time-related Constraints*: this type of rule ensures that newly entered values for certain attributes of an object satisfy certain conditions relative to their previous values. For example, when an employee is promoted, his new rank (and possibly salary) is greater than his previous rank. In specifying this class

---

[2] Assuming that *storage_city* has primitive type.

[3] The attribute *manager_name* in *Employee* is of type string.

of rules, additional operators (such as *New* and *Old*) are needed, e.g. *on update to rank, New rank > Old rank.*

2.1.2 Inter-instance Integrity Rules

The main difference between this category and the previous one is that on updating any object in a particular class, inter-instance rules must be checked for violation against all objects of the class. This is handled in practice by using some statistics that can be updated at off-peak times of system activity. Examples of these rules are given below.

- *Computational Constraints*: in this category, a computation is required on some value in all instances of a class. This mathematical process could be used to enforce an organisational rule such as: average salary of employees should not exceed 20000, which can be specified as:

  $\forall$ *e in Employee, avg(salary) <=20000.*

- *Non-computational Constraints*: these are constraints that span more than one instance of a class. As an example, the organisational rule: the manager of an employee is an employee, can be formulated as:

  $\forall$ *e in Employee,* $\exists$ *e1 in Employee such that e.manager = e1.name.* [4]

- *Uniqueness Constraints*: this category of constraint enforces every object of a certain class to have a unique value for some attribute(s). Such a facility is desirable in situations where a natural attribute (i.e. not an artificial key) of the class must be assigned a different value for every newly created instance. This case can be exemplified by the patient number, which represents the best known method to identify patients within a hospital, as names and other identifiers can be ambiguous. This example constraint can be specified as follows:

  $\forall$ *Patient p1,* $\exists$ *no Patient p2 such that p1* $\neq$ *p2 & p1.pno = p2.pno.* [5]

2.2 Inter-class Integrity Rules

This category of integrity rules models constraints that involve objects from more than one class. In the relational model, a relationship between two tables is implemented by creating a third table incorporating the primary keys of the first two. This is due to the normalisation requirement posed by the relational model. This artificial mechanism is not needed in the OO model, since the domain of a

---

[4] The attribute *manager* in *Employee* is of type string.

[5] Inequality here refers to object identity.

property can be a class (i.e. not primitive). In OODBs, composition hierarchies are used to model relationships between classes. This is regarded as one of the strengths of OO systems. Nevertheless, the OO model, like the relational model, does not provide implicit integrity checking on these relationships. For example, when a course is deleted from a student enrolment database, there is no guarantee that no students are registered on this course. Such an integrity check must be specified explicitly. Part of our discussion below is based on the work of [17], with some useful additions and remarks.

Inter-class integrity constraints can be divided into four groups:

- *Referential Integrity Constraints*: the aim of referential constraints is to ensure that a reference to an object in the database is always valid. Reference to an object is made through its internal identifier, which users can never update. Reference validity means that after deleting an object, no references remain in the database for that object. This integrity test can be enforced by attaching an appropriate constraint to the class, for example:

  on delete of Address a, ∃ no Person p such that p.address = a. [6]

- *Multiplicity Integrity Constraints*: association between two classes takes different multiplicities according to the role it plays. It can be 1:1, 1:m or m:n. For example, an association that links *Student* and *Course* classes is expressed as: each student must register in at least three courses, which can be specified as: ***count** (student.courses) >= 3*, such that *courses* (in *Student*) is a data structure that holds the object identities of the courses taken by the particular student.

- *Inverse Relational Integrity Constraints*: these can be exemplified by the temporary relationship between a course and its teacher. This is first established when a teacher is assigned the duty of teaching a particular course. This relationship terminates as soon as another teacher undertakes teaching that course. In relational systems, a separate table would be created to model this relationship. Relational integrity is modelled in some OODBs by using an *inverse* construct which identifies the inverse of a property. In our example, the attribute *taught-by* in class *Course* is the inverse of the attribute *teaches* in class *Teacher*. This format is not part of the OO model itself, but some commercial systems do support it. Explicitly, we may specify such a relationship as follows:

---

[6] Notice that '=' here refers to identity equality according to [12, 18].
Deep equality is not used in this particular case since more than one person might be living at the same address. In other situations, however, it might be useful.

$\forall$ *Course c, $\exists$ no Teacher t such that t = c.taught_by and c not in t.teaches.*

- *Navigational Integrity Constraints:* this category includes integrity rules that involve navigation through the composition hierarchy of a class. For example, the rule: employees working in departments that manufacture materials with risk greater than 5 must be at least 35 years old, is represented as:

  employee.dept.manufactures.risk > 5 $\Rightarrow$ age >=35

To complete the discussion, it is important to note that the OO model offers another major advantage to integrity maintenance, in that the OO paradigm supports the attachment of monitors to individual objects. This facility can be utilised in implementing triggers when integrity rules are violated. Thus, in all the kinds of rules discussed above, the designer is able to associate appropriate corrective actions for when undesirable updates are attempted.

This taxonomy is not intended to be exhaustive. Other categories of integrity rules can be invented in various application domains. It is not possible for any practical system to support all these categories. Most DBMSs support very few categories. Nevertheless, a canonical data model must be expressively rich enough to cater for any type of local constraint.

In a heterogeneous environment, inconsistencies and conflicts can occur between local integrity rules that model the same organisational constraint. For example, the *Employee* class at one local node uses the name *salary* to model the monthly payment of personnel, while another site uses the term *wage* to model the same function. The domain of the salary can be defined at one node as $salary \geq 0$ whereas another node constrains this domain with $0 < salary < 100000$. Heterogeneity can take many forms. Therefore, resolving different levels of heterogeneity must be undertaken during the generation of homogeneous federated schemas for a multidatabase environment. Another related issue is where integrity constraints, and triggers, are recorded in the MDBS. These considerations are explored and discussed in the subsequent sections of this paper.

3 The Integrity Merging Process

In this section, we describe our approach to global integrity management. Our federation architecture is loosely-coupled, with any number of homogeneous federated schemas constructed using the concepts and semantics of the OO data model. Unless otherwise stated, heterogeneity in this paper refers to semantic heterogeneity among local conceptual schemas. Data model heterogeneity is resolved when local schemas are translated to the notation of the OO canonical data model, as discussed in section 7. We extend the work reported in [25, 26] by supporting global integrity in a bottom-up manner. In this research, schemas are integrated incrementally in a pairwise iterative process.

3.1 Specification and Modelling of Integrity

Integrity rules can be specified in two different forms, depending on the type of the constraint. Intra-class rules are concerned with objects from a single class, and are preferably implemented within the class definition. Due to the lack of a formal OO model, different systems provide different facilities for integrity specification. In the O++ [1] database language, constraints can be associated with classes by using the *constraint* construct, which also offers the ability to associate corrective actions with constraint violations. The specified constraint is checked every time an instance of that class is updated, added or deleted. In POSTGRES [35], constraints are associated through a rule system; a rule or set of rules is attached to a class to constrain illegitimate data values.

Inter-class rules, on the other hand, can be specified within classes or independently in a schema. In our taxonomy above, examples are given for constraints specified separately from their related class definitions. In [17], a declarative language is used to express inter-class integrity constraints. This language is called CIAO++, a minor extension of the original O++ language. We choose to express inter-class constraints separately from any class definition as it should make for easier processing.

3.2 Constraint Specification Language

During a federated schema generation process, class constructs are parsed and essential knowledge is extracted and stored appropriately. Integrity rules are also parsed and they are represented in a PROLOG [10] compatible format for subsequent use by the merging module, which resolves heterogeneities and generates homogeneous global integrity constraints. In our system, constraints are specified procedurally in the rule syntax used in the POSTGRES DBMS [35]. Declarative rules have to be pre-processed before they can be passed down to the integration module. In a complete MDB environment, the process of translating local conceptual schemas into the syntax of the canonical data model transforms local heterogeneous integrity specifications into a uniform syntax; in which case there is no need for a constraint specification language as it will be part of the MDB canonical model. Figure 1 illustrates two example constraints.

```
on update to company              on update to local_comp
do update company.age             do update local_comp.age
   where age > 20                    where age > 18
```

Fig. 1. Two potentially mergeable integrity rules (from a POSTGRES database)

3.3 Constraint Mergeability

Integrity rules from the eleven categories presented in section 2 can be integrated in six different ways. It is not generally possible to merge constraints from two different categories.[7] We say that such rules are not merge-compatible. The six merging methods are:

1. *Containment*: containment occurs when values restricted by a constraint represent a subset of values restricted by another constraint.

   For example, the two constraints: *age > 19* and *age > 20,* can be merged by selecting the first one at the global level, since the set of legitimate values defined by the second rule represents a subset of legitimate values for the first. The proper decision on which to choose as the global constraint will depend on the class mergeability factor, as discussed in section 4, as well as on the interaction of the global database administrator (GDBA).

2. *Intersection*: this case is encountered when the set of values permissible by one constraint overlaps with the set permissible by the other. Containment is a special case of intersection. In the more general case, the merging process can generate a new global constraint which only eliminates values that are not permissible by either constraint.

   For example: $d < category < k$ and $g < category < p$, can be merged into one global constraint as: $d < category < p$, (where $d < g$ and $k < p$). However, to maintain the genericity of our solutions, we choose to introduce both rules at the federated level.

3. *Equivalence*: equivalence is obtained when two identical rules are used in two candidate mergeable classes.

4. *Disjunction*: when two integrity rules constrain two different semantics, or the same real world semantics but using different domains, or the same semantics and domains but allowing disjunctive sets of values, such rules are said to be in disjunction.

   An example of the first case is: *rank > 10, age > 18*. An example of the second case is: *rank > 10, rank > 'm'*. An example of the third case is: *rank > 10, rank < 5*. Rules of these types are not mergeable. With these kinds of rules, a semi-automatic integration method (as discussed in section 4.1.2 below) is used to guide global integrity management.

5. *Synonymity*: two rules are considered to be synonymous if they model the same real world semantics but use different attribute names.

---

[7] In some cases it is in fact possible to do so, but we ignore this situation in the current paper.

For example, the rules: *status = 'mid'* $\Rightarrow$ *wage > 3000* and *status = 'mid'* $\Rightarrow$ *salary > 3000*, are regarded as synonymous, if *salary* has been identified as a synonym of *wage*. [8]

6. *Negation*: this last case arises when two rules model the same real world semantics by using different operators (or quantifiers).

   For example, the rule: *GPA <= 5*, models the rule: $\neg$*(GPA > 5)*, by using different operators. Rules of this kind can be merged, as in the equivalence case, by choosing either rule for the global level, provided their equivalence can be determined.

4 Merging System Approach

Schema integration is primarily based on investigating class structure, syntax and semantics. Potentially mergeable classes are identified and the designer is consulted iteratively to confirm system decisions. The class is the most basic abstract element in the OO paradigm and is the natural level at which the designer perceives and models the universe of discourse. Figure 2 illustrates the class integration process described in [26]. The approach used is a knowledge-based one in which various heterogeneity cases are resolved by firing the appropriate rule bases, in an intelligent inferential reasoning mechanism.

As stated earlier, each pair of schemas is integrated separately. Likewise, pairs of potentially mergeable classes are processed iteratively. At each stage where the type of class integration has been determined in figure 2, there is a rule base which determines integrity mergeability. The work reported in [25, 26] has been implemented in a prototype tool called the Schema Meta-Integration System (SMIS).

SMIS integrates two heterogeneous database schemas into a single homogeneous federated schema by using knowledge-based and meta-programming techniques. It is implemented in PROLOG [10], which we have found from experience to be ideal for prototyping this type of application. The frame structure is used as an intermediate representation tool to model class and integrity knowledge, in a form which is based on the OMT notation [32] and its extension IOMT [28].

The outputs of SMIS comprise, firstly, a versioned shadow schema which contains copies of local schemas. This versioned schema is useful in resolving naming conflicts and redirecting global queries. The second output of SMIS is a set of query decomposition rules representing mapping paths between global and local schemas. The third output is a homogeneous schema based on the concepts of the OO model.

SMIS was implemented with the aim of resolving normal schematic conflicts. Integrity was not considered in the original version of the system. Therefore SMIS is being extended by our current work to cater for integrating

---

[8] During class and integrity integration, GDBA interaction is essential to resolve these inconsistencies according to real world semantics (RWS).

heterogeneous integrity specifications. Integrity constraints are parsed and represented in the internal IOMT structures during the schema parsing process.

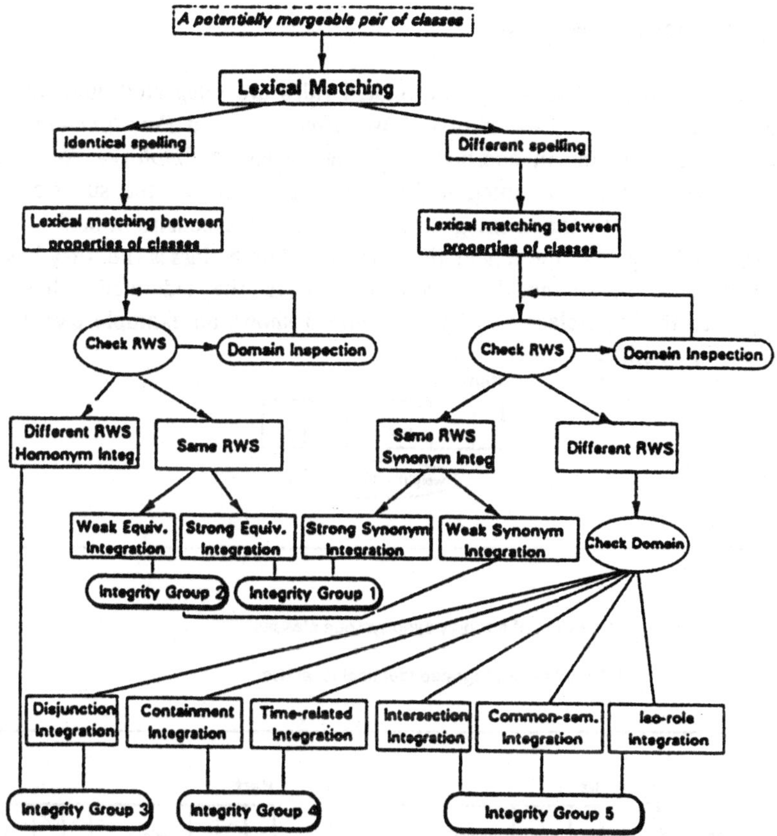

Fig. 2. Integrity rule merging

The original IOMT has been further extended by creating additional slots to model such integrity specifications. In the course of merging integrity constraints, many comparisons take place. These cover attributes, domains, constraint operators and constraint values. Whenever additional semantics are needed to guide the integration process, the SMIS user is consulted. This is achieved through the Schema Meta-Visualisation System (SMVS) component [27] which was developed to enable the users of SMIS to see and interact with the system in a diagrammatic rather than a textual style.

4.1 Rule Integration Methods

The fact that integrity rules can be merged during the integration process in many and various ways was presented in section 3.3. Within the extended version of SMIS, two integration methods are used to cope with these different cases: automatic integration and semi-automatic integration. The discussion below elaborates on these methods, although it is not exhaustive as far as the number of cases that can be processed by each of these methods is concerned.

4.1.1 Automatic Integration

Equivalent, synonymous, and negation-related rules are integrated automatically. Consider for instance the case of two classes *Employee* and *Part-time-employee*, where the latter contains in addition to the attributes of *Employee* some other attributes. These classes are integrated by making *Employee* the super-class of *Part-time-employee*. As far as integrity is concerned, the constraint $sex = 'm' \Rightarrow age < 60$, which is part of the schematic definition of both classes (i.e. they have an identical constraint), is modelled *automatically* in the federated schema by attaching it to the superclass *Employee*. Figure 3 shows an example case that is handled by this method.

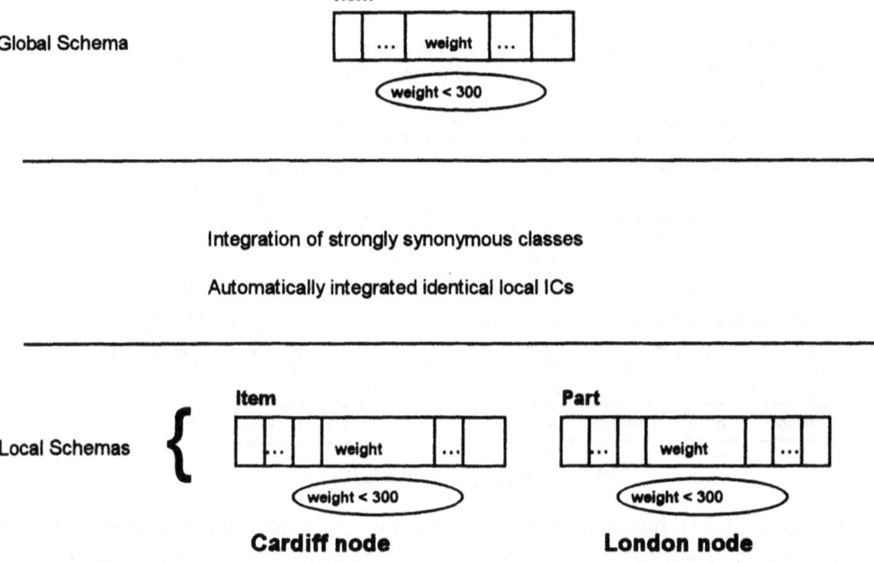

Fig. 3. Automatic integration of identical rules

Automatic integration also takes place in cases where two rules are encountered that constrain different properties or the same property but allowing disjunctive sets of values. Here, both rules are automatically represented in the federated schema. This approach has the advantage of allowing the user to view local conflicting rules in a more homogeneous format, while at the same time providing the global query processor with a copy of the local constraints since they might be beneficial during global query handling [4].

Another case which our system integrates automatically in its current version is that of intersecting rules. Presently, this case is reflected in the federated schema by attaching the two rules, after they are reformulated in an implication constraint style, to the appropriate federated class. Although one could think of a different way to merge the two intersecting rules into one rule, we chose this approach to maintain the genericity of our solutions and to facilitate better processing of MDB queries. Figure 4 illustrates the application of this method on two disjunctive rules.

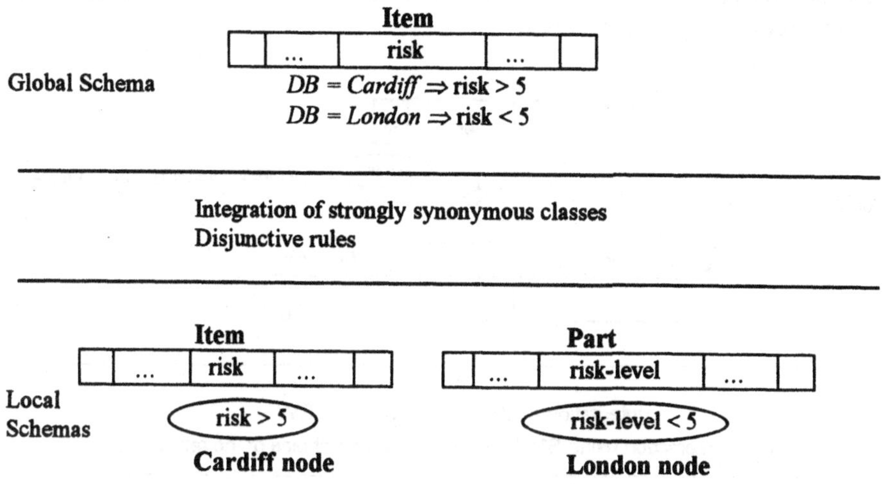

Fig. 4. Automatic integration of disjunctive rules

4.1.2 Semi-automatic Integration

This method is applied when two integrity rules are only partially mergeable. This is the case with containment-related rules. With this method of integration, the user (or DBA) is usually asked to confirm or overrule the decisions proposed by the system.

Most of rules integrated using this method have the same domain but use either different operators or different value limits. The first case is exemplified by the two rules *rank > 1* and *rank >= 1*, while the two rules *salary > 0* and *salary > 1000* illustrate the second. To show how integration of these rules is accomplished by the system, consider two synonymous classes *Doctor* and *Consultant* which have the same set of properties and the two constraints *experience > 4* and *experience > 5*, respectively. The system integrates these two classes by creating one global class (say *Doctor*). By default the system will choose the relaxed constraint *experience > 4* and ask its user to either confirm this decision or modify it according to his understanding of the real world semantics (RWS). In each case, the system will automatically attach a *hidden alerter* to the global integrity rule indicating the site that does not conform to the global rule completely.

This approach has the advantage of enabling the system to assign a single global rule and at the same time consult the shadow schema when both local nodes are involved. The major motivation of this, apart from *reducing* integrity heterogeneity, is that in many cases the global (say relaxed) constraint might be sufficient to answer a query, or to reduce its execution cost.[9] When a user's query requires access to both nodes, the shadow schema is used to adjust the sub-queries created after query decomposition. An example is given in figure 5. In this method the application of SMVS is essential, since GDBA interaction is vital to determine the correct actions to be taken on the variety of conflicts and inconsistencies the system discovers between local ICs.

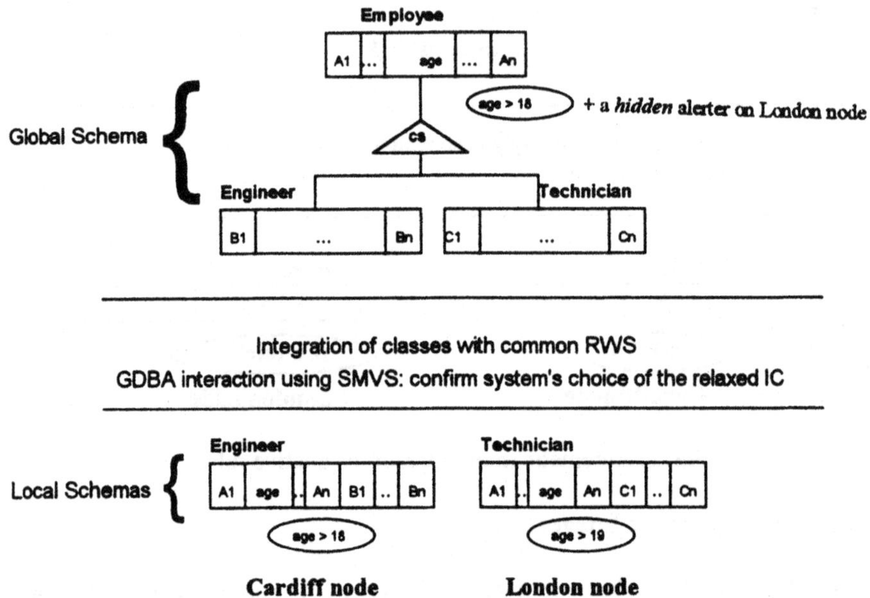

Fig. 5. Semi-automatic integration of ICs

5 Derivation of Global Integrity: Example Groups

For fast prototyping purposes, only two integrity rule categories are utilised in the current phase of our project. These two categories are domain and implication constraints. Additionally, we focus our efforts on rules with numeric domains. This prototype is being used as a testbed for the development of a more generic tool to integrate different types of integrity rules and to investigate a wider range of related problems, such as considering integrity rule context and intelligently deriving new constraints from an integrated set of constraints.

In this section, we show how our six integrity rule-mergeability cases can be facilitated while establishing homogeneous global classes, with their associated integrity rules. Class mergeability cases discussed in [28] are grouped in our augmented system into five groups (as shown in figure 2 above) according to the underlying method of handling global integrity rules. Due to space limitations, only two representative groups are elaborated in this paper.

[9] Details of how this is achieved are discussed in [4].

Integrity Group: 1

When two local classes are strongly equivalent (case 1(i) in [28]) or strongly synonymous (case 9(i)), they are represented in the federated schema by creating a single class (with a proper name) having the attributes of these classes. As for their associated integrity rules, they are modelled globally according to their mergeability, using the classification in section 3.3 above as follows.

Containment: By default, the more relaxed constraint among the two is chosen. In many situations, this is the most desirable option. However, the designer can instruct the system through the visualisation tool to change this selection in a semi-automatic manner.

Intersection: The system automatically attaches the two local rules to the appropriate federated class. An implication IC format is used to model the two rules at the global level.

Disjunction: This case is handled as in the intersection case.

Equivalence: Here, one of the two rules is automatically used for the global level.

Synonymity: Not applicable, since base classes are identical, with the same set of properties and integrity constraints.

Negation: Either of the two rules is automatically chosen for the global level, with preference given to the one with fewer operators (or comparators).

Integrity Group: 5

Classes that share a common set of attributes are modelled in a homogeneous federated schema by creating an inheritance hierarchy in which the common set of attributes is represented by a superclass. The rest of the attributes in each class are left in their respective subclasses. For example, the local classes *Car* and *Truck*, which have some common attributes, are represented globally by creating the superclass *Vehicle* (holding the common attributes) with its two subclasses *Car* and *Truck*, each having their own attributes that are not in the superclass. In [28], by using this approach, three class mergeability cases are modelled in a similar way, namely intersection integration[10], common real world semantics integration and isomorphic role integration (these are cases 4, 6, and 7 respectively). As far as their associated integrity constraints are concerned, various types of rule mergeability require different processing. Notice that in this group we only discuss rules on one of the attributes shared by two classes.

Containment: By default, the superclass is assigned the more relaxed constraint among the two. The designer can instruct the system to change this selection. The subclasses take their local constraints. For

[10] Although this case is modelled in a slightly different way in [28], we argue that the same approach can in fact be applied to these three cases uniformly.

instance, the two rules: *No_cylinders* < *9*, *No_cylinders* < *12*, for local classes *Car* and *Truck* respectively, are modelled globally by assigning the rule *No_cylinders* < *12* to the superclass *Vehicle*, while the global classes (subclasses) *Car* and *Truck* preserve their respective local rules.

Intersection: For the superclass, the system constructs two reformulated integrity rules based on the the two local constraints. The subclasses preserve their local constraints. The common characteristic between this case and the previous one (i.e. containment) is the redefinition of attribute semantics at the subclass level, ICs in our case.

Disjunction: This case is similar to the intersection case. Superclass ICs are not inherited at the subclasses. Instead, local ICs are attached to the two subclasses; so the result is one IC attached to each subclass and two reformulated ICs attached to the superclass.

Equivalence: Here, one of the two rules is attached automatically to the superclass. Unlike previous cases, in this case inheritance is used to define the ICs of the subclasses.

Synonymity: This case is tackled by replacing the two synonymous attributes in the two local classes by one attribute in the superclass. The rule of the superclass is adjusted according to the new name of the synonymous attribute. The subclasses preserve their local ICs. Because of naming differences, this case is handled as an overloading of superclass attributes at the subclass level with new name and semantics, in our case an IC.

Negation: Either of the two rules is chosen automatically for the superclass level, with preference given to the one with fewer operators (or comparators). Subclasses retain their original ICs.

The other three integrity modelling groups of figure 2 (groups 2 to 4) are handled in a similar way to those above.

6 Multidatabase Integrity Maintenance

In this section, we discuss two important related issues. First, we explain how global integrity can be enforced without compromising local autonomy. Second, the issue of maintaining the consistency of global integrity is discussed.

6.1 Local Autonomy vs. Global Integrity

In a multidatabase system, each local node contributes to the federated system under the conditions of being able to determine what data it will share with other sites, what global requests it will service, and when it will join or stop participating in the multidatabase. Local processing has top priority at local nodes. Furthermore, local nodes are not affected by global requirements. This is the ideal case. In practice, however, local nodes have to contribute some of their capabilities to serve global users' requests.

These conditions are made to preserve the autonomy of local DBMSs. Nodal autonomy is defined differently by different authors [23]. However, it is generally agreed that tightly-coupled distributed systems ignore local autonomy. Tight-coupling implies that global functions (data requests) have access to low level internal functions of local DBMSs. Although this may yield efficient global processing, it gives priority to global requests, and therefore, local DBMSs do not have full control over local resources [8]. This is the case with traditional distributed database management systems.

In concept, a tightly-coupled system can still retain a certain level of site autonomy. For example, the component databases in a global schema MDBS, which is usually regarded as a tightly-coupled approach, may be autonomous if they can retain complete control over data and query processing at their sites.

Autonomy is desirable since some local databases may have critical roles in the organisation and it may be impossible from an economic or security viewpoint to change these databases, or to allow external access to influence local operation of their host DBMS. More specifically, autonomy preserves organisational investment in hardware, software and user training when the local database joins the multidatabase, as local applications can continue operating unchanged [8]. Thus, we can conclude from the many definitions of autonomy that the two major factors that must be considered in order for autonomy to be preserved are the safety of the operation of local applications and the freedom of local DBMSs in relation to the MDBS.

This paper regards autonomy as being satisfied if multidatabase transactions are processed by the local DBMSs as if they are local requests. This implies that they are handled through a user/application program interface which guarantees local nodes full control over their low level processing of global queries.

It has been generally concluded that enforcing global integrity constraints in a federated database environment violates local autonomy [13]. We argue that this conclusion is invalid. Our approach to semantic integration of integrity rules is chosen with the fundamental aim of preserving nodal autonomy in mind. We merge local integrity rules, rather than allowing global constraints to be specified explicitly. Our global rules do not require any updates propagated to nodes that are not directly involved in a query[11]. It is these 'side-effects' that make global rules violate local autonomy, due to the existence of interdependencies between database objects [8]. Global ICs have no direct impact on either the operation of local applications or the freedom of local systems to control their resources.

We conclude by claiming that whenever global updates are allowed in a MDB environment, some form of global control has to be practiced, in order that global updates can be accurately executed in a concurrent way. MDB transaction processing is still one of the most challenging research areas.

---

[11] Although this might be a desirable action in some applications.

6.2 Global Integrity Maintenance

Global integrity constraints are derived from heterogenous local constraints. Any modification in the syntax or the semantics of a local schema can affect the set of integrity constraints associated with that schema. In order to preserve the consistency of global integrity constraints, these modifications must be reflected at the global level. Schema evolution maintenance in multidatabase systems is more desirable than in centralised and homogeneous DDB environments since schema changes are more frequent and they can take place without the multidatabase system being informed.

In multidatabases, local autonomy gives local DBAs the freedom to change local data representations without referring to the global DBA. An automatic tool should take the role of propagating changes in local schema and integrity rules to global levels. This tool must be complementary to a federated schema maintenance tool. Developing an automatic integrity monitoring tool implies that local autonomy must be relaxed. We think that allowing such a tool to only monitor schematic modifications of a local DBMS does not have much impact on the operation of that node. In the current version of SMIS, changes are reflected manually in the federated schemas. Research into OO schema evolution [31] provides a good starting point for the development of a tool to propagate changes automatically.

6.3 Assessment

The concepts discussed in sections 6.1 and 6.2 are interdependent in that if we achieve 100% local autonomy, it is at the expense of maintaining global integrity. Thus, there is a tradeoff between nodal autonomy and preserving consistency between local and global integrity rules. We have compromised by allowing a high level of autonomy with a reasonable level of global integrity maintenance. The process of monitoring integrity changes, which are not as frequent as data updates, and propagating changes to the federated schema adds a small burden on local systems, but contributes substantially to preserving consistency and to correctly processing global queries. The exploitation of global integrity during query (and transaction) processing is briefly discussed in the next section.

7 Global Integrity Utilisation

Among the research topics in federated systems, little work has been reported on global query optimisation [11] compared to other topics such as schema integration. This is mainly due to the complexity of this problem as well as the fact that potential returns from global optimisation are not yet clear. Opposers of this research direction base their views on the basic requirement of participating DBMSs, that is local autonomy. Autonomy of the component databases implies that the DDBMS has little control over the actual query processing performed by local nodes. Global queries are very expensive when data transmission is required to accomplish partial result calculation. Even simple distributed queries can have many execution plans which can be evaluated at different costs. We believe that there can indeed be remarkable achievements in performance levels when efficient global optimisers are developed. In [21], an excellent discussion of the merits of global query optimisation in relational systems is provided.

Our discussion in [3] has highlighted a proposed architecture of a global query processor for an OO multidatabase environment. This global front-end prototype is being implemented in PROLOG [10] because of its declarative nature and its power in handling knowledge facts and rules. Many processes are carried out on a query before an optimal global execution schedule is generated. Figure 6 shows the external architecture of our model. Global optimisation has received considerable attention in our work.

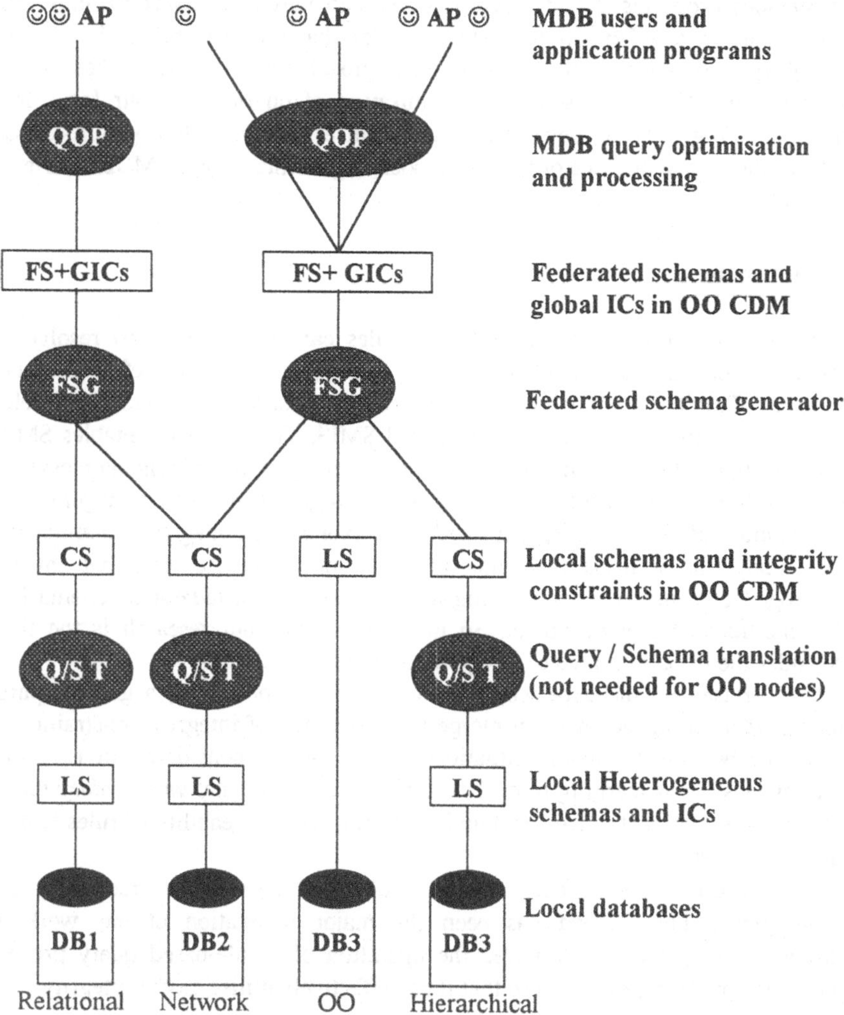

Fig. 6. A model for integrity merging and utilisation

Optimising queries by exploiting application domain semantic knowledge has been investigated by many researchers, such as [33, 36, 9]. Optimisation in its conventional sense utilises syntactic knowledge of operations and storage details to generate better queries, or plans. Semantic processing adds a relatively new dimension to query optimisation by exploiting available knowledge about the data. This knowledge-based query optimisation [36, 22, 16] gains processing efficiency by making use of semantic integrity constraints. These constraints are a profitable organisational resource that should be utilised effectively. Examples of systems that are based on this approach are those reported in [33, 20]. All these research efforts are based on the relational data model for databases and in centralised applications.

In previous DDB methodologies, global integrity has not been utilised for supporting query processing. The role global integrity can play in optimising multidatabase queries has been realised only recently [30, 24]. The major weakness of previous proposals is that they do not explain how integrity constraints can be constructed in a MDB environment, in order that they can be used to optimise global queries. Our work in supporting global integrity establishes a sound infrastructure for global semantic optimisation of queries [4]. Our focus in the future is going to be on developing our optimiser to extend its capabilities and to exploit the rich semantics of the OO model to generate cheaper MDB queries and transactions.

Conclusion

The paper has illustrated how integrity rules can be examined to resolve their inconsistencies and create integrated rules during the integration of heterogeneous schemas. This has been achieved in practice by extending a previously developed prototype schema integration system called SMIS. The extension enables SMIS to consider integrity constraints while testing the mergeability of schema classes. The result of this extension yields a new approach to global integrity management. The contribution of our work lies in providing a taxonomy of integrity semantics in the OO model, as well as the implementation of a generic tool that integrates heterogeneous integrity rules during the generation of a federated schema for an OO multidatabase environment. So far as we know, our research is the first to consider the important area of integrity conflict reconciliation.

Based on the experiences gained with this prototype, a general purpose tool is being designed that can merge a wider range of integrity constraints. This tool will be able to handle situations that were not considered in the current prototype, such as merging rules from different contexts (e.g. when *salary* refers in two rules to different currencies) and exploring the mergeability of rules from two different categories.

Global homogeneous integrity rules are utilised in processing global transactions. This indeed has been the major motivation of our work. Our discussion in [3] has overviewed the operation of a rule-based query processor, which is now being extended so that it can effectively utilise global integrity.

References

[1] R Agrawal, N H Gehani, *ODE (Object Database Environment): The Language and the Data Model*, Proc. ACM SIGMOD, 1989.

[2] R Ahmad *et al*, *The Pegasus Heterogeneous Multidatabase System*, IEEE Computer, Vol 24, No 12, 1991.

[3] R M Alzahrani, W A Gray, N J Fiddian, *A Rule-Based Query Processor for a Heterogeneous Object-Oriented Database Environment - Overview*, Proc. RIDE-DOM'95, Taipei, Taiwan, 1995.

[4] R M Alzahrani *et al*, *Semantics-based Multidatabase Access*, in preparation, 1995.

[5] C Batini, M Lenzerini, S Navathe, *A comparative Analysis of Methodologies for Database Schema Integration*, ACM Comp. Surv., Vol 18, No 4, pp 232-364, 1986.

[6] D Bell, J Grimson, *Distributed Database Systems*, Addison Wesley, 1992.

[7] E Bertino *et al*, *Applications of Object-Oriented Technology to the Integration of Heterogeneous Database Systems*, Distributed and Parallel Databases, Vol 2, No 4, 1994.

[8] M W Bright, A R Hurson, S H Pakzad, *A Taxonomy and Current Issues in Multidatabase Systems*, IEEE Computer, Vol 25, No 3, 1992.

[9] U S Charkavarthy, D H Fishman, J Minker, *Semantic Query Optimisation in Expert Systems and Database Systems*, in L Kerschberg (Ed.), *Expert Database Systems*, Benjamin Cummings, 1986.

[10] W Clocksin, C Mellish, *Programming in Prolog*, 4th Edition, Springer-Verlag, 1987.

[11] U Dayal, *Query Processing in Multidatabase Sysytem*, in W Kim *et al*, *Query Processing in Database Systems*, Springer-Verlag, 1985.

[12] U Dayal, *Queries and Views in an Object-Oriented Data Model*, Proc. 2nd Intl. Workshop on Database Programming Languages, Morgan Kaufman, 1989.

[13] G Fahl, *Object Views of Relational Data in Multidatabase Systems*, Ph.D. Thesis, Linkoping University, Sweden, 1994.

[14] H Garcia-Molina, *Global Consistency Constraints Considered Harmful for Heterogeneous Database Systems*, Proc. 1st Intl. Workshop on Interoperability in Multidatabase Systems, IMS'91, 1991.

[15] M M Hammar, D J Mcleod, *Semantic Integrity in a Relational Database System*, Proc. 1st Intl. Conf. on VLDB, pp 25-47, 1975.

[16] M M Hammer, S B Zdonic, *Knowledge-Based Query Processing*, Proc. 6th Intl. Conf. on VLDB, pp 137-147, 1980.

[17] H V Jagdish, X Qian, *Integrity Maintenance in an Object-Oriented Database*, Proc. 18th Intl. Conf. on VLDB, 1992.

[18] S N Khoshafian, G Copeland, *Object Identity*, in S Zdonik, D Mair (Eds.), *Readings in Object-Oriented Database Systems*, Morgan Kaufman, 1990.

[19] W Kim, *Object-Oriented Database Systems: Promises, Reality and Future*, Proc. 19th Intl. Conf. on VLDB, 1993.

[20] J J King, *QUIST: A System for Semantic Query Optimisation in Relational Databases*, Proc. 7th Int. Conf. on VLDB, pp 510-517, 1982.

[21] H Lu, B-C Ooi, C-H Goh, *On Global Multidatabase Query Optimisation*, ACM SIGMOD RECORD, Vol 21, No 4, 1992.

[22] C V Malley, S B Zdonik, *A Knowledge-based Approach to Semantic Query Optimisation*, in L Kerschberg (Ed.), *Expert Database Systems*, Benjamin Cummings, pp 329-343, 1987.

[23] M T Ozsu, P Valduriez, *Principles of Distributed Database Systems*, Prentice-Hall, 1991.

[24] S Prabhakar *et al*, *Federated Autonomous Databases: Project Overview*, Proc. of Workshop on Interoperability in Multidatabase Systems, RIDE-IMS'93, Vienna, Austria, 1993.

[25] M A Qutaishat, N J Fiddian, W A Gray, *A Schema Meta-Integration System for a Heterogeneous Object-Oriented Database Environment - Implementation in PROLOG*, Proc. 1st Intl. Conf. on the Practical Application of Prolog, 1992.

[26] M A Qutaishat, N J Fiddian, W A Gray, *A Schema Meta-Integration System for a Heterogeneous Object-Oriented Database Environment - Objectives and Overview*, Proc. NordData'92 European Conf. on Information Technology, Finland, pp 74-92, 1992.

[27] M A Qutaishat, W A Gray, N J Fiddian, *A Highly-Customisable Schema Meta-Visualisation System for Object-Oriented (O-O) Database Schemas - Overview*, Proc. 4th Intl. DEXA Conf., Springer-Verlag, 1993.

[28] M A Qutaishat, *A Schema Meta Integration System for a Logically Heterogeneous Object-Oriented Database Environment*, PhD Thesis, Department of Computing Mathematics, University of Wales College of Cardiff, Cardiff, 1993.

[29] S Ram, *Heterogeneous Distributed Database Systems*, IEEE Computer, Vol 24, No 12, 1991.

[30] M P Reddy *et al*, *Towards an Active Schema Integration Architecture for Heterogeneous Database Systems*, Proc. of Workshop on Interoperability in Multidatabase Systems, RIDE-IMS'93, Vienna, Austria, 1993.

[31] Roddick J F, Patrick J D, *Temporal Semantics in Information Systems: a Survey*, Inf. Syst., Vol 17, No 3, 1992.

[32] J Rumbaugh *et al*, *Object-Oriented Modelling and Design*, Prentice-Hall, 1991.

[33] S T Shenoy, Z M Ozsoyoglu, *Design and Implementation of a Semantic Query Optimiser*, IEEE Trans. on Knowledge and Data Engineering, Vol 1, No 3, 1989.

[34] A P Sheth, J A Larson, *Federated Database Systems for Managing Heterogeneous and Autonomous Databases*, ACM Comp. Surv., Vol 22, No 3, 1990.

[35] M Stonebraker *et al*, *Third generation Database System Manifesto*, in W Kent, R Meersman (Eds.), *Object-Oriented Database: Analysis, Design and Construction*, Proc. IFIP TC2-2 Conf., North-Holland, 1990.

[36] C T Yu, W Sun, *Automatic Knowledge Acquisition and Maintenance for Semantic Query Optimisation*, IEEE Trans. on Knowledge and Data Engineering, Vol 1, No 3, 1989.

The Architecture of the

ICL GOLDRUSH MegaSERVER

Paul Watson & George Catlow

ICL, Corporate Servers, West Gorton, Manchester M12 5DR, UK

Abstract. This paper discusses the requirements which are to be met by a parallel computer system if it is to satisfy the requirements of commercial database processing, and describes how one such system - the ICL GOLDRUSH MegaSERVER - has been designed to meet these requirements.

GOLDRUSH is a distributed store parallel processor consisting of up to 64 elements, each of which can co-operate in database processing, exploiting both the parallelism found within complex queries (intra-query parallelism) and that found between queries in On-Line Transaction Processing workloads (inter-query parallelism). The paper discusses the requirements of business critical database applications including high availability, integrity and manageability. It then details the architecture of GOLDRUSH in order to show how a commercially available system has been designed to meet these requirements; this includes resilience to failure of hardware components such as disks and processors, and the provision of system management applications which allow the parallel machine to be managed as a single system.

1 Introduction

Conventional mainframe computers are being pushed to, and beyond, their performance limits by the needs of today's commercial computing workloads. This, combined with the cost of these large systems, is forcing both customers and manufacturers to look at more radical architectural alternatives. Parallel computers have been used successfully for many years to overcome these same problems for scientific computing [ALA89], but it is only now that parallel machines are starting to be produced for the commercial market by a range of mainstream computer manufacturers. Potentially, this market could become far larger than the scientific market: 80% of the worlds large computer systems (those over $1M) are commercial rather than scientific [IDC92].

As these new commercial parallel systems become available, the unprecedented levels of performance they offer will create new opportunities for businesses which utilize them. Already companies are re-engineering their business processes to fully exploit the new technology. One example of this is a financial organisation with a large number of customers, each of which has a number of different types of accounts. Currently, information on each account is held in a different database, on a different computer. This makes it impossible for the organisation to collate information about all the accounts held by a customer. They wish to do this so as to form an overall picture of the financial state of their customers, allowing them to target their services and marketing more effectively. The solution is to move to a parallel system: the higher levels of performance offered will allow them to unify all their information into a single database, on a single machine. The database can be structured to allow information to be accessed by both account number and customer.

The GOLDRUSH system evolved from earlier work carried out in collaborative projects with Universities and other Companies. The two most important of these projects were: the Alvey Flagship project [WAT88] which produced a distributed store parallel system running both Declarative Languages and Databases; and the ESPRIT EDS project [WAT91] which developed a parallel system for Parallel Databases, Language Translation and Declarative languages.

The rest of this paper focuses on the GOLDRUSH parallel system, and is structured as follows. The requirements of commercial parallel database systems are discussed in Section 2. Section 3 then describes the overall GOLDRUSH architecture, including the hardware. Section 4 details the platform software and 5 describes how databases are supported by it. Sections 6 and 7 give details of how two of the key requirements for commercial parallel computers- high availability and manageability- are met. Finally, section 8 contains some of the conclusions we have drawn from our work.

2 Requirements

The challenge for the designers of parallel machines is to give customers the key attributes they have traditionally found in conventional mainframes, but with greater power and lower cost-performance. Customers will not entrust their business-critical applications and data to a machine which does not offer high availability and manageability. The methods which have been adopted to meet these requirements in GOLDRUSH are described in sections 6 and 7.

Another attraction of parallel machines is their scalability; customers can grow their systems by adding units of processing power and IO capability as required. It is important that the design supports this by ensuring that there are no system bottlenecks which reduce scalability.

The need to run commercial relational database systems (RDBMS) places two major requirements on the platform software of the machine. Firstly, there is a need for a globally shared filestore which all processors in the system can access so that each can be running transactions against the same database tables. Secondly, a Global Lock Manager is required to preserve the integrity of shared database tables when multiple processors are performing transactions simultaneously. The design of these two components is described in Section 4.

It is interesting to note that as yet there is no requirement for distributed shared store: current commercial parallel database systems attain parallelism by running a separate server on each processor. They communicate only through the global lock manager, and the globally shared filestore, both of which can be efficiently implemented by distributed, message passing processes.

The implementation of the lock manager and filestore in GOLDRUSH is described in Section 4. The mapping of the database servers onto the system is described in more detail in Section 5.

3 Overall Architecture and Hardware

The GOLDRUSH MegaSERVER is a Database Server, designed to run commercial database back-ends. It stores the database, and services SQL queries sent by external clients such as PCs, workstations and mainframes. Examples of application architectures are shown in Figure 1.

The diagram shows options for Management Information Systems (MIS) generating complex queries, On Line Transaction Processing (OLTP) and Batch Clients. The use of Transaction Processing (TP) protocols in the application architecture is recommended for large systems: Clients connect over a local or wide area network to

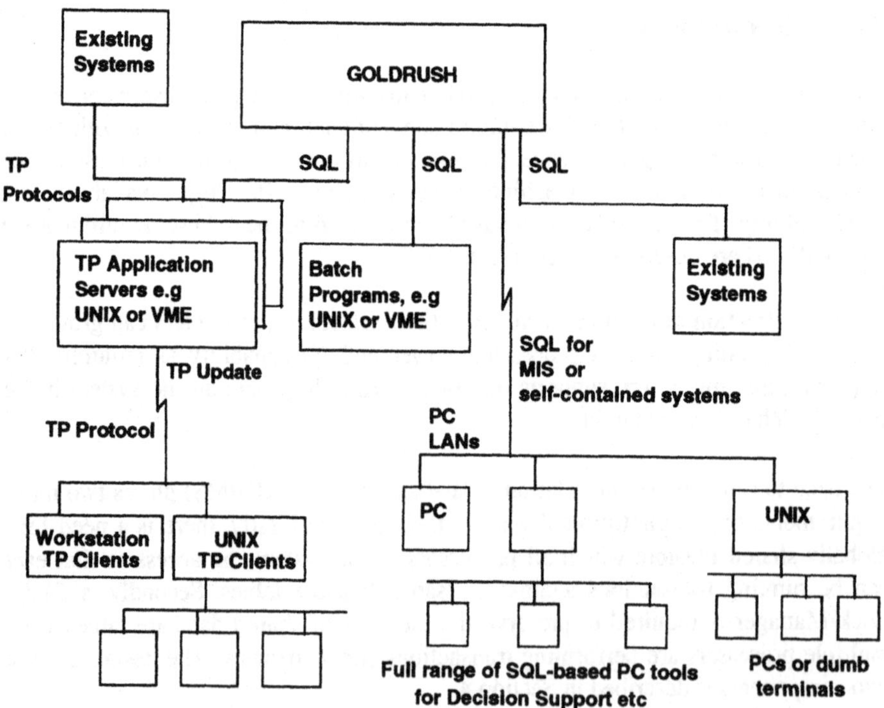

Fig 1. Example GOLDRUSH Application Architectures

an Application server, which generates the SQL. This improves performance as TP sends less data over a wide area network than does SQL; it also offers better security and control of application code. Note that various existing systems can be connected to GOLDRUSH. The applications can remain on these systems, but the database migrates to GOLDRUSH.

The internal architecture of a GOLDRUSH system is shown in Figure 2. It consists of a set of Processing Elements (PEs), Communications Elements (CEs) and Management Elements (MEs) connected together by a high performance network (DeltaNet).

The PE is the most common Element and is designed to run a Database Back-end. It consists of two SPARC RISC microprocessors, one of which runs the database server while the other is dedicated to delivering high performance message passing over the DeltaNet. A very large amount of RAM store is provided in the PE to enable large database caches to be configured: this is very important for achieving high performance database processing. Each PE also has two SCSI-2 (wide and fast) connections, allowing up to 30 disks to be connected.

The Communications Element is identical to the Processing Element except that one of the SCSIs is replaced by two FDDI couplers for Client connection. FDDI was chosen because of its high performance (100Mb/s), and the availability of bridges allowing connection to all other common types of LAN and WAN, such as Ethernet. Multiple CEs can be configured in a system for both performance and resilience reasons (see Section 6).

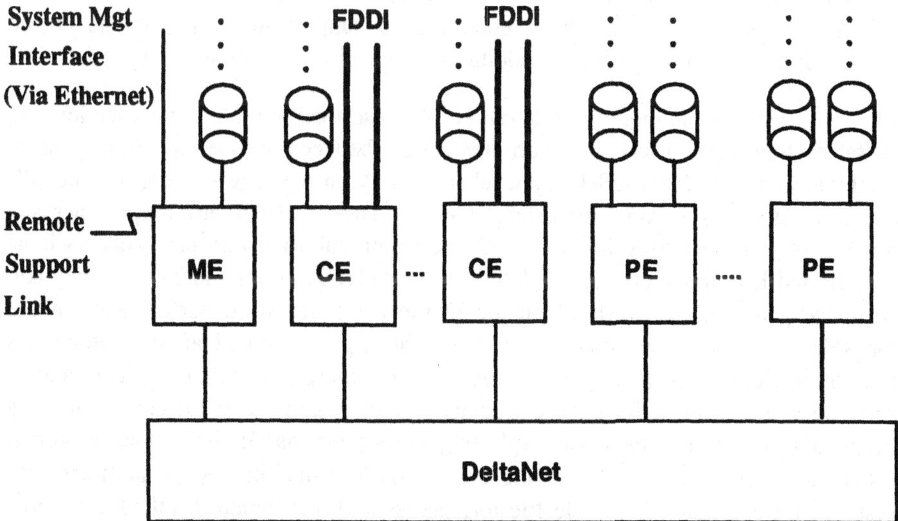

Fig 2. The Internal GOLDRUSH Architecture

The Management Element is a conventional mid-range UNIX processor (currently an ICL DRS6000) which runs the Management Software (which is described in Section 7). It also contains a "Teleservice" modem connection allowing: problem reports to be sent to a service desk; remote problem diagnosis from the service centre; and, software problem fixes to be sent from the service centre to GOLDRUSH.

The DeltaNet is a high performance Delta Network built out of 8x8 router chips. 128 Byte Messages are sent through the DeltaNet between Elements over full duplex links delivering up to 25MBytes per second each way per Element.

For high performance archiving, tape libraries can be attached to the Elements via their SCSI connectors. Multiple Element connections provide high performance archiving by allowing multiple data streams to be archived simultaneously to multiple tape drives.

GOLDRUSH systems can contain up to 64 Elements. Each PE and CE has two 90MHz HyperSPARC processors, with 256MBytes of RAM. PEs can each connect to up to 50GBytes of Disk Store. Because of the reliance on industry standard, commodity components, this specification will be continuously upgraded as new versions of the components become available. These upgrades will include faster processors and larger capacity disks. The first release offers the Ingres, Oracle, Adabas and Informix databases.

4 Platform Software

Figure 3 shows the GOLDRUSH platform software architecture. Each Processing and Communications Element runs a Chorus micro-kernel based SVR4 UNIX Operating System. This has been enhanced to support the requirements of the parallel database processing by the addition of the following sub-systems:

- *Internal Communication Services* : As described in the previous section, the DeltaNet hardware offers fast communication between Elements. In a parallel machine such as GOLDRUSH which relies entirely on message passing for inter-PE communications it is very important that low latency, high throughput message passing is available to software. While conventional transport protocols such as TCP/IP and ISO transport are available for inter-element communications, they add an unacceptably large overhead on top of the basic hardware performance of the DeltaNet. In order to overcome this, a very lightweight communications protocol has been designed. It is made available through UNIX interfaces so that application level software can exploit it; for example database servers can use it for communicating fragments of transactions when exploiting intra-query parallelism. Internal kernel interfaces are also provided, and these are used by a number of the platform sub-systems, for example for remote filestore access and distributed deadlock detection. The bulk of the lightweight comms stack runs on the SPARC processor dedicated to driving the DeltaNet (see Section 3), so minimizing the performance impacts on the other SPARC processor which runs the database server.

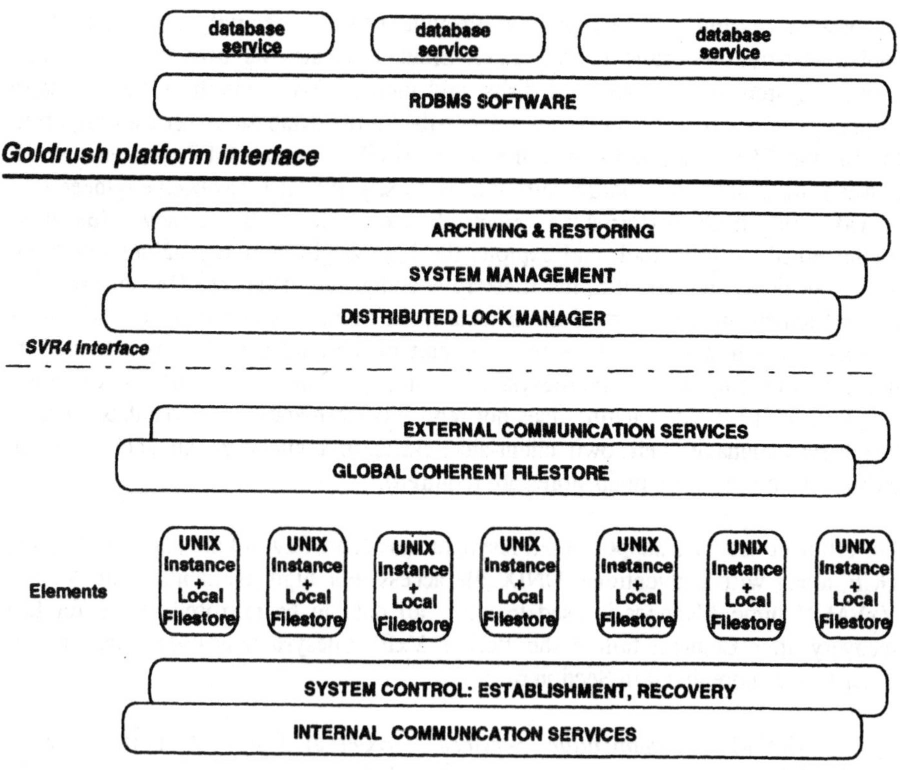

Fig 3. GOLDRUSH Platform Software Architecture

- *System Control* : As was described above, each Element runs a separate instance of UNIX SVR4. It is a requirement that it should not be necessary to manage each UNIX instance separately. Therefore, it is the job of the system control layer to support this: it is responsible for establishing and shutting down the Elements in a co-ordinated fashion. The standard Network Information System (NIS) is used to provide a global method of configuring all the Elements, including users and communications connections. If Disks or Elements fail then this layer ensures that the rest of the system can continue and that applications remain running. This is discussed in detail in Section 6.

- *Global Coherent Filestore* : As described earlier, each Processing Element (PE) runs a separate database server. However, they are all able to perform transactions on the same database simultaneously. This requires that each PE can access all the database tables which are held on disk (details of the mapping of tables onto disks is given in section 5). As was described in Section 3, each Processing Element contains two SCSIs for disk connection. Therefore, physically each disk is attached to one Element only. Some of the space on the disks is dedicated to local filestore which is only required to be accessible by that Element: for example the local UNIX kernel. However, the rest of the disk space is used to hold database data (tables, logs etc.) which must be globally accessible by other Elements if parallel database processing is to be supported. Providing this connectivity is the role of the Global Coherent Filestore (GCF). Each Element creates its own portion of this Global Filestore on its own local disks, and then cross-mounts the global filestore from all other Elements, so making it accessible to the database server running on it. In this, the GCF is very similar to the standard UNIX Network File System (NFS), however there are two important differences. Firstly, the GCF has been engineered to provide very high performance remote filestore access. To achieve this it is implemented in the kernel, and exploits the lightweight communications described above. Secondly, unlike NFS, the filestore is completely coherent. This ensures that if one Element updates part of the database, the updated value is seen by all other Elements which subsequently access that part of the database. This is achieved by implementing only server-side filesystem caching (NFS also has client-side caching). The lack of client-side caching does not reduce performance as the database servers themselves manage their own client-side cache in main store on each Element (which is why the large main stores are required).

For efficient database support, both Asynchronous and Raw IO are supported by the GCF, along with conventional UNIX file access. For high availability, the Veritas VxVM Volume Manager is used to allow all data to be mirrored, while for fast recovery after Element failure the Veritas VxFS Filesystem is used. Their use is described in more detail in Section 6.

- *Global Communication Services* : External Communications between GOLDRUSH and external Clients generating SQL is via the FDDI couplers on the CEs. Both TCP/IP and ISO transport protocols are supported.

It was an important criteria for manageability that GOLDRUSH appeared as a single system to Clients, rather than as a set of individual Elements. The Global Communications Services layer provides this in the following way. For ISO communications the GOLDRUSH machine has a single externally visible address independent of the number of CEs and PEs. For TCP/IP communications each FDDI coupler has a separate address, independent of the number of PEs. PEs wishing to set up communications with Clients "listen" for connections to the service they are offering, and when an external Client attempts to connect to the service, the CE which receives the request routes it to a PE offering the service. If multiple PEs are offering the service then the CE will load-balance the connection requests across those PEs. Once a connection between an external Client and a PE is established, the CE relays the data packets from the FDDI coupler to the PE (and vica versa) using the lightweight communications protocol for efficiency. The Global Communications Services layer can maintain connections in the presence of FDDI coupler, CE or (in some cases) external LAN failure. This is described in Section 6.

- *Distributed Lock Manager:* On GOLDRUSH, database management servers run in parallel on many PEs. It is the job of the Distributed Lock Manager to ensure that they run transactions consistently, avoiding concurrent, incompatible updates to the databases. On a uniprocessor, this job is done by the database server's own lock manager which receives requests to take and drop locks and forces transactions to wait until they have the correct lock before data can be accessed. The Distributed Lock Manager (DLM) must act as a Global Lock Manager for all the database servers running against the same database. It is distributed across all Elements, with an instance running on each Element, so that the processing and communications load is shared, and no one Element becomes a bottle-neck. Each lock is managed by one instance of the DLM and all requests for it are sent to that instance by the PE generating the request. The DLM also provides Global Deadlock detection using a novel algorithm to minimize inter-PE communication [HIL89]. For efficiency, all communication with the DLM is by the lightweight communications protocol. The DLM is also resilient to the failure of any process or Element (see Section 6).

- *System Management:* Section 7 describes this layer.

- *Archiving & Restoring:* One of the key attributes found in mainframes but generally not available in UNIX based solutions is fast archive and restore. This is important as the time taken by archiving may reduce the availability of the system for database processing. Also the time taken to restore from archive will limit the recovery time after a major failure. The latter can be a particular problem as a major failure, unlike archiving, cannot be planned in advance.

The large disk capacity of systems such as GOLDRUSH requires very high throughput rates. Therefore for very high performance, this layer supports the integral, SCSI connected archiving described in Section 3, ensuring that data is archived as fast as the available tape drives can accept it. For lower performance archiving, which may for example be acceptable for small databases, the layer will support archiving to external archive servers connected via the FDDI connections.

5 Databases

The initial release of GOLDRUSH supports the Oracle, Ingres, Adabas and Informix databases. There are two basic mappings onto the GOLDRUSH Architecture. These are denoted as the Shared Access and Distributed Access mappings and are described in this section.

The Shared Access mapping is shown in Figure 4.

In this mapping, each PE runs its own Database Server. The database tables are striped across disks attached to a number of processing Elements; the Global Coherent Filestore allows all Elements to access all fragments of the tables. Each PE has a local database cache in main store, and the Distributed Lock Manager is used to ensure consistency. Figure 4 shows Service 1 running on 3 PEs, and Service 2 running on 2 PEs. When a Client connects to a database service, the CE uses a load balancing algorithm to decide which of the PEs offering that service should take the

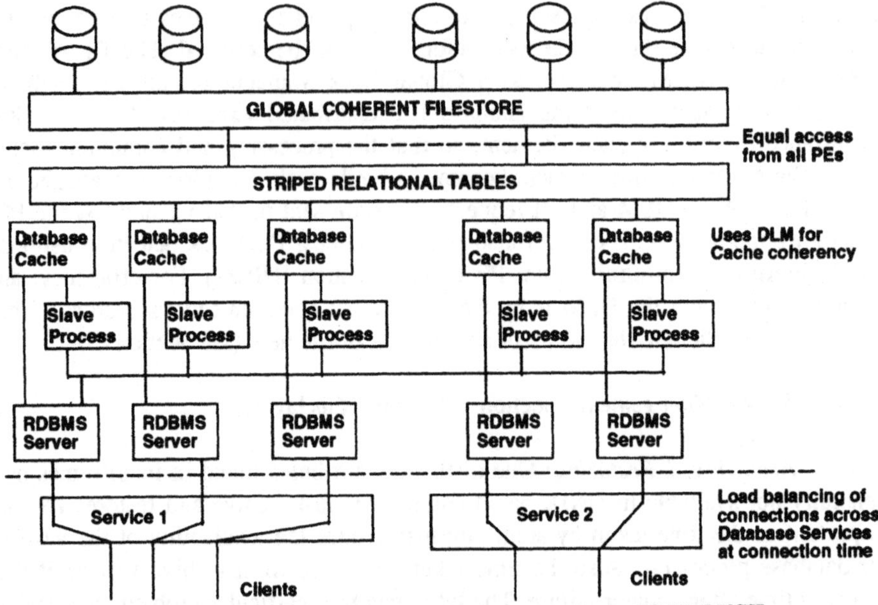

Fig 4. Shared Access Mapping of Databases onto GOLDRUSH

connection. Once the connection is made it remains until the Client disconnects; during that time it services all transactions originating from that Client. Where intra-query parallelism is exploited, slave processes in each PE are used to distribute and manage the execution of the query across a set of PEs.

Figure 5 shows the Distributed Access mapping of database servers onto GOLDRUSH.

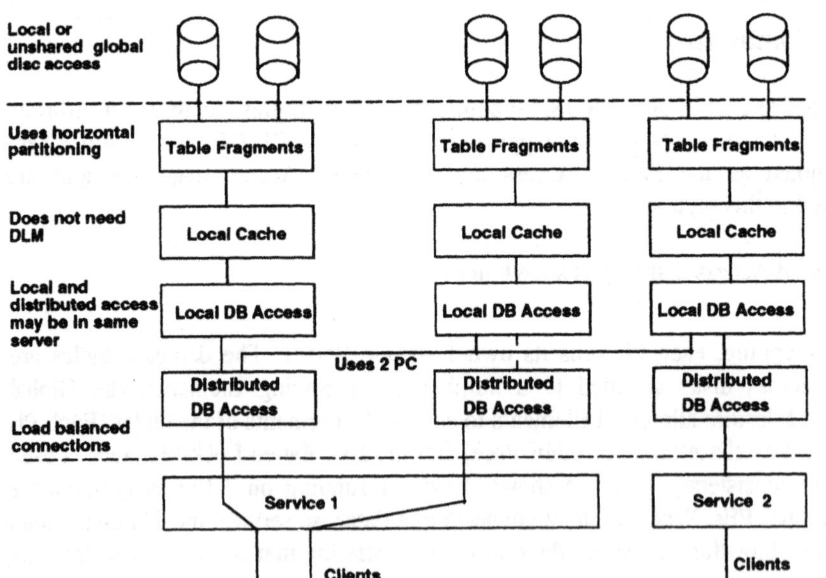

Fig 5. Distributed Access Mapping of Databases onto GOLDRUSH

In this mapping, again, each PE runs its own Database Server and the database tables are horizontally fragmented across PEs. As in the shared access mapping, a Client connects to a PE and sends queries to it. However, each query is decomposed into sub-queries which are distributed such that each PE only has to access the table fragments which are stored on its local disks. The results of these sub-queries are then combined and the result returned to the Client. The main effect of this type of mapping is that there is no use of the Distributed Lock Manager: only one PE (the local PE) can access a particular table fragment and so local locking can be used. However, if a query requires table fragments on more than one PE to be updated then some form of co-ordination such as Two Phase Commit (shown as 2PC in the Figure) is required.

In both the mappings, it is possible for both OLTP and Complex queries to be running against the same database simultaneously. In order to reduce the performance effects of one on the other, different sets of Elements can be used for the two different types of queries- Figures 4 and 5 both show two different services (Service 1 and Service 2) running on seperate sets of elements but against the same database. It is also important that database tables are fragmented across sufficient numbers of disk to ensure that the IO throughput requirements of each type of query are met.

6 High Availability

The GOLDRUSH MegaSERVER is constructed from tens of commodity components such as processors and disks. Machines constructed in this way do not inherently offer the levels of reliability required to meet customers requirements: in a simple parallel machine design, the failure of any one component may bring down the whole machine and halt the customer's application. However, careful design can exploit the parallelism to produce a system in which if one component fails then another takes its place. This may reduce the performance once the failure has occurred, but it will not halt the customer's application.

In this section we discuss how the parallelism of GOLDRUSH is exploited to provide high-availability. The main areas of resilience are:

- *Filesystems:* For high availability, all database data is mirrored; the Veritas Volume Manager VxVM is used for this. Recovery from Disk failure is totally transparent to the database servers accessing the data: when a disk fails, processing continues from the surviving mirror; the data is automatically re-mirrored onto one of the spare disks which are kept in the system for this purpose, and sometime later the failed disk can be replaced (using hot pull and push).

In order to be resilient to Element failures, each mirror is placed on a disk connected to a different Element. Therefore, although when an Element fails the disks locally connected to it become unreachable, all the data on those disks is still available on their mirrors (because they are connected to other Elements).

The use of Veritas VxFS as the UNIX filesystem allows a filesystem which was owned by a failed PE to be very quickly reconstituted on another PE (by considerably reducing the time needed to restore filesystem consistency).

- *Processing Elements:* Each Element in the system runs its own instance of UNIX. This minimizes the dependencies between Elements and ensures that if an Element does fail then others can continue. Any parts of the Global Coherent Filestore which were owned by that Element are logically moved to be owned by another Element as described above. The database transactions being run on the failed Element are automatically recovered by the database software running on another Element using information found in tables, logs and journals. Any Clients connected to a failing PE have to reconnect to the GOLDRUSH server. Those connected to other PEs see a short delay (up to 2 seconds) while the filestore is re-organised, but then processing continues.

- *Communications Element:* If a CE (or FDDI coupler) fails, then SQL connections from a Client into GOLDRUSH will be automatically routed through another CE (or Coupler), provided that there is another route from GOLDRUSH to the Client (and that the Client provides a full implementation of the transport connection protocols). This is achieved by maintaining configuration tables holding information on external sub-networks. Internal polling ensures that the failure of a CE or coupler is quickly detected. Following this, information in the configuration files is used to cause messages to be re-routed through another coupler, if this offers an alternative route to the Client.

- *Fans and Power Supplies:* Spare fan and power supply capacity is present in the GOLDRUSH cabinets so that if one fails then the system can continue running. Uninterruptable Power Supplies can be used to prevent problems due to electricity supply failure.

- *Distributed Lock Manager* : All lock information is mirrored in more than one PE so that the system is unaffected by Element or process failure.

7 System Management

System Management is a vitally important but often overlooked attribute required by Commercial parallel processors. Experience in the computer industry over recent years suggests that companies who downsize from a mainframe to a number of conventional UNIX systems often find that they make no overall savings in their IT budgets because even though the raw hardware and software costs may be lower, the cost of management increases dramatically. This is due to the fact that management tools for UNIX systems are generally more primitive than those available on mainframes, and because there is a need to manage a number of systems rather than just one. The danger therefore is that a parallel processor containing many UNIX Elements will prove to be extremely difficult and therefore costly to manage.

GOLDRUSH management tools have been designed to allow it to be managed as a single system, rather than as a collection of many UNIX systems. The basic architecture of System Management is shown in Figure 6.

Each Element runs an agent which offers local system management functionality, for example running commands and collecting statistics. The Management Element (ME) contains a layer of software which distributes management requests to the agents on the Elements. The agents return results which are filtered and aggregated. Therefore the Management Element (ME) can offer to Management applications a single, high level interface for managing Elements. The applications themselves run on the ME but are controlled from a PC (the System Management Workstation) or an external, possibly Enterprise-wide, Management Server. The Management Applications are designed to offer comprehensive coverage of the key management functions required by a Database Server.

A key concept in the management of GOLDRUSH is the use of named sets of components. Users can define sets of Elements and then use the names of these sets in the system management applications, for example to monitor and administer the

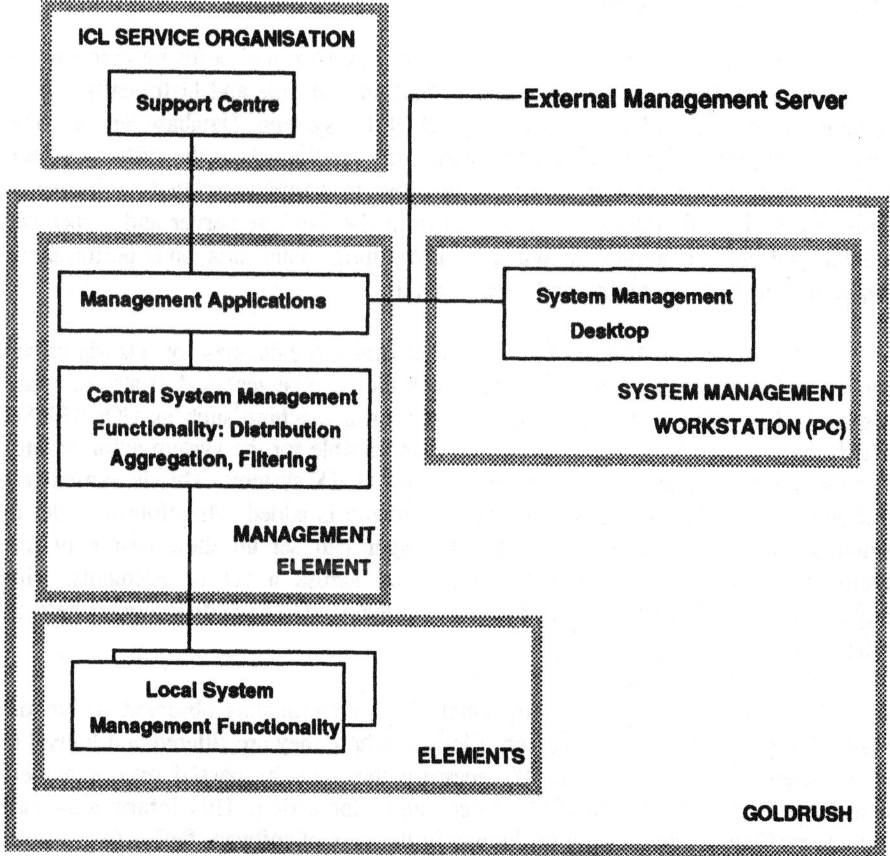

Fig 6. GOLDRUSH Management Architecture

components of the set. Similarly, sets of disks and volumes can be defined and managed. The concept of sets is also key to resilience and tuning: if one Element in a set running a database service fails another can be automatically added to the set. Because the management applications refer to the name of the set, and not the Elements in it, then the change in the set contents is isolated from the manager.

The key management applications designed to provide single-image management of the parallel machine are:

- *Operations Management:* This allows an operator to monitor the current status of all the major hardware and software components (the *managed objects*) of the system through a single pictorial representation. Each managed object is represented as an Icon whose colour represents the current status, and so changes of colour alert the operator of events in the system. Each managed object also has a set of actions associated with it, so allowing the Operator to control it. For example, when a database service is created, a managed object is automatically created for it, and the status of the service (starting, running, in error, stopping...) is represented by its Icon's colour. The object also has a set of actions associated with it to allow the Service to be started, stopped etc.

- *Capacity Management:* All the major hardware and software components can be monitored through this application, both in real time and historically. These components include Disks, Processors, the DLM, Filesystems, Database Servers. The advantage of providing comprehensive monitoring of all levels of the system through a single interface is that it makes it possible to correlate related performance measures, such as transactions per second from the database server and processor utilization from the kernel on which it is running. This aids both performance problem identification, tuning and trend analysis.

- *Configuration Management* : This maintains the database of sets (described above), and provides interfaces through which they can be accessed. It also provides a graphical interface for configuring filestore. In a machine such as GOLDRUSH which may contain hundreds of disks, it is not feasible for the system administrator to configure them one at a time, as in standard UNIX systems. This is particularly true when the complexity of configuring mirroring is added. Therefore in order to simplify the configuration, the system manager can set up the filestore of one Element and have it automatically replicated across a set of Elements. This replication will automatically take into account the need to have disk mirrors held on separate PEs (see section 6).

- *Problem Management* : Information on all problems observed within the system are passed to the Management Element where they are filtered and logged in a customer accessible database. If necessary they can be passed over a modem connected to the ME to the ICL service centre for action. This information may include problem evidence such as dumps. In the case of software faults, fixes can be passed back to the customer site.

- *Administration* : This allows commands to be run on sets of Elements, and provides a tool for installing software packages on a set of Elements.

8 Conclusions

This paper has described the design of a commercial parallel computer system for running business critical database applications. The requirements for such systems are evolving as customers begin to take advantage of the new machines now available in the marketplace. We envisage a positive feedback effect in which these machines will open up new opportunities to users, who will then exploit them and in so doing place new requirements on the machines themselves. In particular, we expect that customers' realisations of the business advantages they can gain through the use of complex queries to analyse their corporate information will lead to increasing performance demands. Similarly, the moves towards multi-media databases, and the advantages of centralizing information in these servers, so making it all available for analysis, will increase the data capacity requirements.

GOLDRUSH is designed to meet these evolving requirements due to its scalable parallel architecture, and its utilization of commodity components whose capacity and performance are continually improving.

9 Acknowledgements

The GOLDRUSH MegaSERVER is the result of the work of a large number of people at ICL, Corporate Servers Division. We would also like to acknowledge our debt to our partners in the Alvey Flagship and ESPRIT EDS projects.

References

ALA89 *Highly Parallel Computing*, G.S. Alamasi & A.J. Gotlieb, Benjamin/Cummings, 1989

HIL89 *Distributed Deadlock Detection: Algorithms and Proofs*, S. Hilditch & C.M. Thomson, Dept. of Computer Science, University of Manchester, Technical Report Series UMCS-89-6-1, 1989

IDC92 Source: International Data Corporation, 1992

WAT88 *Flagship: A Parallel Architecture for Declarative Programming*, I. Watson, V. Woods, P. Watson, R. Banach, M. Greenberg & J. Sargeant. in Proceedings of the 15th Annual International Symposium on Computer Architecture, Honolulu, Hawaii, May 1988.

WAT91 *The EDS Parallel Relational Datbase System*, P. Watson & P. Townsend, in Parallel Database Systems, ed. P. America, Lecture Notes in Computer Science 503, Springer-Verlag 1991.

W-SQL

An Interface for Scalable, Highly Parallel, Database Machines

Jon Kerridge, Dave Walter and Romola Guiton
National Transputer Support Centre, Sheffield, UK
+44 114 276 8740
j.kerridge@dcs.shef.ac.uk

Abstract. The goal of any designer building a scalable database machine is to ensure that the interface between the relational processing part of the machine and the storage system is independent of the actual storage media. The interface should be as high a level as possible to ensure that as much processing as possible can be encapsulated in the storage level components. The interface design should also consider such aspects as backup and recovery, concurrency management, mixed on-line processing and decision support, support for triggered actions and low-level support for the full range of SQL data manipulations. The W-SQL interface provides such an interface which has been demonstrated in operation with a specifically designed hardware component called a Data Access Component that provides the basic building block of a highly parallel scalable database machine.

1 Introduction

The aim of the W-SQL project was to develop a fundamental building block of a highly parallel database machine in which the low-level SQL processing was performed as close to the data storage as possible. The database machine was to provide only a server capability within the client-server architecture now becoming prevalent. This approach to machine design ensures that the interface to the storage sub-system is at a very high level. In fact we wished to achieve a situation where the translation from the source SQL to the W-SQL interface was minimal. At an early stage, and as a result of the IDIOMS project[1,2], it was determined that such a storage sub-system component would not be able to undertake relational operations involving more than one table. Thus the design activity was placed upon the interface between such a storage sub-system and the remainder of the database machine which would undertake the more complex relational operations. The relational processing capability of the storage sub-system component would be restricted to *relational select* and *project* operations upon a single table partition.

Parallelism within the storage sub-system was to be achieved by partitioning a table onto many such storage sub-system components so that each partition could be accessed at the same time to provide data for a query that accessed more than one partition. The sub-component should also be able to support more than one transaction at the same time. Thus we were wishing to support both intra- and inter-query parallelism.

A key aspect of building such a component was that backup and recovery capability should be built in at the lowest level. In systems with large amounts of storage it is vital that backup and recovery facilities are included in the initial planning of the component rather than being added as an after thought. We have therefore taken a great deal of care in ensuring that such facilities are integrated into the basic sub-system component.

Initially, the project was a collaboration between Data Sciences Ltd, the National Transputer Support Centre and Anamartic Ltd. Anamartic were attempting to produce a large semi-conductor based memories that used the complete wafer rather than split the wafer into the individual chips. (Hence the W in the interface name!). The initial design brief was to produce a processor which could be integrated onto the wafer to undertake basic table operations such as reading, writing, updating and deleting rows. The processor should be able to undertake simple predicate evaluation on a single table. With the demise of Anamartic the requirement to keep the processor as simple as possible was removed and we could produce a much more sophisticated interface. This W-SQL interface is now at a much higher level and is able to make full use of current high performance processors and the associated developments in inter-processor communications technology. Towards the end of the project CORAL also joined the collaboration to provide marketing capability. The project was partially supported by a research grant under the UK Department of Trade and Industry's Information Engineering Advanced Technology Programme.

2 Requirements

The basic list of requirements of the interface and the associated storage sub-system component, which is called a Data Access Component (DAC), were as follows :

- Support for all SQL Data Manipulation operations
- Support for basic database management system infrastructure
- Low cost and scalable
- Modular Construction for larger systems
- Concurrent Transaction Processing and Decision Support Queries
- Support for real-time and distributed databases

The relationship between the components of a complete database machine is shown in Figure 1. The W-SQL Interface is used between two different parts of the database machine. An Access Process (AP) provides an interface with the rest of the database machine and in particular provides the connection to the user part of the machine. A database machine would have many of these APs because we presume the rest of the database machine is highly parallel as well. For ease of description we shall presume that each AP is connected to just one DAC, though the interface does not prescribe this. An AP thus makes requests upon a DAC to undertake operations on the table partitions stored in the DAC. The results of these operations are returned to the AP which then passes the result on to the processors making up the rest of the database machine. The W-SQL interface provides the *glue* between the AP and the DAC by specifying a communication and message protocol.

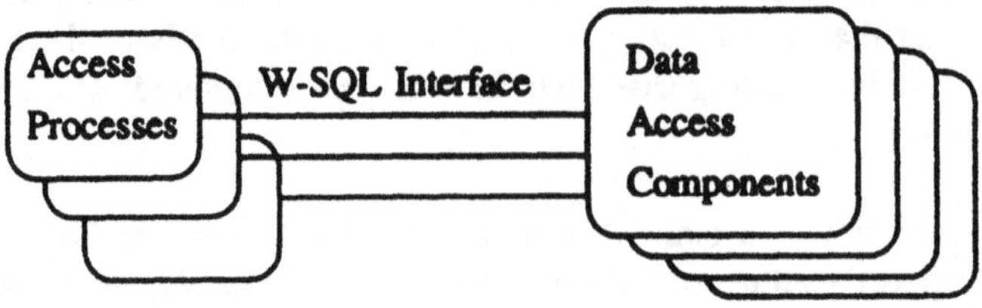

Figure 1

Some results can be determined solely by a single DAC, but some operations may require information from more than one DAC. In this latter case it will generally be possible to undertake most of the processing in the DACs with a final result being calculated from the partial results generated by each of the DACs. The APs will have to communicate amongst themselves in order to determine the overall effect of an operation. We shall briefly review each of the requirements and justify their inclusion.

2.1 Support for all SQL Data Manipulation operations

To be a useful component we must be able to support all SQL manipulations. We restrict this so as to allow only operations which can be performed within a single table. In addition to the basic operations (SELECT, UPDATE, INSERT and DELETE), we also include support for operations such as grouping and aggregation, referential integrity and cursor based operations. These operations are very expensive to implement, thus if we can provide some low-level support we can distribute the processing load over a number of DACs. For a particular query it may be better to undertake some of the processing in the relational processing part of the machine adjacent to the APs, rather than in the DACs. That is a decision that will be made by a query optimiser.

2.2 Support for basic database management system infrastructure

This requirement covers aspects such as support for indexing, concurrency management, backup and recovery and triggered actions.

Indexing is a low-level operation that is specific to a particular table partition. The intention within the requirements specification is not to prescribe the indexing strategy that can be supported, rather to provide a flexible mechanism whereby any appropriate indexing strategy can be incorporated into the DAC. The W-SQL interface would then identify the index that should be used to support a particular query, if any. This need for flexibility is further reinforced when we require the interface to be storage media independent. Thus indexing strategies appropriate for a semi-conductor based bulk table storage may not be useful for disc based storage and vice versa. The database designer needs to be able to chose the most appropriate indexing strategy for the application. Different applications can use different indexes.

Concurrency management results in a great deal of overhead in most database implementations. We wished to construct a component which could provide basic low-level support for this activity. Yet again this influence arose from the ability to undertake such processing in parallel in different DACs. We have chosen to implement an optimistic strategy in the prototype, though the DAC can provide support for the more usual pessimistic locking strategy [3,4]. In either case it is not necessary to store a complete wait-for-graph.

Backup and recovery are key aspects of any database machine which is going to have an availability approaching 100%. Such a consideration means that the backup and recovery system has to be tuneable to the needs of each different application. It also means that the first level of backup and recovery support should be distributed to be as close as possible to the primary storage and that when it is necessary to undertake local recovery or backup it can be done autonomously of the rest of the machine. The design of W-SQL does not specify a particular style of backup or recovery but has captured the essential features such as frequency of backup and the assertion of a quiet point for a full backup so that higher level control can be imposed. The DAC does guarantee that any committed transaction does have recovery information stored on the local backup disc.

The need for triggered actions is increasing as more complex processing is undertaken. Many transactions require knowledge of the state of the database on a regular basis to monitor changes. The DAC provides a mechanism whereby monitors can be defined, in the form of predicates, which actively check the state of the database. If a pre-defined state occurs then a monitor fires and information can be passed back to an application which has been dormant until the state occurs. We have thus provided a mechanism whereby the application part of the system is dormant until the desired state has been activated. The monitor facility provides a very important capability because it means that the DAC undertakes the monitoring of database state rather than a user application having to continuously issue queries to determine the state.

2.3 Low cost and scalable

Many applications of large database machines are not cost sensitive. However, a key aspect is the ability to scale the database machine as the organisation requires more data management capability. Given such capability is required then the costs of such changes in size should at least be reasonable. Another requirement is that the individual parts of the database machine should be individually scalable rather than having to buy a complete unit which contains capabilities which do not need to be scaled. For example, a system should be able to increase the storage sub-system capability without having to scale the relational processing capability at the same time.

Costs can also be reduced by using commodity components. The availability of cheap high performance processors and large memories makes it feasible to produce a reasonably priced basic component. The performance of the DAC component will however be governed by the performance of the backup and recovery system disc. Current commodity disc components tend to use low performance interfaces (e.g. SCSI) and thereby limit the available performance in a system undertaking a lot of short duration update style transactions as frequently occurs in on-line transaction processing systems. There is a need to provide a disc interface which operates at processor communications interface speed [5].

Scalability can also be achieved by using a suitable basic architecture. Thus we chose a message passing architecture with distributed memory which could be implemented on top of a scalable switching and interconnect fabric[6]. The implemented database machine conforms to the shared-nothing architecture, but because we have solved problems such as concurrency management, which normally require a shared memory solution, we have overcome some of the performance limitations of the shared-nothing architecture.

2.4 Modular Construction for larger systems

A modular approach to the DAC was required so that we could provide easy scaling and replacement of malfunctioning components. Customers of such machines require a system that will run reliably at 100% availability. The design must ensure that such systems can be constructed. The demonstrator showed how a reliable system could be constructed using table partition replication. This was achieved in the interface between the APs with the DACs providing the low-level infrastructure.

2.5 Concurrent Transaction Processing and Decision Support Queries

For many organisations the mission critical element of their operation is to support on-line transaction processing. Decision support comes as a second place activity. However, an increasing number of organisations need to undertake decision support on data that is current within the transaction processing environment. We therefore have to ensure that the design decisions within the W-SQL interface and the DAC implementation ensure that we can efficiently support both modes of access concurrently. This aspect is also affected by the SQL definitions for transaction isolation and serializability[7]. The DAC must therefore support these concepts by allowing multiple concurrent transactions each with their own isolation level.

2.6 Support for real-time and distributed databases

The W-SQL interface should not assume any particular style of database. Thus we have ensured that we can support all sizes of database from the relatively small high performance memory based real-time database environment as occurs in control systems and financial trading systems through to the large corporate database system involving large amounts of stored data. Many systems have been distributed through an organisation and though the DAC does not directly support distribution it does not preclude such a style of operation.

3 W-SQL Interface

The W-SQL interface has two different states, initialisation and operational. In the initialisation state the DAC can be loaded with partition meta data, the definitions of indexes and back-up frequency information. In the operational state the DAC can respond to transactions as well as undertaking the dynamic creation of indexes and processing monitors which are used to support triggered actions.

During initialisation the structure of each partition, which a particular DAC stores, is downloaded in a meta data format. This information is stored on the back-up disc (see Figure 2) so that the DAC can recover from failure without needing to fetch the information from a central repository. This meta data will include table and column identifiers, check constraints and default clause specifications and an indication of those columns which are foreign keys to other tables. Those columns which are to be indexed are also indicated together with the type of index to be created. The basis upon which the table is partitioned is also transmitted. In the case of range partitioned tables the partitioning predicate is communicated. Tables can also be hash or round robin partitioned. Also communicated is information concerning the rate at which back-ups should occur.

During the operational phase the main activity is transaction processing, which is discussed later. During the operational phase the W-SQL interface also allows indexes to be created dynamically, say for the duration of a particular query. Further a query can choose whether or not it is going to make use of a specific index or no index at all, or leave the DAC to choose an appropriate index. It may occur that an index is available on a column but use of that index is not appropriate for a particular query. Hence we must allow the interface to indicate what use of indexes is to be made.

Monitors are a mechanism which permits the implementation of triggered actions within the relational part of the database machine. A monitor returns information to a user process through an AP, whenever a specified state occurs within a table partition. The states that can be reported include cumulative changes or changes to a pre-specified value. A monitor can fire before or after a commit. Particular monitors can be activated and deactivated as required and a monitor can be organised that once it has fired it can automatically deactivate itself. The information returned by a fired monitor is specified in the monitor definition.

4 Data Access Component Facilities

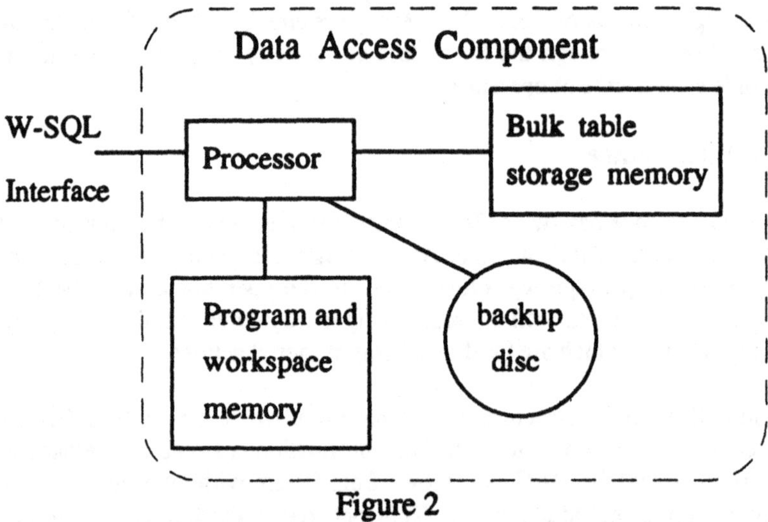

Figure 2

The basic structure of the DAC is shown in figure 2. It comprises a processor which undertakes all the processing and memory to hold the program code and workspace. Bulk storage space is required to hold the table partitions. This storage can be provided by any type of storage media, including semi-conductor memory and disc. A backup and recovery disc is also part of the basic infrastructure. This disc provides the first line of non-volatile backup storage. In a complete implementation we would expect to have another level of backup storage which would be external to the DAC. The DAC should however contain a means of easily connecting to such an external backup storage device. The prototype built in the W-SQL project used semi-conductor memory for bulk table storage and a SCSI disc for backup storage.

A DAC is capable of holding partitions of one or more tables. Some tables may not need to be partitioned over multiple DACs. Some table partitions may be replicated on different DACs. Co-ordination of the modification of such replicas is the responsibility of processing which occurs at the AP level of the database machine architecture. The DAC does provide specific support to enable such a style of operation. A DAC is multi-threaded and can thus support more than one concurrent transaction. Such parallel transactions can access the same or different partitions.

5 W-SQL Transaction Structures

Most communications between an AP and a DAC involve a two-way request - reply message interchange. That is, the AP sends a request to the DAC to undertake some operation and the DAC then responds with some reply or an error message. The only variance to this is the case of monitors. The AP sends a request to activate a monitor and then the AP must create a process which is idle until the monitor fires, at which point it receives a message containing the specified information from the

DAC. A single monitor definition may result in no, one or many firings until the monitor is deactivated.

The basic structure of a transaction is :

transaction initialise
sequence of one or more transaction parts
commit or rollback

The transaction initialisation phase identifies the transaction by means of a unique identifier. This identifier is used subsequently to identify the transaction parts. The unique identifier is required because the AP may be servicing a number of concurrent user requests from other processes which access the DAC by means of one AP. The fact that every request receives a reply does not mean that the AP has to wait for the reply from one transaction's request before it can send another request for a different transaction. Similarly, the DAC can interleave requests and corresponding replies, however, a specific transaction part will always maintain a strict request - reply sequence of messages.

5.1 Transaction Commit

Any transaction that is committed is guaranteed to have transaction recovery information stored on the back-up disc. Both one and two phase commit protocols have been implemented. This was needed so that transactions that involve changes to more than one partition stored on different DACs can use a two-phase commit. In this case the APs have to co-ordinate the responses from each of the DACs to ensure that a transaction is correctly committed. Only one commit will be processed at one time and the DAC orders commits in the sequence in which they were received.

Commit processing is tightly coupled with the concurrency management provided within the DAC. As stated earlier an optimistic strategy has been implemented in the current prototype. This strategy uses version numbers in the following manner. Prior to *update* or *delete*, data is read together with an associated version number, which was incremented as part of the reading process. One or more columns may be associated with a version number. This means that we have concurrency control at the column level within a row of a table. Prior to commit the version numbers of the modified columns are re-read and, provided the version numbers have not changed, the transaction can be committed. During this version number checking phase no other transaction may access the rows that are subject to checking. If the version numbers have changed the transaction has to be rolled-back. If a transaction wishes to operate at SQL isolation level 3, which requires full serialisability, then the version numbers must also be processed when undertaking a read operation.

In addition, the version mechanism we have implemented allows varying granularity on concurrency control. A version number is associated with a segment, which is one or more columns. Thus we can apply concurrency control at the column level at the finest granularity. The coarsest level would be obtained by applying a version number to a complete row. The advantage of the segment concept is that different applications may manipulate different columns within a given row and thus they will not interfere with each other. If version numbers applied to complete rows then such transactions would interfere.

5.2 Basic SELECT Transaction Interaction

The sequence of transaction parts communicated between an AP and a DAC for a basic SQL *SELECT* operation are as follows, ignoring reply messages that are not significant to the understanding of the operation :

AP -> DAC	identify partition and predicate to be evaluated	
repeatedly		
	AP -> DAC	get *n* rows
	DAC -> AP	transfer *n* rows
until		
	DAC -> AP	transfer *r* rows and end of data (r < n)

The first message causes the DAC to determine which partition to access and the predicate which is to be evaluated. The predicate is just a reverse polish expression constructed from the original search condition in the SQL query. It is still represented using column identifiers. The parsing is done by the DAC. Only those parts of the original SQL search condition which refer to the single partition are passed to the DAC. Relational join and set based operations are not passed to a DAC because they involve interaction between two tables. The DAC responds with an accept message if it can parse the expression correctly, otherwise an error message is returned.

The next part of the interaction is carried out repeatedly until all the rows that form the resulting table have been returned to the AP. First, the AP requests that *n* rows are returned and the DAC responds with that number of rows. In some applications it is vital that the first row is returned quickly and that subsequent rows can be returned in groups of say five rows. This can be simply achieved by organising the requests to reflect this. This interaction continues until such time as there are not *n* rows to return. The remaining *r* rows are returned together with an end of data indicator.

5.3 Cursor Oriented SELECT Transaction Interaction

A common feature of most SQL systems is that host languages have to interact with SQL tables by means of a *cursor*. We have therefore provided direct support for this style of interaction. The basic sequence of interactions is the same as the basic select operation described earlier except that the operation is carried out with what is termed *pre-read*. A pre-read causes the data to be accessed and each result row is allocated a row-identifier which is unique to that particular read operation. The AP can then request rows as in the basic case except that the row-identifier is returned to the AP. Once a row has been returned to the AP a positioned update or delete interaction can occur. Such updates and deletes are not restricted to the rows which have just been returned but can refer to any row which has been returned previously within the transaction. In this respect the pre-read capability is more powerful than the normal cursor processing that SQL provides. SQL2 permits forward and backward movement through the cursor but can only refer to the current row[7]. The structure of such a cursor based select is shown below :

AP -> DAC identify partition and predicate to be evaluated with pre-read

repeatedly

AP -> DAC	get *n* rows
DAC -> AP	transfer *n* rows each with a row-identifier
AP -> DAC	optional positioned update and delete commands using row-identifier

until

DAC -> AP	transfer *r* rows and end of data (r < n)

repeat

AP -> DAC	positioned update and delete commands

until

processing completed

5.4 Other SQL Support

The DAC also contains other features which directly support the operation of SQL commands. Referential integrity processing is supported by an efficient implementation of EXISTS and NOT EXISTS predicate evaluation. This processing will automatically make use of any index that may be appropriate. The schema information pertaining to a partition contains any column and table constraint clauses and so any update or insert operation can check that these constraints are not violated.

In a memory based implementation of the DAC we can introduce data structures which would not be viable in a disc based system to support grouping and aggregation functions. We can construct link list data structures so that all rows belonging to a group can be directly accessed. This means that set functions can be more easily calculated. Further more if the same columns that are used for grouping are used for an ordered cursor then the same link list structure can be used to create the sorted order. Obviously, if the grouping results in rows being required for more than one DAC then each DAC has to return a partial result to its AP and then the APs have to co-ordinate to produce the final result.

The W-SQL interface also includes direct support for the bulk loading of tables which makes it much easier to build tables in an empty system. During the loading phase any indexes and other access optimisation data structures are built automatically. This aspect has been tested by loading banking related data from the Sheffield Database Performance Evaluation System[8].

6 Building Database Machines

In collaboration with Data Sciences Ltd we have built a demonstrator that implements the W-SQL interface in an air traffic control application. Data Sciences already had a relational database system called DIOMEDES[9]. Within the W-SQL project they removed from the existing DIOMEDES implementation that part which dealt with storage access and incorporated the necessary calls using the W-SQL interface to access a system with four DACs. The implemented system used full table replication and thus required the construction of a protocol at the AP level to ensure that each replica received any modifications in exactly the same sequence. This protocol was already implemented as part of the application and was easily integrated into the AP part of the database machine. The air traffic control application is highly dependant upon the relative position of aircraft and thus lends itself to the use of monitored events. This aspect of the W-SQL interface and implementation was fully exploited in the demonstration system. In addition, we were able to demonstrate with multiple users that the concurrency control system worked at all levels of the architecture. The two particular cases are, first, two users access the same data at the same time and one user commits their transaction before the other user. The W-SQL system detected the miss-match of version numbers and caused the second transaction to be rolled-back. The second case is more subtle and occurs when two transactions have obtained the same data and attempt to commit the data at exactly the same time. In this case a serialisability error will occur and by synchronised pressing of *enter* keys, by two users, it was possible to demonstrate this phenomenon. In all cases the tables were replicated and each user was accessing a different replica.

6.1 Building Larger Systems

The aim of the project was to build a basic component of a parallel database machine. We are currently undertaking such an exercise with funding from an EU-EUREKA project. We shall here give an outline of the approach which is being adopted. The structure is shown in Figure 3.

A set of DACs is connected to their own local second level back-up storage unit, recall that the disc on each DAC acts as the primary back-up storage media. It would be anticipated that such a unit would be contained in some form of housing which permitted hot replacement of failed units. The unit would be connected to some form of n+1 power supply mechanism to ensure that power failure did not cause a problem.

To ensure full recovery capability it would be necessary to store replicas of all partitions in different incremental units, with the APs undertaking the co-ordination between replicas. A further level of back-up would also be required which would entail a connection from each incremental unit to a third level of storage. A suitable storage device would be some form of cassette based storage based system. The W-SQL interface contains sufficient capability to force check-points to be taken either at pre-defined times or whenever instructed.

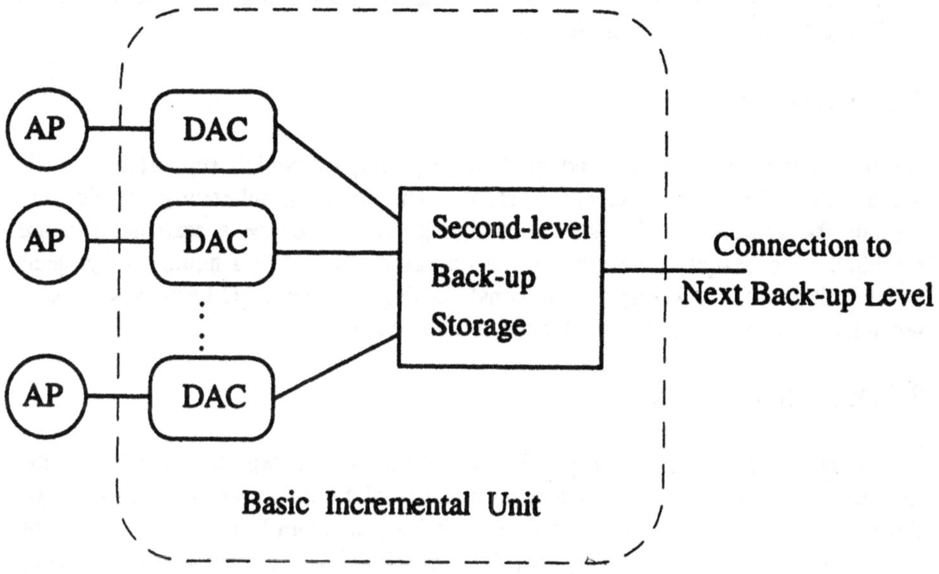

Figure 3

6.2 Comparison of W-SQL with the ICL Goldrush

It is interesting to compare the W-SQL approach with that adopted by ICL for their Goldrush Megaserver database machine [10]. The basic design philosophy of the ICL approach is to build a machine onto which it easy to port existing third-party database products, such as ORACLE, Ingres and ADABAS. This goal would be deemed necessary so that easier penetration into the existing market for relational database products would be easier. It was thus necessary to build a machine to which it would be relatively easy to port UNIX. The ICL machine uses processors which enable this port (Hyper-SPARC). Each processing element contains two such processors, one dealing with data processing activity and the other dealing with communications across an all-to-all connection provided by their delta-network. The mechanism chosen by ICL is to integrate storage access and relational processing into a single processor.

In W-SQL we have similarly assumed that a processor is required to support data storage access but we have presumed that relational processing will take place in other processors. It has been assumed that there will be some form of switch/routing interconnect fabric that will be able to support the communication requirement with very little latency. Such an interconnect fabric could be provided by use of the SGS-Thomson T9000 and C104 routing chip[11]. From the outset, the design philosophy had been to assume that no use would be made of a traditional operating system and associated file management system. The aim of W-SQL was to provide a mechanism which would allow a scalable database machine to be constructed the sole activity of which was to act as a back-end SQL server.

7 Conclusions

We have described how a component can be designed which supports the basic functionality of an SQL database machine. The design is inherently parallel and exploits the advantages that such a design gives to produce a scalable database machine. The design is currently being further developed in a number of projects which will explore how easy it is to construct first, a large DAC based system and, second, a DAC based upon discs for the bulk table storage.

8 Acknowledgements

This work was carried out with part funding from the UK Department of Trade and Industry. We wish to acknowledge, particularly, the support we received from Dr Dennis Henn. We also acknowledge our collaborators from Data Sciences Ltd; Bob Catt, Russell Parkin, Ian Wakely and Alan Sparkes. The project was managed by Roger England of the NTSC to whom we are grateful.

9 References

1. JM Kerridge, The Design of the IDIOMS Parallel Database Machine, in Aspects of Databases, MS Jackson and AE Robinson (eds), Butterworth Heinemann, 128-149, 1991.

2. JM Kerridge, IDIOMS: A Multi-transputer Database Machine, in Emerging Trends in Database and Knowledge-base Machines, M Abdelguerfi and S Lavington (eds), IEEE Computer Science Press (to appear).

3. SW Waithe and JM Kerridge, Deadlock Detection in a Scalable Massively Parallel Concurrency Control Architecture, submitted for publication to Distributed and Parallel Databases

4. SW Waithe and JM Kerridge, A Scalable Massively Parallel Architecture for Database Concurrency Control, June 1994, International Conference on Concurrent Engineering:Research and Applications Pittsburgh.

5. JM Kerridge, The Implementation of Large Parallel Database Machines on T9000 and C104 Networks, in Networks, Routers and Transputers, MD May, PW Thompson and PH Welch (eds), IOS Press, Amsterdam, 1993, 133-149.

6. MD May and PW Thompson, Transputers and Routers: Components for Concurrent Machines, in Networks, Routers and Transputers, MD May, PW Thompson and PH Welch (eds), IOS Press, Amsterdam, 1993, 1 - 14.

7. SJ Cannan and GAM Otten, SQL The Standard Handbook, McGraw-Hill, 1992.

8. JM Kerridge, IE Jelly and C Bates, Evaluation of High Performance Parallel Database Machines, High Performance Computing and Networks, Europe '94, Munich, April 1994, Springer-Verlag, LNCS 796, 424-429

9. PR Tillman, R Giles and I Wakely, DIOMEDES - Multilevel Parallel Processing for a very High Performance Real-Time Database Management, AGARD Symposium April 1988.

10. P Watson and G Catlow, The Architecture of the ICL GOLDRUSH MegaSERVER, to appear in the same proceedings.

11. MD May et al, Networks, Routers and Transputers, IOS Press, Amsterdam, 1993.

AUTHOR INDEX

Springer-Verlag and the Environment

Lecture Notes in Computer Science

For information about Vols. 1–865
please contact your bookseller or Springer-Verlag

Vol. 866: Y. Davidor, H.-P. Schwefel, R. Männer (Eds.), Parallel Problem Solving from Nature - PPSN III. Proceedings, 1994. XV, 642 pages. 1994.

Vol 867: L. Steels, G. Schreiber, W. Van de Velde (Eds.), A Future for Knowledge Acquisition. Proceedings, 1994. XII, 414 pages. 1994. (Subseries LNAI).

Vol. 868: R. Steinmetz (Ed.), Multimedia: Advanced Teleservices and High-Speed Communication Architectures. Proceedings, 1994. IX, 451 pages. 1994.

Vol. 869: Z. W. Raś, Zemankova (Eds.), Methodologies for Intelligent Systems. Proceedings, 1994. X, 613 pages. 1994. (Subseries LNAI).

Vol. 870: J. S. Greenfield, Distributed Programming Paradigms with Cryptography Applications. XI, 182 pages. 1994.

Vol. 871: J. P. Lee, G. G. Grinstein (Eds.), Database Issues for Data Visualization. Proceedings, 1993. XIV, 229 pages. 1994.

Vol. 872: S Arikawa, K. P. Jantke (Eds.), Algorithmic Learning Theory. Proceedings, 1994. XIV, 575 pages. 1994.

Vol. 873: M. Naftalin, T. Denvir, M. Bertran (Eds.), FME '94: Industrial Benefit of Formal Methods. Proceedings, 1994. XI, 723 pages. 1994.

Vol. 874: A. Borning (Ed.), Principles and Practice of Constraint Programming. Proceedings, 1994. IX, 361 pages. 1994.

Vol. 875: D. Gollmann (Ed.), Computer Security – ESORICS 94. Proceedings, 1994. XI, 469 pages. 1994.

Vol. 876: B. Blumenthal, J. Gornostaev, C. Unger (Eds.), Human-Computer Interaction. Proceedings, 1994. IX, 239 pages. 1994.

Vol. 877: L. M. Adleman, M.-D. Huang (Eds.), Algorithmic Number Theory. Proceedings, 1994. IX, 323 pages. 1994.

Vol. 878: T. Ishida; Parallel, Distributed and Multiagent Production Systems. XVII, 166 pages. 1994. (Subseries LNAI).

Vol. 879: J. Dongarra, J. Waśniewski (Eds.), Parallel Scientific Computing. Proceedings, 1994. XI, 566 pages. 1994.

Vol. 880: P. S. Thiagarajan (Ed.), Foundations of Software Technology and Theoretical Computer Science. Proceedings, 1994. XI, 451 pages. 1994.

Vol. 881: P. Loucopoulos (Ed.), Entity-Relationship Approach – ER'94. Proceedings, 1994. XIII, 579 pages. 1994.

Vol. 882: D. Hutchison, A. Danthine, H. Leopold, G. Coulson (Eds.), Multimedia Transport and Teleservices. Proceedings, 1994. XI, 380 pages. 1994.

Vol. 883: L. Fribourg, F. Turini (Eds.), Logic Program Synthesis and Transformation – Meta-Programming in Logic. Proceedings, 1994. IX, 451 pages. 1994.

Vol. 884: J. Nievergelt, T. Roos, H.-J. Schek, P. Widmayer (Eds.), IGIS '94: Geographic Information Systems. Proceedings, 1994. VIII, 292 pages. 19944.

Vol. 885: R. C. Veltkamp, Closed Objects Boundaries from Scattered Points. VIII, 144 pages. 1994.

Vol. 886: M. M. Veloso, Planning and Learning by Analogical Reasoning. XIII, 181 pages. 1994. (Subseries LNAI).

Vol. 887: M. Toussaint (Ed.), Ada in Europe. Proceedings, 1994. XII, 521 pages. 1994.

Vol. 888: S. A. Andersson (Ed.), Analysis of Dynamical and Cognitive Systems. Proceedings, 1993. VII, 260 pages. 1995.

Vol. 889: H. P. Lubich, Towards a CSCW Framework for Scientific Cooperation in Europe. X, 268 pages. 1995.

Vol. 890: M. J. Wooldridge, N. R. Jennings (Eds.), Intelligent Agents. Proceedings, 1994. VIII, 407 pages. 1995. (Subseries LNAI).

Vol. 891: C. Lewerentz, T. Lindner (Eds.), Formal Development of Reactive Systems. XI, 394 pages. 1995.

Vol. 892: K. Pingali, U. Banerjee, D. Gelernter, A. Nicolau, D. Padua (Eds.), Languages and Compilers for Parallel Computing. Proceedings, 1994. XI, 496 pages. 1995.

Vol. 893: G. Gottlob, M. Y. Vardi (Eds.), Database Theory – ICDT '95. Proceedings, 1995. XI, 454 pages. 1995.

Vol. 894: R. Tamassia, I. G. Tollis (Eds.), Graph Drawing. Proceedings, 1994. X, 471 pages. 1995.

Vol. 895: R. L. Ibrahim (Ed.), Software Engineering Education. Proceedings, 1995. XII, 449 pages. 1995.

Vol. 896: R. N. Taylor, J. Coutaz (Eds.), Software Engineering and Human-Computer Interaction. Proceedings, 1994. X, 281 pages. 1995.

Vol. 897: M. Fisher, R. Owens (Eds.), Executable Modal and Temporal Logics. Proceedings, 1993. VII, 180 pages. 1995. (Subseries LNAI).

Vol. 898: P. Steffens (Ed.), Machine Translation and the Lexicon. Proceedings, 1993. X, 251 pages. 1995. (Subseries LNAI).

Vol. 899: W. Banzhaf, F. H. Eeckman (Eds.), Evolution and Biocomputation. VII, 277 pages. 1995.

Vol. 900: E. W. Mayr, C. Puech (Eds.), STACS 95. Proceedings, 1995. XIII, 654 pages. 1995.

Vol. 901: R. Kumar, T. Kropf (Eds.), Theorem Provers in Circuit Design. Proceedings, 1994. VIII, 303 pages. 1995.

Vol. 902: M. Dezani-Ciancaglini, G. Plotkin (eds.), Typed Lambda Calculi and Applications. Proceedings, 1995. VIII, 443 pages. 1995

Vol. 903: E. W. Mayr, G. Schmidt, G. Tinhofer (Eds.), Graph-Theoretic Concepts in Computer Science. Proceedings, 1994. IX, 414 pages. 1995.

Vol. 904: P. Vitányi (Ed.), Computational Learning Theory. EuroCOLT'95. Proceedings, 1995. XVII, 415 pages. 1995. (Subseries LNAI).

Vol. 905: N. Ayache (Ed.), Computer Vision, Virtual Reality and Robotics in Medicine. Proceedings, 1995. XIV, 567 pages. 1995.

Vol. 906: E. Astesiano, G. Reggio, A. Tarlecki (Eds.), Recent Trends in Data Type Specification. Proceedings, 1995. VIII, 523 pages. 1995.

Vol. 907: T. Ito, A. Yonezawa (Eds.), Theory and Practice of Parallel Programming. Proceedings, 1995. VIII, 485 pages. 1995.

Vol. 908: J. R. Rao Extensions of the UNITY Methodology: Compositionality, Fairness and Probability in Parallelism. XI, 178 pages. 1995.

Vol. 909: H. Comon, J.-P. Jouannaud (Eds.), Term Rewriting. Proceedings, 1993. VIII, 221 pages. 1995.

Vol. 910: A. Podelski (Ed.), Constraint Programming: Basics and Trends. Proceedings, 1995. XI, 315 pages. 1995.

Vol. 911: R. Baeza-Yates, E. Goles, P. V. Poblete (Eds.), LATIN '95: Theoretical Informatics. Proceedings, 1995. IX, 525 pages. 1995.

Vol. 912: N. Lavrac, S. Wrobel (Eds.), Machine Learning: ECML – 95. Proceedings, 1995. XI, 370 pages. 1995. (Subseries LNAI).

Vol. 913: W. Schäfer (Ed.), Software Process Technology. Proceedings, 1995. IX, 261 pages. 1995.

Vol. 914: J. Hsiang (Ed.), Rewriting Techniques and Applications. Proceedings, 1995. XII, 473 pages. 1995.

Vol. 915: P. D. Mosses, M. Nielsen, M. I. Schwartzbach (Eds.), TAPSOFT '95: Theory and Practice of Software Development. Proceedings, 1995. XV, 810 pages. 1995.

Vol. 916: N. R. Adam, B. K. Bhargava, Y. Yesha (Eds.), Digital Libraries. Proceedings, 1994. XIII, 321 pages. 1995.

Vol. 917: J. Pieprzyk, R. Safavi-Naini (Eds.), Advances in Cryptology - ASIACRYPT '94. Proceedings, 1994. XII, 431 pages. 1995.

Vol. 918: P. Baumgartner, R. Hähnle, J. Posegga (Eds.), Theorem Proving with Analytic Tableaux and Related Methods. Proceedings, 1995. X, 352 pages. 1995. (Subseries LNAI).

Vol. 919: B. Hertzberger, G. Serazzi (Eds.), High-Performance Computing and Networking. Proceedings, 1995. XXIV, 957 pages. 1995.

Vol. 920: E. Balas, J. Clausen (Eds.), Integer Programming and Combinatorial Optimization. Proceedings, 1995. IX, 436 pages. 1995.

Vol. 921: L. C. Guillou, J.-J. Quisquater (Eds.), Advances in Cryptology – EUROCRYPT '95. Proceedings, 1995. XIV, 417 pages. 1995.

Vol. 922: H. Dörr, Efficient Graph Rewriting and Its Implementation. IX, 266 pages. 1995.

Vol. 923: M. Meyer (Ed.), Constraint Processing. IV, 289 pages. 1995.

Vol. 924: P. Ciancarini, O. Nierstrasz, A. Yonezawa (Eds.), Object-Based Models and Languages for Concurrent Systems. Proceedings, 1994. VII, 193 pages. 1995.

Vol. 925: J. Jeuring, E. Meijer (Eds.), Advanced Functional Programming. Proceedings, 1995. VII, 331 pages. 1995.

Vol. 926: P. Nesi (Ed.), Objective Software Quality. Proceedings, 1995. VIII, 249 pages. 1995.

Vol. 927: J. Dix, L. Moniz Pereira, T. C. Przymusinski (Eds.), Non-Monotonic Extensions of Logic Programming. Proceedings, 1994. IX, 229 pages. 1995. (Subseries LNAI).

Vol. 928: V.W. Marek, A. Nerode, M. Truszczynski (Eds.), Logic Programming and Nonmonotonic Reasoning. Proceedings, 1995. VIII, 417 pages. 1995. (Subseries LNAI).

Vol. 929: F. Morán, A. Moreno, J.J. Merelo, P. Chacón (Eds.), Advances in Artificial Life. Proceedings, 1995. XIII, 960 pages. 1995 (Subseries LNAI).

Vol. 930: J. Mira, F. Sandoval (Eds.), From Natural to Artificial Neural Computation. Proceedings, 1995. XVIII, 1150 pages. 1995.

Vol. 931: P.J. Braspenning, F. Thuijsman, A.J.M.M. Weijters (Eds.), Artificial Neural Networks. IX, 295 pages. 1995.

Vol. 932: J. Iivari, K. Lyytinen, M. Rossi (Eds.), Advanced Information Systems Engineering. Proceedings, 1995. XI, 388 pages. 1995.

Vol. 933: L. Pacholski, J. Tiuryn (Eds.), Computer Science Logic. Proceedings, 1994. IX, 543 pages. 1995.

Vol. 934: P. Barahona, M. Stefanelli, J. Wyatt (Eds.), Artificial Intelligence in Medicine. Proceedings, 1995. XI, 449 pages. 1995. (Subseries LNAI).

Vol. 935: G. De Michelis, M. Diaz (Eds.), Application and Theory of Petri Nets 1995. Proceedings, 1995. VIII, 511 pages. 1995.

Vol. 936: V.S. Alagar, M. Nivat (Eds.), Algebraic Methodology and Software Technology. Proceedings, 1995. XIV, 591 pages. 1995.

Vol. 937: Z. Galil, E. Ukkonen (Eds.), Combinatorial Pattern Matching. Proceedings, 1995. VIII, 409 pages. 1995.

Vol. 938: K.P. Birman, F. Mattern, A. Schiper (Eds.), Theory and Practice in Distributed Systems. Proceedings,1994. X, 263 pages. 1995.

Vol. 939: P. Wolper (Ed.), Computer Aided Verification. Proceedings, 1995. X, 451 pages. 1995.

Vol. 940: C. Goble, J. Keane (Eds.), Advances in Databases. Proceedings, 1995. X, 277 pages. 1995.

Vol. 941: M. Cadoli, Tractable Reasoning in Artificial Intelligence. XVII, 247 pages. 1995. (Subseries LNAI).

Vol. 942: G. Böckle, Exploitation of Fine-Grain Parallelism. IX, 188 pages. 1995.

Vol. 943: W. Klas, M. Schrefl, Metaclasses and Their Application. IX, 201 pages. 1995.